S0-BSD-917

DATE DUE

*Citizenship, Political
Engagement, and Belonging*

# Citizenship, Political Engagement, and Belonging

## IMMIGRANTS IN EUROPE AND THE UNITED STATES

*Edited by*
DEBORAH REED–DANAHAY
CAROLINE B. BRETTELL

RUTGERS UNIVERSITY PRESS
*New Brunswick, New Jersey, and London*

LIBRARY OF CONGRESS CATALOGING-IN-PUBLICATION DATA

Citizenship, political engagement, and belonging : immigrants in Europe and the
United States / edited by Deborah Reed-Danahay and Caroline B. Brettell.
    p. cm.
  Includes bibliographical references and index.
  ISBN 978–0–8135–4329–1 (hardcover : alk. paper) — ISBN 978–0–8135–4330–7
(pbk. : alk. paper)
  1. Immigrants—United States—Political activity.  2. Immigrants—Europe—Political
activity.  3. Political participation—United States.  4. Political participation—Europe.
5. Citizenship—United States.  6. Citizenship—Europe.  7. United States—Emigration
and immigration—Social aspects.  8. Europe—Emigration and immigration—Social
aspects.  I. Reed-Danahay, Deborah.  II. Brettell, Caroline.
  JV6477.C58 2008
  323.3'2912094—dc22                                   2007037877

A British Cataloging-in-Publication record for this book is available from the British Library.

This collection copyright © 2008 by Rutgers, The State University

Individual chapters copyright © 2008 in the names of their authors

All rights reserved

Visit our Web site: http://rutgerspress.rutgers.edu

Manufactured in the United States of America

# CONTENTS

# ACKNOWLEDGMENTS

THE IDEA FOR this book emerged from field research that we are currently conducting on citizenship and civic engagement in two immigrant populations, Vietnamese and Asian Indians, in the Dallas-Fort Worth metropolitan area. We are grateful to the Russell Sage Foundation for their support of this research. We have both previously done research in Europe, and are, thus, interested in transatlantic comparisons. To create a forum for our own thinking, we decided to assemble a group of anthropologists working on similar issues in both the United States and Europe for an organized session, cosponsored by the Society for the Anthropology of Europe and the Society for Urban, National and Transnational Anthropology, at the 2005 annual meeting of the American Anthropological Association. The session was well attended and we are grateful to the audience for their questions and comments, as well as to David Kertzer and Nancy Foner who served as discussants. We also want to acknowledge the hard work of all the contributors who revised their papers for this volume, as well as the anonymous reviewers who offered helpful suggestions.

Our deepest gratitude is extended to Adi Hovav of Rutgers University Press who saw the significance of the book and, in particular, of anthropologists weighing in with their methods and insights on a topic often associated more closely with other disciplines in the social sciences. She has been a wonderful editor with which to work at Rutgers University Press. We would also like to thank Marilyn Campbell, Alicia Nadkarni, and Heath Renfroe, our copyeditor. Deborah Reed-Danahay would like to thank the University of Texas at Arlington, where she was teaching when we started this book project, for many years of support and SUNY College at Buffalo for a supportive climate regarding her research and work on this book starting in fall 2006. She would also like to thank her research assistant Bethany Hawkins for her help in the preparation of this manuscript. Caroline Brettell would like to thank Southern Methodist University for their support of her work over the years, and particularly Julie Adkins who assisted with the index for this book, and Lenda Callaway, assistant to the dean of Dedman College, who made it easier to continue with her scholarship as she assumed the role of dean ad interim.

*Citizenship, Political Engagement, and Belonging*

# Introduction

*Deborah Reed-Danahay and Caroline B. Brettell*

THE POLITICAL ENGAGEMENT and political incorporation of immigrants is a topic of pressing concern in both Western Europe and the United States. Political incorporation entails not only naturalization and the rights and duties of legal citizenship, but political and civic engagement (or forms of "active citizenship"). While rates of immigration, and numbers of nonnative-born residents, are comparable between the United States and Western European nations, Europe has been slower to recognize both the presence of immigrants and the issues that immigration presents for newcomers and their host societies. The recent introspection about national identity and citizenship in Europe provoked by the fall 2005 demonstrations and political unrest in Paris, the London bombings in July of 2005, and the failure of France to ratify a new EU constitution in spring 2006 illustrate new questions being raised about what it means, for example, to be French or British. In the post-9/11 context of the United States, with a new Office of Homeland Security pushing for closer scrutiny of both visitors and immigrants, there are ongoing debates about immigration reform, border control, and the role of immigrant labor in the economy. On the streets of major metropolitan streets across the United States, thousands marched in April and May 2006 to protest various proposals (especially those of HR 4437) for immigrant reform and to plead for immigrant rights.

Little dialogue between anthropologists working in Western Europe and in the United States has yet taken place, despite these issues that touch both sides of the Atlantic. There is, however, a growing body of work among anthropologists doing research in Europe on issues of immigration and citizenship, which complements the more established ethnographic traditions of research among immigrant populations in the United States (Foner 2003c). This book contributes to such a dialogue by bringing together scholars working on both sides of the Atlantic and exploring common themes in the experiences of immigrants within the institutional contexts of various nation-states. Two other recent books look comparatively at issues of immigration and citizenship (Tsuda 2006 and Portes and DeWind 2007), but not with a specific focus on ethnographic approaches. We explore the contributions that ethnographic studies "on the ground" can make to our understandings of current processes of immigration, political behavior, and citizenship.[1] Anthropological studies of immigration underscore the need for an approach to political incorporation that looks not only at naturalization and the rights and duties of legal citizenship, but also at political and civic engagement (or forms of "participatory citizenship").[2] The chapters in this book focus attention on the social agency of immigrants as well as the structures in which they operate. There are formal legal and jural frameworks that determine possibilities for immigrant belonging or exclusion, and there are formal practices such as naturalization and voting. At the same time, there are "on the ground" vernacular practices employed by immigrants and those who come into contact with them.

As Stephen Castles and Alistair Davidson (2000: 1) have aptly put it, being a citizen was until recently a "common sense" notion, that involved rights like that of voting and obligations like those of paying taxes, obeying laws, jury duty, and, in several European countries, serving in the military. Why, they ask, "this sudden interest in something that seemed so obvious?" (2000: 2). Will Kymlicka and Wayne Norman (1994) have pointed out, along similar lines, that after issues of citizenship fell out of fashion mid-century, political theorists were consumed with them by the 1990s. There was also a rise in interest in citizenship among anthropologists in the 1990s (see Verdery 1996), particularly those working among U.S. immigrant populations whose behaviors and experiences belied discrete notions of citizenship based on what Rogers Brubaker has called the "international filing system, a mechanism for allocating persons to states" (1992: 31). The view of citizenship defined by Brubaker as bounded and context-independent (29), or as an "abstract, formal construct" (30) must be rethought in the situations of real social actors and their behaviors. Although nations define individuals in terms of discrete citizenship categories, the ways in which citizenship is enacted, understood, and expressed may vary considerably.

Several writers have distinguished between forms of citizenship that might be thought of as legal citizenship vs. participatory citizenship. Étienne Balibar (1988: 724) usefully makes a distinction between citizenship in its "strict sense"—"the full exercise of political rights"—and in its "broad sense"—"cultural initiative or effective presence in the public sphere (the capacity to be 'listened to' there)." Angus Stewart likewise points to the distinction between "state citizenship" and "democratic citizenship"—the first having to do with legal status recognized by a nation-state and the second having to do with the community participation of citizens as "political actors constituting political spheres" (1995: 64). Kymlicka and Norman (1994: 353) phrase this in terms of "citizenship-as-legal-status" vs. "citizenship-as-desirable-activity." Castles and Davidson (2000: 84) distinguish this in terms of access to citizenship ("becoming a citizen") and substantial citizenship ("being a citizen"). Takeyuki Tsuda (2006) places useful emphasis on forms of substantive citizenship that can be considered "local citizenship"—"the granting, by local governments and organizations, of basic sociopolitical rights and services to immigrants as legitimate members of these local communities" (7). Even when immigrants do not have national citizenship or even permanent resident status, they may have their rights expanded at the local level, often facilitated by NGOs.

As increasing attention has been paid to citizenship, a variety of terms and concepts has arisen to distinguish between different modes of political incorporation. While citizenship describes at its most basic level the legal status of rights and duties associated with membership in a nation-state, Tomas Hammar (1990) has coined the term "denizens" to refer to those immigrants who have the recognized legal status of having permanently settled in a host country and who have some economic and social rights, but who are not naturalized, legal citizens. Although they do not use the term "denizens," James Holston and Arjun Appadurai note that "legally resident noncitizens often possess virtually identical socioeconomic rights and civil rights as citizens" (1999: 4). Caroline Brettell (this volume) looks at the category of noncitizens in terms of their political behaviors as "netizens" who mobilize in cyberspace. The political incorporation and civic engagement of noncitizen immigrants helps to broaden our understanding of the meaning of citizenship, to recognize the differences between legal and substantive citizenship, and, by extension, to underscore the significance of citizenship practice.[3] The term "margizens," introduced by Marco Martiniello (1994), refers to those who are illegal immigrants but may enjoy some civil and social benefits even as they may be ultimately at risk for deportation.

Changes in both U.S. and European immigration policy since the mid-twentieth century have informed research on immigration and citizenship. Much of the new ethnographic work on immigrants in the United States addresses immigrants who have entered the country since 1965 when the National Quota Act, in place since 1924, was lifted. A policy emphasizing family reunification and labor qualifications was put in place. While immigration streams were relatively small in the immediately ensuing years, after 1980, and especially after 1990, the number of newcomers began to increase dramatically. The main attraction was a booming economy, which has brought both well-educated, highly skilled workers (Indians, Chinese) and less well-educated, low-skilled workers (Mexicans, Central Americans) to the United States. Free trade laws and improved transportation and communication are additional factors that have influenced the volume and source of flows. The United States has also admitted substantial numbers of refugees from Southeast Asia (Vietnamese, Cambodians, Laotians), from Cuba, and most recently from Africa.

Although U.S. citizenship laws have remained stable throughout this period, other laws have been adjusted in the face of rising numbers of undocumented workers or economic downturns. Some of these laws have affected basic rights as well as the opportunity to become a legal citizen. Among these is the Immigration Reform and Control Act (IRCA) of 1986, which extended amnesty to large numbers of Hispanics who had entered the country without legal papers and put them on a path to legal citizenship. Other laws have been amended in response to economic downturns and pressures on social services. The best example is the 1996 Illegal Immigrant Reform and Immigrant Responsibility Act (IIRIRA), which imposed restrictions on benefits to "legal aliens" among other things and ultimately prompted another spurt in citizenship applications. Finally, new dual citizenship laws in countries such as India and Mexico are also a factor to be considered in any attempt to understand new forms of political behavior and citizenship practice among the post-1965 immigrant populations in the United States.

The study of immigrants, political behavior, and citizenship in Europe must be placed within the context of three related changes in European society since the middle of the twentieth century. First, as is the case in the United States, there are new trends of immigration since the mid-1960s that have created new debates and social policies within nations. Second, economic restructurings since World War II connected to neoliberal politics and the lessening of the welfare state affect the social services available to immigrants and their children. Third, the growth of the European Union and its own citizenship policies at the supranational level has implications for individual national citizenship laws and vice versa.

While rates of immigration, and numbers of nonnative-born residents, are comparable between the United States and many Western European nations,[4] European nations were slower to recognize both the presence of immigrants and the issues that immigration presents for newcomers and their host societies (Grillo 1985; Lucassen 2005; Noiriel 1996). Recent post–World War II migrations, and particularly changes since the 1990s in Europe, have led even those nations that were historically sites of emigration (Spain, Italy,

Greece) to join those that have always been characterized by high rates of immigration (France, Germany, England, the Netherlands). One of the major changes in immigration facing Western Europe is that while most of the previous migrants were from other European nations (Portuguese or Italians to France, for example; or Irish to England), many current migrants come from Muslim countries and are viewed as non-Western. There has also been a shift from migration based primarily on labor (frequently associated with colonialism) to the migration of refugees and asylum-seekers. The growing "Islamicization" of Europe related to immigrant streams from Turkey (to Germany), North Africa (to France) and Pakistan and Northern India (to England), as well as newer immigrations of African populations to nations such as Italy (Cole 1997) or Ireland (see Smith in this volume), has led to new forms of racial categorization (Al-Shahi and Lawless 2005; Modood and Werbner 1997; Silverstein 2005). These late twentieth- and early twenty-first-century changes in global flows of immigration, as well as the circumstances in which immigrants now arrive in their host nation-states, has led to renewed interest in the meanings of citizenship among policy makers and scholars. Laws on how one becomes a citizen, through such criteria as birth, naturalization, or marriage, are currently being rethought in the European context. Attention has also recently been placed on dual citizenship laws and their implications for both sending and receiving societies (Koslowski 2000).

## Legal Frameworks of Citizenship

The political behavior of immigrants is shaped in part by the laws of immigration and citizenship in the host country. The study of citizenship and citizenship theory has already claimed much attention among political scientists, sociologists, and historians. Several authors have discussed the implications of citizenship laws for immigrants (Brubaker 1989; Castles and Davidson 2000; Joppke 1999b; Joppke and Morawska 2003; Soysal 1994). Some recent studies of changing immigration laws and policies in Europe conclude that new forms assimilation to the nation-state are occurring and that the "postnation" of transnational flows may not be so close on the horizon (Joppke and Morawska 2003). An ethnographic focus on immigrants as social actors, resisters, and transnationals must not ignore consideration of the ways in which the host society's policies and discourses of immigration shape the modes of political incorporation experienced by immigrants. Several of the chapters in this book look closely at such issues (especially Stanley, Smith, and Gibb).

In her article on the meaning of citizenship in the United States, Linda Kerber (1997) points out that although "the definition of 'citizen' is single and egalitarian, . . . Americans have had many different experiences of what it means to be a citizen; indeed, over the centuries since 1780 the number of different categories of experience has increased" (837). Despite the Fourteenth Amendment to the constitution, which defined all persons born or naturalized in the United States as citizens of the United States and of the state wherein they reside, thereby guaranteeing them equal protection of the laws, many groups in ensuing years have not been equally treated with regard to citizenship rights. These include women, African Americans, and immigrants, especially those from Asia who, throughout much of U.S. history, have been denied the right to naturalize. The evidence for the racial construction of citizenship became most apparent in the 1920s when several Asian groups, including the Japanese, Filipinos, and those of Hindu faith, were declared by the Supreme Court to be nonwhite and hence ineligible for citizenship (843). The historian Martha Gardner (2005) also draws attention to the fluidity of U.S. citizenship, arguing that it has been shaped by changing ideas not only about race, but also about gender. The legal citizenship of immigrant women was particularly limited and in 1907, as a result of "derivative citizenship," American women who "married noncitizens became noncitizens" (123).

Today U.S. citizenship by birth involves two legal principles—*jus soli*, citizenship resulting from being born in the United States, and *jus sanguinis*, citizenship resulting from having an American parent or parents in the United States.[5] Citizenship can also be acquired through naturalization. The United States offers a fairly easy adjustment process from one visa status to another and citizenship through naturalization can occur after five years as a legal permanent resident (green card holder) upon demonstration of some English-language competence, knowledge of elementary civics, and a clean criminal record.

Many legal permanent residents have access to the same benefits accorded to citizens, with the exception of voting, making it possible to enjoy a host of rights without becoming naturalized citizens—a fact that has been used to explain the low rate of naturalization in the United States, although this varies by groups. Mexicans and Canadians naturalize at lower rates than Asian and European immigrants. The 1996 Immigration Act (IIRIRA) began to erode some of these rights, pushing many people toward naturalization.[6] While the oath of citizenship asks individuals to "renounce and abjure" allegiance and fidelity to any "foreign prince, potentate, state or sovereignty of whom or which the applicant was before a subject or citizen," in practice this is hard to regulate in an era of globalization and widespread possibilities for dual nationality extended by other countries. By comparison with many other Western democracies, scholars have labeled legal citizenship in the United States "thin" because it is relatively easy to acquire (Heller 1997; Joppke 1999a).

Kerber (1997) suggests that while political theory has had much to say about the rights of citizenship, there has been much less emphasis on the obligations beyond those of voting, paying taxes, refraining from treason, obligatory service in the military (until 1975 when the United States introduced a volunteer military), and participating on juries. Indeed, very often one of the sole measures of citizenship, and hence the political incorporation of immigrants, is voting behavior. And yet, citizenship, as civic engagement, is a much more complex practice that involves individuals, as agents, in the public sphere. While some ethnographic research on immigrants and citizenship in the United States has focused on the process of acquiring citizenship and hence on citizenship status and citizenship rights, more attention has been directed to the practice of citizenship.

The most innovative and insightful ethnographic research on legal citizenship is directed to an understanding of why immigrants choose to naturalize and how they "live" the process—in essence the study of citizenship from below rather than from above. In their study of a single multigenerational Dominican extended family, Greta Gilbertson and Audrey Singer (2003) discuss differences in the attitudes toward and experiences of naturalization between the first and second immigrant cohorts. However, they conclude that across all cohorts, naturalization is often an action pursued defensively (in relation to legal changes such as those that occurred in 1996 as part of the Illegal Immigration Reform and Immigrant Responsibility Act) and that it does not necessarily obviate participation in the sending society.

Brettell (2006) uses the term pragmatic citizenship to cover a host of very practical reasons for naturalizing (including the facility of travel or the ability to sponsor family members),[7] but she argues that this does not diminish a powerful sense of American identity and political belonging or eradicate a bifocal outlook that sustains an attachment to the culture and country of origin. In her analyses of the naturalization process as seen through the eyes of Salvadoran immigrants, Susan Bibler Coutin (1998, 2003a, 2003b) coins the phrase "additive citizenship" to encompass the same dual sense of belonging. One of Coutin's (2003a: 154) informants told her "Becoming citizens, we don't lose anything. We remain Salvadoran at heart."

As in the United States, citizenship in Europe can be acquired either at birth or through naturalization. There have been recent changes to citizenship laws in European nations that reflect the new immigrant presence and changing ideologies of belonging and national identity. The basis for national citizenship through birth in Europe varies from country to country, with the two extremes of Britain and Germany historically providing the touch points for comparison. As Brubaker (1992: 81) points out, most Western European countries employ some combination of the two principles of jus sanguinis (citizenship based on descent) and jus soli (citizenship based on territory). In Britain, as in the United States, citizenship is a simple matter of being born within national territory. Prior to the new citizenship law of 1999 (Germany Info 2001–6), birth on German soil had no bearing on German citizenship and only the children of citizens could become citizens at birth. Germany's system was based purely on jus sanguinis, but now incorporates some elements of jus soli, and represents a shift in the direction of what has long been the law in France. It is still, however, more restrictive than the French policy. A child born in Germany after January 2000 who has at least one parent who has been a legal permanent resident in Germany for the past eight years, may file for full citizenship at age twenty-three (but must denounce any dual citizenship claims). France has taken a position between the two extremes of Britain and Germany, so that a child born in France or its overseas territories who has at least one parent also born either in France or in one of the former colonies (preindependence) may take citizenship at birth. Moreover, any child born in France to immigrant parents has the right to become a citizen at age eighteen if they have resided in France for at least the last five years and do not have a criminal record. France recently changed its citizenship and naturalization laws during the summer of 2006, making them more restrictive. While this law makes the recruitment of skilled laborers and foreign students easier, it places new restrictions on access to citizenship through naturalization.

There have also been recent changes in citizenship laws in Sweden (Gustafson 2002) that respond to international migration and permit dual citizenship. In her comparative study of new immigration from Eastern Europe and non-Western nations to Italy, Spain, and Greece, Anna Triandafyllidou (2001) points out that these countries have different models of what she calls "national community." Whereas Greece has an "ethnocultural" model, Spain has a model based more on "civic identity," and Italy bases its concept of the nation on both ethnic and territorial aspects.

An important factor in Europe is that European citizenship, which grants rights to travel, study, and work freely across nation-state boundaries as well as the right to vote in European elections, automatically follows from citizenship in any country that is a member of the EU. Therefore, each member nation has an "interest" in the citizenship laws of other nations within the EU. This has led, particularly in European research, to considerations of the relationship between nationality and citizenship. As Balibar has pointed out (2004; see also Reed-Danahay 2006) European citizenship is stratified, and has varying implications related to social class, immigration status, and other factors.

In her discussion of European Union citizenship, Catherine Neveu distinguishes between nationality and citizenship and provides some helpful insights on citizenship from the perspective of Europe. She points out that the common understanding of the English term "citizenship" as a legal status is misleading: "in some European countries, you can thus be a citizen without being a national, i.e., you can enjoy political rights, like voting rights, without being a national (what in French is called 'un ressortissant'). This is the case for instance for Pakistani or Indian nationals residing in Britain, who while not having a British passport can nevertheless, under certain conditions, vote and be elected in local or general elections" (2000: 120).

Neveu (2000: 123; see also Neveu 1995) also argues that horizontal and vertical citizenship be distinguished (vertical having to do with the citizens' relationship to the polity and horizontal with their relationships among themselves). The challenge for European Union citizenship is how to create a sense of belonging among people without an idea of a shared national culture. This question leads, as Neveu points out, to the need "to explore how different levels of citizenship, both as practices and as representations, and different types of identity are mobilized or stimulated, how they interrelate and how they contradict or reinforce each other" (2000: 132). Stewart (1995) has made a similar point about the importance in the European context to separate the nationality and citizenship connection. Speaking of what Neveu would term horizontal citizenship ties, Stewart remarks that "political communities are the product of citizenship practice" (74).

## Being a Citizen

There are both descriptive (models of) and proscriptive (models for) analyses of different modes of "being a citizen." For example, multicultural citizenship (Kymlicka 1995) and differentiated citizenship (Young 1990) are models for societies in which different ethnic populations participate in citizenship through their group membership rather than individual rights. These models argue against the assimilationist state. A related concept is that of cultural citizenship formulated by Renato Rosaldo and William V. Flores (1997: 57) as "the right to be different (in terms of race, ethnicity, or native language) with respect to the norms of the dominant national community, without compromising one's right to belong, in the sense of participating in the nation-state's democratic processes." Cultural citizenship (Rosaldo 1994: 252; see also Rosaldo 1997) "stresses local, informal notions of membership, entitlement and influence," and takes into account what

Rosaldo terms "vernacular notions of citizenship"—that is, the claiming of distinctive and special rights, representation, and cultural autonomy that is different from official or unitary models of citizenship. For example, Rosaldo suggests that among Latinos the notion of *respeto* is linked to concepts of cultural citizenship. And as Rosaldo and Flores (1997) point out, immigrants frequently draw on forms of cultural expression to claim recognition and political rights. A counterdiscourse from within this community is used to redefine illegal status. Sunaina Maira (2004), writing about cultural citizenship among South Asian Muslim youth in the United States, describes young people who "negotiate multiple social identities and structures during their college years." In her study of Sikh youth in Britain, Kathleen Hall (2002) similarly finds the relationship between ethnic identity and citizenship to be one of negotiation in educational settings.

These notions that "complicate" citizenship and point to the various ways of "being" a citizen are connected to the idea of belonging. Individual social actors can belong to more than one polity or social group, they can move back and forth between identities, even if a particular state system defines them in only one way. Our current problems with belonging in the current era stem, as many have argued, from the legacies of nation-states that attempted to reify belonging into notions of formal citizenship. Nation-states construct our identities through what Pierre Bourdieu (1992) called "rites of institution" (such as identity papers, ID cards, etc.), and the nation-state sought to bind together and assimilate people believed to have a shared identity. Much recent research on issues of citizenship has also drawn attention to the ways in which Western nation-states worked to construct a sense of belonging based on geography and a sense of place and boundedness. In the nation-state, historically, territory and polity are one. Yet immigrants as individuals, families, or groups, may transcend these boundaries and operate in various social and political fields.

## HYBRID, TRANSNATIONAL IDENTITIES

In his analysis of changing constructions of the immigrants in European discourses, Paul Silverstein (2005) identifies the two most recent ones as that of the hybrid and the transmigrant. The hybrid is seen as liminal and epitomized by the second generation immigrant who is "in-between" cultures (373); while the transmigrant is someone with "enduring cultural orientations to homelands elsewhere" (375). Silverstein points out that these ways of talking about immigrants travel across national boundaries of scholarship and also are used by immigrant activists in their own discourses of identity (see also Silverstein in this volume). Flexible, transnational, and diaspora citizenship are other concepts that have emerged in the context of ethnographic research among immigrant populations. Much of this research has taken place in the United States, but it has influenced scholarship on European immigration.

Based on her research among the elite Chinese business class in California, anthropologist Aihwa Ong has introduced the term "flexible citizenship" to describe a type of identity that arises from the "cultural logics of capitalist accumulation, travel, and displacement that induce subjects to respond fluidly and opportunistically to changing political-economic conditions" (1999: 6). Ong defines citizenship as a "cultural process of 'subject-ification,' in the Foucaldian sense of self-making and being-made by power relations that produce consent through schemes of surveillance, discipline, control, and administration" (1996b: 737). Ong (2003) has more recently explored how Cambodian refugees negotiate becoming American, focusing her attention on how the state makes Cambodians into good citizens in the context of institutions—economic, political, religions, biomedical, and legal—they encounter.

New forms of what Nina Glick Schiller calls "long-distance nationalism" (see also Anderson 1992) are also expressed in the terms "trans-border citizenship" (Glick Schiller and Fouron 2001) and "diasporic citizenship" (Laguerre 1998). These concepts of citizenship take into account a changing terrain of geographic mobility and mass communication that enhances continued attachment to the homeland for immigrant groups. They describe the simultaneous participation in citizenship practices within and across the borders of nation states and hence the expression of a transnational identity.

Clearly these studies of the process of naturalization, as experienced by immigrants to the United States, address the question of transnational or diasporic citizenship mentioned above as well as the transnational political field that Michel S. Laguerre defines as "a system in which the political process of the nation-state encompasses both actors who live inside as well as those who live outside its legal and territorial boundaries" (1998: 158). Indeed some anthropologists have recently argued that the transnational arrangements constructed by "ordinary migrants, their families and their friends, have undermined both the political dominance exerted by the state and its cultural authority" (Rouse 1995: 358). Glick Schiller and Fouron describe long-distance Haitian nationalists who engage in transborder citizenship by which they mean individuals who "act as substantive citizens in more than one state" (2001: 25). These authors note that the difference between legal citizenship and substantive citizenship is important, the latter referring to practices of claims making to belong to a state, as well as collective organizing "to protect themselves against discrimination, gain rights, or make contributions to the development of that state and the life of the people within it" (2001: 25). In their essay in this volume, Nina Glick Schiller and Ayse Caglar develop further these varying notions of citizenship, focusing in particular on the concept of social citizenship that they define as the process whereby individuals assert rights to citizenship substantively through social practice rather than formally through law.

Some research demonstrates that the participation in homeland politics that is often characteristic of transborder citizenship in fact promotes political incorporation in the society of immigration. These are precisely the issues addressed by Karen Richman and Bernard Wong in their chapters in this volume. But their writings build on earlier work. For example, Anna Karpathakis (1999) argues that it is concern about Greece that mobilizes Greek immigrants in the United States to naturalize, to vote, and to become involved in and organize around activities that influence America's foreign policy toward Greece. The same can be said of Cuban immigrants in Miami, as well as the Vietnamese populations in several cities across the United States (Reed-Danahay in this volume; Gold 1992; Hein 1995; Stepick et al. 2003).

Taking a slightly different approach, Luin Goldring (2001) has explored the transnational citizenship practices of Zacatecan migrants in Los Angeles. She conceptualizes citizenship to include both formal rights and substantive citizenship practices exercised in relation to different levels of political authority and different geographic sites within transnational spaces. Of significance is her finding that while women are excluded from citizenship practices in transnational spaces, they are active in the practice of social citizenship in the United States. Goldring further suggests that the state can shape transnational citizenship practices. "The Mexican state is pushing Mexicans living in the United States to naturalize while retaining close affective ties to Mexico, in the hopes of perpetuating investment, remittances, and 'international cooperation projects.' . . . This amounts to pushing transmigrants to orient their substantive or de facto social and civil citizenship rights toward Mexico and their *de jure* political and social rights toward the United States" (2001: 525). Arturo Escobar (2004) identifies similar trends within the transnational organizations founded by Colombian immigrants in the United States and in the role played by the Colombian state through its governmental and economic institutions.

As James Holston and Arjun Appadurai have pointed out, "cities remain the strategic arena for the development of citizenship" (1999: 2), if not the only arenas and not always strategic. They point out that the flows of goods and persons to urban centers of nation-states has created a "wedge between national space and its urban centers," so that cities are tied to global processes in ways that differ from rural or suburban spaces (3). This has been noted by scholars working in the urban spaces of U.S. cities, which shape the process of political incorporation and civic engagement. Pamela M. Graham (1998; see also Pessar and Graham 2001) argues that the concentrated patterns of settlement characteristics of Dominicans in New York City, as well as the nature of federal and local laws that affect political districting, are as important as ties to the homeland in explaining their political activities. Despite the fact that their rate of naturalization is low and their level of poverty high, immigrants from the Dominican Republic have been actively involved in city- and state-level politics, managing to elect representatives of their group to two major offices in the 1990s. Graham describes a gradual process of involvement (1998: 56). It has also been, she argues, a springboard for broader panethnic engagement. As a result of their increasing involvement Dominicans have arrived at a more expansive understanding of "the political" "to include problems of family survival, neighborhood crime and police brutality, and deteriorating schools, housing stock and public services" (Pessar and Graham 2001: 264). Whether as citizens or noncitizens they are using the appropriate channels to fight for their rights. In a recent ethnographic study that examines the intersections of labor and politics, Christian Zlolniski (2006) challenges the view that undocumented Mexican immigrants will not engage in political mobilization in the United States to improve their conditions.

## IMMIGRANT ASSOCIATIONS AND CIVIC ENGAGEMENT

A number of ethnographic studies, including several in this volume, have pointed to the associative behavior of immigrants, including that which occurs within religious organizations, as vital to political education, the development of leadership skills, and civic engagement. Several works, including that of Robert Putnam in both Italy and the United States, point to the role of associations in fostering social cohesion. In her study of North African immigrant associations in France, Camille Hamidi asks, "are associations places of democratic socialization and of politicization? Are they places where people learn to take care of other people's interests, where people develop broad solidarities and where they learn how to discuss issues in a spirit of communication and tolerance? Are they places that develop civic virtues?" (2003: 318–19).

In the United States, hometown clubs and other associations are an important context for political activity and citizenship practice. For example, in her work on the Chinese in New York City's Chinatown, Jan Lin (1998) discusses a series of militant and advocacy associations, some emerging from radical student organizations. These organizations offer ESL and citizenship classes as well as legal support to Chinese immigrants. Many Chinese, because of their workplace niche, are also involved in organizations like the ILGWU (International Ladies' Garment Workers' Union). These organizations, writes Lin, "have been the most influential in providing services, advocating for rights of workers and residents, and organizing collective action in the community" (1998: 132).

In research on the Vietnamese, Hien Duc Do (1999) also locates some of the roots of political engagement within student organizations on American university campuses (see also Reed-Danahay in this volume). In his research on the Vietnamese, Jeremy Hein (1995) identifies three realms of Vietnamese political involvement: (1) MAAs (Mutual Assistance Associations); (2) grassroots, mainstream, and international political arenas; and (3) legal disputes and courts. Examples of Vietnamese political activity cited by Hein range from protests against political repression in Vietnam, to activism aimed at establishing a separate Vietnamese Catholic parish in San Jose, to court challenges to housing discrimination. Steven J. Gold (1992) emphasizes generational differences—the older generation of Vietnamese in America is more concerned with homeland politics, while the younger groups have become more engaged in domestic issues

Madhulika Khandelwal (2002) argues that an interest in national politics did not really emerge among Indian immigrants in New York City until the 1990s, but even then was largely focused on fundraising for Indian candidates or for American politicians who had a pro-India policy record. Asian Indians, she argues, have been less interested in local politics and the number of politically oriented organizations is small. Most of their other organizations were focused on cultural and religious activities and did not promote broader civic participation. However, in other urban contexts, researchers (Brettell 2005; Rangaswamy 2000) have identified broader activities of civic engagement and political mobilization among Asian Indian immigrants.

Robert Smith (2001), who defines political mobilization not only as political activity focused on engagement with U.S. institutions, actors, and structures but also participation in community organizations, suggests that mobilization is limited among Mexican immigrants because of their legal status, residential dispersal, and low paying jobs. But in the context of anti-immigrant politics they have become more active, and much of this mobilization has occurred in the context of religious organizations. Often, of course, the organizations in the United States engage immigrants, Latinos, and others in homeland politics (Hardy-Fanta 1993; Jones-Correa 1998; Escobar 2004).

European research on immigrants has also focused on immigrant associations (see especially Gibb and Garapich in this volume). Most of these studies have been conducted in or near major European cities, the primary sites for immigrant settlement. One of the first ethnographic studies of political behavior among immigrants in Europe was Gisèle L. Bousquet's 1991 work on Vietnamese in Paris. Her study looked at the "dual political identity" of the French Vietnamese groups concerned with homeland politics in Vietnam yet having high rates of naturalization, and also with factions within the Parisian Vietnamese population. Rather than seeing these factions in terms of interethnic processes and ethnic leaders, she situates the political behavior of Vietnamese in Paris within an international context involving not only Vietnam but also the anticommunist Vietnamese in the United States. In this Bousquet nuances previous work among scholars in other disciplines that focuses on immigrant leaders and their role in mobilization. Hamidi's more recent ethnographic work on immigrant associations in France, which focuses on social associations among North African immigrants in the neighborhood of Saint Denis, looks at a mutual aide association, a sewing association, and a dance/music association. While these are not explicitly political and are "officially apolitical" (2003: 324), they have what Hamidi calls "indirect political effect" (329) in that some members of these groups who started out volunteering went on to more formal political types of collective action. While Hamidi does not see these voluntary associations as necessarily leading toward democratic practices and civic education, they may encourage people to see themselves differently, more as social actors than passive victims, and this may encourage civic engagement.

Gerd Bauman's study of the multiethnic town of Southall, near London, deals with the ways in which concepts of community and culture are used strategically by the various ethnic groups (South Asian Sikhs, Hindus, Muslims; Afro-Caribbeans; and Irish Whites) who interacted in this sphere. This study is therefore about claims to identity, discourses about culture as political resources. Bauman shows how various "cultural communities" in Southall and their leaders, through their associations, compete with each other for civic and social resources. This study shows the site of immigrant political behavior to be a social field in which various ethnic groups work out their positionings vis-à-vis each other and with the wider dominant society.

Gökçe Yurdakul's 2006 study of two Turkish political associations (one more conservative than the other) in Berlin similarly shows that there is variation between associations and immigrant elites. This recent work points to a shift in the receiving societies, which "have gradually begun to take these immigrant associations seriously and to consider them as representative and consultative bodies in immigrant issues" (436). Yurdakul argues for a view of immigrant associations as having a vital role as key political actors in the host country's political decisions. This is a different stance, the

author argues, from that which sees immigrant associations as passive victims of the receiving society's policies or of macrolevel theories (i.e., Soysal
1994) on the postnation that do not take into account the mobilization
work of these associations and assume that immigrants appeal to "universal
rights" apart from claims of ethnic or class legitimacy. Ethnographic studies
of immigrants have also looked at the role of labor unions and other local
associations (Cole 1996) in the context of immigrant political mobilization.
Robert Gibb's chapter in this volume on SOS Racisme similarly looks at
groups that advocate on behalf of immigrants and the role these play.

### BOOK CHAPTERS

The chapters in this book draw from immigrant populations in urban
centers of the United States and Western Europe. Although Latino immigration has been the major focus of immigration studies in the United
States, the examples here draw from other immigrant populations—from
Haiti, India, Vietnam, China, and Africa. While the chapters by Silverstein
and Gibb focus on the well-known issues of North African immigration
to Paris, offering new insights, other chapters based on research in Europe
point to newer flows of immigration—Africans to Italy, Germany, and Ireland, and Latin Americans and Poles to the United Kingdom. There are
large variations among these populations in terms of the historical relationship between their country of origin and their country of immigration; their
political, economic, and social capital; and their "transnationality." Race
plays a prominent role in many of these case studies. The authors study immigrants and members of the "host" society in those spaces in which they
interact—immigrant associations, college campuses, social service agencies,
maternity hospitals, transnational political movements, churches, Internet communities, and high-tech industries. Although these ethnographic
studies are sited or multisited in specific spaces (including cyberspaces), the
social actors involved have networks and frames of reference that are globalized and transnational, as are the structures in which they find themselves. These transnational spaces are increasingly important to immigrant
practices of citizenship. As Riva Kastoryano notes: "the country of origin
becomes a source of identity, the country of residence a source of rights, and
the emerging transnational space, a space of political action combining the
two or more countries" (2000: 311).

This book is divided into three sections, and brief section introductions
precede each group of chapters in order to highlight the major themes that
emerge from each case study. These sections organize the chapters according to themes of discourses of belonging, political mobilization, and "new
spaces" of citizenship. Cases from the United States and from Europe are

grouped together to underscore differences and similarities in immigrant civic engagement across national borders.

NOTES

1. The chapters here were presented in earlier versions at an invited session at the American Anthropological Association meetings in December 2005, cosponsored by the Society for the Anthropology of Europe and the Society for Urban, National, and Transnational/Global Anthropology. The editors of this book organized that session.
2. The term "participatory citizenship" is also used by Irene Bloemraad (2005).
3. The political scientist Mark Miller (1989) has identified five areas of extra-electoral politics with which noncitizen immigrants engage: homeland participation; consultative voice; unions and factory councils; political, civic, and religious organizations; and extraparliamentary opposition. See also the work of political scientist Michael Jones-Correa (1998).
4. The proportion of the foreign born in the total U.S. population was 7.9 percent in 1990 and 11.1 percent by 2000 and had risen to 12.4 percent by 2005. The major Western European nations have comparable figures (Meunz 2006), approximated here as: Ireland (14 percent), Germany (12 percent), Sweden (12 percent), France (11 percent), the Netherlands (10 percent), and the United Kingdom (9 percent).
5. There are restrictions on these principles. Children born in the United States to foreign diplomats are not U.S. citizens, for example. The laws are also liberal. Children born to tourists and illegal aliens who are in the United States are U.S. citizens by birth. There have been a number of amendments to citizenship law during the latter half of the twentieth century, the most recent in 2000.
6. The 1996 Illegal Immigration Reform and Immigrant Responsibility Act was not only an effort to control illegal immigration but also limited some benefits to noncitizen legal immigrants.
7. Jacqueline Maria Hagan (1994) also finds that the practical benefits of citizenship are paramount in people's minds as they consider naturalization.

# PART I

# Inclusion and Exclusion

## Discourses of Belonging

THIS FIRST SECTION of the book deals with immigrant belonging, with examples from the host nations of France, Italy, Ireland, and the United States. In the chapters that follow, we can see that the particular history of a country and its historical relationship to the immigrant populations entering its borders affects the modes of belonging possible for immigrants. The careful ethnographic work exhibited in these chapters illustrates the ways that belonging is a fluid process produced through relationship between the social practices of immigrants and the historical, structural, and cultural conditions within which they find themselves. The authors of these chapters, all of whom have conducted ethnographic fieldwork, based their analyses not only upon detailed social interactions, however, but also place them within the wider contexts in which immigrants as social actors negotiate their place in the new host society. Sources from media, law, public opinion, and formal institutions provide such contexts. Different sites in which belonging is enacted, discussed, or rejected are examined—including sport, music, social service agencies that deal with immigrants, maternity hospitals, and university campuses. Both explicit forms of protest and more informal ways of learning how to negotiate one's position are discussed by the authors as modes of social agency on the part of immigrants. At the same time, the power of the dominant society to undermine the ability of newcomers to "belong" is never ignored.

At a time when immigration has become such a visible and controversial topic, the issue of belonging for those of non-European ancestry who settle in both Europe and the United States is fraught with struggle and contest. Discourses of race, even when hidden in the "new" racism that does not explicitly use a racial vocabulary, are an integral part of discourses of belonging. When we talk about immigrant belonging, we can be talking about various things—possibilities of becoming a citizen in the formal legal sense, possibilities of belonging in a more vernacular sense ("cultural citizenship"), or possibilities of transnational belonging in which the immigrant has two "homes" (the new host country and the country left behind). In the chapters to follow, all of these ways of belonging are addressed.

Paul Silverstein addresses the performance of racialized citizenship in what he calls "Algerian France," especially in Paris. The relationship of North Africans, especially Algerians, to metropolitan France is one in which citizenship and belonging are not congruent processes. During the time that Algeria was a colony of France, legislation granted French citizenship to inhabitants of Algeria—although this was a form of second-class citizenship compared to that of "native" French. After the war of independence, the issue of gaining French citizenship was more complex. The racialized nature of Algerian citizenship in France persists. Starting with the case of Zinedine Zidane, of the French soccer team, who has Algerian parents, Silverstein shows how citizenship is surveilled by the dominant society and also performed by the immigrant. Another example, that of the disenfranchised North African youth of French housing projects, illustrates the rejection of belonging to France on the part of alienated youth who practice a form of what Silverstein calls "politics without politics." At the same time that they reject France, they also make use of images from the storming of the Bastille in their protests.

Flavia Stanley similarly takes up the idea of race and citizenship in her study of social services for immigrants in Rome. Italy as a nation has always recognized its internal regional diversity and sharp contrasts are still drawn between southerners (stigmatized as backward) and northerners. Its historical formation from a fragmented series of smaller states gives it a different national flavor than France, for instance, which has asserted its homogeneity and underplayed its regional cultural distinctions. In her fieldwork, Stanley paid attention to talk about immigrants among social workers and also paid attention to immigrant responses to the intake interviews and Italian language school in which they participated as part of the process of incorporation. A distinction between citizenship and nationality comes across clearly in her study, so that "Italian-ness," an aspect of nationality, becomes a category of belonging not easily entered by immigrants. Italy's anxieties about immigration, despite its relatively low level of immigration compared to other European nations, are, Stanley suggests, related to its marginal status in the European Union.

Angèle Smith's chapter looks toward changing laws of citizenship in Ireland that altered the relationship between motherhood and belonging for asylum seekers, the largest group coming to Ireland in recent years being Nigerians. Ireland presents a slightly different case from the chapters on France and Italy. While France has long had a history of immigration, from Italy and Portugal as well as from North Africa, and Italy has had a lot of diversity within its borders, Ireland is a country with a very strong notion of its homogeneity. It was also a sending society for many generations, and only recently has experienced the economic boom that attracts immigrants. Ireland changed its citizenship laws recently in response to asylum-seeking mothers who prompted concerns about "nonnationals" giving birth in large numbers in Irish hospitals. These "citizenship tourists" were seen to undermine the historical notion of what it means to be Irish. The law now does not grant automatic citizenship to children born on Irish soil (jus soli), but only to children whose parents were born on Irish soil. Smith provides a recent case of the processes of inclusion and exclusion at work in contemporary Europe. The above cases focus on European nations, showing the European Union's presence in recent considerations of citizenship and belonging in Europe. Any citizen of a member nation is automatically a European citizen, which grants liberties of travel, education, and other benefits, not to mention voting in EU elections. Therefore, the surveillance of citizenship in any member nation has consequences for the wider supranational entity of the European Union.

In chapter 4, Deborah Reed-Danahay's case of Vietnamese Americans in the United States presents a contrast. Reed-Danahay's focus on immigrant belonging through "communities of practice" emphasizes the social learning that is part of belonging in a host society. While most Vietnamese immigrants do not face legal barriers to formal citizenship, due to their somewhat privileged status as refugees based on U.S. involvement in the Vietnam War, there are other racial and cultural aspects to belonging that intervene. Reed-Danahay's chapter calls attention to the ways in which immigrants learn to become part of a society, to belong, but also to the constraints on belonging that can develop both internally and externally to the Vietnamese American population. She blends together the concepts of community of practice (Lave and Wegner 1991), cultural intimacy (Herzfeld 2005), and social capital (Bourdieu 1986) in order to better theorize the contexts and modes of belonging and exclusion that operate in contexts of immigration. Her chapter also has implications for the role that college campuses can play as settings for the enactment of immigrant inclusion or exclusion.

CHAPTER 1

# Kabyle Immigrant Politics and Racialized Citizenship in France

*Paul A. Silverstein*

ON JULY 9, 2006, the national football teams of Italy and France met in the championship match of the World Cup finals in Berlin, Germany. While both countries had previously won World Cups, the presence of France in the final match came as a surprise, particularly given its first-round exit in the previous World Cup finals in 2002, and its poor showing during the preliminary rounds of the 2006 competition. Indeed, before its round of sixteen victories over Spain, most French fans and experts had all but written off the chances of their national side, *Les Bleus*. Searching for scapegoats, commentators from the political Far Right blamed the team—consisting largely of black and North African players, several of whom had been born outside of the *metropole*—as nonrepresentative of the French nation.[1] Zinedine Zidane, the center-midfielder hero of France's 1998 victory who was born in Marseille to Berber-speaking Kabyle (Algerian) parents, was particularly singled out for criticism both for his lackluster play and, more egregiously, for his apparent lack of patriotism as evidenced by his not publicly singing the national anthem ("La Marseillaise") at the beginning of matches.

However, after brilliant performances against Spain and Brazil—in which Zidane was remarked to have been the only "Brazilian" on the pitch in terms of his display of creativity and virtuosity normally associated with South American football (Delerm 2006)—and a gritty victory over Portugal—in which he scored the only goal from the penalty spot—Zidane had suddenly emerged as a renewed national hero, and expectations for a French victory charge led by Zidane were running high.[2] Such expectations were nearly fulfilled deep in overtime when, with the match locked at 1–1, Zidane redirected a header toward the goal in nearly identical fashion as he had done to score the winning goal in 1998, with the ball only to be brilliantly saved by the Italian keeper. Several minutes later, with only ten minutes to go in the match and penalty kicks looking inevitable, Zidane, in a spectacular gesture that will remain indelibly linked to the 2006 World Cup and Zidane's lasting legacy, seemingly inexplicably lowered his head and felled Italian defender Marco Materazzi.

In the weeks that followed, Zidane's "head-butt" (*coup de boule*) became the source of a veritable social drama over race, racism, and violence in France that all but overshadowed the outcome of the match.[3] On replays, it was clear that Zidane reacted most immediately to a sustained verbal tirade from Materazzi, the exact words of which were subject to much debate, but about which there was some general agreement that the comments were racist in tenor, with some (including Zidane's own brother) claiming that Materazzi had called Zidane the "son of a terrorist whore."[4] Regardless of the exact words said, Zidane's reaction was itself racialized in the press, taken as a sign of his rough-and-tumble upbringing in the housing projects (*les cités*) of La Castellane (Marseille) and, more particularly, of his Algerian "sense of honor" (see Kessous 2006).[5] Far Right ideologues gloated in the downfall of *Les Bleus* provoked by the "little hooligan" (*voyou*) of "Zidane the African" (Forcari 2006: 10).

In addition to such reracialization of Zidane, the head-butt was immediately decried by a number of French commentators in the mainstream press (including *L'Equipe* and *Le Monde*) as setting a negative example for children across the world, and particularly from the suburban cités of France (see Caussé 2006; Droussent 2006).[6] Such criticism was magnified by the recent memory of urban violence among France's racialized youth, particularly in October-November 2005, when, after the electrocution of three Muslim children from the Parisian suburb of Clichy-sous-Bois, confrontations between local youth and police raged for three weeks across 280 municipalities, resulting in 10,000 torched cars and 4,800 arrests.[7] Moreover, Zidane's Algerian background recalled the disastrous France-Algeria match of October 2001, in which young Franco-Algerian men and women in the stands whistled during "La Marseillaise" and, in the seventieth minute with France leading 4–1, invaded the pitch waving Algerian flags. Accordingly the head-butt was read by many as a de facto act of sabotage of French national dreams and an index of Zidane's suspect loyalty to the French nation—and via him the suspect citizenship of all Franco-Algerians. Only after Zidane issued a public apology, with a particular note of regret for the "children" who had seen his final performance, was he generally forgiven by the French president Jacques Chirac and the majority of polled French men and women.

This chapter explores the embedded racial dynamics of citizenship and national belonging in France to which the social drama around the surveillance of Zidane's public actions—his nonsinging of "La Marseillaise," the head-butt, his televised apology—attests. In theory, French republican ideologies of citizenship explicitly exclude diacritics of race and ethnicity in the determination of political subjectivity and the attribution of rights and duties. However, this official discourse belies a set of gendered, racialized practices that outline different forms of political belonging for first and second-generation immigrants—as well as other racially or ethnically hyphenated men and women—in France.[8] These practices of institutional suspicion of immigrant legality and loyalty effectively constitute a racial and spatial divide—what Étienne Balibar (2004) terms "apartheid"—between "rooted French" (*Français de souche*) and French citizens of color treated as "second-class citizens," between those who can claim what Ghassan Hage (2000), writing of Australian nationalism, calls "governmental" or "managerial" belonging empowered to accept and forgive, and those who must constantly apologize for their presence (Sayad 2004: 252, 290). Moreover this racialized divide is in no way stable, but must be continuously made and remade—or, as Judith Butler (1990), following J. L. Austin (1962), claims, "performed"—through public, perlocutionary words and deeds that have pragmatic effects. Through an examination of the various, conflicting ways in which primarily male North African immigrants and their children speak and do politics, I argue that citizenship—when taken as a practical, lived, everyday, vernacular experience rather than simply as a legal syntax (see Reed-Danahay in this volume)—should less be understood as a set of enacted formal criteria of group membership than as a repetitive, surveilled performance of national belonging.

In particular, this chapter outlines a constitutive ambivalence at the heart of immigrant political practice in France, which opposes two modalities of "doing politics" as simultaneously crucial yet mutually contradicting performatives of Franco-Algerian citizenship. The first modality—what I have elsewhere described as "transpolitics" (Silverstein 2004a; see also Richman in this volume)—involves the politicization of cultural practices—from religious dress to musical production to public language use—that transcend the formal political sphere and occur within the larger space of transnational engagement that unites spatially noncontiguous polities and state structures across the Mediterranean (see Glick Schiller and Caglar in this volume for a parallel case of transnational engagement). In this chapter, I will focus on the Berber cultural activism and party politics of Kabyles from northeastern Algeria in France. The second modality—which I am here glossing as "politics without politics"—concerns the performative denial of these self-same transpolitical practices as themselves "political," which is to say as self-serving or interested, as oriented toward the advancement of individual political careers. This chapter will examine such denials of the political field in the ghettocentric, localized cultural politics of French hip-hop.

That these two modalities of racialized citizenship performance can coexist in Algerian France is perhaps not in and of itself surprising, as they seem to be but a specific case of a cyclical, if not global, generational shift, where new social actors attempt to redefine the political as a space of ethical engagement in a way that provides them room for personal mobility and distinguishes them from their (presumably careerist) forebears. However, in the case of immigrants—and particularly male Muslim immigrants in France—whose citizenship, if legally recognized, is perpetually surveilled, the stakes of this generational rupture are significant.[9] Indeed, the intersection of a transpolitics and a "politics without politics" in the practice of immigrant vernacular, practical citizenship constitutes a central dilemma within a larger social drama over the changing contours of the French nation, over the incorporation of immigrant agency into a shifting field of French national politics.

Thinking about immigrant politics and citizenship in light of recent upsurges in racialized violence on the French urban periphery requires an expansion of our understanding of the "political." For, if there is anything that characterizes the confrontations between housing project young men and the French police, it is the *lack* of any explicit or coherent political ideology in the general "rage" or "hate" (*haine*) of the French "system" viscerally expressed by these French citizens (many of whom are of Algerian parentage) inhabiting the cités. These young men feel alienated from the political process; they feel that voting is, in the words of local, St-Denis hip-hop artist Joey Starr, no better than "pissing into the wind." Moreover, they view any formal relationship with the state as inherently delegitimizing, as "selling out." Such a delegitimation of the political is exactly the problem faced by local community activists and self-appointed (or government-appointed) spokesmen and women, who view the political apathy of the younger generation as a major impediment to their integration as full-fledged citizens of France, and hence as a not insignificant underlying factor magnifying their rage (see interviews collected in Bouamama, Sad-Saoud, and Djerdoubi 1994). The efforts of these local actors to motivate their juniors thus requires a recontextualization, if not de facto mystification, of their own political engagement. It is in this sense that Zidane's *coup de boule* can be read as a public performance that invokes particular claims and denials of national belonging that reinscribe racialized divides within citizenship.

## RACIALIZED CITIZENSHIP

Citizenship in France is a racially contested terrain. Scholars of immigrant incorporation and naturalization have generally treated citizenship as an "abstract, formal construct," which has developed historically and which may or may not involve determinants of "ethnocultural nationality" (Brubaker 1992: 30). Yet, as Étienne Balibar (2004), Nicholas De Genova (2005), and Ghassan Hage (2000) in different European, American, and Australian settings suggest, citizenship retains a racialized dimension, both in terms of its criteria of access (often mediated by ties of genealogy) and in terms its ongoing "unequal politics," which maintain informal, embedded distinctions between "homely" and "naturalized" citizens. For Hage, behind the "institutional-political acceptance" of citizenship that formally erases internal distinctions lies an informal, unequal distribution of "practical cultural nationality" that leads to the creation of "national aristocracies" and the underwriting of white supremacy in societies like Australia (2000: 51–62). This white aristocracy maintains a sense of "governmental" or "managerial belonging" according to which they believe themselves to be the "enactors of the national will" and exercise a "nationalist practice of exclusion" on racialized Aboriginal and Asian cocitizens (46–47). In De Genova's study of Mexicans in the United States, this exclusion is reinforced through the legal construction of "illegality," and the racialization of Mexican immigrants in relation to the "hegemonic polarity of whiteness and Blackness" as temporary laborers and as potentially deportable (2005: 6–9; see also Chavez 2001). Balibar discusses the ways that such mechanisms of informal exclusion maintain the "discrimination and hierarchization of populations" in Europe such that "once an immigrant, always an immigrant, with the unlimited possibilities of exploitation that status allows" (2004: 63). The endgame, for Balibar, is the construction of a "virtual European apartheid" within "European citizenship" (x).

In the case of France, while abstract principles of *jus soli*—according to which rights devolve from territory rather than blood—have theoretically extended legal citizenship to those born on French soil at the age of maturity, questions of morality and loyalty have historically determined the parameters under which such citizenship rights have been adjudicated. As Mahmood Mamdani (1996) and Ann Laura Stoler (1997) among others have demonstrated, fears of moral decay and the degeneration of cultural-*cum*-racial purity underwrote colonial debates over the incorporation of indigenous subjects into French legal belonging. In colonial Algeria, Muslims were denied French citizenship on the basis of their religious "local civil status," in spite of the fact that Algeria was administratively assimilated as part of France after 1880, and thus subject to the same juridical regime as the metropole. To a certain extent, one might rightly understand this hesitation in legal incorporation as part of a larger French Islamophobic discourse that regarded (and in many ways still regards) Islam as incompatible with secularist modernity; however, colonial arguments on this issue frequently returned to the proposition that the loyalty of Muslim subjects was inherently suspect, as they owed principal allegiance to a set of political-legal orientations derived from shari'a courts, imamate religious decrees (or fatwas), and an absent (if potentially reconstitutable) caliphate. When in 1891 the Third Republic considered naturalizing all Algerians, a violent debate broke out within the Parliament, with one senator, Mr. Sabatier, opposing the reform on the grounds that it would implicitly condone "Coranic" civil and familial practices which "escape French laws, not to mention French morality" (cited in Borgé and Viasnoff 1995: 18). To achieve French citizenship, Muslim "nationals" were required to engage in a linguistic primary performative (Austin 1962: 7, 32), to verbally apostatize themselves and deny their subjection to religious precepts before a representative of the colonial civil administration.

While Muslim Algerians gained French citizenship with the adoption of the Constitution of the Fifth Republic in 1958, a racialized distinction in legal status and representation was maintained (Ruedy 1992: 152; Shepard 2006: 46–49). After independence, Algerian citizenship superceded French legal belonging, with nationality replacing racial-*cum*-religious status in setting divides between populations. This was particularly consequential given the long and turbulent history of Algerian emigration to France that, during the colonial period, had primarily consisted of a circulation of male migrant laborers on short-term contracts for manufacturing, mining, and agricultural concerns, but during the violence of the 1954–62 Algerian war of decolonization had increasingly become more settled, with families increasingly joining male immigrants. By 1973, when France closed its borders to future economic immigrants from Algeria, the Algerian immigrant population in France had reached 800,000, making it the second largest immigrant group in the country. Ongoing policies of family reunification, asylum, and the attribution of citizenship status at birth to children born in France to parents having been born in colonial Algeria, have contributed to the growth of the French-Algerian population to an estimated 1.5 million today, of which a substantial minority (approximately 40 percent) are Berber speakers originating in Kabylia.[10]

Algerian immigration, particularly given its charting of the violence of colonialism and decolonization, has been subject to repeated martial representations within French political discourse, with immigration portrayed as an "invasion." Moreover, the housing projects that immigrant families have largely occupied since the 1960s have been characterized in the media and state urban renewal discourse as spaces of criminality, delinquency, and violence, as "outside of the law," if not sites of "jihad" (Battegay and Boubeker 1993; Pujadas and Salam 1995; Silverstein 2004a: 109–11; Wihtol de Wenden 1991). Given such enduring anxieties, the parameters of French citizenship and immigrant naturalization have been subject to repeated debate. In 1993, under the aegis of conservative Interior Minister Charles Pasqua, the Code of Nationality was reformed. New provisions required those born in France to noncitizen immigrant parents to make a formal request for citizenship and declaration of loyalty to the French nation between their sixteenth and eighteenth birthdays. Although the code was seen as punitive and was rescinded when the Socialists regained control of the government in 1996, several criteria were maintained that continue to highlight morality and loyalty as parameters of French citizenship: namely the requirement of uninterrupted residence of the applicant in the national territory during the preceding five years and the need to demonstrate an absence of any previous revocation of citizenship rights either through verbal statement or due to a felony conviction. Moreover, in 2004 these checks have been augmented by the creation of a "Contract of Integration," which, as of 2006, all immigrant applicants for French residence permits must sign, declaring their "willingness to integrate into French society and to accept and respect the fundamental values of the Republic" (Clarkin 2005). And, following the 2005 suburban confrontations, Prime Minister Dominique de Villepin further announced that "mastery of the French language" would likewise be required for the granting of future long-term residence permits.

The existence of these criteria underlines the publicly suspect nature of naturalization as a procedure of immigrant incorporation. As Abdelmalek Sayad has emphasized, the "original sin" of immigration is suffered as a "genetic crime" by hyphenated French citizens who, as "ambiguous agents," "blur the borders of the national order" and are thus subject to "perpetual anxiety" and "collective suspicion" (2004: 291–92). Distinctions between white autochthones (*Français de souche* or "rooted French") and racialized allochthones (*Français de papier* or "paper French") remains a mainstay of French political discourse, whether in terms of media reporting of youth from the cités as "immigrant," regardless of the fact that many are French citizens born and raised in France; or in terms of Jean-Marie Le Pen's populist xenophobic fantasies concerning the "repatriation" of immigrants. The general nonrecognition of North African French citizens as full compatriots is not lost on the objects of such suspicion, whose own antiracist demands for social, economic, cultural, and religious equality and inclusion have been premised on their declaration of membership in the *patrie*—the Republican *pays légal* of post-Revolutionary universal citizenship, if not the traditionalist *pays réel* of French village culture (Lebovics 1992).

This visceral understanding underwrites the language of "rights" appropriated into what became known as the "Beur Movement" of the early 1980s, when Franco-Algerians advocated for "equality" and "civil rights" in a series of public concerts, demonstrations, strikes, and occasional confrontations with police.[11] In particular, participants in these events protested the extrajudicial killings (*bavures*) and deportations of cité residents by French police and state authorities, acts that effectively denied these young men and women citizenship and reduced them to a bare life of disposable bodies. The question of deportation, in particular, proved to be an important rallying point for the construction of Beur political subjectivity. In 1981, Franco-Algerians in Lyon staged a series of hunger strikes in opposition to recent legal regimes of deportation: the Barre/Bonnet law of December 1979, which enabled the detention and expulsion without trial of noncitizens in violation of immigration laws; and the Stoléru Circular of May 1980, which sanctioned the expulsion of documented immigrants unemployed for a six-month period. When, in spite of these protests, a young woman from the Lyon suburb of Saint-Dizier was deported to Algeria, neighboring Les Minguettes exploded in a flurry of approximately 250 violent confrontations between young residents and the police. Known colloquially as "rodeos," these confrontations played out as public spectacles in which local youth stole expensive cars, engaged police in a chase, and then abandoned and burned the vehicles. Similar incidents occurred two years later in nearby Vénissieux, and afterward periodically across the urban periphery. While the Barre/Bonnet and Stoléru decrees were subsequently annulled by President Mitterrand in the early years of his presidency, deportations continued apace under the auspices of even tougher legislation against undocumented immigrants.[12] Indeed, recent civil disobedience by and in support of undocumented African immigrants and their young families—including pitched battles over asylum sanctuaries in churches and association locales—follows very closely upon this earlier history of public protest. In both cases, allochthony is in large part determined through a legal construction of what Nicholas De Genova has termed "deportability" (2005: 8).

While struggles with police over spaces of residence and sanctuary have left an indelible mark in the larger immigrant political imaginary, a more banal form of citizenship surveillance involves the everyday police stops of young Franco-Algerians. Such "random," but clearly racially profiled (*à faciès*) identity checks, pat-downs, and detainments, as practiced by the

Anti-Criminal Brigade, have been for many years a regular feature of every-day housing project life, and have only been exacerbated with the security elaboration of France's post-September 11th "war on terror" and the crimi-nalization of gatherings in cité spaces like the entryways and basements of estate buildings. Even earlier, following the enactment of the Vigipirate security plan after the 1995 subway bombings, transportation centers had become similar spaces of heightened watchfulness, with roving patrols of riot police and military gendarmes imposing millions of identity checks on racially profiled subjects. In choosing their subjects, the security forces naturalize particular gendered bodily features (such as the "Beur look" of track suits and baseball caps) as markers of identity and, consequently, of suspect allegiance. During these stops, those detained are required to pro-duce their residence permits and/or national identity cards, thus publicly attesting their legality and/or nationality. In these performances of belong-ing, a racialized form of second-order citizenship is effectively recreated through the threat of violence.

A third site to examine the performance of racialized citizenship is in the contest over the speaking position of the "citizen," which occurred dur-ing the 2003–4 debates around the banning of headscarves from French public schools. The wearing of the "Islamic headscarf" (or *hijab*) by young Muslim women in France had been the subject of public debate since the 1989 dismissal of three French-Moroccan girls from a public middle school (*collège*) in the Parisian suburb of Creil for refusing to remove their heads-carves in class. A 1992 high court ruling later allowed for the *hijab* except when the dress was either ostentatious and interfered with the educational environment or represented an act of proselytism. However, as these criteria necessitated the interpretation of school teachers and administrators, the issue remained open and repeatedly came to a head every fall with the dismissal of students wearing *hijab*. Moreover, the *hijab* was further linked to fears of an Islamist insurgency among French Muslims, a fear magnified by the 1995 subway bombings linked to the Algerian Armed Islamic Group, and in which a French-Algerian citizen of Lyon had taken part, and the arrest after September 11th of Zacarias Moussaoui as the "twentieth hijacker" and the discovery of a number of French citizens among the Taliban in Afghanistan. In 2004, President Chirac, as part of his growing arsenal in the "war on ter-ror," ratified a sweeping law on *laïcité* (state secularism) that banned "signs that ostensibly manifest religious belonging" (including the *hijab*, the Jewish *kippa*, and excessively large crosses) from French public schools.[13]

In protest, women wearing *hijab* demonstrated throughout France, poi-gnantly carrying French flags, marching with banners evoking "Liberty, Equality, Fraternity, Laïcité," releasing blue-white-red balloons, and even wearing headscarves emblazoned with the French tricolor. They faultlessly sang "La Marseillaise" including, as reporters remarked with amazement, verses seldom heard at national celebrations. Their verbal acts similarly deployed the language of (religious) citizenship, with protestors declaring themselves "proud to be French and Muslim" (*"Française, musulmane et fière de l'être"*). Protesters in Nice intoned, "We, French Muslim women, we defend the Republic, liberties, and *laïcité*." In perhaps the most evocative display of citizenship, demonstrators throughout the country waved their national identity cards while invoking some version of "one headscarf = one vote." Thus, as in the cases of Beur activism and police stops, we see that citizenship, when taken as surveilled performance rather than a set of formal rights, remains the racially contested terrain on which the future of the French nation is being determined.

## TRANSPOLITICS

Having examined the general racialized terrain of immigrant citizenship practice, I now want to turn to the ambivalent modalities of transpolitics and "politics without politics." These modalities structure the political engagements of immigrant social actors in France, with the new generation engaged in the simultaneous politicization of cultural practices and the denial of said politicization as being about "politics." I will examine this constitutive ambivalence by taking two examples: one that tracks the national and the transnational; the other that mediates the local and the national. The first instance involves the enactment of Algerian civil war politics on French soil; the second concerns the ghettocentric politics of French hip-hop. Both examples underline how citizenship, when viewed as a social practice rather than as a set of formal rights and duties, emerges out of a set of embodied (and often linguistic) performances.

The first case concerns that of Algerian civil war electoral politics as it is played out among Berber-speaking immigrants from Kabylia and their children in France. Following the 1988 liberalization of Algerian politics that brought an end to the single party state of the revolutionary National Liberation Front (FLN), a multiplicity of political parties were formed representing the entire political spectrum: from Islamist to Berberist to feminist to Trotskyist to centrist, and so on. This political process was interrupted from 1992 to 1995 after the army took power to block the Islamists from gaining electoral control of the parliament, resulting in a ten-year civil war in which over 100,000 people perished in battles between the military and various Islamist militias.[14] During the war, all but the outlawed Islamist parties remained organizing forces both at home and among the Algerian diaspora in France. In particular, the two

Kabylia-based political parties—the Socialist Forces Front (FFS) and the Rally for Culture and Democracy (RCD)—were active presences in France during the presidential elections of 1995, 1999, and 2004; the legislative elections of 1997 and 2002; and the various national referendums called for the approval of constitutional reform (1996) and amnesty laws (1999 and 2005)—whether participating directly in the voting or actively calling for boycotts. They both operated through immigration wings in France calqued on preexisting village and cultural associations.

The FFS and RCD's domination of Kabyle political life since 1989 constitutes a classic dual classification system as described by Lévi-Strauss (1963) (see Silverstein 2003: 95–96), insofar as their binary division constituted and organized the sociopolitical field of Algeria. In terms of civil war politics, the FFS consistently espoused a position of reconciliation with the outlawed Islamists as the only possible means to resolving the civil war. It was a cosignatory with the FIS of the Sant'Egidio platform that called for a negotiated, multiparty solution and a civil peace; it boycotted the 1995 presidential elections and consistently refused to take part in the various military governments that have ruled Algeria since 1992. In contrast, the RCD took part in national elections in 1995 and 1999, and participated in the coalition government under Abdelaziz Bouteflika, who became president in 1999. More significantly, the RCD advocated a hard-line (*éradicateur*) position that has rejected any dialogue with Islamist forces.[15]

Beyond these divergences in the enactment of civil war politics, the FFS and the RCD were understood by many Kabyles I interviewed in France to function as rival village clans (*lessfuf*, sing. *ssef*), as embodiments of the ritualized antagonism that is written into village social relations and spatial arrangements, and that occasionally results in violent encounters read as wars of "honor" (*nnif*). More broadly, these *lessfuf* often come to represent, in the structuralist logic of dual classification systems, two opposed moral universes, often designated with left-hand/right-hand terminology (Khellil 1984: 33–34; cf. Hart 1999). In the case of the *lessfuf* of Kabyle politics, the FFS and RCD were firstly seen to correspond to two opposed political generations, with the FFS drawing its symbolic capital from the war of national liberation and the RCD attempting to claim a monopoly over those who came of age in the Berber Spring. Furthermore, they were seen as having discrete territorial claims, with the FFS claiming geographical prominence in the province of Bejaïa (the eastern district of Kabylia) and the RCD dominating the *wilaya* of Tizi-Ouzou. Finally they were seen as corresponding to two distinct classes, with the FFS drawing from the ranks of maraboutic (i.e., localized saintly) lineages, while the RCD, with its avowed secularist ideology, clearly appealing to the larger population of the laity.

Obviously these distinctions were ideal and only approximated the complex reality of civil war politics, where Kabyle brothers and sisters found themselves on opposite sides of the divides between the military government, the Islamists, and the Berberist parties, not to mention internally between the FFS and RCD. Nonetheless, these popular perceptions, coupled with the irreconcilable political platforms of the two parties, resulted in the fragmentation of the larger ethnonationalist Berber Cultural Movement (MCB) into factions aligned with each party, making concerted political action difficult. For instance, a 1994–95 boycott of public school classes with the goal of forcing the teaching of Berber language (Tamazight) broke down prematurely due to internal strife between the MCB factions. Subsequent popular mobilizations for political and economic autonomy in 1998 and 2001 have likewise found themselves bifurcated and weakened by the constant doubling of organizational committees, marches, and demands. Increasingly these same political divisions mapped onto Berber cultural associations in France, with the two major associations of mid-1990s Paris, the Association de Culture Berbère (ACB) and Tamazgha, as well as their sister associations in the suburbs and provinces, allied with the RCD and the FFS respectively. Even the transnational World Amazigh Congress (CMA) fractured along the two lines after the entrance of RCD-affiliated associations after 1999.

Such political infighting, alongside the evident careerism of various leaders, like the FFS's Hocine Aït-Ahmed and the RCD's Said Sadi, increasingly discredited the parties in the eyes of many Kabyles. This was particularly evident during the April 2001 "Black Spring" demonstrations in Kabylia, when angry young men fed up with the ongoing social and economic marginalization (*hogra*) of Kabylia fire-bombed party headquarters alongside their attacks on the police stations, town halls, and other edifices of the Algerian state. The parties were completely ineffective in their calls for calm, and it took the emergence of a new organizational body—a confederation of local village assemblies—to negotiate an end to the violence. Likewise, in France there was increasing popular disgruntlement with the inability of the FFS and RCD in effectuating concrete changes. While an overwhelming number of Kabyle immigrants and their dual national children participated in the 1995 presidential elections in spite of the FFS's call for boycott—to the extent that one unaffiliated militant complained to me about the excessive patriotism of Kabyles, that they were too tied to questions of citizenship—this participation dropped off substantially in subsequent elections and referendums.

Beginning in the late 1990s, Franco-Kabyles started forming associations that sought to escape the FFS/RCD party divisions and reorient transpolitics away from the practices of formal citizenship to an enactment of multicultural belonging. Such was the explicit discourse of one Argenteuil-based association, MCB-France, a group whose communiqués embrace the transnational dimensions of immigrant culture while pointing to the daily exigencies of life in France. A charter member of the transnational World Amazigh Congress, the association reached out to Berber groups beyond the narrow confines of the Algerian political scene. Moreover it actively sought to forge ties with other cultural movements initiated by regional and immigrant groups in France, including inviting Occitan and Breton activists to its public events and conferences. Its goal was to appeal to the younger generation growing up in the suburban housing projects surrounding Argenteuil, young men and women whose already distant ties to Algerian society had been further attenuated due to the travel difficulties imposed by the civil war violence. Moreover, by shying away from the sphere of formal politics, the association sought simultaneously to appeal to these young members' parents who were understandably anxious about their children joining any political organizations, fearing the effect this might have on their futures whether in France or in Algeria. While individual members were engaged militants, its public gatherings focused on the aesthetic, literary, and ritual dimensions of transnational Berber culture. In so doing, it outlined a form of political engagement that could effectively deny its own political character.

### GHETTOCENTRICITY

If Algerian civil war politics outlined the transnational dimensions of citizenship performance, hip-hop points to its hyperlocal dimensions. Since the mid-1980s, French hip-hop has been an emergent genre of musical, dance, and artistic performance that has succeeded in bridging ethnic and racial divides among the inhabitants of France's marginalized urban periphery (see Bazin 1995; Durand 2002; Prévos 1996). On the one hand, it has been incredibly flexible to the incorporation of different stylistic forms that emerge from the various immigrant trajectories—whether it be North African raï or gnawa rhythms, Roma vocalizations, or sub-Saharan African dance movements—merging them with various African American musical traditions from funk and soul through ska and reggae. On the other hand, the immediate object of hip-hop's critical engagement has been the everyday life in the housing projects, the structures that bind together the different ethnic, racial, and religious "communities," such as they are. Rap artists in particular have underlined local ties over national or international ones, organizing themselves around interracial "posses" of fellow residents of their natal housing projects who often serve the groups as managers, promoters, security guards, and back-up singers. They invoke locality in

tags, cover art, and song lyrics that reference their particular cité belonging. For example, one group, Suprême NTM, consisting of one white and
one black rapper, constantly references their native St-Denis, or the larger
administrative department of Seine-Saint-Denis—and its short-hand postal
code 93—in song as well as in the name of their posse and graffiti tag. For
other groups, the reference is Aubervilliers (Tandem), Creil (Alliance Eth-
nik), Les Ulis (Diam's, Sinik), Marseille (IAM, Fonky Family), Sarcelles
(Ministère Amer), or Vitry-sur-Seine (113).

This "ghettocentricity," as Robin D. G. Kelley (1996: 136) has called
it with reference to American gangsta rap, is evidenced both in the themes
of French rap focusing on life on the streets (including realistic portrayals
of violence and drug dealing) and in the musical and linguistic tropes used
in the songs. Indeed, the vocal style of the rapping (their "flow") often
explicitly mimics everyday speech in the cités not only in terms of the use
of various slang expressions, but also in rhythm, enunciation, scansion,
and prosody that can denote very specific localities and origins. Lyrically
hardcore rap artists attest to having a "cité culture" or "ghetto heritage"
(*patrimoine du ghetto*) that supercedes any sense of belonging to the French
nation or any other society with which their parents identify (see the com-
pilation album, *Patrimoine du Ghetto*, 2005). In his 2006 composition, "Si
Proche Des Miens" ("So Close to My Own"), Sinik revisits the refrain,
"I make music for my people ('cause that's my people)" from NTM's 1998
anthem, "That's My People," and reaffirms his own identity as "just a
rapper representing his town," as well as his ongoing loyalty to those who
have supported him. In another song on the same album, he specifies his
representational priorities as "One for my street, two for my block, three
for my hall," followed by shout-outs to his friends in jail, in "the biz," and
those fighting the cops ("Zone Interdite" ["Forbidden Zone"], 2006).

Ghettocentric identification is further attested through the rap artists' deployment of a gendered kinship idiom in which their age-mates
are addressed as classificatory "brothers" and "sisters," and the larger cité
community as their "family" or "clan."[16] To a great extent, this refer-
ential practice emerges from the larger structuring of cité community
networks of economic exchange and social reciprocity through ties of fictive kinship. In particular, young men in their twenties and thirties tend
to act as "older brothers" (*les grands frères*) with social authority over the
younger generation in the housing estates, serving as surrogate guardians
for immigrant parents culturally or linguistically marginalized from their
younger children, and garnering support from municipal officials seeking local intermediaries in their various wars on crime, drugs, and terror
(Duret 1996).

If rap artists acknowledge this socially prescribed role as older brothers, they work to carve out a space for themselves free from state cooptation. Indeed, the fraternity they invoke is contrasted explicitly with the *fraternité* of the French national triptych that they depict as racist and hypocritical: "That is France: Liberty to shut up and be deported (*fermer sa gueule et prendre son charter*). Equality for whom? My fraternity starts with my brothers" (La Clinique, "Est-Ce Ça La France?" 1998). They repeatedly express solidarity with their "brothers" killed by police violence, as well as with others who decide to take to the streets in (sometimes violent) protest (cf. Sniper, "Nique le Système" ["Screw the System"], 2003). They promise to remember the trials of their parents—the "bloodied years" of colonial violence, debilitating factory work, and wartime antiimmigrant pogroms (La Rumeur, "On M'a Demandé D'Oublier" ["They Asked Me to Forget"], 1998)—and vow either to "re-pay the blows" (*rendre les coups de baton*) that their parents had received (La Rumeur, "Pedateur Isolé," 2002) or demonstrate that they are "capable of working together to stop the violence" altogether (Fonky Family, "Sans Faire Couler Le Sang" ["Without Drawing Blood"], 1997). Finally rappers hope for "one day of peace for our sons, one day of peace for our daughters" (113, "Un Jour de Paix" ["A Day of Peace"], 2005) and express their desire to "watch my son grow up, hoping that we can build an empire and fly the flag of our family, our hands on our heart" (Sinik, "Si Proche des Miens," 2006).

In these ways, the invocation of familial belonging and community solidarity proposes local patriotism in the place of national identity. 113 refers to Vitry-sur-Seine as "my nation" (*ma patrie*) ("Les Evadés," 1998), and Assassin famously claimed: "My only nation is my posse. . . . The flag of unity is planted in the 18th" ["arrondissement of Paris from where the group hails"] ("Kique ta merde," 1993; see Cannon 1997: 162–63). Such a politics of locality tends to dismiss, rather than engages, the formal national and international political sphere. While some groups like Assassin or La Rumeur do espouse radical agendas of transformative politics, most simply see themselves as street journalists, as "amplifiers" for the extant rage in the cités. NTM's Joey Starr has claimed in an interview that "It's not up to me to explain what there is to do . . . We're just a reflection of what's happening . . . We don't throw stones at cops, only words. . . . Some people think we exaggerate; I'd say we tend to understate" (*Le Monde* 16 November 1999). Rather, rappers highlight in their texts and self-presentation the figure of the antipolitical, individualistic *caillera* ("gangsta"), the urban, postindustrial incarnation of Eric Hobsbawm's "social bandit" or "primitive rebel" (1959, 2000). Such rebelliousness is focused on local contests for value and authority established through spectacular acts of violence against symbolic

material property (cars, state buildings, shopping centers) and in direct confrontations with the police. Their general call is, as in NTM's 1995 anthem,
"What Are We Waiting For?" ("Qu'Est-Ce Qu'On Attend"), "to burn the
whole place down," or, in Sniper's 2003 version, to "screw the system,"
rather than to a play a role in it or transform it. Indeed, for Joey Starr, like
for most of the young cité residents he is amplifying, French governmental
structures have lost all credibility: "For people like me, a government of the
Left or the Right is the same" (*Libération* 26 January 1999). Voting, much
less direct engagement in the formal political process, is, for Joey Starr, like
"pissing in the wind."

However, this general apathy with regards to formal or revolutionary
politics should not necessarily imply the complete depoliticization of the
cités or the quiescence of its immigrant residents. If the young cité residents who took to the streets across France in October–November 2005 in
their own enactment of the storming of the Bastille expressed an avowed
contempt for the French "system" and the formal political practices that
underwrite it, they nonetheless engaged in a repetitive, public performance
of legal belonging, waving their French identification cards to the ever-
present television cameras. Indeed, Bastille imagery is replete in rap albums
cut after the 2005 uprising, with MacKregor/Hematom's 2006 collection,
*Insurrection*, juxtaposing historical images of the Bastille siege with present,
computer-generated images of the Place de la Bastille on fire, a painting of a
revolutionary sans-culotte with a contemporary black, *indigène de la République* labeled as "sans culotte 2006." The back cover of the CD case underlines this remaking of France from within by picturing a full-scale national
identity card featuring the photos of the various, multiracial rap artists and
replacing the identity number with "93 Hardcore" (the departmental code
of MacKregor's hometown Aubervilliers).

Moreover, beginning in the mid-1990s, rap artists were imploring their
listeners to counter the electoral success of the Front National through constituting an antiracist electorate. Monsieur R's *Sachons Dire Non* collections
(1998, 2003, 2006) contain multiple tracks calling for such a "no" vote:
"Son, you have to vote against [them], in the city and the countryside. You
have to vote for your own in the city centers, even if the others aren't going to" (FAF la Rage, "FAF à la Rage," 1998). In 2001, Sniper similarly
saw antisystemic violence as only a step in the appropriate direction, that
taking over the government was better than simply burning it down: "We
don't give a damn about the Republic and its freedom of expression. Better
to change the laws and see soon Arabs and Blacks in power at the Elysée"
("La France"). In the aftermath of the 2005 urban uprising, they repeated
their claim that the best way to "incinerate these assholes" (*connards*) was to

vote them out of office ("Brûle" ["Burn"], 2006). Indeed, the music video of "Brûle" features the trio and their posse waving their voter registration cards and closes with a black screen and the words: "2007 Vote!" In like fashion, Diam's 2006 *Dans Ma Bulle* (*In My Bubble*) album was issued with an accompanying pamphlet that describes in detail how to register to vote and that constitutes a veritable call-to-citizenship: "We, children of the republic, whether by birth or by adoption, are neither represented nor understood by the politicians who run our country. One vote = Ten Molotov cocktails. . . . 2007 presidential elections: We will vote."

Zebda, a crossover, multiethnic musical group led by Franco-Algerians and strongly identified with its native Toulouse, has furthered this logic of political engagement.[17] In 1997, Zebda—whose name is a transidiomatic play on "Beur," the ethnonym for Franco-Maghrebis, (with the Arabic *zebda* translating into the French homonym *beurre*)—entered into the formal political arena, using the proceeds from its platinum album sales to finance a grassroots development association, Tactikollectif, and later a political party, Motivé-e-s, to run in the 2001 Toulouse municipal elections. Campaigning on a far-left, antiglobalization platform that emphasized local investment, racial equality, and civic participation in the cités, Motivé-e-s garnered a surprise 12.4 percent of the vote in the first round of the elections before allying with other leftist parties in hopes of unseating Toulouse's rightist mayor. Inspired by their success, other "alternative lists" were organized in Rennes, Marseille, Grenoble, Lille, and Strasbourg, cities with significant housing projects (*Les Echos* 26 February 2001; *Le Monde* 16 March 2001).

How did Zebda's politicization of musical practice and urban reform escape the scorn of local youth? For one, the central members of the band refused candidacy on the party ticket, preferring to work either behind the scenes in developing approaches and platforms or alongside the candidates as intermediaries with the larger cité world of Toulouse. Their willingness to ally with other parties, in this respect, represented as much a pragmatic decision designed to maximize a voting block in the municipal assembly, as it did a symbolic act intended to demonstrate that they were not simply playing a game of personal prestige. Secondly, and perhaps more importantly, Zebda worked hard to maintain an identity for themselves as outsiders, as political pirates deploying the "system" to effectuate meaningful change without being part of the "system" itself. The 1997 album that launched the political involvement—titled *Motivés* and cofinanced by the Revolutionary Communist League (LCR) political party—was a collection of revolutionary songs from the Spanish civil war through the contemporary Algerian civil war, highlighted (of course) by a mandatory version of "Hasta Siempre," the famous paean to Che Guevara.

However, perhaps more central to the figure of the revolutionary in Zebda's musical work, as with that of the hardcore rap groups discussed above, is that of the recurring character of the *caillera*, the social bandit, who, as in the song "Je Crois Que Ça Va Pas Être Possible" ("I Believe That Will Not Be Possible"), suffers discrimination at the hands of racist bankers and real estate agents, but in the end gets his just revenge by inviting the offending parties to his birthday party and not letting them leave before they each receive a kick or two. Zebda's self-portrayal as marginal heroes effecting justice is further reinforced in the cover imagery on their 2002 album *Utopie d'Occase (Second-Hand Utopia)*, which features a child of color dressed as Zorro, slashing through a map of the world charting unequal economic development. Throughout, their political engagement through local agency is premised on a denial of political incorporation or personal careerism. Voting or even holding public office can thus be completely compatible with a "politics without politics."

CONCLUSION

In examining these two cases that both ambivalently negotiate between what I have called "transpolitics"—e.g., the transnational politicization of cultural practices that transcend the formal political sphere—and "politics without politics"—e.g., the representation of said politicization as being disinterested and of local, practical, social relevance—I am trying to understand how immigrant and hyphenated French men and, to a lesser extent, women situate their political actions within a system they find to be alienating and exclusionary. While the two cases are certainly ethnographically specific, my hope is that the pitfalls of immigrant politics to which I point can be understood as part of a more general predicament, which subaltern social actors face in their surveilled performances of citizenship. When the "nation" comes to be discredited in the eyes of these actors through civil war or institutionalized racism, their sphere of political engagement moves to the local or transnational levels.

However, if the performative delegitimation of the formal political sphere can become a powerful means of community organization within marginalized communities, it can also underwrite the continued marginalization of said actors from central decision-making bodies. In other words, if cultural associations and hip-hop posses constitute effective forms of community building for men in the French housing projects—and can even serve as interlocutors between the French state and immigrant populations—they remain forever identified as "immigrants" or as self-proclaimed *indigènes de la République*, in other words as not quite or only suspect French. Like Zidane, their every move is scrutinized by a larger (white) public who feel completely at home and authorized, in their "managerial" or "governmental" national belonging (Hage 2000), to accept or deny such actions as legitimate or in the larger national interest. In the context of perduring moral criteria of citizenship within the postcolonial metropole, the self-marginalization of Kabyle or cité residents can underwrite a racialized just-so-story of the French exception that maintains its own implicit ethnic hierarchies in spite of an explicit discourse that denies the existence of said divides. In the end, the expansion of localized performances of "politics without politics" on national peripheries points to the de facto fragmentation of supposedly universal models of citizenship based exclusively on formal rights and duties. It is exactly this racialized fragmentation of political engagement to which anthropologists of immigrant citizenship should attend.

## Notes

1. Front National leader Jean-Marie Le Pen in particular publicly questioned whether, "there are too many blacks on the French team" (Forcari 2006: 10). Similar positions had been articulated as early as the late 1990s, and most notably, in the wake of the October-November 2005 riots, by conservative French Jewish philosopher Alain Finkielkraut who remarked that the national soccer team, "composed almost exclusively of black players," was the "ridicule" of Europe (interview in *Ha'aretz*, November 18, 2005).

2. Indeed, former French national coach Aimée Jacquet later remarked that even as the match wore down toward penalty kicks, he remained absolutely convinced that Zidane would score the winning goal.

3. Much has been written on the incident and its aftermath. My analysis is indebted to numerous conversations with other scholars and observers of France and soccer, as well as to a comprehensive unpublished manuscript by Laurent Dubois, "Coup de Boule, Coup de Théâtre: Zidane, Thuram, and the Empire of French Football."

4. See Jaxel-Truer 2006. Materazzi later revealed that the comments centered on Zidane's sister. Materazzi even claimed that he was too "uncultured" to even know what a "terrorist" was.

5. The sense of the head-butt as reconfirming Zidane's Algerian or Kabyle identity was similarly invoked by Algerians (and Kabyles in particular), many of whom had previously disavowed Zidane's success and criticized him for being a "virtual Arab" (*arbi mzowar*) or the "King of France" who had turned his back on his natal culture and allowed himself to be deployed by the French state as an example of integration (see *El Watan* (Algiers) 11 July 1998; *Le Monde* 13 July 2006).

6. This concern over the effect of Zidane's actions on the *banlieue* youth was repeated in the international press as well, most famously, in Adam Gopnik's article in the *New Yorker* (2006).

7. The violence built on a history of earlier confrontations stretching back to the early 1980s, the majority of which followed the police killing (*bavure*) of a local resident. Such earlier conflicts—termed "riots" (*émeutes*) abetted the growing media and state representation of the cités as violent spaces "outside the law," which had augmented a security discourse and the progressive militarization of

these areas (Silverstein 2004a: 106–9). For a discussion of the structure and effects of this uprising, see Le Gouaziou and Mucchielli (2006) and Silverstein and Tetreault (2005).

8. There is increasingly an important critical literature that addresses the enduring dynamics of race and racialization in the presumably raceless French Republic. See Bancel, Blanchard, and Vergès (2003); Fassin and Fassin (2006); Keaton (2006); Ndiaye (2005); Peabody and Stovall (2003); Saada (2002); Thomas (2007); Wilder (2005). See Stanley (in this volume) for a parallel case of the racialization of immigrants in Italy.

9. The generational shift from the Beur Movement of French North African cultural activism of the 1980s to a transpolitical present in many ways mirrors the experiences of the civil rights movements of blacks in Britain (Gilroy 1991) and Chicanos in the United States (Muñoz 1989).

10. The exact population is subject to debate as French law prohibits the collection of any data on race or ethnicity in censuses. Emigrants from Kabylia were among the first Algerians to come to France and originally constituted a significant majority among the Algerian community.

11. "Beur" is an ethnonym as a term of self-reference by French North African suburban youth during the late 1970s. The term was later appropriated by the media and academic world and since disavowed by French North Africans. "Beur" likely derives from a double syllabic inversion of "Arab," according to the French colloquial language game, *verlan*. Other local actors have linked "Beur" directly to the large Kabyle presence in North African immigrant France, interpreting it as an acronym for "Berbers of Europe" (Aïchoune 1985).

12. For histories of the Beur political and social movement, see Bouamama, Sad-Saoud, and Djerdoubi (1994), Boubeker and Abdallah (1993), Gibb (in this volume), and Jazouli (1986).

13. For a further discussion of the law and the larger debate around the *hijab*, see Bowen (2006) and Silverstein (2000, 2004b).

14. For a general discussion of the Algerian civil war, see Martinez (1998), Quandt (1998), Roberts (2003), and Stora (2001).

15. For a thorough discussion of Kabyle politics in Algeria and France, see Chaker (1998).

16. Stomy Bugsy's "J'Avance Pour Ma Familia" ("I Move forward for My Family") (1998) is a good example of the metaphorization of "family" as local community, with all its gangster (mafia) intertextuality. 113 and Lunatic make similar use of the "clan" trope to refer to both their posses of production personnel and allied musicians, and more generally their larger worlds of supporters and listeners (see 113, "Main Dans La Main" ["Hand in Hand"], 2000; Lunatic, "HLM3" and "Mauvais Oeil" ["Evil Eye"], 2000). Sinik is particularly explicit in his use of fictive kinship, referring to himself as having "over forty brothers, though parenthetically not related" (*une quarantaine de frères, en parenthèse sans liens de parenté*) ("Si Proche Des Miens," 2006). On Sniper's track, "El Dorado" (2006), the two Franco-Maghrebi rappers actually play two brothers on a tragic voyage of clandestine migration (Ar. *hareg*) across the Mediterranean.

17. For a comprehensive, book-length study of Zebda's political trajectory from neighborhood association to electoral movement, see Marx-Scouras (2005).

# CHAPTER 2

# On Belonging in/to Italy and Europe

## CITIZENSHIP, RACE, AND THE "IMMIGRATION PROBLEM"

*Flavia Stanley*

THIS CHAPTER LOOKS at the meanings and notions conveyed by the keywords "citizenship," "nationality," and "race" in transnational Europe and in Italy. While movements of people across national borders are certainly not new phenomena, many academics have noted that current trends in transnational migration have had the effect of creating more ethnic diversity in countries not usually host to permanent settlements of immigrants. The discourses surrounding nationality and citizenship cast transnational populations into the disparate categories of national, citizen and noncitizen. In Italy, those who look and act "Italian" are assumed to be citizens whereas those who look and act "other" are assumed to be noncitizens. Thus the use of "national" as a category is utilized to denote difference in what it means to "be" Italian, whereas the category of citizen refers to those who deserve the privileges allotted to them for "being Italian." "Italianness," then, is more than a cultural identity; it also implies a political and legal belonging not automatically ascribed to the non-Italian and non-European immigrant. This distinction has serious implications for the immigrant resident. Examples from fieldwork conducted in Rome are used to posit that the process of citizenship making in Europe and in Italy is participatory in the creation and protection of racial privilege.

In the past twenty years, Italy has become host to an unprecedented number of immigrants and transitioned from a nation of emigration to one of immigration. Italian citizens grapple with fears about the very future of Italy and "Italianness" prompted in part by demographers, the media, and politicians, citing, for example, the nation's record-low birth rate. In

addition, Italy faces the pressure to comply with the demands and responsibilities of participating in the European Union. These tensions and anxieties regarding changing demographics and transnational global flows have
pushed issues of national identity and immigration policy into the forefront
of heated political and social debate.

In general, despite the fact that immigrants consist of no more than 3.5
percent of the entire population (Castles and Miller 2003: 244), the issue
of immigration is often cast as an unequivocal (and perhaps irresoluble)
problem by the popular media, one that poses a threat not only to Italy and
"Italianness" but also to Europe and "Europeanness." For example, Elizabeth Krause (2001: 595) notes that the low birth rate of Italians is often
juxtaposed in media reports against the growing non-European immigrant
population and becomes linked to fears about the demise of the Italian
"race" and to the disappearance of European culture. Nicola Mai (2002:
77) reports that in a 1991 poll of Italians regarding immigration, 78 percent of respondents stated that the number of foreign immigrants was too
high while only 43 percent of those surveyed were aware of the actual dimensions of foreign migration. Where does the disjuncture between "real"
numbers and public opinion come from? What kinds of fears and beliefs are
provoked by the presence of immigrants in "Italian" space and where are
ideas about immigrants formed? To get at some of these questions, I discuss
some of the larger political and geographic changes in Europe and reflect on
my fieldwork to get at a more nuanced understanding of how ideas about
immigration in Italy are learned and reproduced.

## DESTINATION EUROPE

Unpacking the positioning of immigration as a threat may yield clues to
current shifting notions of national (and transnational) identities, as member
countries of the European Union respond to pressures of sustaining boundaries "in a world ever more open to cultural flows" (Foster 1991: 237; see
also Ong 1999). In the context of Europe, immigrants "are often distinct
from the receiving populations [with] the position of immigrants marked
by a specific legal status, that of the foreigner or non-citizen . . . [with] differences between groups often summed up in the concepts of ethnicity and
race" (Castles and Miller 2003: 14). The "imagined community" of the
nation-state is typically realized through the invention of traditions (Anderson 1983; Hobsbawm 1983) that create illusions of unity among people
via language, history, and culture. Phil Marfleet (1999) notes that national
identity is usually a "construction of the ruling elite" (18) and that the
project of nation building creates powerful national myths. One effect of
this is that immigration and ethnic diversity threaten ideas of nationhood as

they "create a new social reality of people without common ethnic origins" (Castles and Miller 2003: 15).

Furthermore, the countries of destination in Europe have no myths of nation building that might incorporate culturally and physically distinct groups (e.g., the "melting pot" myth in the United States). The metanation building project of the European Union is one example of the expansion of socioeconomic boundaries beyond the historical boundaries of the nation-state. To many theorists, such global changes have attendant shifts in the meanings of citizenship and nationality, not only to the citizens of nation-states, but especially to the increasing numbers of transnational immigrants who reside in those nation-states.

Recent concern and attention by scholars, such as Vera Stolke (1995), Cris Shore (2000), and Étienne Balibar (2004), situates the project of European unification and the creation a European citizenry as an emergent problem that is in need of investigation, interpretation, analysis, and eventually, perhaps, critical intervention. Balibar cautions that the processes and projects of European unification necessarily exclude nonnational residents of member EU countries, such that "the exclusions proper to each of the national citizenships united in the EU will inevitably produce an explosive effect of apartheid, in flagrant contradiction with the ambition of constituting a democratic model on the continental and world scale" (2003: 44). Shore similarly elaborates that the creation of the European Union "discriminate(s) against non-EU nationals—thereby raising the prospect of an ever more exclusivist 'Fortress Europe'"(2000: 79).

Smith (in this volume) and Cole (1997) write of the anxieties that arise from the coexistence of "outsiders" in another's borders, as the presence of the "other" presents a potential threat to national identity. Such anxieties often lead to the creation of new boundaries among and between people as well as to a reimagining of identity. Furthermore, Theodora Kostako-poulou writes that new definitions of citizenship and immigration need to be theorized, as the "EU is not a suitable plane for the application of existing theoretical paradigms on citizenship, immigration and community—for these have been firmly rooted in the spatial framework of the state" (2001: 8). Kostakopoulou's point, that new forms of social, economic, and political organization require new understandings and theories, is valid despite conflicting notions regarding the totality of, and the effects of, globalization and transnational global flows. It is therefore important to investigate how the intersections of immigration, citizenship, nationality, and race are understood, defined, and experienced in local national contexts. This chapter attempts to add to the ethnographic literature regarding the intersections of these keywords (see Williams 1983), specifically in the context of Italy.

## ITALY AND THE "IMMIGRATION PROBLEM"

Although Italy's struggles with immigration are relatively well known, most academic literature has focused on the reactions of "the core" EU member countries such as France, Britain, and Germany to increasing immigration. Such research suggests that different EU member countries have responded very differently to immigration. (Donald and Rattansi 1992, Smith and Brinker-Gaber 1997) It is therefore important to broaden the inquiry of the effects that immigration has had on the European Union's "periphery nations," such as Italy.

Much of the scholarly literature on immigration in Italy tends to focus on the impact (including statistics, changes in policies and laws, migratory patterns of certain groups) that immigration has on the host society (Cotesta and De Angelis 1999, Blion 1996; Barjaba, Dervishi, and Perrone 1992). Anthropological work also includes descriptions of the lives of immigrant groups in a new society and how immigrants are affected by host country policies and prejudices (Angel-Ajani 2000; Carter 1997). Aside from Jeffrey Cole's (1997) ethnography, *The New Racism in Europe,* which examined the responses of southern Italians to the increasing presence of immigrants, an area needing further elaboration is how host-country citizens themselves are reacting to immigration. It is therefore important to look at, in the case of Italy, the ways that Italians see their lives and identity being challenged and affected by the presence of non-Italian foreigners.

Italy has always been infused with the cultural politics of difference. Tensions between regions, particularly well documented regarding the "Southern Question," have existed at least since Italy was unified in 1861. In fact, depending upon the social and political contexts, a person's regional identity or affiliation may be more pronounced than his/her national identity (Schneider 1995; Cole 1997). Regionalism then is still a factor regarding interrelations between Italians. It ranges from more quotidian concerns such as cuisine or dialect, to larger and potentially fracturing realities such as the social and economic marginalization of southern Italians, to the continuing efforts of (and growing political support for) the Northern League to separate itself both geographically and economically from the "rest" of Italy. In contrast, "Italianness" then is mainly tangible in the context of the non-Italian and particularly regarding interactions with the non-European immigrant.

This chapter is based on fieldwork I conducted at an immigrant service organization, Servizi per Immigrati (SPI), in Rome in 2001 and 2004.[1] According to Janis Steele (1997), social service workers (e.g., social workers, teachers, community workers, etc.) act as front-line cultural mediators who are in a unique position to construct and negotiate difference in their encounters with foreigners. By interviewing and observing social service workers at SPI and their interactions with immigrant clients, I hoped to find out whether Italian identity is reified in such spaces. Indeed, I found that the social service workers at SPI are not neutral. Instead, they engaged in everyday practices that serve to reinforce categories such as "Italian" and "foreigner."

## On "Italianness" and Boundary Maintenance at SPI

SPI was just one of many potential sites where meanings and notions of Italianness and otherness are formed and transmitted. I chose SPI because it is one of the largest and most well-known service organizations in Rome. SPI is a popular destination for recently arrived immigrants because SPI provides a multitude of services to immigrants. It runs soup kitchens and shelters in Rome and provides referrals to lawyers, health services, dentists, and potential employers. It is popular even among those not seeking specific services, as each person is issued a SPI card. The card is laminated, has a picture of the person and most importantly, includes the date of the immigrant's first visit to SPI. These cards have served as proof, to authorities, of an immigrant's date of residence in the event of a declaration of *"sanatoria"* (amnesty), which enable illegal immigrants to obtain a *"permesso di sogiorno"* (permit of stay) if they have proof of residence before a certain date.[2]

The *"centro ascolto"* (the listening center) is the first necessary stop for an immigrant seeking any kind of service provided by SPI. Here, they wait in line, show their passports and begin the process of getting the SPI card. The process usually takes the better part of a day. Here and throughout an immigrant's interactions with SPI, the barriers between immigrant and Italian are both physical and symbolic. Those waiting are walled off from the service providers, and the only space of interaction is the *"sportello"* (teller window), a bullet-proof window underneath which exists an opening just large enough to slide papers through. While their information gets processed, immigrants are called one by one for the first of two intake interviews. These occur in a separate room, the immigrant on one side of a desk and the interviewer on the other. The purpose of the first interview is to weed out anyone who might not need any of the services SPI provides (i.e., to make sure the sole purpose of the immigrant is not the SPI card itself). If the person is cleared to receive the SPI card, and hence access to services, they are given an appointment for a more thorough interview up to two weeks later.[3]

The second interview consists of volunteers who fill out a four-page form that is kept on file at SPI. After the interview, the completed forms are filed according to country of origin so that all the files of each country

are organized together into one filing cabinet.[4] The form includes information about the immigrant: names and locations of any dependents and/or
family members, the date of their arrival in Italy, why they came to Italy,
what their needs are, as well as the impression the interviewer has about the
character of the interviewee. After the interviewer listens to and takes notes
regarding the personal history of each immigrant, s/he is asked what kind
of services s/he needs from SPI. Virtually every immigrant is encouraged
to go to the Italian school and gets permission to do so. Any services sanctioned by the interviewer result in a stamp on the SPI card. At SPI soup
kitchens, for example, one must present the SPI card with the appropriate
stamp in order to get a meal.

The second interview again takes up the better part of a day. All those
being interviewed must show up by 8 AM and are served one at a time until
all the interviews of the day are completed. This time all the interviewers and
interviewees are all in the same room. One side of the room contains folding
chairs for those waiting. On the other side of the room is a line of desks where
the interviews take place. While there is an obvious utility to the desk during the interview, the set up of the room clearly demarcates and separates the
service providers from the immigrants. Furthermore, the physical distance
of the desk is seldom crossed by the interviewers. Out of the fifteen interviewers on staff I only observed one, Mauro, who made a conscious effort
to bridge the distance between interviewer and interviewee and shook the
hands of his interviewees, both before and after the interview.[5] This gesture
was symbolically powerful. Because of its rareness, it seemed to render the
boundary between Italian and immigrant more obvious. In fact, many immigrants showed visible signs of surprise when offered Mauro's hand. Such
demarcations and boundaries between service provider and service recipient
are of course commonplace in many social service organizations. They are
often so familiar that they take on a common sense feel. However, such barriers at SPI (and arguably at any service organization) are symbolic. In this case,
the boundary between "us" and "other," between Italian and non-Italian, is
firm and rarely transcended.

### *"LA SCUOLA ITALIANA"* (THE ITALIAN SCHOOL)

The only service provided onsite at SPI is the free Italian language school
for immigrants, which they can attend regardless of their legal status. The
classes are taught by volunteers (predominantly retired school teachers) and
range from beginning to advanced and each immigrant progresses at his or her
own pace. The classroom in particular is an important site where meanings
and notions regarding Italianness and otherness are formulated and transmitted. Researchers such as Deborah Reed-Danahay (1996), Signathia Fordham

(1996), and Oriole Pi–Sunyer (1992) have looked at classrooms as rich sites of the articulations and contestations of national interests and identity. Donald Carter elaborates on the Gramscian notion that in society the school is the "context of everyday life in which the social and political contours of . . . the community are negotiatied, transformed, and lived" (1997: 9).

At SPI, teachers made constant reference to the foreign status of the students. Such references varied in form and content. For example, in an effort to highlight the differences in usage between the verb *"essere"* (to be) and the verb *"avere"* (to have), a teacher said, "I don't *have* the SPI card because I *am* Italian. You (pointing to the students) *have* the SPI card because you *are* foreigners." While most teachers interviewed pointed to Italian language proficiency as primary to the success and incorporation of immigrants into Italian society, the boundary between Italian and non–Italian is clear and marked.

Notions of cultural difference between Italians and immigrants were also made tangible in the form of lessons and workbook pages copied from a handbook used by SPI's Italian school. The handbook was written by a collective of Italian teachers who taught Italian to immigrants in Bologna. The overall purpose was to create lessons that incorporate the experience of the immigrant and to show a vision of Italy as a multicultural society that includes non–Italians. Despite the intent, essentializing presumptions of the culture of immigrants are embedded in many lessons. Often they promote views of immigrant life that express commonly held fears among Italians regarding the dangers of increased immigration.

For example, in a lesson for vocabulary associated with family rela–tionships, two families are introduced to the student. One family is ob–viously Italian (all the members have Italian names—Giuseppe, Antonio, Maria, Rosa, and so on). It consists of a chart showing the relationships between three generations of one family. Two of the Italian couples have two children, one has three children, and one has one child. The next page is entitled *"La mia famiglia e numerosa"* ("My family is numerous"), and is a portrait of a Muslim family (expressed via the names, Aziz, Leila, Majdo, and by the mother's veil) that has come to Italy to find work. The Muslim family consists of the two parents and five children. The underlying mes–sage of cultural difference is marked.[6] This particular example reproduces notions of immigrants having more children than Italians and recalls fears associated with Italy's low birth rate.

The classroom then is a site where boundaries and notions of "us" and "them" are necessarily denoted, both for the Italian citizen and the immi–grant. General boundaries, whether physically demarcated at the *"sportello"* and the intake interview sessions or articulated in the classrooms, only stress such differences. At the same time, such distinctions actually produce a solid notion of "Italian" identity. Again, while expressing regional loyalty is still very much part of interactions among Italians, the presence of the non-Italian (especially the non-European immigrant) in the daily life of Italians creates a sense of national belonging.

## On the Differential Ordering of Immigrant Groups

While the demarcation of Italian and non-Italian can be tangible in the classroom, intake interviews, and even in the mundane interactions between SPI employees and their clients, SPI workers also communicated ideas about differences between immigrant groups. "Race" and a person's national affiliation played an important role in the construction and reproduction of difference. This differential ordering of immigrant groups was usually hierarchical, placing groups of people into categories of, for example, more trustworthy to less trustworthy, more hardworking to less hardworking, and from more dangerous to less dangerous. Such notions about the differences between groups seemed informed more by popular ideas of such groups produced in the media and in discussions among Italians than by actual interaction with immigrant groups.[7]

Before discussing specific examples at SPI, it is necessary to outline popular notions of immigrants in Rome, in general. The spaces that different groups occupy in Rome are distinct. If one pays attention, even one day in Rome will yield evidence of how bounded and distinct immigrant spaces are. Most obvious is the presence of street vendors. While many groups engage in vending as a primary source of income, the items different groups vend are specific to each group. For example, Bangladeshi immigrants are rarely, if ever, seen working as anything but vendors, most typically selling roses in restaurants and tourist areas, but increasingly as pay-per-service photographers for tourists. Chinese immigrants vend as well, usually plastic toys and lighters. Many African groups vend handbags, perfume, and wooden African statues along popular pedestrian areas in historic parts of Rome. Especially in Rome, where factory work is hard to find, one rarely sees immigrants integrated into the formal economy. Instead, they must find work informally, even those who may have working papers. Similar to the history of immigrants in the United States, the most common and productive means of finding work is via one's own group network of previously settled immigrants.

There is a correlation between this segregation and common assumptions about the culture of immigrants' nationality, in the Italian imagination. Briefly, Ukranian and Filipino women are typically seen as trustworthy enough to find work in Italian homes as nannies, cooks, and to care for the elderly.[8] Some African groups (Senegalese in particular) are seen as hard-working, though they rarely find domestic work (usually deemed the most desirable form of employment); instead they must usually settle for vending items illegally or as low-skilled, low-paid factory laborers. Most interestingly, the distinct spaces and employment that different groups occupy are rarely challenged or transgressed.

One close informant, Alpha, from French Guinea, tried very hard to find some sort of domestic placement. He wanted to clean, shop, or cook for an Italian family or individual. While through underground networks he found potential employment, each time, instead of being refused outright, he was offered a salary that he simply could not live on. I spoke to a potential employer on the phone one day (Alpha's Italian was rudimentary at the time) to help set up a meeting and he said, "He's African, right?" I found myself responding without thinking, "Yes, but he's very reliable." When I translated for Alpha what had happened (including my response) he laughed. He met with the man and was again offered a low hourly wage. Alpha's example is just one of many that I heard from different immigrants at SPI.

Aside from how hard it is for an immigrant to transcend the space allotted to him or her by Italian society, it can be very hard to talk with Italians about immigrants (as the above example shows) without acknowledging or reproducing in some way dominant views on immigrant groups. This may be partially due to the fact that Italians in general do not hold back their ideas and views of different immigrant groups because it is not viewed as racist to do so. Therefore, such expressions of difference between immigrant groups, based on their country of origin, become so commonplace it seems natural.[9]

At SPI, a service worker's views of what an immigrant's nationality represents can also have deterministic consequences. At the first intake interview, for example, a person may be denied a second interview (and therefore the SPI card and any access to SPI's services and resources) if they do not seem needy enough or if are assumed to have a steady source of income. One intake interviewer, Giovanni, said "I watch out for Albanian and Romanian men. They make a lot of money through the black market . . . many of them are with the mafia. A lot of them have more money than I do! I have to figure out who needs SPI and who doesn't. And they already speak Italian well, so they don't need the Italian school."[10]

The service information and referrals distributed during the second interview process is entirely up to the discretion of the interviewer. A few interviewers had a policy of giving information and referrals to anyone who asked for particular services. Other interviewers, however, seeing SPI's resources as limited, might deny access to certain resources, even if those resources were requested. For example, Chinese and Bangladeshi immigrants were often denied access to soup kitchens. One interviewer, Paola, referring to why she usually does not give soup kitchen referrals to Bangladeshi or Chinese immigrants explained "even if we give them the stamp to use the soup kitchen, they won't go . . . they don't like Italian food, so it would go to waste . . . they eat rice and other things . . . they think Italian food tastes weird."

Sometimes the debates over resource allocation grew antagonistic. People who were seen as overly pushy and/or faking desperation were frequently denied any services at all. One young man from India, Deepak, originally had come to SPI for the Italian school. After one month, he requested to be reinterviewed because he realized he needed assistance with food, clothing, and medical care. The person in charge of the decision denied his request, believing Deepak to be exaggerating his situation. Deepak then went directly (violating protocol) to the person who had given him the second interview and demanded an increase in services. The interviewer denied his request as well and a loud debate ensued, resulting in Deepak being removed from the premises and told not to return.

After the altercation, the interviewer told me that he simply did not believe Deepak's story, that he was just taking advantage of SPI and that Deepak was living with family who were taking good care of him. Deepak's story (told to me in English) differs substantially. When he first was signing up for services, he felt that he should not ask for too many things. At the time, he felt that his family (his father's brother's family) was happy to take care of him. However, because he was having a hard time finding work, he felt that he was becoming a burden on them and wanted to seek alternative sources for food and clothing. While Deepak's nationality may not have been a factor in this particular case, his situation serves as an example of how a service worker's personal view on an immigrant can determine his or her access to resources.

Notions of success are also embedded in different service workers' views of immigrants. I had noticed in my observations at the Italian school that the beginning classes had a mixture of many different nationalities, but that the intermediate or advanced classes were primarily made up of South and Central Americans and Africans. I asked the supervisor for the Italian school, Francesca, what she thought about my observation. She asked me to speculate and I offered up my interpretation, that perhaps the other nationalities (predominantly Russians and Ukrainians) found employment more easily, which was the primary reason that people stopped coming to Italian school. Francesca countered with "Maybe it's because they (Ukrainians and Russians) learn Italian very fast . . . they come from very determined and hardworking cultures. Yes, they do also find jobs but it is because they try very hard to find work . . . people from South American and Africa don't care as much about work. They come from more fluid cultures." Such ascribed behavioral characteristics also play a role in an immigrant's treatment in Italian society. In Alpha's example, notions of what Africans were like prevented him from finding certain employment; being Albanian or Romanian may exclude a person from vital services. Being locked into a certain space in Italian society is not the only potential problem that emerges from such notions, however. This differential ordering also tends to naturalize the economic and social marginalization of certain groups, who like Alpha and countless others, have a hard time finding viable employment.[11]

Notions of difference among immigrant groups certainly vary from individual to individual and some Italians certainly challenge and work against dominant notions. What is remarkable though, regardless of how an individual might feel, is the ease with which s/he can describe how a particular immigrant group is viewed in Italian society. The language teachers at SPI, for example, were much less likely than either the interviewers or office workers to make blanket statements about the culture of an immigrant. However, most recognized and could detail popular conceptions of certain immigrant groups.

Despite the differential imaginings, many of my Italian informants asserted that Italy is not a racist country. Many pointed to the more favorable treatment of certain "nonwhite" African groups, such as the Senegalese, over certain "white" groups, such as Albanians, as proof. Scholars on race in Italy have noted the tendency of Italians to think of themselves as immune to the racist ideologies that occur in the United States and in other Western European countries (Cole 1997; Bocca 1988). Academics have posited that the (mis)treatment of non-European immigrants in Europe consists of a "new" racism (Balibar 1989; Barker 1981; Cole 1997).

This "new" racism shifts from dominant notions of race, historically based on biological difference, to difference based on nation and culture. Grosfoguel (1997) locates the change in racial ideology: "after the defeat of the Nazi occupations in Western Europe and the 1960's Civil Rights struggles in Britain and the United States, global racial discourses shifted from biological racism to cultural racism" (409). New racism (or cultural racism) is the kind of racism where "The word race is usually not even used. Cultural racism assumes that the metropolitan culture is different from ethnic minorities' cultures but understood in absolute, essentialist sense [but] . . . it is always related to a notion of biological racism to the extent that the culture of groups is naturalized . . . [and] articulated in relation to poverty, labor market opportunities, and/or marginalization" (412). Certainly, as Grosfoguel notes, the differential ordering of immigrant groups carries an

assumption of the incompatibility of an immigrant's culture with that of
the host society. Italians do, for example, pinpoint "culture" as a means of
defending their notions of different immigrant groups. The assumption of a
foreigner's nationality and the attendant cultural notions becomes a means
of distinguishing one group from another and makes the distinct spaces
immigrant groups occupy, both socioeconomically and within the Italian
imagination, seem natural.

However, although the existence, and some of the effects, of this differential ordering of immigrant groups can be documented, possible underlying reasons for it are much harder to determine. Why, for example, does the
differential ordering in the Italian context seem so different from the racial
hierarchies prevalent in countries such as Canada and the United States
(which tend to associate threat with skin tone)?

Mai notes that part of Italian reactions to immigrants may also be due to
a sense of insecurity about Italy's "social capital" within the European Union.
Michael Herzfeld (1987), Elizabeth Krause (2001), Oriole Pi-Sunyer (1992),
and Giovanna Zincone (1999) refer to the fact that Italy, along with other
nations in Europe's "southern periphery," hold a less secure status in the European Union, given Italy's history of economic marginality and "relatively
late industrialization and attendant social dislocations and transformations"
(Pi-Sunyer 1993: 77). Russell King and Krysia Rybaczuk (1993) report that
migration became a source of tension that divided Western Europe from the
South. Part of the problematization of immigration and subsequent policies
to curb and control immigration are therefore linked to Italy coming into
compliance with the rest of Europe (Cole 1997: 12; Krause 2001). In the
case of Italy, protecting Italians from non-Italian foreigners may then be
related to the project of protecting Europe from non-Europeans.

### EUROPEAN CITIZENSHIP AND IMMIGRATION

The terms "citizen" and "citizenship" have broad and varying meanings depending upon context; at the broadest level, to be a citizen of a
certain space/place confers a kind of relationship of belonging and behold-
enness. Citizen then may or may not imply a "political rights" relationship.
The term citizen can mean, "an inhabitant of a city," (in which case illegal
and unnaturalized immigrants are citizens), as much as it can refer to people
who have full political privileges as members of a state (in which case "illegal" and unnaturalized inhabitants of a state are not citizens). The term
"citizen" can also refer to anyone who is affected by governmentality of any
kind, so that citizen becomes synonymous with "subject" (see Cruickshank
1996, and her use of the term citizen/subject), in which case, everyone is
a citizen of some kind, regardless of his or her actual political rights. For

the purpose of this project, I refer to the meanings and notions conveyed by the keywords "citizen" and "citizenship" as they relate to the creation of political and social "ingroups" and "outgroups," in the geopolitical realms of the European Union and in Italy. The terms ingroup and outgroup are borrowed from Teun van Dijk (2001) who views the two groups as resulting from any ideologically based discourse that polarizes the representation of "us" and "them."

As Shore (2000: 66) notes, the Maastricht Treaty of 1993 created, legally, the category of "European Citizenship," by conferring to any (legal) citizen of the European Union's member states an official belonging to Europe via the title "Citizen of the Union." While what this means is unclear, as there are no parameters (or certificates or papers) regarding exactly what rights and responsibilities this new citizenship entails, Shore posits that "in establishing 'European citizenship' as a status in law, the EU has . . . also created a de facto new form of nationality" (66). In this context then, "citizenship" and "nationality" exist necessarily in relation to one another. Furthermore, as "international law does not recognize the distinction between citizenship and nationality and regards the first as completely determined by the second"(66, quoting Scruton 1982), the two keywords have been conflated in certain contexts for some time.

The keywords citizenship and nationality certainly are related. They both refer to identities (as well as legal statuses) that are both embraced by and bestowed upon populations. The discourse, and legal/political apparatuses, surrounding nationality and citizenship, help make the nebulous matter of "populations" into nationals, citizens, and noncitizens; into de facto ingroups (those who are conferred the rights and obligations of belonging) and outgroups (those who exist outside the nexus of belonging). Socioculturally, however, citizenship and nationality have different nuances especially in the context of a Europe of increasing transnational global flows. It is therefore important to distinguish between them.

In a culturally pluralistic society, nationality can also have a similar connotation to "ethnicity," which exists entirely outside the issue of citizenship. For instance, in the United States, ethnicity is used more than nationality to refer to someone's country, or people, of origin. While the use of "ethnic" does reveal a person's deviation from the norm of whiteness in the United States, one who is ethnic is not necessarily assumed to be a noncitizen. The reverse seems to be true in the context of increasing immigration and the existence of more culturally diverse populations in Italy.

In Italy, one's assumed nationality becomes the primary means of differentiating between Italian and other, even if one is also legally an Italian citizen. For example, one who phenotypically and/or culturally deviates from

Italian, one who is differentiated because of an assumed non-Italian national-ity, is also likely to be assumed to be a noncitizen. Nationality and citizenship, while related, then have significantly different meanings in Italy.

Contrasting the United States with Italy here is to show that, due to different histories regarding immigration and so on, an ethnic (nonwhite) person in the United States, while still seen as a racial/ethnic other can still be assumed to be a U.S. citizen. This is not to say, however, that the potential to recognize the political belonging of ethnic groups is realized in many contexts as in the case of Mexicans and Arabs. Reed-Danahay (in this volume) writes of the social learning many Vietnamese Americans must undertake in order to minimize their exclusion as "foreigners" in the United States. The same is true of other European countries; Silverstein (in this volume) writes of the suspect citizenship of Franco-Algerians who are racialized and constantly surveilled in the process of maintaining French national identity.

However, I contend that in Italy, and in contrast to the United States and France, those seen as physically distinct from Italians, regardless of their performativity, also carry the assumption that they are not citizens of the Italian state. Because citizenship is an assumed, as well as an actual, status in the Italian context, perhaps the use of nationality rests on ascrib-ing difference in the presence of internal non-Italian others, whereas citi-zenship helps create and bind an ingroup with the rights and privileges of being Italian. In this way, being "Italian" is more than a cultural identity, as it, in this context, also implies a political citizenship.

The pronouncement by the European Union that all citizens of mem-ber countries are also European citizens further complicates the issue of citizenship. As Shore notes, "there can be little doubt that European citi-zenship was inserted . . . as an instrument for instilling European con-sciousness among the masses" (2000: 77). Citizenship in the context of the European Union, according to Shore, is more (at this point in time) a cultural than a political project.

Unmasking citizenship as a cultural *and* a political category is help-ful in understanding the treatment of immigrants in Italy. What is inter-esting about the hierarchy of immigrant groups in Italy is that it departs from other racial/immigrant hierarchies (as in the case of the United States where the darker your skin tone, the more subject you are to differential treatment). Perhaps what exists in the case of Italy is a boundary put into place to protect something, rather than just to "otherize."

On one level, the presence of certain groups may undermine a sense of Italian identity as Italy tries to maintain its status in the European Union. Perhaps, Eastern European immigrants, such as Romanians and Albanians who are viewed as particularly untrustworthy, represent the possibility of "racial assimilation" that is less likely for groups such as Africans, Bangladeshis, and Filipinos who look phenotypically very different from Italians. In *Building Europe,* Shore outlines the effort on the part of the EU policy makers to create a European citizenry/identity that relies more on cultural than on political benefits. Balibar's caution that conditioning EU citizenship upon the national citizenship of EU member countries consists of exclusionary practices that may result in an apartheid in Europe. Perhaps then the boundary that is set firmly between Italians and immigrants, especially those with the potential for one day "passing" as Italian, exists partly to secure and protect the identity of belonging to Europe.

Shore elaborates that "EU policy statements consistently conflate issues about immigrants, foreigners and border controls with fears about drugs, terrorism and crime . . . this category represents all those who show 'disrespect for Europe's frontiers' . . . culminating in . . . a host of initiatives designed to fortify Europe's southern and eastern frontiers against illegal immigrants" (2000: 80). This dynamic of being and becoming part of the European Union, and of Italian citizens also being declared European citizens, may help explain the differential ordering and treatment of immigrant groups in Italy. While thus far, the term citizenship in the European and Italian context has been discussed as being both political and cultural, the project of creating ' European citizenship' may also mask the formation and protection of a racial identity.

Citizenship's necessary byproduct is the classification of an ingroup (citizen) and an outgroup (noncitizen). More simply, the legal and political benefits of being a citizen include political rights and responsibilities and the possibility of the citizen to influence state policy. Allegiance is owed to the state via taxes and military service and, in exchange, the citizen receives protection from the state (Shore 2000: 66, 70). Citizenship may then be an example of a "Mauss–ian gift." In that there are "no free gifts," the acceptance of citizenship as a valid category, one that bestows differential benefits to different populations, has conditions.

On the one hand, as a citizen, one can reap the benefits of the social and cultural capital associated with belonging. On the other hand, as in the case of European citizenship, one may also participate (albeit unintentionally) in the reification of racist and xenophobic ideologies and policies. One may also have to accept the existence, and (mis)treatment of, the noncitizen other as common–place and natural. Furthermore, because certain privileges of belonging are associated under the category of citizen (a seemingly race/gender/class-less term) prejudices and differential treatment can often be ignored or overlooked.

58 FLAVIA STANLEY

As stated before, one's assumed nationality can have a deterministic effect on a foreigner's treatment in Italian society. Certainly even if one's assumed nationality is dubbed as "less dangerous" than others, being seen and treated as foreign has adverse effects. At the very least, one may be barred from certain economic and social structures, while at the worst, one may suffer mistreatment and even violence. The issue of citizenship is closely related to nationality in this case; if one's nationality is assumed to be non-Italian, then one is most likely assumed to be a noncitizen as well. The notion and nuances of identity then are firmly embedded in notions of citizenship.

As Shore notes, the success of the European Union relies heavily upon the (re)creation and (re)invention of a pan-European identity. In other words, for Europe to succeed as a political and economic force, people need to start identifying themselves as (also) European. The European Union's legalization of the status European citizenship in 1993 is but one step in the process. While this proclamation has done nothing to undermine the national and regional identities of Europe's member countries, it has had the effect of relegating the non-EU national to even more precarious positions (Shore 2000: 80). Shore notes that European citizenship has had the odd effect of both forging a pan-European identity in relation to non-EU nationals and strengthening national identity, combined with renewed popular support for separatist and regionalist movements across Europe (Shore and Wright 1997: 27–28).

Balibar (2002:107) reminds us that citizenship is the gateway to access political participation, suffrage, and the opportunity of access to the elite and protected individual rights. On an everyday level, those who can be assumed to be citizens are privy to certain advantages and protections. In the case of Italy, if one who looks non-Italian (or is prevented from passing due to distinct immigrant spaces and opportunity structures) is assumed to be not only a non-Italian noncitizen but also a non-European noncitizen, then in this scenario, isn't privilege or disadvantage associated with phenotype? Rather than framing the differential ordering of immigrants as a "new" racism, what may be at work in Italy, in order to reap the benefits of belonging in (to) Europe is the (re)creation and bounding of an identity, a citizenship, that is Italian, European, and white.

ACKNOWLEDGMENTS

Betsy Krause, Enoch Page, Julie Hemment, and Agustin Lao-Montes, who make up my dissertation committee, deserve a big thank you for their support, guidance, and wisdom. The European Field Studies Program at The University of Massachusetts provided funding and a space for discussion among colleagues undertaking fieldwork. This project would not have been possible without the patience of the workers and teachers and immigrants at SPI. Thanks especially to Sara and Mouctar for the chance to dialogue about my ideas and observations. I also owe many thanks to my friends and family and especially to Jon Zibbell, Lisa Modenos, and Kaila Kuban for their intellectual support and friendship.

## NOTES

1. I have changed the name of the organization to protect my informants and to limit any potential negative consequences that may arise from my research.
2. By 2004 the SPI card no longer served as proof of residency in Italy and because of its more restrictive policies toward resource allocation, demand for services had decreased from previous years. However, SPI continued to be a popular destination for immigrants seeking services.
3. At the time of the first interview, immigrants needing services are provided with interim, short-term referrals.
4. The form includes two numbers as well as a code for the person's country of origin. The first number indicates the latest person served at SPI overall since a census was instituted in 1990, and the second number refers to the latest person served from that particular country of origin. A form reading 297121 ALB 7207 would indicate that the person was the 297121st person served at SPI since 1990, and is the 7207th person from Albania to pass through SPI's "*centro ascolto.*"
5. The names of the people mentioned in this chapter have been changed.
6. It is also interesting that the Muslim family is "generically Muslim," in that no specific country of origin is mentioned for Aziz's family. This may indicate another general boundary between Muslims and Christians or it may refer to an unspoken assumption of Italian identity as Christian.
7. Despite the fact that SPI workers interact with immigrants every day, as noted previously, there are distinct barriers regarding such interactions. This limits the ability of the workers to form relationships that might challenge dominant notions of different immigrant groups.
8. A widely circulated joke (in 2001) is that the typical middle class Italian family is made up of four people: a mother, a father, one child, and a Ukrainian.
9. When a person's country of origin is not known outright, it is usually assumed and based on phenotypic and cultural clues such as dress and accent. People are also lumped into geographic regions (African, Eastern European) if a specific country of origin is hard to place. Sometimes one country becomes synonymous for an entire group, so that people seeming vaguely Eastern European will be "Romanian," Asians will become "Chinese," and so on. As Angel-Ajani (2000: 339) notes, the term "Marrochini" (Moroccans) is often used to signify a person of color, regardless of his/her actual nationality.
10. Unless otherwise noted all interviews have been translated from Italian.
11. Evidence that immigrant groups occupy distinct and hard to transgress economic and social spaces are similarly documented by, for example, Angel-Ajani (2000), Carter (1997), Cole (1997), Mai (2002).

# CHAPTER 3

# The Irish Citizenship
# Referendum (2004)

## MOTHERHOOD AND BELONGING IN IRELAND

*Angèle Smith*

Joanne has found the first two years of her life in Ireland
an uphill struggle. "Sometimes I feel like killing myself,"
she says, her voice breaking. "Only for my children, I don't
think I could cope."

—Quoted in Bracken 2005

"Oh yes, I do get depressed and sometimes I cry," says
Odette. "But like I say before, you have to put on a brave
face for them." She looks at her eight-year-old daughter,
dressed in a navy school uniform, playing at the sink. "You
go to your friends here to spill your problems. But you are
helpless. You have no control. It is like you are at the mercy
of the system."

—Quoted in Holland 2005

IDEAS OF CITIZENSHIP are ideas of belonging. In this chapter I examine how female asylum seekers in Ireland attempt to find some
sense of belonging in their host country at a time when the Irish state has,
through changes in Irish citizenship laws, changed what it means to belong in Ireland. In June 2004 a referendum was held to determine whether
a change in the Irish Constitution should be made to redefine one's rights
to citizenship and hence belonging in Ireland. The vote outcome was 79
percent in favor of the amendment (BBC, 13 June 2004). As the best local
election turnout in nearly twenty years, it suggests the overwhelming wish

of the Irish public to change the Irish citizenship from one based on place of birth on the island of Ireland (jus soli) to one based on being born in Ireland of at least one parent who is a citizen of Ireland (jus sanguinis).

That Irish citizenship had been associated with birthplace and the rights of the land is not surprising given that a deep-seated ideology grown of a long colonial history, links Irishness and a sense of place. Under colonial rule, the Irish were disenfranchised from the right to their land; they were marginalized within their own home. The consequence was a divide between the Irish and the British colonizer based on a sense of belonging to the place of Ireland.[1] In Ireland there is an ideology that the outside "Others" have long been their neighbors, the British. As a corollary, there is an ideology that Ireland has always been homogenously white. What happens then when the newcomers seeking asylum are nonwhite? What happens to the sense of Irish identity? To say that Ireland has never known a multiethnic community within its borders is historically not accurate. Yet with ministers of government being quoted saying that "today in Ireland, as never before, there is racism and discrimination," the message is clearly that the current immigration into Ireland is somehow different and more threatening. That threat led to changing citizenship laws to be about birth- and not place-rights, thus effectively excluding female asylum seekers' children born in Ireland.

Michael Dummett writes that "it is from the concept of citizenship that our prevailing notions of the rights and duties of a State derive" (2001: 80). These rights and duties include the rights to residency and to vote, and the duty to pay taxes and abide by the laws of the country. Citizenship determines who is considered part of the national community and who is to be excluded. Thus the concept of citizenship is inextricably linked to a sense of identity (see Anderson 1991; Gellner 1983; Hutchinson and Smith 1994) as David Cesarani and Mary Fulbrook explain:

Identities have been forged on the basis of many possible imagined attributes: the myth of common ancestry, the inheritance of blood, the binding force of tribal tradition, custom and belief are historically among the most widespread. With the rise of nation states in the late eighteenth to late twentieth centuries, new elements of definition begin to emerge: notions of citizenship defined by common ideals and the right to reside in the country of birth rather than of ancestry began to overlay or displace the primacy of kinship. Perceiving something of a sea-change in bases of identity in the modern era, historians and social scientists have for some time been grappling with an attempt to define the concept of national identity (1996: 1).

Far from merely being defined within the confines of law, citizenship is about belonging: belonging to a place and belonging to a community (see Silverstein, Stanley, and Reed-Danahay in this volume for further discussions of "cultural citizenship" and its practice/performance).

Feminist geographer Catherine Nash suggests that "Thinking critically about nationhood, gender and sexuality is never simply about women but about understandings of Irish history, culture and identity" (1997: 111). I argue here that to think critically about citizenship and belonging, we must explore the understandings of women and motherhood by understanding Irish history, culture, and identity. As I will show, pregnant asylum seeker women are stigmatized. This stigmatization is an extension of the long history of feminizing colonial Ireland. I will return to this point at the end of the chapter.

Why Ireland? Ireland's asylum policy may be compared to and certainly has been influenced, indirectly and directly, by the asylum policies of other countries, most notably Britain, and by the guidelines of the European Union. As the European Union works toward harmonizing all asylum practices, it is likely that there will be increasing standardization and similarities across European countries. However, that does not mean that the experiences and meaning of these practices will be the same in each of these countries. Ireland's experience and practice of asylum policy is unique from those of other European countries for a number of reasons, including: first, that Ireland itself has a long history of being a colonized place; second, Ireland was a place from where people emigrated (i.e., immigration in any significant numbers is a recent postcolonial development); and third, until recently Ireland was an impoverished and politically marginal country within the European context (see Stanley in this volume for similar discussion of the effect of Italy's marginal status in the European Union on Italian citizenship and identity). For these reasons, the fact that Ireland has become a "new place" of immigration allows for a careful exploration of the processes and negotiations of identity, belonging, and citizenship.

In this case study of Ireland, I am drawing from a number of sources, including: fieldwork I conducted in June 2005 (personal interviews and participant observation associated with asylum seeker accommodation centers and activist support groups); analysis of newspaper coverage; and relevant court cases, state policy, and legislation. The structure of the chapter will begin with a short history of the rise of immigration in Ireland along with an overview of who is seeking asylum; this is followed by a discussion of how women asylum seekers are specifically targeted for discrimination and segregation. The next two sections cover how the issue of motherhood was a direct catalyst for calling the citizenship referendum and the debates of the referendum. Before concluding, there is a discussion of asylum seekers' response to the citizenship changes in terms of backstreet abortions, deportations, and the negotiation of the state's Residency Program. In the face of the state's control over citizenship, belonging, and even motherhood, asylum seeker women aim to find ways that best meet their needs of security and safety as they seek to "belong," "settle," and "have a life" in Ireland.

## IMMIGRATION TO IRELAND

While immigration into other European countries is a common and long-established phenomenon (see Anthias and Lazaridis 2000; Brandes 1975; Dummett 2001; Freedman and Tarr 2000; Schonwalder 1996), immigration to Ireland is relatively new. In the last decade Ireland has witnessed a remarkable change in its immigration rates. How Ireland's immigration compares with the rest of the European Union, whether similar or dissimilar, is of interest, but perhaps more significantly is that as a "new place" of immigration the Irish state has had to deal with the issue of its citizenship and what it means to belong to Ireland in a way that it has never had to do before.

In this chapter, I focus on the asylum seeker in Ireland. Definitions may vary from country to country, but for Ireland an "asylum seeker" is one who comes to the country seeking to be recognized as a refugee under the 1951 Geneva Convention on the Status of Refugees, while a "refugee" is one who has been legally granted the status of refugee by the state. Refugees are legally permitted to reside in Ireland and if they then choose, they can claim citizenship through the "naturalization" process, which requires five years residency in the country (though their years in the asylum process are not counted). There are other categories of migrants to Ireland, including economic migrants (who voluntarily leave their home country with the appropriate visas, if necessary, to seek work in Ireland) and illegal migrants who do not have the legal right to be in the country (no visa and/or not in the asylum process). Why I choose to focus on asylum seekers here is because most are not seeking "citizenship," per se, but rather are seeking permission to reside in and perhaps are hoping for a sense of belonging to Ireland as a new home. Unlike refugees, as asylum seekers their status is ambiguous and their association with the state (a state that is largely inexperienced with managing asylum seekers) is itself "in process." Thus this allows for an interesting case study in the negotiation of citizenship and belonging.

In 1999, at the European Council of Tampere, it was decided that there should be a common asylum policy throughout the European Union (European Commission 2004). The first phase of establishing this "Common

European Asylum System," completed in April 2004, set EU common minimum standards and limited the member states from initiating their own
asylum legislation and policy. The standardized EU asylum legislation and
procedure to grant status will not be set in place until the second phase
is undertaken. This effort will seek to create minimum standards in the
treatment and process of asylum seekers across the European Union, and
certainly there are, even now, similarities across some countries, such as
Ireland and Germany, which both prohibit asylum seekers from working.
Despite such similarities, there are still variations in the application of the
asylum policy and process. For example, both Ireland and Britain have opted
to retain the right to decide on a case-by-case basis whether or not they will
accept EU legislation on immigration. As will be shown throughout this
chapter, Ireland's handling of immigration is linked to an understanding of
citizenship and Irish identity.

Once a place of emigration, Ireland has become a destination place for
many asylum seekers. How did this change come about? There are a number
of interrelated causes including the Celtic Tiger of the 1990s and the 1998
Good Friday Agreement signed by the Republic of Ireland, Northern Ireland, and England. These events resulted in growing prosperity and closer
political ties with the European Union. Further the peace accord signaled
an effort to bring an end to the violence and thus promoted a new political vision for the whole island, which further helped to boost the economy.
From one of the poorest countries in the European Union, Ireland is now
one of the most economically thriving (Crowley and MacLaughlin 1997;
MacSharry and White 2000).

Though Britain, France, and Germany are the top receiving countries in the European Union, when these numbers are examined relative
to the size of the hosting country's total population, Ireland is one of the
top five receiving EU countries (UNHCR 2004). For example, in 2002,
Britain received the highest number of asylum seekers with 110,700 applications, followed by Germany with 71,127 applications. However, when these
numbers are compared to the country's population, the ratios of asylum
seeker applications in Austria, Norway, Sweden, Switzerland, and Ireland
rank much higher (ECRE 2006). Further, over the ten-year period from
1992–2002, while France's intake of asylum applications almost doubled
and Britain's increased by three and a half times, and Germany's intake
decreased by more than six and three quarters times, Ireland's asylum applications increased by almost three hundred times. That is, in 1992, only
thirty-nine individuals applied for status in Ireland; four years later in 1996,
that number had increased to over 1,000 applications. By the year 2000,
roughly 1,000 applications were being sought per month or near 12,000 for

the year. This remained a constant rate of applications (USCR 2003) until 2005 saw a decline in numbers.

Who are these asylum seekers? In Ireland, the statistics of the Office of the Refugee Applications Commissioner (ORAC 2004) give the breakdown of asylum seekers by age and gender categories, as well as record the top six countries of origin. Over the last six years, the nationality with the highest number of asylum seekers in Ireland was Nigerian, making up approximately 39 percent of the total number of applicants. The second largest group has been either Somalians or Romanians, each group comprising another 5 to 10 percent of the refugee applications. Other countries represented in the "top six" have included Sudan, Democratic Republic of Congo, Zimbabwe, China, Moldova, Ukraine, and, more recently, Iran and Georgia. The remaining nationalities represented make up less than 2.5 percent each (ORAC 2004).

The reasons why Nigerians are seeking asylum are more identifiable than the reasons why they have chosen Ireland as their new home. Though requiring further investigation, it can be assumed that the introduction of shari'a law, or Muslim-based law, in many states of northern Nigeria in 2000 has been a factor contributing to increased emigration (especially for Nigerian women). In addition, there has been an escalation of violence in areas of the non-Muslim population and increased interethnic conflict. The political and economic impact of the multinational companies such as Shell and Exxon has further added to the plight of locals, especially in the oil-rich Niger delta region in southern Nigeria (Levin 1997; Uwazurike and Mbabuike 2004). When asked why she chose Ireland, Catherine, a young Nigerian woman, stated that she had heard from friends that there were already many Nigerians making a life in Ireland and that it was "easy to get in." There are anecdotal accounts that Nigerians are seeking asylum in Ireland because they know of Ireland from the Irish Catholic Missions in their country. However, the explanations are likely more multifaceted and complex, perhaps even unique on a case-by-case basis.

Of those who come to Ireland seeking refuge, many are women. The Irish 1996 Refugee Act recognized that women comprise a significant category of persecuted persons, whether because they are singled out as political activists and community organizers, because they are sexually targeted, or because their home country's national identity is so closely linked to gender identity, that any divergence from social norms is seen as a national threat (Yuval-Davis and Anthias 1989; Yuval-Davis 1997). Taken from the statistics on Nigerian migrants alone, the ratio of women to men arriving in Ireland since 1998 averages approximately two women for every one man (USCR 2003). In part because the numbers of women asylum seekers in

Ireland are very high, they became the target for racism and discrimination. This is important for understanding the state's asylum policy, how the asylum situation came to be considered a "crisis," and how asylum seeker women (Nigerian as well as other ethnicities) were held responsible for the "crisis" of Irish identity and citizenship.

## WOMEN AND THE ASYLUM PROCESS: SEGREGATION

Yeti, a Nigerian mother of 10-month old twins born in Ireland, says: "I know why I left my country, but the way I am being treated now is as good as being back in Nigeria. I have lost my self dignity, even to walk on the road now I am so embarrassed, I think everyone is looking at me and I feel very inferior."

—Deegan 2003

Grace, also from Nigeria, has three young children and is bringing them up alone in Ireland (she does not know where her husband is, or if he is alive). "I find everything, from A to Z, difficult here," she said. "I would like to go to a busy place like Dublin where everything is not so far away."

—Healy 2003

In the report "African Refugees Needs Analysis," it was documented that almost nine out of ten African asylum seekers and refugees have experienced racism in Ireland (NCCRI 2002). This discrimination has taken the form of verbal abuse, refused service, as well as physical abuse, and has been suffered at the hands of landlords, security personnel, welfare officials, the gardaí (police), and strangers on the street (see Fanning 2002; Lentin and McVeigh 2002). Since the late 1990s, newspaper coverage of racial incidents has increased to an unprecedented level (see the detailed discussions of racism in the case studies of Silverstein's and Stanley's chapters in this volume). Frequent hostile sentiments are voiced against asylum seekers as the source of diseases such as TB and AIDS, as well as the source of crime and begging. Others still react by complaining that asylum seekers and refugees "take Irish people's jobs" (though asylum seekers are not permitted to work) or, if they are not working, that they abuse the social welfare system of the state. In another report, less than one-third of Irish people surveyed said they would welcome asylum seekers or members of ethnic minorities into their communities (NCCRI 2002).

However, that is seldom a problem as asylum seekers are not permitted to integrate into the local community but rather are kept apart from the society. Once entering the country and the asylum process, asylum seekers are placed in state-operated Direct Provision Accommodation Centres that are dispersed around the countryside (IRC 2002; IRC 2004). These centers are often in old hostels or hotels and most (more than 90 percent) are located outside of Dublin. Some are located in other sizeable cities: Cork, Limerick, and Galway. But many are in remote small towns. Either way, all are distanced from Dublin where all aspects of the official asylum process for the claimant take place.

The backlog of asylum claims means that asylum seekers can be housed in these accommodation centers for as long as three years before their status is determined. During this time, the asylum seeker is neither allowed to work nor to go to school. It is a "waiting time." When asked how she spends her time, Odette looking away and staring ahead, replies "[I] Sit and think. I think too much." Salome, a development support worker in Athlone comments that: "They [asylum seekers] feel so segregated. They feel they are seen as bad people, that they must be hidden away. It definitely reinforces racism" (quoted in Holland 2005).

Rontin Lentin, in her article "Pregnant Silence: (En)Gendering Ireland's Asylum Space" writes that "Pregnant asylum seekers are specifically targeted for racial harassment" (2003: 314). That the marginalization of asylum seekers is especially aimed at women asylum seekers has been well documented and theorized (Anthias and Lazaridis 2000; Buijs 1993; Simon and Brettell 1986). Nira Yuval-Davis and Floya Anthias (1989) argue that women as child-bearers, responsible for the biological reproduction of a community, are ideologically symbolized as the "mothers of nations/cultures/identities." If these nations/cultures/identities are at odds with the dominant society, pregnant asylum seekers become the focus of discrimination; symbolizing the culture identity "crisis," they may become the catalyst for changing definitions of belonging and laws of citizenship (see Friedman 2005; Werbner and Yuval-Davis 1999).

## MOTHERHOOD AS CATALYST TO CHANGE: THE PATH TO THE CITIZENSHIP REFERENDUM

The catalysts to a changing understanding of citizenship are directly linked with the politicalization of birth and motherhood. This change is witnessed in Ireland in two ways: a series of court cases concerning the rights of nonnational parents with Irish-born children; and the so-called crisis in the maternity hospitals of Dublin. The former illustrates how individual "nonnationals" used the legal system and courts to actively engage with the political process of citizenship and while the majority of asylum seekers do not take such overt political action to gain their rights to belong, these cases nevertheless affect the majority because they led up to the 2004 Citizenship Referendum. (It should be noted that the terms used during these "crises"—national vs. nonnational or "Irish-born children"—are euphemisms hiding the deeper message that continues to "otherize" and deny some a sense of belonging in Ireland.)

In 1990 there was the landmark case of *Fajujonu vs. Minister for Justice, Equality and Law Reform* (High Court of Ireland 1990 2IR 151). In this case the court held that an Irish-born child had the right to the company and care of his or her parents within the family unit and that there must be "predominant and overwhelming" reasons for breaking up a mixed family of nonnationals and Irish citizens (for example, by deporting the nonnational parents). The focus was primarily on the rights of the child (especially because the child was an Irish citizen) and the right to reside in the Irish state (see Fraser 2003). As a result of this decision, nonnational parents of Irish-born children could apply for residency in Ireland.

However, on 23 January 2003, in the case of *Lobe and Osayande* (usually referred to as L & O) *vs. Minister for Justice* (Supreme Court of Ireland 2003 IESC 3), the Supreme Court of Ireland restricted the almost automatic residency rights for nonnational parents of Irish-born children. This decision claimed that—"in the interest of the common good, which was held to include the integrity of the asylum process"—the minister could deport the nonnational parents of an Irish-born citizen, even if this resulted in the de facto removal of the Irish-citizen child from the state. This ruling held that the protection and care of the Irish child could be fulfilled outside of the state (see Fraser 2003; Ryan 2005). Following this landmark decision, the minister announced that none of the 11,000 families in a similar situation would be given residency based solely on being the parents of Irish-citizen children, but that decisions would be made on a case-by-case basis. This caused chaos in the system as many families subsequently received deportation notices and filed complaints with the high court over the ruling.

The Chen case was one such challenge to the L & O decision. Ms. Chen, six months pregnant, came from China to the United Kingdom with her husband, seeking asylum. Ms. Chen moved to Belfast and there gave birth to Kunquian Catherine Chen. Applying to the European Court of Justice, Chen sought the right to reside in the United Kingdom based on her daughter's Irish citizenship and therefore EU citizenship. The Advocate General of the European court gave a preliminary judgment in favor of Chen, a decision that legal experts interpreted to mean that non-EU parents of Irish-born children could live anywhere in the European Union except in Ireland (according to the L & O ruling). The judgment states that as long as the claimants did not pose a financial burden on the host state, they had the unrestricted right of movement throughout the European Union. The Irish government considered the residency situation politically unsustainable, and while the Chens had substantial financial resources, the ruling implied that the same rights would not be awarded to poor claimants. Given that asylum seekers in Ireland are not allowed to work during their asylum process, all asylum seekers could be regarded as a burden on the state and thus not qualified to receive the rights of residency despite having Irish-citizen children.

The "crisis" of citizenship that led to the 2004 referendum is, in all of these court cases, a crisis of birth and motherhood. The matter is not so much that there are Irish-born children citizens but that the mothers of these children are able to "slip in the backdoor" though they are not Irish-born themselves nor have been granted status and the right to reside in Ireland through the asylum process. That this is the situation is evident in the controversy surrounding the Dublin maternity hospitals in which it was claimed there was a "crisis" in the high number of nonnationals having children (O'Halloran 2004).

As early as 2002, the number of nonnationals giving birth was being examined. "Officials" stated that 80 percent of the asylum seekers were visibly pregnant during their application for refugee status. Dr. Michael Geary, master of the Rotunda Maternity Hospital in Dublin, voiced concern that many of these women were arriving in Ireland, late in their pregnancy, with no medical records and with little or no previous prenatal care. This soon became an alarmist situation in which the "authorities" worried that the "high numbers of non–national births occurring in Dublin hospitals meant that women were targeting Ireland because of its automatic citizenship rights of children born in the state. This was labeled "citizenship shopping" and the women were called "citizenship tourists" or "maternity tourists" and constituted a threat to the "integrity of Irish citizenship" (Brennock 2004a).

Thus, in March 2004, Justice Minister Michael McDowell claimed that a referendum should be held because of the Chen case in the European Court of Justice, but also because the masters of two main maternity hospitals in Dublin had "pleaded" with him to make constitutional changes in relation to the status of nonnationals. These two denied that they had approached the minister, saying that they were being used as scapegoats in the government's push for a citizenship referendum. Further the doctors argued that there were not "massive flows" of pregnant nonnational women and that many of those "foreign" mothers having children in the maternity hospitals were in fact legally living and working in Ireland—i.e., they "belonged" in Ireland. Minister McDowell insisted that the masters did alert him to the potential crisis in medical services if the citizenship laws were not changed and his Justice Department produced a study reporting that 60 percent of female asylum seekers over age sixteen are pregnant at the time of application and that 25 percent of the births in the Dublin maternity hospitals were to nonnationals, signaling a "real problem" with the citizenship laws (Brennock 2004a). In response, in May 2004, thirty doctors across Ireland banded together to call for a "No" vote in the citizenship referendum the following month. They claimed that a "Yes" vote would be nothing more than scaremongering as Ireland was not being "swamped with refugees."

The citizenship referendum was promoted as the legal (and medical) regularization of citizenship laws so that Ireland would not merely be the backdoor of Europe. This "path to the poll" (see *Irish Times* 2004) that I have outlined here suggests that while immigration issues were seen as a crisis linked to women; citizenship issues were largely seen as a crisis linked to nonnational mothers who did not belong in Ireland.

## THE CITIZENSHIP REFERENDUM

The Citizenship Referendum took place on 11 June 2004 and asked the Irish public whether they supported a change in the constitutional definition of Irish citizenship from *jus soli*, that granted citizenship to a person based on being born in Ireland, to *jus sanguinis*, that grants citizenship based on one's parent being a national or citizen of that state.[2] The proposed amendment would require that Irish citizenship be granted only to those children who had at least one parent of Irish citizenship, thus changing the citizenship tradition of Ireland created in 1921 (under the first Free State constitution) (Irish Statute Book 2004). In doing so, Ireland was complying with the Maastricht Treaty which allows each EU member state to self-determine who "belongs" to their nation, while simultaneously practicing extreme control of the European external borders (termed "Fortress Europe").

The government's argument for the citizenship law revision was to curb the abuses of the existing system, effectively prohibiting the "citizenship tourism" feared to be occurring regularly with nonnational women choosing to have their children in Ireland in order to get Irish and EU citizenship through the backdoor. When the minister of justice, Mr. McDowell, claimed that "hordes of impoverished women and babies will start moving between EU states" (Brennock 2004b), this created a clear image of thousands of pregnant women burdening the overstretched Irish hospitals. However, the Irish Refugee Council reported (2004) that of the 60,000 babies born in Ireland in 2003, less than 1 percent were born to nonnationals arriving at hospitals late in their pregnancy. Undoubtedly there were some who were abusing the system; however, instead of dealing with those few, the government's course of action was to target a whole group of people and vilify their intentions, where to be non-Irish and a woman could only mean that she would use her biological ability to have children as a weapon against the state.

Another of the government's arguments was that Ireland's citizenship laws were at odds with the European Union's "Fortress Europe" policies. It is perhaps not surprising, then, that the Irish Fianna Fail government of Bertie Ahern promoted a Yes vote in the referendum while Ahern was holding the presidency of the European Union. Other EU member states, such as Italy and to some extent Britain and until recently, Germany, do not practice *jus soli,* but *jus sanguinis.* Thus the line of reasoning was that Ireland should not be the means through which non-EU citizens could gain entry to other parts of Europe. (However, though the new Irish citizenship laws might uphold the spirit of the EU policy, there are no EU laws that require or pressure national governments to alter their constitutions. In fact, the European Union specifically declares that citizenship laws are solely the responsibility of the national governments.)

A fundamental opposition to changing the citizenship laws was that it equated to the creation of two categories of children born in Ireland, those with citizenship and those without, and that this would be the basis of discrimination between them (Fraser 2003). If the legislation makes the provision that citizenship rights are only granted to the children of those parents legally resident in Ireland for three years (not including any time spent in the asylum process), then what of the children of the migrant worker who has lost residency through no fault of their own?

What the Citizenship Referendum means for these women's sense of belonging and sense of identity in Ireland is reflected in their experiences of backstreet abortions, deportations, and trying to negotiate the Residency Program (called the Irish Born Children '05 Scheme) (Department of Justice 2006).

## WOMEN'S RESPONSES TO CITIZENSHIP CHANGES
### *Backstreet Abortions*

Media accounts continued to fuel the idea that nonnational births were solely the result of trying to cheat the system, as they reported on women seeking abortions after the referendum decision. An *Irish Times* article entitled "Abortion & Isolation: Crisis Pregnancies Among Non-Nationals Increasing" explains that "There have been cases of foreign-national women traveling to Britain for an abortion and then trying to 'sneak' back through Northern Ireland . . . [and that] a Nigerian national in this situation . . . was that desperate she risked being deported. Given that asylum-seekers are entitled to just €19.10 per week, few could take up even this option" (Holland

2004a). Many asylum seeker women are in the accommodation system with no family around them, no social supports to fall back on and little money to afford traveling to Britain for abortions (legal abortions in Ireland occur only in the most extreme cases). Thus, on the same day, another article in the Irish Times reports that gardaí (the police) were investigating abortions involving foreign women: "refugees and asylum-seekers existing on €19-a-week and illegal workers who clearly felt that they could not leave this country, were now in what could only be described as a kind of hidden Ireland lacking in social protection to such an extent that they had felt it necessary to have illegal back-street abortions and put their health at such risk" (Walsh 2004).

Though these news accounts, on one hand, could be interpreted as sympathetically trying to make the general public aware of the harsh conditions experienced by pregnant asylum seekers, there is also another message being presented. In a country that has a long and complicated history surrounding the legality (or illegality) of abortion (even to the point of opposing EU sanctioned laws on the subject), these accounts of backstreet abortions by asylum seekers reinforces the view of opportunistic nonnational women and only serves to bolster and justify the recent changes in the citizenship laws.

### Deportations

Deportations of failed asylum cases existed long before the Citizenship Referendum and deportation rules were written into many of the new immigration and refugee laws of the 1990s (Anderson 2003). In fact, the Citizenship Referendum should have nothing to do with deportations, let alone increased deportations. However, some asylum seekers had been legally advised (prior to the referendum) that since they had Irish-born children, they would have a clear case for residency based on their child's Irish citizenship and therefore should remove themselves from the asylum process. After the referendum, these women became an ambiguous category: neither asylum seeker, nor resident. Thus, what *was* different after the referendum was that asylum seekers *felt* an increased threat of deportation.

Rose, from the Cameroon, arrived in Ireland four years ago and now has a two-year-old Irish-born daughter. She has completed a number of courses to, as she says, "get work for a better life. [Yet] I am very worried now that I could be deported. There are bad ones taking from the system, but there are lots of us who are trying to build up something for themselves here, and I hope the Government will see that" (Deegan 2003).

Peter O'Mahony of the Irish Refugee Council reports that while the minister of justice is "vigorous" in his pursuit of immigrants, there are numerous cases where children are separated from their parents when the parents are wanted for deportation (Holland 2004b). Amnesty International's 2005 report also raises the question of the plight of Irish-born children whose asylum seeker parents are being deported (CADIC Amnesty 2005). When asked where the children who are left behind stay in Ireland, Sr. Paula of a refugee support group answered, "I'd say they are staying with friends or contacts. I think there are ways and means of finding out where they are staying but the state doesn't know where they are and isn't caring for them. They would have to go to school but they are totally traumatized from losing their parents."[3]

Though deportations are understood by most as a necessary part of the system, Amnesty has criticized the use of prisons to hold people facing deportation (Healy 2005). Others have drawn attention to the harshness of certain deportations. In one case, a Burundi woman and her two young children experienced a night-time deportation, in which "Members of the Garda Immigration Unit called to the hostel in which Olivia and her two daughters were staying, at 10.30 P.M., packed their belongings into plastic bags and drove them to Dublin by car. They were transported to Heathrow Airport the next morning, and interviewed by British Home Office officials"(McConnell 2004). Such night-time deportations then become, as Rose had worried, a threat to all in the asylum process. That threat increased with the decision made in the Citizenship Referendum and was reinforced by the minister for justice's statements about "bogus asylum seekers' cock-and-bull stories." He had said he would like to meet all asylum seekers at the airport and send them back home, but "unfortunately, the UN convention requires me to go through due process in respect of all these claims" (Holland 2005).

## The Residency Policy Program

Called the Irish Born Children '05 Scheme (IBC/05), this policy was introduced by the minister of justice in January 2005 as a consequence of the citizenship changes (Ryan 2005). It stated that parents of Irish-citizen children born before 1 January 2005 were entitled to submit applications for residency based on their parentage of Irish-born children, if they could prove that they had been continually resident in the state since the birth of the child and were actively fulfilling their role as a parent (Department of Justice 2005). This meant that any asylum seeker in the state-run accommodation system with a child born in Ireland, would have the necessary proof, could submit their application and, if successful, could remove themselves from the asylum process altogether. In submitting an application, they must also declare that they will uphold state law and will "make every effort" to become economically viable within two years of being granted residency. Further, they must waive their right to try to bring into Ireland their spouse or children who are still in their country of origin.

Margaret, of a refugee support group,[4] explained to me, "There was a scheme set up specifically to cover those people who got stuck in the loop-hole. To be honest with you, the reason why that happened was because there were thousands and thousands of people backlogged, so one of the main reasons is to get rid of these off their desks. And most of them will get leave to remain" (meaning that they will be granted residency). Margaret speaks of "tens of thousands." Eighteen thousand claims were submitted by the deadline in March 2005. By June almost 7,000 had been processed and of those only about forty had been rejected because of severe criminal charges (Department of Justice 2006).

These new residents will be able to apply for citizenship by naturalization if they stay in Ireland for five years (not counting their years in the asylum process). Applying under this scheme can be seen as asylum seeker women practicing the political process and using what means are available to them to gain citizenship and belonging in Ireland. However, there are some significant problems with this residency scheme. Again, Margaret explains, "Well, it's very difficult. They have to swear that they won't bring their families over. Our receptionist, Marian? Her husband and her three-year-old child are still in Nigeria. She had to sign a sworn statement that she won't bring them over on a family reunification program. So, she will never see them again . . . She never stops thinking about it. It's a very difficult choice to have to make. But given the option, most people would stay here."

Another critical problem is that these women and their young children have only lived in the state-run accommodation centers where they are not allowed to cook or care for themselves. As asylum seekers they are neither permitted to work or attend school. They may have been in Ireland for as long as three or more years, but until now, they have never had a chance to be part of the local Irish community. While they still will receive small social welfare checks, they are ultimately on their own with few social services available to their specific needs. And after two years out of the asylum process they must prove that they have become "economically viable" (Ryan 2005). Many of these women will not be able to afford daycare if they go out to work; and though some are professionals (especially nurses and teachers) in their home countries, their qualifications are not recognized in Ireland and so what work they find might not be any more than minimum wage.

In July of 2005 I participated in an Information Session on Residency given by the local asylum support group at an asylum seeker accommodation center in Galway. The women gathered in what had been the bar and dance room of the old hotel but was now dingy, worn, and empty. The talk was of procedures for finding and renting lodgings once the women had received their residency papers. The support worker Michelle was emphatic, "don't borrow money for the deposit because the social welfare officer needs to approve the flat and sign off on the deposit voucher . . . don't be intimidated by the landlords trying to tell you that you don't have rights . . . don't agree to one 'official' price and then give the landlord extra money . . . it's a landlord's market—many are known to be nasty and the gardaí are no help as many of them are landlords themselves." One Nigerian woman, Christine, asked if she would be allowed to choose housing outside of Galway. "No, that wouldn't be easy—you need to deal with the social welfare officer in the area, you know the one here in Galway and you wouldn't know the officer somewhere else." Christine's friend, Emily, asked about taking training as a nurse, "I did nursing back home [in Nigeria]; could I train here and work as a nurse?" Again, the answer was negative, "You have to be a citizen or else you will have to pay foreign student fees. How will you pay for that when you need to pay for your flat, food, childcare, and your bills?"

Many of the women seated in the circle, their children playing around them, had no idea what they would be facing once out on their own. When budgeting was discussed, Michelle talked about being careful with how they spent their money,"your oil heating for instance, turn on the heat for half an hour in the morning and two hours at night, but don't have it on all day or you'll use up your whole tank very quickly and you'll want to try to make it last all through the winter" (all this, considering that these women are used to hotter climates, and that many will have to stay at home all day long to care for their children). One of the most telling questions was when Simone, looking at the budget guidelines that had been handed out, asked, "what is ESB?" It stands for the "Electric Supply Board" but as it is always referred to by its acronym, the session leaders fumbled for a way to explain. They looked at each other wide-eyed; this was so basic a term that it never occurred to them that someone wouldn't know what it meant. Later, outside on the steps of the accommodation center, the session leaders were shocked, "how scary it is to think of these women trying to learn how to fit in and handle all that will be new to them in their daily lives. How scary to think how *easy* it will be to scam these women trying to get homes and get work in order so they can prove 'economic viability' within two years."

Before the session, Ada, a Romanian woman with two children ages five and two-and-a-half, sat down beside me. She was nervous and agitated. She wanted to know if I could tell her about receiving her residency status. She had not heard yet and while I reminded her that the government had not yet processed half of the applications, this did not calm her. She had been pregnant with her second child when she arrived in Ireland three years ago. She had lived that entire time in this accommodation center: "my son has only ever known this hostel; my daughter knows this place as home. But what kind of home is this? I need a home of my own to raise my children. Why have they [the government] not contacted me about my residency? What will I do if I don't get it?"

## CITIZENSHIP, MOTHERHOOD, AND BELONGING IN IRELAND

The politicization of birth and motherhood led to the 2004 referendum and thus to the changes in defining Irish citizenship. By biologizing Irish citizenship laws, it effectively prohibits making a place for newcomers in Irish society. Many nonnational women having children are single mothers. Citizenship rests then not, as the legalese would have it, on the rights of the parents but of the mother. In this way, it is the mother's status that thus creates a second class of Irish-born but not Irish-citizen children. It is the mother who is burdened with this marginalization. She and her children do not belong.

In many ways the stigmatization of pregnant asylum seeker women (many, if not most, of whom are of color) is an extension of the feminization of Ireland that has a long history: (1) polarizing the concepts of female/ male, savage/civilized, chaos/order; (2) using images of women as symbols of vulnerability, charity, and corruption; and (3) supporting long-standing Western associations between nature, land, fertility, and femininity (Nash 1997). Thus during the colonial period, Ireland was figured as a female subject to be controlled and subordinated; Irish women were seen as sexually promiscuous and free and therefore a threat to English cultural purity by reducing the cultural distinctiveness between colonizer and the colonized. This is common in colonial discourse. And it echoes in the current climate that talks about the "fear" of the increasing number of nonnational births. The government's solution is to withhold the legal right for these women and their children to share a sense of Irishness and belonging in the Irish society, a society that is ideologically masculine and white.

For the asylum seeker women I spoke with, what was important was to have a sense of belonging to their new country and to "have a life" in Ireland. Emily, at the information session said, "I want to find a way that I can be here and raise my kids and start over; have a new life here. I will do whatever it takes. If the government tells me I can be a resident because my girl was born here then I will work and stay here. Whatever it takes." Asylum seeker women must negotiate their sense of belonging in Ireland as the state controls and changes the definition of belonging and citizenship. Ireland is not unique in this sense, but as a "new place" of immigration, with its own unique colonial history and its recent departure from its politically and economically marginal position within the European context, it provides a telling study in how the processes of inclusion and exclusion are operated and experienced.

NOTES

1. An example of this, is that the mother of the family I live with in Ireland has been married and lived on the same farm in the same community for almost forty years, and yet she is still considered a "blow-in": though she is Irish (and Irish-born) she was not born in this place, in this community, and so though accepted (she has raised five children here) she will never fully belong to this "new" place.
2. An interesting note is that as Ireland was making its citizenship laws more restrictive, Germany was making theirs somewhat less restrictive. However, as mentioned before, comparison of Ireland's citizenship (and asylum/migration) policies with those of other European countries though relevant and of interest is far too complex to attempt here (see Cesarani and Fulbrook 1996) as each country's legislation is rooted in a long and deep national/cultural history.
3. Sr. Paula (a pseudonym) was interviewed by the author in June 2005.
4. Margaret (a pseudonym) was interviewed by the author June 2005.

# CHAPTER 4

# From the "Imagined Community" to "Communities of Practice"

## IMMIGRANT BELONGING AMONG VIETNAMESE AMERICANS

*Deborah Reed-Danahay*

### INTRODUCTION

ONE OF THE WAYS to theorize the nation and a sense of belonging to it is that of Benedict Anderson's (1983) concept of the "imagined community"—the idea that belonging to a group that one cannot see or interact with directly is based on imagining the greater unit and coming to identify with it through various media such as newspapers and novels. Anderson writes also of the sense of simultaneity necessary to nationalism that is created not only through these print media but also through rituals. If a nation is an "imagined community," then how can immigrants imagine their place within it? This is a question that Leo Chavez (1991) has asked about undocumented Mexican immigrants in the United States. He places them "outside" of the imagined community of America, and analyzes their experience of travel to the United States in terms of Arnold Van Gennep's rites of passage. Chavez suggests that Mexicans go through stages of separation (from home) and liminality (in the United States after they first arrive), but not necessary that final stage of incorporation. There are parallels in the circumstances of refugees, who also make a separation from home (often quite abruptly) and are then in a liminal state while in refugee camps and after initial arrival in a host country. Vietnamese refugees who have settled in the United States differ from the undocumented Mexicans studied by Chavez in that they have been granted rights to permanent residence and eventual citizenship. The degree to which Vietnamese Americans are now making the transition to incorporation in U.S. society is based not only on formal citizenship but also on their participation in the public sphere ("participatory citizenship") and on modes of belonging imagined for them by the dominant sectors of society. Although they are not necessarily "outside" of the imagined community, it may be more useful to view Vietnamese Americans in terms of a process of moving toward being "inside."

I suggest that although the nation may very well be an "imagined community," it is through "communities of practice" that are face-to-face, tangible units of sociality that immigrants come to experience a sense of belonging and citizenship.[1] The concept of a community of practice can, therefore, complement the notion of the imagined community by paying more attention to social agency, social learning, and lived experience. The concept of a community of practice, developed by Jean Lave and Etienne Wegner (1991) originally in the context of studies of learning and cognition, is one that theorizes the relationship of newcomers to an already established unit of social interaction. A community of practice is a site for "situated learning," a view of social learning adapted from work on apprenticeship learning that incorporates an emphasis on social practice and also uses a vocabulary of newcomers. These concepts of situated learning and community of practice have been used primarily in the contexts of work, education, and voluntary associations—contexts in which the term newcomer does not have the specific connotations associated with an immigrant but that of any person new to some form of social practice. One can conceptualize an association, a club, a classroom, a neighborhood, a political party, or wider social unit as a community of practice. Rooted in the anthropology of apprenticeship, a mode of informal learning, and based in a practice-oriented approach that sees learners as having social agency and not passively being taught, the concept of a community of practice, with its focus on situated learning, seems well suited to helping answer questions about how immigrants learn things about "belonging" in their new host country. It is a way of thinking about how newcomers can move from the outside to the inside, or from the periphery to the core, and also about the barriers to doing so. As Lave has written:

"Newcomers become old-timers through a social process of increasingly centripetal participation, which depends on legitimate access to ongoing community practice. Newcomers develop a changing understanding of practice over time from improvised opportunities to participate peripherally in ongoing activities of the community. Knowledgeable skill is encompassed in the process of assuming an identity as a practitioner, of becoming a full participant, an oldtimer" (Lave and Wegner 1991: 68).

Lave and Wegner define the process of "legitimate peripheral participation" as a form of situated learning that "provides a way to speak about the relations between newcomers and old-timers, and about activities, identities, artifacts, and communities of knowledge and practice. It concerns the process by which newcomers become part of a community of practice" (1991: 29). Lave and Wegner oppose peripheral and full participation as opposite ends of a continuum so that one can study the "learning trajectory" of a person moving along this in relationship to a community of practice. Each person participates in multiple communities of practice, so that the notion of community in this theory is not fixed in that sense (Wegner 1998).

How do immigrants learn to become citizens in the broadest sense of that term ("full participants," as Lave writes)? How and in what contexts does an immigrant experience the identity shift that leads to feelings and practices associated with citizenship in the new host society? How does an immigrant learn to become civically engaged? And what are the barriers to this? These are questions that explore the connections between individual experience and sociocultural and structural locations or dislocations. They are vital to understanding the notion of "belonging" for immigrants.

Immigrants actively learn about becoming civically engaged through both individual and shared experiences. While there has been much important research on the institutional, socioeconomic, and cultural factors involved in immigrant incorporation (variously conceived of as integration, assimilation, adaptation, etc.),[2] there has not been sufficient attention paid to the *processes* through which people come to take part in the public sphere—which is a form of learning. Certainly public schools have long been part of the picture of immigrant incorporation in modern nation-states, primarily because they have intentionally been designed to create citizens, and there has been much attention paid already to civic education in such institutions.[3] There are, however, multiple ways in which people acquire knowledge of the public sphere and learn to participate in it. My interest in this chapter lies in those less formal channels through which newcomers learn ways of operating (Certeau 1988) and modes of civic participation in their host countries.[4] Here I draw upon Renato Rosaldo's (1997; 2003) notion of vernacular or cultural citizenship. This has to do with whether or not people feel they belong, or feel they are considered "second-class citizens." These forms of vernacular citizenship occur within the context of "interactions in everyday environments—such as the workforce, church, schools, friendship and family networks" (Rosaldo 2003: 3).

The case of Vietnamese American immigrants/refugees in north-central Texas, a newcomer group to U.S. society, is one in which we can usefully draw upon the concept of the "community of practice" to interrogate the ways in which people learn and practice vernacular forms of citizenship. We can see this both through the personal stories of "learning" how to adapt to life in the United States—to the wider community of practice that is the civic sphere, and through the ways in which ethnic populations interact with U.S. institutions through their own communities of practice (social networks, ethnic associations). In this chapter, I will first look at some cases of personal experience and discuss their theoretical implications, before turning to the ethnography of a conflict over the use of Vietnamese flags on a college campus.

### Communities of Practice, Situated Learning, and Cultural Intimacy: Personal Stories

One of my research participants, Mr. L., a self-proclaimed Vietnamese American community activist who arrived in the United States as a young adult refugee soon after the fall of Saigon in 1975, told me about two mistakes he made as he learned to participate in U.S. civic life. "When I first arrived, I got a job as a social worker. I thought that was really great because I would be working for the government. In Vietnam, any job that is part of the government is a good job and you are treated well. But I soon realized that I was wrong. A social worker here in the United States has low wages and is not respected; it was the opposite of the situation in Vietnam." He eventually went back to school and trained as an engineer. The second error Mr. L. mentioned to me happened a few years later, before the 2000 U.S. Presidential elections, and after he had become a naturalized U.S. citizen and started to participate more in politics—an area of great interest to him. "I got a call from someone very important in the Texas Republican Party asking about my support for the upcoming elections. This was before the primaries were over. They asked me who I supported, and I said that I thought John McCain would be a strong candidate." He explained that he was thereafter written off as an insider to the party, because in Texas George W. Bush would be the favored candidate. He was surprised that his honesty was not respected and told me that he has learned a few things about politics in the United States through this experience. He describes himself, a recent arrival having fled a Communist regime, as having naively acted as though the openness of a democratic society meant that one could freely voice one's opinions.

In the example of Mr. L., we see how a newcomer stumbles as he learns about participation in U.S. society, as he struggles to "belong" and become an active participant. By telling me about his experiences of confusion prompted by his missteps both in choice of occupation and in choice of candidate, Mr. L. was not simply displaying his earlier naiveté about U.S. society, he was telling me about becoming privy to U.S. forms of cultural intimacy. As Michael Herzfeld has argued, these are the secrets that members of a society tell themselves about themselves, and form a counternarrative to the more seamless front they offer to outsiders. Cultural intimacy involves "the recognition of those aspects of a cultural identity that are considered a source of external embarrassment but that nevertheless provide insiders with their assurance of common sociality, the familiarity with the bases of power that may at one moment assure the disenfranchised a degree of creative irreverence and at the next moment reinforce the effectiveness of intimidation" (Herzfeld 2005: 3). The story of democracy and freedom of speech that is part of the narrative of U.S. society becomes understood later by the immigrant as more nuanced and dependent upon "politics" in sense of strategy, manipulation, and so on. Organizations, such as the state, appeal to forms of cultural intimacy as a way to reinforce the emotional ties of their members. These are "self-stereotypes that insiders express ostensibly at their own collective expense" (3).

While Mr. L had originally been influenced by models (presented to newcomers, children, and outsiders) of democracy, freedom of speech, and the like that would have indicated that you could be open and honest about your political views in the Untied States (as opposed to in Communist Vietnam), he was learning the dirty secrets of Texas politics—that if you wanted to be onboard in the Republican Party at that moment in time, you had to support George W. Bush. This is the type of cultural intimacy about Texas politics that someone like the late columnist Molly Ivens expressed very well. Mr. L. was learning the cultural intimacy of U.S. life. And he was expressing this to me (a coparticipant in U.S. society) in our conversations about what he has learned since his arrival thirty years ago. But we must not take Mr. L.'s expression of bafflement in the reaction of party members to his response about his preference for a political candidate completely at face value. Mr. L. is himself an astute political observer and agent, who may have his own reasons for telling these stories about his experiences in the United States—for adopting the posture of the naïve immigrant who is dismayed to learn that the United States is not always the open democracy it purports to be. In Lave's terms, as he has moved more from the periphery to the center of U.S. life (from newcomer to insider), he is able to voice the "dirty secrets" of Texas politics. And I suggest that it is in the context of communities of practice that cultural intimacy is expressed and learned.

At the same time that Vietnamese immigrants learn about U.S. cultural intimacy, they also invoke in-group talk about their own versions of cultural intimacy—for example, jokes about the cultural practices of Vietnamese, similar to the "self-deprecating Jewish diaspora humor" that Herzfeld suggests helps to find "common ground with the encompassing society" (2005: 3). One example of this in the Vietnamese case is the notion of "Viet time" frequently cited by my informants. It is in relationship to the norms they perceive to be prevalent in the United States that this self-recognition occurs. That things always start late, are poorly organized until the last minute, and usually involve just a few key actors who get things going, are common refrains among my informants. "Like at a wedding," one Vietnamese American student told me, "you always tell the invitees that it will start an hour before it will actually start. People will come an hour later." Or another young woman told me, "We don't make appointments to get our hair done like Americans; we just go and stop in and if they are busy, we come back another time." There is also the common notion that the Vietnamese are too busy working and too focused on their families to get involved in the Vietnamese community, let along the wider U.S. society. This, too, is an aspect of the "cultural intimacy" shared by this population as a community of practice. It is part of the sense of identity among Vietnamese Americans, and when I have pointed out to some informants that I found a similar sense of time among the rural French families with whom I previously conducted fieldwork, this has been an unwelcome comment—it undercuts the sense of uniqueness and of shared culture (warts and all) of the Vietnamese. That they are not so unique after all in their approach to time may also be viewed as part of cultural intimacy among the Vietnamese in America, a recognition of their shared marginality with other groups within a competing system where being "on time" and keeping to a schedule is highly valued.

The concept of cultural intimacy can be viewed in the context of communities of practice, as part of the shared repertoire of meanings within the group. Each individual may participate in several communities of practice, and switch back and forth between them. In his study of craft apprenticeship in Crete, Herzfeld (2003) brought these two concepts together to articulate the ways in which Crete is marginalized within the overall Greek society. Although he is not dealing with immigrants, per se, and is looking at a specific location related to artisanal production, the analogy with immigrants is apt considering that we can see them as also serving a form of apprenticeship after arriving in the host country. Moreover, artisans and immigrants both occupy a subaltern status. Herzfeld writes that "apprenticeship emerges as a training in the mastery of cultural intimacy at multiple levels from the most local to the international" (2003: 51–52). The apprenticeship of artisans in Crete, he argues, is not just about learning a trade, but about learning about being Greek. In my previous work in rural France, I was similarly concerned with the issue of how rural children in the region of Auvergne learn to be "French" and learn to manipulate various forms of identity (local, regional, national, and, increasingly, supranational in the context of the European Union). I turned to a concept used by my informants themselves, *se débrouiller*, which I gloss as a form of strategic action aimed at both "making due" (coping or "getting by") and "making out" (profiting through ruse) to illustrate the forms of social manipulation, flexibility, and cunning that are often associated with straddling various social worlds (which I might now refer to as "communities of practice"). We can see the immigrant as newcomer, Mr. L. for example, working to *se débrouiller* (to "make due" or cope with new social rules and constraints, but also to profit from them, or "make out").

Not only can we see communities of practice as places for learning, as sites for a shared repertoire of cultural intimacy, but also as a resource for social capital. It is by gaining access to the resources of groups, Pierre Bourdieu argued, in which forms of what he called "social energy" can be appropriated, that social agents enhance what he called their "social capital"—their network of resources and relationships (Bourdieu 1986). Because such groups (and here one could insert the phrase "communities of practice") aim to reproduce themselves, and to maximize their material and social profits, and also because they face questions of the ways in which they are legitimately represented, "members of the group must regulate the conditions of access to the right to declare oneself a member of a group and, above all, to set oneself up as a representative of the whole group, thereby committing the social capital of the whole group" (Bourdieu 1986: 251). This maximization of social and material profits is not necessarily either consciously or overly pursued, so that the individual comes to experience his or her obligations to the group as emotions, "feelings of gratitude, respect, friendship" or as rights guaranteed by membership. When new members are inducted, "the whole definition of the group, i.e., its fines, its boundaries, and its identity, is put at stake, exposed to redefinition, alteration, adulteration" (1986: 250). By bringing Bourdieu's perspectives on the ways in which groups include or exclude potential members into the picture of the incorporation of newcomers into communities of practice, any romanticized notion of a community as a necessarily open and receptive site for new members is challenged.

According to Bourdieu, groups try to recruit members who are already a good fit and who already have a shared habitus and sufficient cultural or symbolic capital to contribute. If we borrow this framework, originally discussed by Bourdieu primarily in terms of the family and educational institutions, in terms of immigrant incorporation, I think there are some fruitful avenues to pursue in understanding the barriers to civic participation and the modes through which it can occur. Bourdieu argued that it is the social agent whose habitus is already most receptive to the ethos of the group that gets "chosen" by a group and is able to enter its sphere. I think we can make an analogy here to immigrants and their children. In my studies of Vietnamese Americans who have taken on leadership roles outside of the ethnic community, I have learned that many of them were mentored by members of the community who "recognized" some potential in them. Bourdieu would say that these immigrants (or social agents) were acquiring forms of symbolic capital and displaying the capacity to acquire the proper secondary, dominant habitus required of those in leadership positions in the community.

Examples from my fieldwork illustrate these processes. As my informants have recounted their life stories to me, I have been listening for the ways in which they learned to become engaged in U.S. civic life. Linh, a single professional woman born in 1968, arrived in the United States with her family in 1981. Growing up in Texas as the second youngest child of five, her elder siblings had already left the house when she was in high school. She told me "I raised myself . . . my parents worked so hard, all the time. I came home from school, did my homework, and then watched prime time TV for three hours every night." She did not participate in Vietnamese organizations until college, when she was drawn into a student association (a community of practice) by her sister. After graduation, Linh worked for several years in her profession with little direct connection outside of her family and coworkers. She traveled widely to other countries, and eventually was drawn to seek out other Vietnamese professionals and "get back to her roots." Linh is now active in many civic activities in Texas aimed at encouraging Vietnamese youth to keep their ethnic identity and contributes time and money to efforts to improve health and education in Vietnam. This example shows the ways in which someone moves from the periphery of Vietnamese American communities of practice (established here in the diaspora setting) to full membership and leadership. As a newcomer to the United States who arrived as a child, Linh was drawn into civic participation through ethnic Vietnamese communities of practice—first through a Vietnamese student group and then through a professional group. Although she has contact in her job with other ethnic groups, she still lives at home with her parents and most of her social activities involve other Vietnamese.

A different scenario is found for Hien, who also arrived in Texas as a child. He and his family originally settled in the Texas Gulf Coast area before later moving to the Dallas-Fort Worth region. He was in elementary school when he left Vietnam in 1975, landing first in refugee camps for a brief period. His family was sponsored, through Catholic Charities, by five U.S. families in the Gulf region. He told me that his family learned things by carefully watching. For example: "OK, Americans mow their lawns on Saturday; we'll do that, too." Each weekend, one of the children in his family would spend a weekend alone with one of the U.S. families. He said he would just watch and copy what they did—"how they used utensils, how they ate, how they brushed their teeth . . ." Little by little, he kept observing and eventually learned enough so that he is now a high school teacher, engaging with students in one of the poorest and most ethnically diverse schools in his district. This young man was illustrating the kinds of apprenticeship learning studied by anthropologists in which someone peripheral to a community of practice gradually learns the social practices of the group and comes to participate more legitimately in it. As with many of the very first wave of Vietnamese, he and his family did not have a ready-made Vietnamese American community with which to connect. His insertion into U.S. society was through participation in the community of practice of more mainstream U.S. families. Hien eventually trained as a teacher and now works in a public high school, in one of the most central and institutionalized "communities of practice" for Americanization. On the wall of his classroom is a plaque naming him a Teacher of Year by Wal-Mart. Although he is close in age to Linh, Hien's experience of belonging in U.S. society has been more mediated through "mainstream" communities of practice than has hers.

In another example of even more recent immigration among someone who is also similar in age to Linh and Hien is that of John.[5] John is a Vietnamese male in his late twenties who I have come to know and interviewed in depth about his civic involvement. He is highly active in mainstream north Texas politics, which is unusual among the Vietnamese American population in that region. He has only been in the United States since the early 1990s, a little over a decade, having left Vietnam as an older teenager. While most of the Vietnamese in Texas who are involved in religious institutions are either Catholic or Buddhist, John, who practiced no religion in Vietnam and told me he had been an atheist, converted after arriving in Texas to the Evangelical Christianity that is highly prized in various circles of Texas politics. It was through church contacts that he became involved in civic issues. As he became increasingly interested in civic life, he was mentored by an Anglo neighbor active in politics and gradually brought into the sphere. He now holds several important roles in his electoral district, is active in both homeland and local politics, and works actively on mainstream candidates' elections. John hopes to run for office one day, but for now, as he told me "I am paying my dues." This is in some ways an exceptional story of the immigrant experience, of someone who not only arrives as a newcomer with limited language skills and acquires education and a good job, but also becomes intimately involved in the formal political system and is accepted by the "insiders." His case is a prime example of what Bourdieu identifies as that of being "recruited" to enter a group based upon the perception of a good fit between the person and the group. John has acquired some forms of cultural capital that fit with local Texas Republican politics.

Unlike Mr. L., who has learned about U.S. civic life mostly through his own experiences of trial and error, John was guided and helped by a mentor. Using the theory of habitus we can see that John has acquired a secondary habitus and adopted a world view, dispositions, and ways of operating that enable him to effectively participate in the public sphere (and be "recognized" by it). It enabled him more access to the community of practice of local Texas politics than other Vietnamese immigrants. This may have resulted primarily from his conversion to Evangelical Christianity and his adoption of a worldview based upon it. He has started to enhance his own social capital in the United States through a network of political contacts and exchanges that also ultimately rely upon his own secondary habitus that enables him to operate within and be recognized as a legitimate member of these networks.

### VIETNAMESE IN TEXAS

The life experiences narrated above take place within a fairly recent wave of immigration in Texas. Before turning to an ethnographic example of group protest, it is helpful to place this population in its geographic and historical contexts. Texas has the second-largest concentration of Vietnamese immigrants in the United States, after California. Most of the Vietnamese immigrants in Texas live in the Houston region, an area that has elected and recently reelected a Vietnamese American state representative, Democrat Hubert Vo, a former refugee. The second largest settlement in Texas (and fourth largest in the nation) is in the Dallas-Fort Worth (DFW) metropolitan region. There are close to 50,000 Vietnamese in that CMSA (Consolidated Metropolitan Statistical Area) overall, according to the 2000 census, but the entire ethnic group would be larger when U.S.-born children are included, and the Vietnamese themselves use the figure of 80,000. My research has focused on Tarrant County, which is located within the DFW region, and in particular on the cities of Fort Worth and Arlington.[6] Tarrant County is the third-largest county in Texas, and has a population of almost 1.5 million. Its population is increasingly diverse as a result of immigration, particularly since the 1990s, and the Vietnamese population is the second-largest immigrant (nonnative born) group after Mexicans. According to the racial categories of the U.S. Census, the majority in this county are white (71.2 percent), but almost 20 percent are Hispanic or Latino, and 12.8 percent are black. Approximately 3 percent of the total population is composed of nonnative born Asian immigrants.

According the U.S. Census, there are between 18,000 and 26,000 Vietnamese living in the Fort Worth-Arlington PMSA (Primary Metropolitan Statistical Area). The total population for this unit is close to 1,773,000 (U.S. Census 2002). The largest concentration of Vietnamese in Tarrant

County is in Arlington, the seventh-largest city in Texas, with a total population of approximately 362,805 (according to recent data from the 2005 ACS [American Community Survey]). It is a suburban city, increasingly ethnically diverse, and located midway between Fort Worth and Dallas. The Asian-born population of Arlington is 6 percent of the total population overall and Vietnamese total almost half of the entire Asian population. There are close to 10,000 Vietnamese living in Arlington. Along with their U.S.-born children, the Vietnamese former refugee population is a growing presence in this region of Texas.

Many Vietnamese came to Fort Worth originally as part of refugee resettlement programs hosted there, with Catholic Charities playing a prominent role, and movement to Arlington came a bit later. Secondary migration of Vietnamese in the United States (from California and from other states, including Louisiana) as well as new immigration based on new visa rules has led to a doubling of the Vietnamese population in this metropolitan region since the 1990s. Those who have migrated to north Texas from other regions of the United States cite the climate, relatively low cost of living (compared to California and the East Coast) as well as the large Vietnamese ethnic population (with its ethnic restaurants, churches and temples, associations, and stores) as factors. Arlington has major Vietnamese businesses, numerous restaurants and retail centers, and two major grocery stores that sponsor events in the community and attract shoppers from throughout the DFW region.

The Vietnamese refugee experience in the United States is one that provides a good example of the modes of civic learning among newcomers. The Vietnamese are a diverse group, and one of the newer Asian groups to migrate to the United States, following the wave of professionals from East Asian nations that arrived starting in the 1960s (Anderson and Lee 2005: 6). Most of the Vietnamese who came to the United States did so as refugees fleeing a Communist regime after the fall of Saigon in 1975, and even those arriving more recently are here because of the legacy of the war in Indochina (many families who have recently arrived were permitted visa status owing to the former imprisonment of the father or because a Vietnamese mother has an Amerasian child whose father was a U.S. soldier). The diversity of the Vietnamese population is important to note, both in terms of the three waves of settlement and accompanying generational issues and in terms of the ethnic and linguistic divisions within Vietnamese society (Do 1999; Freeman 1995; Gold 1992; Hein 1995; Kelly 1977; Rutledge 1992). They have arrived in different stages. Although some Vietnamese did settle in the United States earlier, having come as students, the first major immigration cohort was those elite Vietnamese who arrived right after the Vietnam War and who had high educational levels and good language skills.

Next were the so-called Boat People who arrived after 1978 and included many ethnic Chinese. Those who have arrived more recently, post-1989, tend to have lower educational levels. Many of them also spent a long time waiting in refugee camps. Representatives of all of these groups, including the Amerasians who have arrived most recently, are included in the Tarrant County population. The Vietnamese in this region, therefore, include people of different ages, genders, and social-class backgrounds in Vietnam. Although most refugee families arrived with no material resources, having either spent what fortunes they may have had on the passage, or leaving it behind, some brought various types of cultural or social capital from Vietnam that may not translate well in U.S. society, but that carry weight within the Vietnamese population.

The Vietnamese experience in the United States differs from that in other nations, especially in Europe (Dorais 1998), because immigration to the United States took place primarily after the end of U.S. involvement in the Vietnam War. This means that most Vietnamese Americans are staunchly anti-Communist. In France, for example, which has a longer association with Vietnam through earlier colonialism in Indochina, there were earlier waves of immigrants from Vietnam to France, and both vocal Communist and anti-Communist factions exist (Bousquet 1991). The Vietnamese American identity is one based on a diaspora identity for the most part. As Anderson and Lee point out, "this ethnonational self-definition, which ties the immigrant subject to a specific (if sometimes only imagined) national homeland rather than to a collective ethnic or racialized U.S. history is deeply embedded in the discourse of diaspora" (2005: 9).

INTERNATIONAL WEEK AND VIETNAMESE AMERICANS:
A CASE OF AMBIGUOUS BELONGING

At a fashion show during the week of events that make up the International Week on a large university campus in north Texas, representatives of various student groups were to perform their identity through a display of clothing. For a group of Japanese students, this was a display of hip, urban style. For the Vietnamese Student Association, the fashion show performance included traditional dress (the *au dai*) for the females and military fatigues (evoking the Vietnam War) for the males. As the crowd assembled for this event, the presence of a large group of Vietnamese adults in the audience became increasingly evident. With the other attendees, this group poured into the auditorium. Reporters from Vietnamese print and radio media were also present. The audience sat patiently and admired the various groups that came on stage, applauding and smiling at the students who performed. When the Vietnamese students came on stage, many of the Vietnamese adults began to stand and wave small South Vietnamese flags (yellow with red stripes) and some came close to the stage waving these flags. Several non-Vietnamese students also waved these flags in support. Although there were university security police in attendence who seemed on guard for some sort of incident, the conduct of the audience was orderly and quiet. As the Vietnamese students left the stage and another group came on to perform, the audience sat back down and watched the rest of the show.

This incident raises several questions about immigrant belonging and civic engagement and illustrates the ambiguous status of Vietnamese Americans in the United States. The actions of those who waved flags during the fashion show cannot be read simply a display of ethnic pride, as some observers may have conjectured, but was part of a protest organized by VAC (Vietnamese American Community) of Greater Fort Worth.[7] The organizers of the festival knew it was going to happen and had been warned by VAC. This protest occurred at an early stage of a process that was to spread out over the course of the spring, into the summer and fall. A number of events took place over this period, including teach-ins, evening gatherings in front of the university library, and a large rally and protest march on the university campus that brought over 3,000 supporters. The protest was provoked by the university's designation of the Vietnamese flag (the flag of the current Socialist Republic of Vietnam) as the flag to represent Vietnamese students in the parade of nations/flags that opened the International Week a few days before. There are several aspects to this incident that I am exploring in my overall research project, but in this chapter I focus on its implications for immigrant belonging.

This incident illustrates the problem of moral claims to a Vietnamese identity in contemporary America. At this university, a major research university that intensely recruits "international" students for its science and engineering programs, the annual International Festival is organized by the International Student Organization (which is sponsored through the Office of International Studies). Although membership in this group is open to any student, its leadership and membership draw primarily from students who are categorized as "international" by the university (primarily because they are paying tuition and fees as an international student and are in the United States on a student visa.) On this campus, there are Vietnamese students who arrived in the United States as the children of refugees—some were born in the United States and others arrived as children. Most of the "domestic" students are from families who live locally in the DFW region and many live at home and commute to the university. There are also "international" Vietnamese students whose families live in Vietnam and who are studying in the United States but plan to return home eventually. Although there is some blurring of these lines in individual families residing in the United States (for instance, college-age relatives from Vietnam sometimes now come to stay with their Vietnamese American aunts or uncles while studying in America), the lines at the university are drawn along political lines, primarily. The first group numbers among its members many who are strongly anti-Communist; the second has the children of Communist Party members in its ranks.

VSA (Vietnamese Student Association) is a student group composed almost exclusively of Vietnamese American students (those who are not Vietnamese are from other ethnic groups but not Vietnamese nationals), most of whom are U.S. citizens either through birth or naturalization. This group was founded by first-generation Vietnamese refugees who were students at the university in the 1970s. During the 2005–6 academic year, the VSA president was a young woman who had spent many of her childhood years in refugee camps before finally coming to the United States in her teens. She is a U.S. citizen and in the Army reserves. A cheerful and easy-going person, she told me that she is not someone easily influenced by politics and prefers not to get involved in that. The president of the International Student Organization that year, also a female and about the same age as the president of VSA, was a Vietnamese International Student from Hanoi. Her English was excellent and she had been sponsored by a Christian group (although she is not a convert) to attend high school in Texas before attending college. Although she moved freely and comfortably within her surroundings in the United States and was interested in learning more about its language and culture, she told me that she did not see this in terms of becoming "Americanized" and that she avoided and resisted anything related to that. She intends to eventually return home after her studies. She also feels quite removed from the Vietnam War, which was over more than a decade before her birth.

The ways in which these two young women, and the student groups of which they were a part, were inserted into the identity categories set up by the university and also reflecting the wider society, differ. Students who are labeled "international" by the university, perhaps precisely because they are international students, who are not staying in the United States permanently, but will return home, and, therefore, pose little threat to U.S. identity, are freely embraced by the university. They are celebrated through the international festival and were, until the events of this protest, honored with the display of their national flags during a parade of nations. This is not so as to incorporate them within the United States polity, but, rather, to foreground their foreign status and to acknowledge the global consciousness they confer to the home-grown students with whom they come into contact. The monetary advantages to the university that come from recruiting international students (who pay higher tuition and fees and do not receive state aid) are never explicitly recognized in this system, but play a back-stage role and provide some impetus for the attention paid to these students. There is a social division on campus, whereby the Vietnamese national students are under the umbrella of the Office for International Students, and the domestic students with Vietnamese ethnicity are under the umbrella of the Office of Multicultural Affairs. This international/multicultural divide is slippery and complicated, which was made clear through the events of the flag protest. The presence of international students is not defined by the university as being about the multicultural nature of American society, but, rather, about U.S. influence, reach, and standing abroad. In this system of thought, they represent U.S. dominance in the world, underscored by the presence of international students who want to profit from its excellent system of higher education, improve their English, and experience the United States first hand. International students make no claims to "belong" to U.S. society, as the label of "international" makes very clear; they are constructed in this system as people who will return home to their own country after their studies. In the "imagined community" of the United States, the lines are drawn between those Vietnamese who are considered outsiders and those who have claims to being insiders.

Where do Vietnamese American students fit into this picture? How do they "belong"? The role of Vietnamese American students is ambiguous on campus. They are associated with the Office of Multicultural Affairs (along with other U.S. ethnic populations—in the context of Texas, especially Mexican Americans and African Americans) more than with the International Office, and yet they were invited to set up a table about their "culture" for the International Week and to participate in the fashion show. The table is part of a large exhibition visited by school groups during the International Week, in which various "international" groups display cultural artifacts and symbols. The betwixt and between status of Vietnamese American students as "multicultural" *and* "international" both calls into question such easy demarcations of identity and highlights their newcomer status in the category of U.S. ethnic group. The ambiguity is underscored by the fact that while the VSA played a role in the protest over the display of the Vietnamese Socialist flag, this association also won first prize for the best recipe in the annual (and very Texan) chili contest organized by the Office for Student Activities on campus that same spring!

The event that provided the catalyst for the entire protest over the flag was a dispute over the table display about their culture that the VSA was setting up prior to the festival week. That weekend, a few students were in the room setting up their table and decorating it partly with South Vietnamese flags (also called the "Freedom and Heritage" flag) that symbolize for many Vietnamese Americans in north Texas their diaspora community of former refugees. This flag is displayed at many events organized by various Vietnamese American associations in the region, often, for instance, just to point to the location of the event at the entrance to a parking lot. This flag is also displayed next to the U.S. flag at public ceremonies of the Vietnamese community, such as the New Year Festival (Tet). One Vietnamese informant explained to me that this is just like when in Texas schools, the Texas state flag is placed next to the U.S. flag—to show that they are both Texan and American. As the students were preparing their table, one of the staff of the International Office came over and told them that they would not be able to have those flags displayed and that they should be removed. The explanation was that only one flag could represent Vietnam in the festival, and it had already been decided that the official flag of the Socialist Republic of Vietnam, recognized by the United Nations, should be that flag. The staff member noted that it would, moreover, be confusing to the school children coming through the displays to see two different Vietnamese flags and not understand the background.

This act of asking the students not to display what they call the "freedom and heritage" flag at their table set off a whole series of events and mobilized a wider network of Vietnamese social activists. Eventually the Vietnamese activists (those from within the Vietnamese student organization and from outside community groups) demanded that the university take down the flag of the Vietnamese Socialist Republic from a permanent display in a Hall of Flags on campus. The university responded by hanging the South Vietnamese "Freedom and Heritage Flag" in addition the official Vietnamese flag, but later took down all flags as a result of the growing controversy. The local and national Vietnamese ethnic media became highly involved and photos of the fashion show protest and later protests became front-page news. Students who had been peripheral to the Vietnamese Student Association became involved in this cause, and moved from periphery to core of the student group. In many ways, the protest group developed out of a "community of practice" for political mobilization among Vietnamese Americans that was already established. The Vietnamese American students were the newcomers to this community of practice. Web sites were developed by Vietnamese and non-Vietnamese to chronicle the growing dispute. A committee was eventually formed by the president of the university to examine the issue, and the issue of how best to "honor" international students continues to be grappled with as this book goes to press. The two female presidents of the student groups involved, reluctant at first to enter into this social drama, were increasingly drawn into the controversy and unable to find any common ground—despite their shared language and ethnicity as Vietnamese.

Although this incident can be analyzed from many angles, including that of political protest (and is not the only time Vietnamese Americans have rallied to protest the display of the official Vietnamese flag in the United States [see Ong and Meyer 2004]) it is also telling about modes of immigrant belonging. What does this incident say about the ways in which Vietnamese Americans, individually and as a group, express their civic engagement with U.S. society? It is very "American" to be anti-Communist, and so in their protest against the official Vietnamese flag that represents a Communist regime, the Vietnamese Americans were operating in a sphere that was understandable to many Americans in the wider community beyond the university. And there were expressions of support for their protest from local politicians. There were threats that certain legislators would withdraw support for some programs at the university if they did not take down the flag of the Vietnamese Socialist Republic. Although one could argue that the protest was an example of "homeland" politics connected to a diasporic identity and represented a lack of engagement with U.S. society, this case illustrates something a bit more complicated. In the clash with university policies and practices regarding international students, the barriers to "belonging" for Vietnamese Americans as an ethnic group on a university campus were made explicit. Several "communities of practice" were involved in this—that of the student organizations, that of the community organizations that got involved, that of Vietnamese activists, that of the wider university, and that of the city in which the event took place. Although the protest was about the flag, and about anticommunism, it was also about the place of Vietnamese Americans. It was not just the Vietnamese American activists who rallied to mobilize the protest who "internationalized" Vietnamese Americans by referring to their ongoing struggle to undermine the Vietnamese government, but the university campus that was not sure where to place the Vietnamese American students. They were neither fully "international" nor fully "domestic."

By using forms of protest that simultaneously address the on-going anti-Communist politics of diaspora Vietnamese in the United States and the ambiguous position of Vietnamese American students on a college campus (both foreign and domestic), we can see Vietnamese American social actors seeking to establish their own "communities of practice" in the U.S. context and to challenge their exclusion from mainstream society (as when they are positioned in the same category as foreigners or "international" students). There was disagreement among Vietnamese Americans about how to respond to the university's actions, with some maintaining that the politics of anticommunism are stale and not relevant to the newer generations born and raised here. It is not helpful, therefore, to reify the Vietnamese American community as one unified community of practice anymore than one can theorize the United States as a community of practice.

## CONCLUSIONS

The identities of Vietnamese Americans are, in Bernard Lahire's (1998) terms, "in the plural." As they come to participate in the public sphere, either through formal political participation (as in the case of John), through ethnic associations (in the case of Linh), or U.S. civic institutions such as public schools (in the case of Hien), or through group protest on a college campus, it is useful to conceptualize this in terms of their participation in multiple communities of practice—communities that can also be viewed as networks of resources, sites for acquiring social skills and knowledge (including varieties of cultural intimacy) and forms of social capital. An immigrant's movement from periphery to core, from newcomer to old-timer, from outsider to insider, is never complete, but is one of social learning as an active participant in meaning construction. A community of practice, just like a nation, may select its members based on their seeming "fit" with its image of itself, it may patrol its borders, and it may exclude some while including others. At the same time, immigrants themselves are active participants in the process of learning to become a member, who learn to *se débrouiller* within a wide range of social settings and systems of meaning. Like Mr. L., they learn new forms of cultural intimacy that may challenge reifications.

By keeping within our focus both the "imagined community" of the nation and "communities of practice," we can see that immigrants and refugees learn not only ways to imagine the nation that has become a new home for them, but ways to strategically interact within it, moving from newcomer to old-timer. It is useful to apply the perspective of a continuum between being on the periphery or at the core to the nation itself. In this way, we can work against the aims of the nation to "fix" identity and to articulate a firm border between those who are citizens and noncitizens, by seeing a more fluid process, connected to social learning, of becoming and being a citizen. Rather than think in terms of being inside or outside of the "imagined community" of the nation, the concept of situated learning within communities of practice helps us think in terms of moving toward or away from vernacular citizenship.

ACKNOWLEDGMENTS

This research was generously funded by a grant from the Russell Sage Foundation. I would like to thank Michael Herzfeld for comments and suggestions on this manuscript, as well as the input of anonymous outside readers for Rutgers University Press. I would also like to thank those who offered questions and comments from the audience in a talk I gave to the Anthropology Department at the University of Buffalo, where I presented some portions of this chapter. I heartily thank many Vietnamese American research participants, who remain anonymous in this work, for sharing their experiences with me and welcoming me at various events. Le Me Linh, Do Uyen-Thu, Ton Quynh Anh, Bethany Hawkins, and Marilyn Koble have been invaluable research assistants on this project.

NOTES

1. It is not without a certain self-consciousness that I draw upon analytical concepts that employ the term "community," given all of the problems associated with using a word so loaded with commonsense understandings in everyday life (see especially Amit 2002 and Creed 2006). I avoid any deployments of this term in my own uses of it that depend upon romanticized visions of community and am in other writing projects engaged in considering the implications of a phrase translated into "community" (Cộng Đồng) by Vietnamese Americans (Reed-Danahay 2006).

2. There are numerous examples of this. To name but a few most relevant here: Bloemraad 2005 and 2006; Bousquet 1991; Brettell 2005; Gibson 1989; Kiang 2000; Shiao 2002; Stepick and Stepick 2002.

3. Although there are many works that could be cited here, two relevant studies of citizenship and education include Hahn's (1998) international overview of civic education and Foner's (2001) historical perspective on this. See also Spring 2003.

4. I have made a similar argument about the need to look beyond schools to learn about citizenship learning in my work on education and European citizenship (Reed-Danahay 2003 and 2006).

5. All of the names used in this paper are pseudonyms. I have tried to protect the anonymity of my research participants as much as possible in this research, by avoiding the use of names or other personal information that might identify them. I chose an "American" name for John but Vietnamese names for the other informants to reflect their own uses. Most of my Vietnamese American acquaintances who are either second generation or 1.5 generation have both Vietnamese names and what they call "American names." The latter are often used at work and at school. It is a mark of cultural intimacy to know the Vietnamese names. John has started to increasingly introduce himself with this American name to Vietnamese audiences as well as more mainstream ones, while the other people mentioned here are known among other Vietnamese with their "Viet" names. Obviously this name-switching makes for complications in fieldwork as I have had to learn two names for most people. This is an interesting topic in and of itself, and one I am pursuing in my research.

6. This research is part of a collaborative project "Practicing Citizenship in a New City of Immigration: An Ethnographic Comparison of Asian Indians and

Vietnamese," funded by the Russell Sage Foundation. In this project, Caroline B. Brettell is working with Indian immigrants in counties to the north of Dallas and I am studying the Vietnamese population in Tarrant County.

7. The VAC is a nonprofit organization formed in the 1990s. It has a community center, a board of directors, and an executive committee headed by a president or chairman (the Vietnamese term is variously translated into both of these words). Similar organizations exist in other major U.S. cities.

# PART II

# Political Mobilization and Claims Making

THE FOUR CHAPTERS in this section explore political mobilization among immigrant populations with special attention to associative practices and to factions that form as various claims to authority are made within these groups. All four chapters also illustrate the advantages of an ethnographic approach that combines close observation of political behavior "on the ground" with considerations of wider political debates and processes. The chapters by Davide Però and Michal Garapich examine Latin Americans and Poles in the United Kingdom, respectively, providing interesting comparisons about the ways in which generation and other elements of "infrapolitics" within these populations affect both their civic engagement in London and involvement in transnational political behavior.

Però both engages and critiques the concept of political opportunity structure as part of his analysis of how the newest immigrant population in the United Kingdom, Latinos, have become political actors. He emphasizes the multidirectional politics of migrants that engages the country of origin, that of arrival, and no country in particular. The latter involves activities such as disseminating information and advice on legal issues, resettlement matters, housing and health availability, as well as protesting racism, sectarianism, and political exclusion. Some of these activities are carried out in the context of organizations that are bounded and hierarchical or loose and horizontal. Però, here, notes what several other scholars of migration are beginning to note—the significance of voluntary associations to civic and political life (see, for example, Brettell and Reed-Danahay 2008; Fennema and Tillie 1999; Hamidi 2003; Odmalm 2004; Tillie 2004). Però focuses his analysis on two associations: the Latin Front, a loose organization founded by two middle-class Columbian women to represent the interests of Latin Americans in the United Kingdom, and the Latin American Workers

Association (LAWA), founded by four Latino trade unionists. The Latin Front directs its attention to influencing political parties in the United Kingdom through claims making and identity politics while LAWA primarily addresses issues of economic exploitation, workers' rights, and employment abuse. concludes that structural constraints as well as opportunities explain mobilization, but equally important are social capital, networks, political socialization, and perspectives.

Michal Garapich, who, like Però, engages the concept of political opportunity structure, offers an intriguing analysis of the differences between Socialist and post-Socialist migration streams from Poland to the United Kingdom. He focuses in particular on the construction of a Polish emigration ideology about the "good" and "moral" migrant (the political exile) and how this shapes a form of political participation and identity that is different from that among more recent economic migrants, who are constructed as individualistic. He also draws a careful distinction between ethnic- and class-based discourses in public claims making, whether in the host society context or in the transnational arena. Polish émigrés in London have taken it as their mission to remind the British about the sacrifices made by Polish soldiers and the Polish people during and after World War II in the struggles against fascism and communism, but their voice is becoming weaker as they find themselves sharing an historical identity with new immigrants from a different class background and with a different political project. Garapich draws on Frederik Barth's (1969) ideas about boundary construction as he analyzes the significance of these internal differences within the Polish diaspora. These differences are reflected in the institutions and organizations that have emerged among Polish immigrants in the United Kingdom, and in particular political positions that are taken toward such issues as voting rights abroad.

With Robert Gibb's chapter we are transported across the English Channel to France, a European country that has been much in the news in relation to the politics of immigration and to the political activism of immigrants. Like Però, Gibb also offers an analysis of immigrant associative practice in his discussion of SOS-Racisme, an organization founded in the early 1980s by Paris-based students and political activists to combat racism. Gibb traces the contested history of this organization and places it in relationship to other immigrant associations in France and to the legislative and other institutional contexts within which it operates. In particular he explores the forms of civic engagement promoted by SOS-Racisme and how these activities are viewed by the Franco-Maghrebi population. Also of note are his efforts to situate SOS-Racisme in the context of conspiracy theories that "imagine" politics as confrontations between a majority and a minority and that draw distinctions between outward appearances and "true" reality. The larger questions here are the relationship between SOS-Racisme and the French Socialist Party, on the one hand, and its agenda in relationship to the National Front Party of Le Pen, on the other. By extension, Gibb's analysis puts the issue of immigration itself at the center of political action and national party politics. Ultimately it is the more *sui generis* immigrant associations that were undermined and marginalized by the activities of SOS-Racisme.

The final chapter in this section, by Karen Richman, takes us back and forth between Haiti and the United States to examine the struggles over political authority and voting rights between Haitian immigrants in the United States and those in Haiti who solicit their support for homeland politics. Like Garapich, she emphasizes how nationals abroad become "contested constituencies." The "transterritorial" entity of Haiti is a sphere of contestation and possibility in which new understandings of political participation for Haitians in the United States and "at home" is being forged. Richman compares the activities of Haitians to those of Mexicans who are also involved in what she labels transborder citizenship. Haitian Americans have become politically empowered and have successfully run for and been elected to local offices, especially in the state of Florida where there is a substantial population. They are also involved in home town associations, which have become arenas for civic participation in several cities of the Unites States where Haitian immigrants have settled. Although Haitian leaders reach out to nationals abroad, the empowerment of the Haitian diaspora has not been fully realized in the form of dual citizenship and absentee voting rights. Haiti, here, is behind Mexico, which has taken particular steps to create true transnational political subjects. Richman elucidates the contrast by describing the political ambitions and activities of two immigrant food magnates, one Haitian and the other Mexican, who have involved themselves in homeland politics. But she concludes that in both these cases there are still nationalist barriers to transborder citizenship.

Collectively the chapters in this section call into question narrow definitions of citizenship and political participation for immigrant populations that draw from the expectations of the new host country. They do so by showing that modes of civic participation are complicated by ethnic politics within and among immigrant groups, between immigrant groups and broader national political movements and parties and within a transnational space that is influenced by homeland politics.

CHAPTER 5

# Migrants' Mobilization
# and Anthropology

REFLECTIONS FROM THE EXPERIENCE OF
LATIN AMERICANS IN THE UNITED KINGDOM

*Davide Però*

INTRODUCTION

ANTHROPOLOGISTS HAVE ENGAGED little with the topic of
collective action and with the relevant social scientific literature. This chapter
seeks to respond to recent calls made within the discipline to engage with
both. Drawing on fieldwork carried out among Latin Americans in London,
this chapter shows how their mobilization is shaped by a multiplicity of factors and not merely by the political opportunity structure of the country of
arrival, as the prevailing approach to migrants' mobilizations seems to contend. In addition to indicating some of the other factors that influence migrants' mobilization, the chapter makes some suggestions for rethinking the
notion of political opportunity structure in more inclusive, loose, flexible,
and pluralist terms. Last but not least, this chapter offers an account of how
Latin American migrants are responding collectively to the difficulties they
experience in Britain.

*Researching Latinos' Politics in London*

Since the early 1990s the United Kingdom has experienced a new immigration flow that—differently from that of that of the postwar years—is
mostly from non-Commonwealth countries. As pointed out by Steven Vertovec (2006), the United Kingdom is increasingly characterized by: a sizeable
migrant population from developing countries with no direct colonial link
to the United Kingdom; a greater linguistic diversity (over 300 languages

spoken in London); a proliferation of smaller groups (e.g., Colombians, Ru-
manians, Ghanaians, Kurds, Afghans, etc.) alongside large and longstanding
"ethnic communities"; a more fluid duration and greater variety of legal statuses; the sustenance of greater transnational connections (social, religious,
political, etc.) on the part of migrants. This emerging scenario suggests that it
is no longer appropriate to treat the United Kingdom as a "postimmigration"
country as much research and policy-making activity has been doing. The
United Kingdom is a country of new immigrations—like Italy or Spain—but
with a greater preexisting, ethnocultural heterogeneity. This development in
British society has been branded by Vertovec as "super-diversity" (2006).

Parallel to the new immigrations, Britain has in the second half of the
2000s experienced a growing "neoassimilationist" wave that has put "multiculturalism"—the prevailing public and policy attitude—on the defensive.
This "backlash against diversity" (Grillo 2005), has not only come from
the Right, but also from important sectors of the Left that are now arguing
that: the United Kingdom is too diverse; diversity undermines cohesion
and solidarity; multiculturalism leads to separatism; minorities should sub-
scribe more strongly to British national values and way of living.[1]

In addition to neoassimilationism, the British public discourse on integration treats migrants and minorities as objects of policy and governance[2]
and ignores their political agency. It also includes—at best—voices from
ethnic minorities but not those from new migrants. Unlike the public and
policy discourse on integration, this chapter prioritizes the perspectives of
the new migrants by focusing on their collective efforts to improve their
conditions in the United Kingdom.

### The Significance of the Latinos

In "super-diverse" Britain a migrant group that has received little attention despite its numerical significance is that of Latin Americans.[3] Unlike in
the United States where the Latin American population is on the whole much
more established, in the United Kingdom Latinos are, for the most part, a
"new immigrant group" for whom there are not yet reliable official statistics. In my fieldwork I have repeatedly come across Latin Americans estimat-
ing their presence around 500,000. This estimate figure is made up by some
250,000 Brazilians, 200,000 Colombians, and 50,000 Ecuadorians and other
Latin American nationalities.[4]

Latin Americans arrive in Britain through a broad range of immigration
channels and hold a variety of different statuses including many students, unau-
thorized/irregulars (e.g., over-stayers, forged papers, etc), asylum seekers, and
refugees. The majority of Latin Americans came primarily for "economic" reasons (e.g., poverty and lack of opportunities for self-development) although, as

often is the case among Colombians, migration can be the result of the combination of economic and "political" reasons.[5] Apart from a sizeable group of refugees, there are many people who left Colombia for the generalized climate of violence, fear, and instability that—with poverty—characterizes vast geographical areas of the country.

In Britain, Latinos are predominantly residing in London, with significant concentrations in Lambeth, Southwark, Islington, and Camden. They are heavily employed in the cleaning sector where they work for subcontracted companies (often multinationals) cleaning commercial and public buildings (offices, hospitals, and so forth) often under very exploitative conditions.[6] They have also developed a wide range of "ethnic" commercial and cultural activities.

Not being from Commonwealth countries, Latinos do not speak English as a second language. As many of them recognize, their linguistic competence at their arrival is on average rather poor and tends to improve slowly over the years.

Their voice in the British media and public discourse is absent. In spite of such marginalization, the Latinos have an impressive and growing ethnic or "community" media in Spanish that includes several radio programs and news magazines, widely and freely distributed, that cover developments in Latin American countries as well as in the United Kingdom. By addressing the entire Spanish-speaking Latin American collective in the United Kingdom, the Latino media are simultaneously facilitating the Latino population in the United Kingdom to imagine themselves as a "community" (Anderson 1983; Chavez 1991).

Latino immigrants—unlike Commonwealth and EU ones—are not entitled to vote in any type of UK elections. This situation makes it particularly compelling to adopt a notion of politics that transcends the voting and standing for election typical of certain branches of political science and to include a broader range of collective political initiatives.

An important point to make here is that the wide range of social, cultural, and economic initiatives and exchanges just outlined promotes physical and virtual encounters and networks among Latino migrants not only from the same nationalities but also from different ones. These encounters and exchanges are forging a growing sense of a Latino identity, which—as we will see—has recently begun to be deployed politically.

## MIGRANTS' COLLECTIVE ACTION: JUST A MATTER OF OPPORTUNITY STRUCTURES?

The study of collective action is a story of scarce interdisciplinary exchange and cross-fertilization. The few anthropologists engaging with this topic have paid limited attention to the work done in other disciplines and scholarly fields and vice versa. In anthropology, the first author to highlight the disciplinary neglect of the topic has been Arturo Escobar (1992). He attributed such shortcomings to the following five reasons: "the concentration on representation as a political arena during the 1980s, which, although of great importance, shifted attention from other political terrains; an individual-oriented notion of practice; divisions of labour within the academy; the [sociopolitically detached] nature of [anthropological] research; and perhaps even the decline of collective action in the United States during the same decade" (400).

This scarce anthropological concern with social movements seems to be part of a wider "problem" that the discipline has been having with politics for quite some time. According to Jonathan Spencer (1997), anthropology has addressed the political as something separated from the cultural until the early 1970s and then abandoned the study of politics and political institutions altogether. Paradoxically by the time other scholars—primarily sociologists—were beginning to discover the significance of the cultural dimension in the study of politics (e.g., Touraine 1971; Melucci 1985) anthropologists—at least according to Spencer's account—had already written it out.

Although Spencer's article does not mention explicitly social movements, it is not difficult to see how—as suggested by Gibb (2001a)—the restricted and rigid understanding of politics that came to characterize political anthropology may have contributed to the disciplinary neglect of social movements. A decade after Escobar's critique the situation seems largely unchanged as pointed out by Edelman (2001) and Gibb (2001a) and more recently by Nash (2005).

With regard to migrants and minorities, this limited disciplinary engagement has been even more acute. A reason for this seems connected to the relatively late engagement of the discipline with the study of migrants and migrations (see Brettell 2000; Foner 2003b). Concerned with the studies of "cultures" as territorialized and bounded units (Brettell 2000) and informed by a "sedentaristic metaphysics" (Malkki 1997), anthropologists merely focused on people who stayed put and ignored migrants.

If anthropology has paid scant attention to migrants' collective action, the interdisciplinary field of migration studies has only in part been more attentive. Like policy makers, most migrationists have considered migrants as objects rather than subjects of politics (Kofman et al. 2000; Zontini 2002). One reason for that is that migrants have been considered from the perspective of the nation-state and government of the receiving countries. Another reason is connected to the influence of the structuralist and Marxist paradigms, which have represented individuals and their behavior as mechanistically determined by structural constraints (Martiniello 2005). A further reason for not looking at migrants as political actors is connected to the migrants' lack of formal political entitlements (the only feature that can turn them into formal political actors) and to the prevailing understanding of political engagements as being restricted to electoral behavior and politicians' activity. As suggested by Patrick Ireland: "Such a lack of formal political rights and other political resources at first led scholars, like host-society public officials, to see foreign workers as largely unorganized and largely apolitical components of the economy" (1994: 4). Clearly this reductive conceptualization of migrants' political engagements is inadequate to account for their political initiatives that take place in the absence of voting rights.

Despite the tendency in policy and research to consider migrants as objects rather than subject of politics, a number of recent studies have, nevertheless, focused on migrants as political actors. For the purpose of this chapter, such studies can be distinguished between those concerned with explaining migrants' political behavior and those addressing other aspects of their politics. It is only with the former that this chapter engages.

The dominant approach characterizing the studies that seek to explain migrants' political behavior is that of the political opportunity structure (POS). The POS approach was originally developed to study social movements and protest and in particular to explain their emergence. Its contribution consists of highlighting the role of the institutional and policy set up of a country in shaping its residents' collective political initiatives. The POS approach builds on the Resource Mobilization Theory (RMT) approach that conceived collective action as the result of actors' rational calculation of cost and benefits as well as their ability to mobilize resources as a precondition of mobilization. POS complements and advances the essentially internally oriented focus of RMT by locating collective action in its political context and correlating it with its external environment (Koopmans and Statham 2000).

The POS approach was initially applied to the field of migration studies by Ireland (1994). Ireland's work developed from dissatisfaction with preexisting explanatory models of migrants' collective action based on class and ethnicity. Such models saw collective action as being deterministically produced, respectively, by the unequal capitalist organization of production and by the ethnocultural characteristics of migrant groups. Ireland replaced class and ethnicity with political opportunity structure as the key factor (the "independent variable") for explaining migrants' mobilization.[7] Indeed, class and ethnicity are not mobilizing factors, per se, as their greater or lesser salience is itself the effect of the politicoinstitutional environment that migrants encounter. Drawing on comparative research carried out in France and Switzerland, Ireland explains variations in political participation of the same ethnic groups across localities with the different political-institutional set up that they encounter in the different localities.

Subsequently the POS approach has been adopted by a growing number of scholars (e.g., Garbaye 2000; Koopmans and Statham 2000; Odmalm 2004) who, for the primacy that they attribute to the institutional environment in explaining migrants' collective action, have been identified as "neoinstitutionalists." Arguably POS is now the prevailing approach to the study of migrants' political mobilizations. The following pages will explore how Latin Americans' mobilization in London "fits" the theoretical approach just outlined.

### LATIN AMERICAN MOBILIZATION IN LONDON: AN OVERVIEW

A schematic way of conceptualizing Latino mobilizations in the United Kingdom is to consider them as made of two parallel ideal-typical streams coinciding with initiatives directed respectively toward Latin America and the United Kingdom. However, in practice peoples and organizations are often simultaneously involved in multidirectional politics targeting the country of origin, that of arrival, and even a third country, or no country in particular. The nature of such politics need not be the same, so we can have organizations or individuals who articulate Marxist politics vis-à-vis Latin America while, at the same time, being involved in the apolitical and "charitable" activity of service provision in the United Kingdom.

The first forms of Latino mobilization in the United Kingdom are considered those of the Chilean refugees of the 1970s who constituted a small but active and well organized group primarily involved in opposing Pinochet's dictatorship. In subsequent decades, and especially since the 1990s, with the arrival of "economic migrants" and asylum seekers from other Latin American countries (especially Colombia)—the bulk of Spanish-speaking Latino migrants in Britain—the number of Latino initiatives grew further. Alongside homeland and transnational politics, political initiatives increasingly entailed the provision of information, advice and support on resettlement matters such as legal procedures, access to housing, health and other welfare provisions to their users and the adoption of the nonpolitical organizational status of charities and public subsidy.

In recent years, the most significant developments in Latino mobilization seem to reflect the growing concern with issues of long-term integration such as exploitation, marginalization, lack of recognition, legal status, racism, religious sectarianism, drug addiction, domestic violence, political exclusion, and so on.

With no claim of exhaustiveness, here I provide a sketchy account of the political and organizational complexity and heterogeneity I encountered in my fieldwork. I have deliberately omitted or disguised names of individuals and organizations to avoid exacerbating the divisions, rivalries, misunderstandings, and polemics that characterize Latino initiative alongside collaboration, support and solidarity.

One form of organization is the "orthodox Communist." This type of organization tends to engage in homeland politics and have an exclusively Latino membership. They are hierarchically and rigidly organized and distrust more horizontal and open Leftist organizations (seen as "Trozkists") that, they claim, have no idea of what a "real" political struggle is. In turn, these organizations are seen as dogmatic, "Stalinists," closed to debate, sectarian, centered on their leader, and having a top-down idea for the organization of struggle. They are also seen as "machistas," with women having access only to subordinate and executive roles and tasks, as well as homophobic.

Among the organizations with a more loose and horizontal structure, we find "Latin Americanist" ones. These organizations are British-led and have a predominantly British membership. They are sometimes criticized for giving Latinos little space and secondary roles. They have also being criticized for cooperating too little with each other for reasons that are connected to their position in the British political arena and that—from a Latino point of view—are unhelpful. Despite these criticisms, there is a wide appreciation among Latin Americans for the work and commitment of these organizations and their members. It is not uncommon for British members of these organizations to have a Latino partner or spouse.

A relatively loose and horizontal structure also characterizes Latino youth organizations. These organizations are predominantly involved in "cultural politics" that entail artistic and cultural productions like staging plays on the condition of the Latino migrants in London. They question many other Latino organizations for being insensitive to and unsupportive of issues and concerns of young and second generation Latinos. These organizations are sometimes criticized for the "too liberal" and "relaxed" lifestyle of some of their members.

There are also "women-only" organizations engaged in the protection and promotion of Latino women in the United Kingdom. These organizations provide an important service that ranges from career development training to support for the victims of domestic violence. Highly structured and efficiency-driven, these organizations embody well the professionalized British-NGO style. These organizations have been criticized (by the same women who criticized and left some of the *machistas* organizations mentioned above) for being excessively separatist, dogmatic, and even a little heterophobic in providing what otherwise they consider a crucial field of initiative.

Many are the organizations that—with varying degrees of professionalism and efficiency—are involved in the delivery of services and assistance connected to immigration, housing, health, and access to welfare. These organizations constitute the bulk of the Latino civic and community organizing. They can be very different in terms of gender sensitivity and equality among its membership. Some of these are being criticized from within the "community" for being mere service-delivery, depoliticized, divided, in competition with and jealous of each other, and incapable of innovating to address issues of integration that go beyond the arrival stage.

The collective initiatives of Latin Americans presented so far are "progressive" in character. With regard to "conservative" Latinos' engagement, it seems that this does not get articulated through civic and political organizations to the same extent. If "progressives" tend to privilege face-to-face collective initiatives and organizations, "conservatives" seem to prefer popular (and populist) radio programs and news magazines. Prominent "conservative" figures appear to be economically well off and to own profitable commercial activities. Their politics seems to consist of encouraging disengagement, and laissez faire attitudes, stigmatizing the initiatives that seek to alter the status quo in a more equitable and participatory direction. "Conservatives" are also said to be working more closely than "progressives" with the diplomatic institutions of their sending country. There is, however, some "conservative" face-to-face organizing which, I was told, is connected to the activities of Latin American evangelical churches.

While clearly schematic, the above account of the Latino associative sector provides a sense of the several manners of differentiation that separate many Latino migrants while uniting others. This already broad and heterogeneous scenario has diversified further in recent times. Since mid-2004 a sort of new wave of markedly political initiatives directed at improving Latinos' conditions from a longer-term perspective of integration started to translate into collective action. As one of my informants pointed out:

> We are realizing [*toma de consciencia*] that it's time to do something about our conditions here rather than just keep thinking about Colombia, as here we are having many problems like marginalization, lack of opportunities, education, religion (with the "Christian" sects), drug-addiction . . . and it's not just the society here the cause of the problems but the mentality of the Latinos, too. . . . We are realizing that a new way to approach politics in this country is necessary . . . rather than supporting the Labour

Party automatically we are realizing that we need to become more demanding and become aware also of our political and electoral weight for using it as a bargaining tool.

The following sections will examine two important instances of these new collective initiatives.

## THE LATIN FRONT

Arguably the most ambitious political initiative of the Latinos in Britain, the Latin Front (Frente Latino or LF) came into being in the second half of 2004 on the initiative of two liberal and middle-class Colombian women. The intent was to represent politically the interests of Latin Americans in the United Kingdom. Its official goals included: creating a sense of community; achieving recognition as an ethnic group; lobbying British and European institutions to promote the rights of Latin American residents including the regularization of those with an irregular status, working rights, social security rights, voting rights, health and education, and citizenship for the children of Latinos born in the United Kingdom; and quantifying the Latino political "weight" (for purposes of political bargaining).

At least in the first year of its existence, the LF successfully intercepted and expressed the growing concern among Latin Americans for recognition as an ethnic minority and for the improvement of their living conditions in a long-term perspective as well as for the regularization of many of its members whose irregular/unauthorized status had confined them to a situation of great precariousness, insecurity, vulnerability, and marginality. With a loose organizational structure and a great deal of proactiveness and entrepreneurship, the Latin Front started off as an umbrella organization/movement with the ambition to federate Latinos' civic organizations and initiatives, create a strong unitary and representative "community voice," and lobby British political institutions. As one of its founders defined it, the Frente Latino is a "political but not party political group." For this reason the possibility of acquiring the "charity" status had been discarded.

The political background of the Latin Front activists is quite heterogeneous. The two founders have a liberal and centrist identity. One of them has been simultaneously active with the Liberal Democrats in Britain where she stood as candidate for councillor at the local 2006 elections, and with liberals in her country of origin where—taking advantage of electoral law changes—she has tried to be appointed candidate MP for one of the abroad constituencies.[8] The majority of the activists involved, however, seemed to be of left-of-center orientations. Among these, those who had the status of refugee or had left their country of origin due to political violence were prominent. Some also had taken part in political and civic initiatives in Britain, some in local political parties, others in Latino community organizations. On the whole the Latin Front, at least in its first year of activity, was a collective initiative developed by a group of people that had a diverse political socialization, sensitivity, and identity.[9]

From the outset, the Latin Front has also carefully dealt with Latin American diplomatic institutions and personnel in the United Kingdom. In order to retain full autonomy, a courteous distance was deliberately kept to prevent powerful and skilled diplomats from interfering with national and home-country agendas.

### The Politics of the Latin Front

The main field of initiative in which the Latin Front operates is the party-political. Lobbying all the main British political parties and institutions has characterized the Latin Front from the outset. In its first year or so of existence, its activity culminated with the organization of three major public events with such parties and with a meeting with the home secretary. The public events were held in the hall of one of the main Latino shopping malls of London with a lay out and arrangements designed to present the Latin Front and the wider Latin American collective in an authoritative and powerful way.

The substantive politics being articulated by the Latin Front has been primarily directed at gaining recognition. The Latin Front mobilized to make Latin Americans visible and recognized as an "ethnic minority" in Britain. It also mobilized for the regularization of unauthorized Latin Americans living and working in Britain and of their children, especially those born in the United Kingdom.

In trying to widen its support basis and construct a powerful image vis-à-vis British institutions, the Latin Front deployed a shrewd identity politics based on a strategic use of the "Latino" category. This is a category that (by and large) becomes salient outside Latin America to indicate some shared ethnocultural background vis-à-vis the rest of the population. Until then, the Latino category had circulated spontaneously in the everyday social arena in London but had not yet been deployed contentiously. Other civic organizations had used the term Latino to appeal to a wider population of potential users or members, but not for purposes of explicit political claims making at least on such a large scale. Thus the Latin Front is the most forceful and grand-scale attempt to date to introduce Latino as a category of contention in the British political arena by making the most of the existing Latino identity, networks, and resources. By clustering together all Latin American nationalities (and even southern European), this strategy has sought to convey the idea of the existence of a large and politically organized collective that is comparable to those of the established ethnic minorities and that therefore deserves similar attention from British institutions. It is a strategy that reflects the multicultural set up of the United Kingdom and its encouragement to organize around ethnicity.

However, this organization around ethnicity was not just instrumental and derived from a cold assessment of costs and benefits, but also by a genuine belief that organizing as Latinos is an intermediate stage necessary to create a larger and confederated migrants movement to protect migrants interests. As Ubaldo put it: "we must learn to organize politically among Latinos and then begin to collaborate with other immigrant communities. If we can't unite among ourselves, how can we unite at a wider level?!"

The identity politics of the Latin Front extends not only horizontally across ethnic/nationality lines but also vertically across class lines seeking to appeal to Latinos from all classes and backgrounds. Little identifiable along the Left-Right continuum and in a somewhat populist and ambiguous fashion, the LF makes of political transversalism and ecumenism its own political flag. Indeed, the Latin Front leadership appears to conceive Left-Right divisions unhelpful to the goal of creating a single strong Latino ethnic community voice in Britain. This transversal character of the Latin Front represents in the eyes of many a good thing given that many Latinos (of any political affiliation) are likely to experience similar difficulties in the United Kingdom.

As one of its founders once said in a meeting, "All the efforts of the Latin American organizations must converge in a broad and strong bloc." I found this view shared by many other Latinos who were not actively involved in the LF. As Juana said, "it exists a common interest among many Latinos to have one voice representing us . . . for example many work and pay taxes and would like to be regularized or that there were an amnesty."

Despite the popularity achieved during its first year and the support of much of the Latino media, not everybody within the Latino "community" subscribed to the idea of confederating under the overarching framework and leadership of the Latin Front. Indeed, the majority from the civic and political Latino organizations steered away from the LF invitation to join in. Reasons for such lack of support included reservations about the LF ambiguous political nature, and the personal agenda and political affiliation of part of its leadership, including in relation to their home country (many Leftist Latin Americans also rejected the idea of a transversal and interclassist organization organized around ethnicity and opted for alternatives; see below). Some also saw the leadership of the LF as too involved in "politicking" and "vote exchange" both here and in Colombia.

One way in which Latin Front activists explained the lack of support from many Latino community organizations was jealousy, competition, and fear of being overshadowed and losing the visibility, status, and benefits acquired by carving out a niche for themselves over several years. They also explained the lack of support for the obsolete participatory model subscribed to by most existing community organizations, which entailed specialization in the provision of advice/assistance on issues of immigration, accommodation and access to welfare but clearly failed to respond to emerging preoccupations such as those of more long-term integration (e.g., education, marginalization, and voting rights).

Despite the above criticism and while not achieving its objectives, the initiatives of the Latin Front have made Latin American migrants more visible in the eyes of the local and national British politicians and administrators. The LF has also conveyed the impression of certain organizational and mobilization skills and resources, even if they are still not considered as adequate interlocutors by the local authorities, as the following quotation from a Lambeth Labour councilor shows.

> Question: "What did you think of last year's event organized by the LF in the shopping mall?"
>
> Answer: "Well I was very impressed first of all by the scale of it, that was very good that there was such a large turn out of people. . . . But in terms of a working event it's not the way to bring people together. . . . nevertheless it gave an indication that there's a sizeable community that needs to be factored into the political process, and to try and make that happen you have to try and bring a crowd together and say to the politicians from all parts 'here we are' . . . So as a starting point it was a useful opening point. But in terms of a practical way to dwell below the issues and then set up a machinery to make it happening from there on it hasn't done much to take that process forward."

Finally, after the Latin Front initiatives of 2005 some of its leaders have become part of mainstream public committees, such as the Refugee & Asylum Seekers Listening Group (which features the London Metropolitan Police). Even if such "recruitment" may have had a cooptative dimension it still denotes some degree of recognition on the part of the British institutions and represents a significant institutional forum where concerns and demands can be voiced.

The Latin Front has also given Latin American migrants themselves an empowering feeling, especially through the public meetings it arranged. It raised the awareness and boosted the confidence that they possess the resources and skills that can turn them into a collective capable of positively influencing their integration in the United Kingdom.

## The Latin American Workers Association and the Transport and General Workers Union

The Latin American Workers Association or LAWA was set up by three Colombian and one Chilean trade unionists as part of the British Transport & General Workers Union (or T&G) in the second half of 2004, after they had existed in a more informal way for several months.[10] Forming LAWA was seen as a necessary step to protect and support more effectively the large number of Latin American workers experiencing superexploitation and abuses of various types at the work place. Until the creation of LAWA employment had been a crucial aspect of life, which was left "uncovered" by the existing Latino organizations. In the words of one of its creators: "The LAWA is the product of a necessity, which has emerged progressively after that many Latinos had solved their immigration, housing, and benefits problems. . . . Besides addressing some of the exploitative aspects experienced by Latinos workers in Britain, LAWA struggles for helping the Latinos workers coming out of the invisibility with dignity not by 'asking' (*pedir*) but by 'demanding' (*exigir*). Together with other workers organization—the Portuguese, the Turkish, the African—we share the same class need [necesidad de clase]."

LAWA started out of an urge of Marcelo and Arturo to combat the many abuses experienced by Latin Americans at work. Together with Fernando and Pedro they looked for support in the British trade union movement in order to do that more effectively. The view that needs play a key role in the emergence of LAWA emerged also in an interview with another activist, Irene.

> People mobilize because they have needs otherwise they don't mobilize. For instance, in the case of immigrant workers here [the United Kingdom], they organize because they have a need. And what is the need? The exploitation being perpetrated by the cleaning companies and by the Colombian themselves, Latin Americans [supervisors and managers] who exploit other Latin Americans [cleaners]. There is a need and it is not because they are providing structures, structures are there but people don't know them because it is a community which is immigrating and there is new people in the country and none of these characters [managers] is going to tell them "you are entitled to this and that," on the contrary they tell them that they have no entitlements. It is out of necessity that people get organized: "they are stealing my salary, they are underpaying me, they

are sacking me without a justification, they are violating my rights" this is why people get organized. If people had it all they wouldn't organize.

The kind of problems that Latin Americans experience and the nature of LAWA's activity are illustrated by Ines: "Sexual harassment, psychological maltreatment . . . abuses concerning working time, verbal abuses and discrimination of all sorts. Essentially all that happens because one doesn't know the [British] laws . . . and people [employers and managers] take advantage of that and abuse the power they've got. . . . I myself had a case and after solving that, I stayed on working with them [LAWA] as a volunteer. I was abused verbally and psychologically by my managers. . . . It happened in a clothes shop for which I worked." Indeed, Ines saw her decision to mobilize with LAWA as being connected to her working conditions but also to her civic and political identity, formation and values.

> Yes . . . it was like a means of protecting myself, because not only was I getting affiliated to protect myself in this case [see below] but also in future situations. It is a way of protecting oneself here as a worker, as an individual and as a human being. . . . I also always wanted to collaborate to my community . . . It's not possible that this [exploitation/abuse] is happening in a developed country and people just ignore it. . . . So I said:"my community needs it [trade union work], the volunteers are few and also I am passionate about this kind of work" . . . When I arrived here, after something like three months I started voluntary work with Initiative . . . I was with them for about two years . . . I also worked with my church doing social work and at some point the opportunity with the trade union [LAWA] came up . . . I've always had the urge to help politically the people since high school. . . . My mother always told me that I was "the lawyer of the poor," that I always went out to defend this and that.

Although support in the field of employment was, in principle, available to Latino workers through the existing British trade unions, such support was not, in practice, accessible to them, for reasons of communication/language, trust, lack of relationships, or links between T&G and the Latin collective and lack of adequate efforts on the part of the union to reach out to migrant workers.

An important concern in setting up LAWA was the preservation of its autonomy. LAWA founders had always been determined to form a political, rather than a civic or community charitable organization. They wanted to avoid relying on public funding—as these organizations often do—because this would entail economic dependence on the state (an institution that they did not see as promoting the interests of working people and in particular of migrant workers) and political restrictions (for receiving public funding and a charitable status). In the end, the four founders' guess about the need for LAWA proved right and the organization boomed straight away (and with it Latino affiliations to the T&G) to the extent that after a few months of activity LAWA already struggled to keep up with the demand for assistance.

In terms of background, political socialization, and experience, the four founders all had previous experience in trade union activism in their country of origin, which was also connected to the reasons for which they left their respective countries. The other members of the directive committee also had a history of activism in their home country, although not necessarily in the trade union movement strictly speaking. LAWA has also begun to recruit activists among young people with a more limited political experience (if only for their younger age), as in the case of Ines.

Before setting up or joining LAWA, all its activists had been involved in one or more Latino civic organizations. Some became immediately active once in the United Kingdom, while others took longer as they went through a period of withdrawal, partly connected to the discouraging social environment (made of kin and acquaintances) in which they arrived and partly due to their contingent psychological situation. In fact, some of them lived forcedly separated from their closest family members and friends, in a country where they did not even speak the language and in which their qualifications were not being recognized. Fernando pointed out how before setting up LAWA, and while working full time as a cleaner (despite his post–A-level qualifications), he had been involved in some Latino NGOs but was not fully satisfied. While recognizing the importance of civic-communitarian work, he explained that it is the sociopolitical work through trade unions that really fulfils him and that he is really good at, in addition to the fact that Latinos in London strongly need protection on this front.

As these organizers did not know each other in Latin America, it was their participation in the Latino civic and political circuit that brought them in contact with each other and that they now—through the set up of LAWA—are in turn making more comprehensive and stronger. This relationship of symbiosis with the Latino associative circuit is sustained by LAWA's members participating in other Latino organizations that, in turn, contribute to LAWA's growth by referring people with work-related problems to them.

### LAWA Politics

The field of political initiative in which LAWA operates can be described as sociopolitical. LAWA is neither interested in party politics nor in lobbying national and local politicians and officials (like the Latin Front does). They privilege political initiative in the socioeconomic sphere around issues of workers' rights and, more generally, material justice. In addition to the protection of Latin American workers in the United Kingdom, they are connected to the initiatives of Social Forums and of the Global Justice movement. For example, in 2004 they participated to the European Social Forum in London. They have also been developing international/transnational links with trade unions in Latin America.

In terms of identity politics LAWA articulates a particular blend of class and ethnicity. They are promoting greater ethnocultural recognition of Latin Americans within the class framework of the trade union movement. Overall LAWA considers it important to be fully part of a large and organized British trade union, but feels there are ethnocultural specificities that require a customized treatment; hence their organization as Latinos within the T&G. However, as Fernando said, "the objective and the essence of the struggle, as well as what unites us with other immigrant groups, is a question of class." The attitudes that LAWA members have toward unauthorized migrant workers further help us to form an idea of LAWA's political vision. In Irene's own words, "Work is a right that all human beings have, if they are illegal or not is not something that makes any difference to us . . . and this is why we also fight for illegal immigrants."

In addition to the cases attended to at their office, LAWA has been involved in a number of initiatives for workers' welfare in London that ranged from supporting the strike and protest of the cleaners of the British House of Commons (figure 5.1) to the organization of training on working rights for its membership.

It is important to point out that Latin Americans are also becoming increasingly active through the "mainstream" T&G (rather than through LAWA). For many Latin Americans this involvement developed largely as a result of the recent large-scale efforts—like the Justice for Cleaners campaign—to organize migrant workers in the cleaning sector. Although not centered around ethnicity (like the Latin Front), the trade union is a growing form of Latino engagement, which is not only important in itself but also crucial to recognize if we want to avoid the "ethnicist" (Brah 1996) or "culturalist" (Vertovec 1996) reductionism of certain literature on migrants and minorities that considers them only as merely ethnocultural subjects overlooking all their other political identities, relationships, and engagements. In terms of politics this mobilization represents a rather classic form of class politics, i.e., one in which the socioeconomic component is paramount and the ethnocultural is complementary but still relevant (expressed for instance by the resorting to migrant organizers). This is also a politics that targets all workers independently of their ethnocultural background, who

5.1. Migrant cleaners striking at the House of Commons. London, July 20, 2005. Photo by Davide Però.

in the cleaning sector happen to be essentially migrant (with a significant quota of Latin Americans). Recently the T&G has also started to strengthen its promigrant stand by starting to campaign for a regularization of unauthorized migrants as it recognizes that their immigration status renders them vulnerable to superexploitation and abuses and condemns them to exclusion and marginality. As for LAWA, the prevailing attitude within the T&G toward unauthorized migrants is inclusionary; they are seen as workers regardless of the legal status attached to them by the state.

In terms of achievements LAWA and the T&G have unionized a remarkable number of Latin American workers (nearly one thousand). This process has happened in a relatively short period of time and by overcoming a number of fears and prejudices including those of deportation (recurrent and yet unjustified among unauthorized migrants) and those of dealing with philo-*guerrilleros* (recurrent among Colombians). The second achievement is the operationalization of the Latino workers protection that both LAWA and T&G have performed. Thirdly, they have also gained a greater visibility and popularity in the eyes of the Latin American collective and among employers who are becoming aware that there is an increasing chance to face the trade unions if they abuse migrant workers. Finally, all this activity has strengthened the overall integration of Latin American migrants into British society, particularly in the sociopolitical sphere.

## CONCLUSIONS

Unlike the prevailing treatment of migrants as passive objects of policies, this chapter has approached them as political actors, taking Latin Americans' collective action in London as a case study. Latinos have always been politically engaged, since their early arrivals in the 1970s when they were still numerically few. Moroever Latin Americans' mobilization has progressively grown and diversified to include home-country politics, transnational politics, arrival (short-term oriented), and integration (long-term oriented) politics in the receiving society. This chapter has focused on the last of these forms of politics by examining two of the most significant collective efforts recently articulated on this front: the Latin Front and the Latin American Workers Association. Latin Americans in London are not only politically active[11] but also increasingly engaged in overcoming the marginalizing practices they are being subjected to. The ethnographic material presented has given a sense of *what* Latin American migrants mobilize about in the United Kingdom and *how*. By and large their mobilization reflects the conditions of both the invisibility and exploitation they experience. Through collective action taking place broadly outside the formal political system, they struggle for recognition (both as an ethnocultural minority and as residents) *and* material justice (dignified working and living conditions).[12]

At a more theoretical level, it is evident that the political opportunity structure of the receiving country is significant, and this structure in the United Kingdom has helped Latino migrants to channel their collective action. For example, we saw how the British multicultural set up tailored around large, long-standing ethnic communities has encouraged many Latin Americans from different nationalities to mobilize around a common Latino ethnic identity in the Latin Front. We also saw how the presence of trade unions, such as the T&G, has facilitated other Latin American migrants to mobilize around class, setting up the Latin American Workers Association as an integral part of the workers movement.

However, the ethnographic material also indicates some limitations in the POS approach. One concerns issues of diversity and change. In fact, while such an approach explains variations in the mobilization of a given ethnic group across localities with the different institutional environment of such localities (e.g., Ireland 1994), it has little to say about the diverse and changing mobilizations of a given group within a single and stable institutional environment, as in the case of the Latinos in London.[13] If anything, by treating ethnic groups as homogeneous entities, the POS approach denotes a certain ethnicist tendency.

Another limitation concerns the narrowly and rigidly defined range of forms that POS can assume. At present these are limited to the institutional and policy apparatus of the receiving society, but the material presented above calls for a broadening and loosening of what constitutes POS so as to include in it both migrants' movements and collective actions themselves as well as the wider cultural attitudes to difference of the receiving context.[14] For example, after being set up, thanks (in part) to the opportunity provided by the T&G, LAWA itself came to represent an opportunity for the mobilization of many Latin American migrants. Similarly the Latin Front's strategy to mobilize as an ethnic minority around the Latino identity is influenced not only by specific institutions and policies but also by the wider "multicultural culture" that characterizes the United Kingdom and that—in spite of the mounting neoassimilationist wave—still encourages ethnic identification and mobilization.

In addition to the failure of conceiving the structure of political opportunities transnationally (Østergaard-Nielsen 2003a),[15] the current narrow and institutionalist conception of POS reveals a problematic approach to theorizing that tends to take institutions and governments as key referents at the expense of people (e.g., migrants). This tendency compels us to (re-)think who and what we are ultimately committed to when we theorize and how we, as researchers, position ourselves in relation to the governmental process.

The ethnographic material also indicates the presence of further influences that suggest that the explanation of collective action is more complex than the POS approach allows for. One is migrants' political socialization, backgrounds, experiences, and values. For example, someone who has been active in the workers movement and whose world view is characterized by a class vision (like Fernando) is more likely to reflect such repertoire in the mobilization he/she undertakes in the country of immigration. Conversely somebody who has had a more liberal trajectory (like Isabel) is inclined to reflect this trajectory in his/her mobilization in the receiving country. Similarly those who are accustomed to undertaking critical or antagonistic stands are more likely to mobilize differently from those who are used to endorsing governmental or hegemonic views.

Another influential factor is that of the living conditions experienced in the receiving contexts. For many Latino migrants in London, these conditions are characterized by exploitation, marginalization, and exclusion. When I asked my informants what made them mobilize, all of them made reference to the problems and difficulties the Latin American collective on

the whole suffered from. To them it was actually more the structural constraints than the opportunities that made them mobilize. Indeed, it seems
that their determination to change this situation was such to make them go
against the wind and resist the institutional encouragement to organize as a
publicly funded charity.

A further influential factor that my ethnographic case has suggested concerns the migrants' networks and social capital. It is through the networks,
circuits, and social capital that they developed within the Latino and with the
wider community that they often made contacts, met, discussed ideas, got
involved and found out about opportunities to mobilize, and so forth.

This list of factors that—alongside and in interaction with the political
opportunity structure as well as with each other—shape migrants' mobilization is to be considered tentative, in progress and open to alterations and
developments. It is not meant to encapsulate the definitive typology of mobilizing factors, but only an indication of the influences at play in migrants'
participation. To be sure, by compiling this tentative list, this chapter is not
seeking to discard political opportunity structures as irrelevant but merely
suggesting a rethinking in more comprehensive, loose, actors-oriented and
interactive terms so as to avoid monocausal institutional determinism.

Future research on the topic should explore further the range of factors
that influence migrants' collective action and how they interact. Given their
traditional care for detail, microdynamics, and the demotic perspective, anthropologists are in a good position to make a significant contribution to
the interdisciplinary development of research on collective action and in so
doing get out of their marginal position in relation to this important topic.

ACKNOWLEDGMENTS

I wish to thank all my informants for the precious information they have
shared with me. I hope that they will find my representation of things accurate enough despite my sometimes critical considerations. I also wish to
warmly thank David Kertzer, Deborah Reed-Danahay, and Elisabetta Zontini for their comments on earlier drafts of this chapter.

NOTES

1. A good example of "progressive" neo-assimilationism is Goodhart (2004). For
   a critical discussion see Grillo (2005), but also Back et al. (2002), Cheong et al.
   (2005), Però (2007a; 2007b), Vertovec and Wessendorf (2005).
2. For an anthropological discussion of "governance" in the context of migration
   see Però (2005a; 2005b).
3. Soon after beginning fieldwork with Colombians, the realization that much of
   their collective initiatives directed at the United Kingdom (the focus of research)
   involved people from other Spanish speaking Latin American nationalities as

well and was being branded as "Latino," made me shift my attention from Colombians to Latinos.

4. At least for the Colombians, these estimates are consistent with those reported in Bermudez (2003) and Macilwane (2005). The number of people with a Latino background in the United Kingdom is also likely to grow further because of their high birth rates (Lewenstein 2006: 2).

5. See Macilwane 2005.

6. For an analysis of Latin Americans' involvement in the contract cleaning sector, see Lagnado (2004).

7. In arguing his case Ireland draws attention to the fact that POS take up different forms in different localities producing different types of migrants' participation from the same group.

8. This reveals how so-called host and home-country politics can be articulated not only simultaneously but also in synergy.

9. In terms of the work activity of its main activists the Latin Front included: journalists and media professionals, students, teachers, cleaners, doctors, shop owners, and law advisors.

10. In the "pre-T&G" period much of LAWA's activity was conducted in coffee shops, fast food restaurants, and private homes.

11. As Martiniello (2005) observed, the "presence in trade unions" and the "creation of collective actors" constitute indicators of political participation.

12. Interestingly material justice is a matter that is being overlooked in the current public and policy debate counterpoising "multiculturalists," who defend the existing British way to integration, and "neo-assimilationists" (see Però 2007a).

13. See also the case of Polish migrants presented by Garapich in this volume.

14. This suggests that the line separating POS from movements is blurred, contextual, and perspectival.

15. The transnational dimension of POS has been illustrated—if briefly—in this chapter when describing how one of the Latin Front's leader engaged across borders in a synergic way.

# CHAPTER 6

# Odyssean Refugees, Migrants, and Power

## CONSTRUCTION OF THE "OTHER" AND CIVIC PARTICIPATION WITHIN THE POLISH COMMUNITY IN THE UNITED KINGDOM

### Michal P. Garapich

### INTRODUCTION: POLES APART . . . AGAIN

SINCE THE COLLAPSE of communism in Eastern Europe, the region regained its status as one of the major supply areas for migrant labor to Western Europe. The recent enlargement of the European Union and the principle of the free movement of labor have legitimized a long existing, albeit often illicit, dense web of migration networks. The sudden increase in public attention focused on migration from Accession Countries, and especially from Poland, marks a change of perception rather than reality on the ground. Suddenly it is fashionable to talk about Polish migrants. But the semantic play offered by the double meaning of the word "Pole" is being uncreatively overexploited by the British media, which is covering the recent influx of Polish immigrants in articles with titles such as "Poles Apart," "Pole Position," and "Opposite Poles." Unintentionally, however, this reveals an important characteristic of the Polish presence in the United Kingdom. There are diverse groups of Polish migrants shaped by at least three generations of migratory history between Poland and Great Britain, multiple patterns of mobility, and diverse diasporic identities (Duvell 2004); Garapich 2006; Górny and Kolankiewicz 2002; Janowski 2004; Patterson 1964; Sword 1996; Zubrzycki 1956, 1988), which are also observable in the United States (Erdmans 1998; Mucha 1996; Schneider 1990). Complex cultural, generational, social, and structural differences between migrant cohorts result in a particular set of relationships of power between groups and particular symbolic articulations where ethnicity, constructions of homeland, social class, and national ideologies are being negotiated and sometimes clash. This, in turn, has a direct outcome for issues of civic participation, inclusion, and integration in the host society since various groups may compete for recognition and the status of the "official" and "true" community. It puts official, formal associations of the established groups in a particularly privileged position of power to impose specific meanings of citizenship, belonging, and national identity. By definition then, the formal diasporic associations become a tool of exclusion and symbolic violence where specific meanings, performances, and discursive habits are reproduced and reinforced. Newcomers can opt for submission to and acceptance of these unequal power relations or contest in various ways the dominant position of those in power. Polish migration to the United Kingdom in the last decades thus offers a fascinating insight into contemporary dynamics of white immigrants' associational life where states, transnational networks, and individuals participate in complex practices of place making, long-distance nationalism, and the reconstruction of relations between the state and the individual. At the heart of these processes lies the emergence of European transnational citizenship (Castles and Davidson 2000: 179–82) that contests nationalistic and state-centric notions of citizenship and belonging. The main argument of this chapter is that this process takes place not only between states and supranational institutions, but also within ethnic group institutions and associations, thereby directly affecting immigrants' civic participation and use of their transnational citizenship.

The internal diversity of contemporary Polish migrant groups raises important methodological questions for studies of the active civic participation of immigrants or ethnic group mobilization more generally. It offers a powerful case against an "ethnicist" (Brah 1996, see also Però in this volume) approach that essentializes ethnic minorities and equates them with interest groups with a clearly defined identity, based on a shared cultural or political agenda. The case of Polish migration to the United Kingdom described in this chapter supports Hassan Bousetta's critique of Patrick Ireland's (1994) one-dimensional institutionalist approach to the dominant role of the "political opportunity structures" framework in determining both the political mobilization of ethnic groups and the importance of the infrapolitical layer of this mobilization.[1] The concept of infrapolitics derives from work of James Scott (Scott 1990) and refers to political action undertaken off-stage, away from public scrutiny where the stake is control over the community/group political agenda and resources. Hassan Boussetta (2000), Gerd Bauman (1996), and John Eade (1989; see also Eade, Fremeaux, and Garbin

2002) have in various ways emphasized that the internal heterogeneity of immigrant community dynamics, as well as identity politics within the group should always be kept in mind when looking at immigrants' civic participation and community construction. By stressing the institutional framework of the host country as the dominant factor shaping participation and representation in the host society, Ireland's approach intentionally rei-fies ethnic groups, viewing them as bounded objects with clearly defined essences. This not only legitimizes and fixes power relations within one particular group, but also denies the ability of individuals within one group to contest a given social structure and dominant discourses. Methodologi-cally the only way to penetrate the reified body of the group is through a careful and prolonged ethnographic study that is attentive to the symbolic aspect of all human political action (Cohen 1974). This "insider" perspec-tive is often crucial in understanding *who* decides and *why* to participate in public life, who takes the role of the leader, why some sections of the group are being excluded or why one group chooses to use an ethnic- or class-based discourse in public claims making.

Second, what most social policy makers focus on are the outcomes of their policy provisions regarding integration and incorporation. But, as men-tioned above, internal power structures in a group may at times have greater bearing on participation patterns and civic inclusion. Furthermore, immi-grant sending states in this interconnected world—Poland in this case—may act as powerful players impeding or encouraging participation by directly funding certain activities of their citizens abroad or by constructing part of this imagined community (Anderson 1991) in a particular way. As will be shown later in this chapter, the silence of Polish ethnic and religious organi-zations on the new voting powers gained by immigrants after EU enlarge-ment, along with state withdrawal from the issue, are powerful examples of how state-centric nationalistic discourses may come into conflict with the notion of "postnational" citizenship (Soysal 1994) being constructed within the European community. The active policy of the Polish state toward its population abroad demonstrates additionally how diasporas are increasingly becoming "contested constituencies" (Adamson 2004) where a complex in-terplay of nationalist, class, and diasporic discourses set an agenda for a con-temporary transnational politics.

This chapter draws on data gathered during fieldwork undertaken in the United Kingdom since 2003 and during the Economic and Social Research Council funded study on recent Polish migrants in London (conducted be-tween 2005 and 2006). The chapter is divided into three parts. The first establishes the current dynamics of Polish migration to the United King-dom, especially in the context of EU enlargement. This is followed by an anthropological analysis of the social and cultural role played by migrants, and by diaspora and transnational politics in Polish history. The role of emigration in the process of Polish national identity construction is explained using the notion of "emigration ideology." The second part examines how discourses around Polish diaspora are being replayed in everyday relations between different cohorts of migrants. At the core are, on the one hand, an established, highly institutionalized and organized group, which uses the symbolic power of World War II veteran and political refugee status and, on the other hand, new migrants, who bring a different set of cultural values and attitudes and thereby challenge the power of the established diaspora. In the concluding section I examine these relations in terms of the tension between groups occupying different power positions and the consequences of this tension for civic participation.

### Transnational Poles—Been There, Done That

In the enlarged European Union, Poles quickly became the heroes or antiheroes of public opinion debates about immigration. The referendum on the European Union constitution in France was lost partly because the Polish migrant, in the form of a mythical plumber undercutting local workers, captured the imagination of the French, reminding them (apart from clear gendered and sexual connotations) of two major challenges that modern liberal democracies face: immigration and market liberalization. In the United Kingdom, a country that decided to open its labor market, the welcome has been much warmer and Polish migrants were even praised by a traditionally xenophobic press.[2] Since then, Britain continues to be one of the favored destinations of Polish migrants after Germany and the United States.[3]

According to Home Office statistics, between May 2004 and March 2007 almost 400,000 Poles registered to work in the United Kingdom. However, this figure does not include the self-employed or people working in the informal economy (Accession Monitoring Report 2007: 5). It is difficult to estimate the total number of migrants not only because of inadequate statistics, but also because of the dynamism and circularity of these flows. Twenty-two percent of the respondents in a survey of 500 Poles conducted in July 2006 identified themselves as seasonal migrants, and a third of them stated that they intended to stay less than two years in the United Kingdom. Only 15 percent admitted that they had moved to the United Kingdom permanently.[4] Bearing in mind the high seasonality of these flows, (generally more in summer and less in winter), the overall number of Polish nationals hovers around a half a million. Leaving exact numbers aside, these flows are substantial enough to create a perception of Poles as the fastest growing ethnic minority in the United Kingdom and to compare the influx with the Huguenot migrations of the seventeenth century (Swinford 2006). While the reliability of the statistics is debatable, it appears that 80 percent of Polish arrivals are below thirty-four years of age; most are single; and the majority work in construction, hospitality, catering, domestic service, as well as in health services, education services, and finance (Accession Monitoring Report 2007).

Despite the visual symbolism of the 1st of May when Poland entered the European Union, it is important to stress that from the perspective of migration networks and transnational social fields between Poland and the United Kingdom, the opening of the British labor market accelerated a migration process that was already well underway. Since the early 1990s Polish nationals have been allowed visa-free entry to the United Kingdom as visitors but with limited access to the labor market (for Polish migration to the whole European Union, see Triandafyllidou 2006). As Franck Duvell and Bill Jordan show in their research on Polish migrants (Duvell 2004; Jordan 2002; Jordan and Duvell 2002), Poles during the 1990s were one of the immigrant groups most commonly associated with illegal employment and visa overstaying. Post-Accession data show that around 30 percent of people who registered in the first six months after EU enlargement were already in the United Kingdom and hence illegal (Accession Monitoring Report 2004, 2005). A majority of migrants who have established the ethnic economy or "migration industry" (Cohen 1997; Hernandez-Leon 2005), which is presently booming in London, came before enlargement. Thus from the perspective of flows and transnational migration networks, EU enlargement was not a zero point of departure. The gate was already open and significant numbers of individuals had already walked through it.

In fact, this migration stream has been in operation much longer. In the 1980s thousands of Polish Solidarity dissidents found their way to London, pushed out by the martial laws imposed by General Jaruzelski in the winter of 1981. That migration was facilitated by the substantial diasporic institutional structures that had been set up in the United Kingdom at the end of World War II. London was the home of the government-in-exile. Around 150,000 Polish soldiers and displaced persons (DPs) settled after the war (Sword 1996; Zubrzycki 1956) and schools, churches, the press, ministers, presidents, and even a special self-taxation system resulted in a very high degree of institutional completeness (Breton 1964). Today, having played an important political role, this migration cohort has been described by Keith Sword (1996) as "declining" both in numbers and vitality. Its political *raison d'être*—the independence of the Polish state—has been achieved and it has been hard to find a new political issue on which to focus.

These three, broadly described cohorts constitute what may be termed "Poles in the United Kingdom" or a "Polish ethnic group." There are numerous links between them and their members interact regularly in social spaces such as churches, shops, streets, or workplaces. Thus a considerable level of experienced commonality exists. There are particular social environments where these commonalities become more meaningful than differences and occasions where generational boundaries are temporarily withdrawn. Transnational networks that bind these cohorts together support the idea that, despite being divided into different groups, migrants are sometimes part of the same migration chains (Patterson 1977; Burrell 2004; Garapich 2006). However, at the discursive and performative level a highly visible feature is the powerful boundary that divides "political" and "economic" emigrants. This division goes well beyond the simplistic issue of individual motives for leaving the home country. It constitutes and defines the individual's relationship with land, ancestors, and the wider collective and is an important element in Polish identity construction. The cultural meanings behind these processes of symbolic boundaries construction are rooted in history.

Christian Joppke and Ewa Morawska (2003: 21), in an effort to challenge the "novelty" of transnationalism (Glick Schiller, Basch, and Szanton Blanc 1995) have pointed to the great migrations during the nineteenth and twentieth centuries from Eastern Europe, which were also marked by circularity and transnational networking. Poles played an important part in these movements, migrating to work in the mines and factories of the industrializing world of the nineteenth and twentieth centuries. Many thousands also emigrated as sort of nineteenth-century revolutionary nomads plotting insurgencies in Poland in almost every capital of Europe, from Istanbul to London, and also, like Pulaski and Kosciuszko, in the United States. In Polish history transnational politics is indivisible from domestic politics and Poles surely can claim to have the largest number of governments-in-exile in the last two centuries. The act of emigrating, deeply entangled with Polish national identity, is also a widespread archetypical notion present in literature, the arts, religion, and political thought. Through the literary work of poets in exile emigration is thickly woven into a national narrative of land, belonging, family, and loss.[5]

Not surprisingly considerable contributions to nationalist identity construction were made by nationalist leaders abroad. As with Italians (Bean 1989), Polish immigrant leaders in the nineteenth and twentieth centuries, mostly in France, Belgium, and the United States, had significant success in developing and constructing a national identity among people from rural areas (Walaszek 2001). Since Poland has been a sending country for a couple of centuries, a particular set of cultural meanings has developed around the act of migrating. We could describe the set of values attached to migration as a form of emigration ideology. What is crucial is that the ideology is based on a dichotomy between migrating for political, as opposed to economic, reasons. That division embodies and generates all the necessary meanings and symbols that enforce and reproduce the boundaries between the collective and the individual, duty and freedom, the self and the imagined community, the material and the ideal. It is also a class-based division, separating refugees from the gentry classes who were fighting for independence, on the one hand, and "simple folk" (peasants and the working class) who were seeking a better life abroad, on the other. During the nineteenth and twentieth centuries, this emigration ideology served as a nationalistic tool for identifying the population. In that ideology there was little place for minorities migrating from Poland—or for Jews, Romas, Germans, Ukrainians, and many others.

Polish national identity developed in opposition to the state but with a strong affiliation toward territory, religion, and language. The dominant role played by the land-owning gentry in this opposition reinforced the tragedy implicit in the act of leaving one's land. Poles living abroad have a ready residue of symbols, traits, concepts, and historical references that define the immigrant's place in an alien environment. Nationalistic discourse uses strong notions of what Liisa H. Malkki has called "sedentarist metaphysics" (Malkki 1997) that naturalizes attachment to the land. From this perspective all mobility and movement is seen as pathological and contradictory to human nature—people are biologically connected with the soil. Additionally mobility is a threat to the moral order since the source of national morality lies in the national bounded territory and soil.

The collective character of nationalism ensures that in official Polish historical discourse emigration is perceived in moral terms (Erdmans 1992). Migration for political reasons has higher moral status than economic migration since it entails sacrifice and submission to the collective. In Polish emigration ideology, political exile is a sacred act in the fight for freedom while economic migration is a necessary evil, a manifestation of weakness or simply cowardice, egoism, and an ambiguous act of turning away from the fate of the nation. This ideology plays on a Christian/Platonic dualism between the ideal and the material, the soul and the body, patriotism and narrow egoism. What is crucial is that by reducing individual motivation to a moral dichotomy of "ideas" vs. "bread," the emigration ideology has the capability of creating a hierarchy of migrants.

As a "myth of origin" (see Robert Gibb in this volume), this dichotomy between political and economic migrants functions as a fixed and reified definition of one's moral value since it relates to the reified past—the primary reason of being removed from the national territory, replayed over and over through commemorations, rituals, and debates. Its determinism and historicism means that individual experience should be understood in terms of passive internalization of nationalistic narratives and humble acceptance of the dominant historical processes, rather than personal choice and agency. People who migrated to the West for political reasons a half-century ago, are then seen as morally superior through their suffering and sacrifice, even if the initial reasons for migration are rendered void due to, for example, the achievement of the political goal of an independent nation state.

As with all cultural meanings, the Polish emigration ideology requires constant nurturing in the form of memory construction, performative actions, rituals, and discursive practices. As we will see, that symbolic construction of the national narrative dichotomizing the emigration experience as either political or economic, is a powerful cultural resource used and manipulated in Polish diasporic groups. Its importance is essential to understand the dynamics of civic participation and power relationship within the group.

## THE ESTABLISHED AND THE OTHERS—
## DIASPORA AS A FORM OF EXCLUSION

London has been the seat of a government-in-exile that preserved the legal continuity of prewar Poland, a role acknowledged by the first freely elected Polish President Lech Wałęsa, who received the presidential insignia in 1990 from the last president-in-exile, Ryszard Kaczorowski. The London diaspora may, therefore, be regarded as a paradigmatic example of Polish émigré patriotism and a "sacred" spot in Polish emigration geography. Not surprisingly the activity of this group concentrates on memory revitalization, preserving and reproducing memories of wartime experience, staging rituals that emphasize the role played by the Polish government-in-exile, and maintaining the prestige associated with veteran status. Apart from strengthening the integration of the group and reproducing the "primary" motivation of emigration, these activities are directed toward Polish and British authorities who are reminded constantly about the Polish contribution to the World War II effort.

Considering that the émigré culture of representation is based on the cultural politics of reminding the British hosts about the sacrifice made by Polish soldiers, part of that representation includes an emphasis on the distinctiveness and total separation from other migrants from the same ethnic group; that is, migrants arriving after 1989. Every researcher will hear from members of the old Polish diaspora in the United Kingdom an identity statement similar to the one expressed by an eighty-year-old lady in a letter to the *Polish Daily,* the newspaper catering to this diaspora: "We are different, we came from a country that does not exist any more." These kinds of statements are constantly made at meetings, in the press, and even through the church. They are always accompanied by a mainly negative description of newcomers (on the same issue, see Sword 1996; Janowski 2004).

As a result of the constant influx of Polish migrants after 1989, accelerated by EU enlargement, Polish émigrés found themselves in the difficult position of sharing a common historical identity with people with different social, class, and even sometimes ethnic identities. Daniele Joly (2002) coined the term "Odyssean refugees" to denote a distinct refugee identity that may come into conflict, based on class difference, with people from the same ethnic group. She defines Odyssean refugees as: "Actors who were not just victims of the structure of conflict in their country of origin but were positively committed to the political struggle and project of society in their homeland; they also brought this project with them into exile so that they are committed to a collective project in the homeland despite the defeat they have suffered . . . for Odyssean refugees include not necessarily all nationals of the same origin but all who were engaged in the same political struggle" (Joly 2002: 9).

The generation of Poles that arrived in the United Kingdom at the end of World War II is a perfect example of how this form of identity can be developed. Mostly representatives of prewar Polish elites with a strong leaning toward the Right, they embodied a particular political project. However, the boundary maintenance required a lot of ideological, cultural, and institutional effort. Most of the diasporic institutions were formed in the 1940s and 1950s when most of the refugees still believed in a quick return to Poland triggered by another international conflict, possibly a third world war. The threat from Communist police infiltration was real and the air of suspicion present in publications of the time reflects a power struggle between the Polish regime in Warsaw and the survivors of the prewar Polish state structures who found themselves in disarray.

This suspicion of everything that originated from Communist Poland helped to maintain group loyalty and defend the ideological values from outside influence seen mainly in terms of a pro-Soviet but sometimes vaguely also pro-Left global conspiracy (Mach 1994). This is why potentially anything coming from Communist Poland was ideologically "stained" by communism—from books, to ideas, to people themselves who therefore needed to be kept separate. Along with the preservation of prewar Poland political symbolism, the conservation of political values, or the "political project," became the goal that could be achieved only by excluding every influence from

Poland, which could corrupt the purity of the ideal. As a result, Polish émigré groups in the United Kingdom see themselves as the only true, uncorrupt examples of the finest version of Polish patriotism and romantic freedom fighters. The dichotomy was all too clear: an immoral, un-Polish,[6] corrupt, and Eastern regime suppressing a healthy but oppressed nation, on the one hand, and a virtuous, Polish, patriotic, free diaspora, on the other. The boundary obviously requires someone on the other side. As Frederic Barth notes it is the process of intergroup contact that generates cultural meanings through a boundary dividing *us* from *them* (Barth 1969). We need, therefore, to look at "the ethnic boundary that defines the group not the cultural stuff that it encloses" (15). Akhil Gupta and James Ferguson (1997) link this approach to an anthropological analysis of power relations. For them difference construction is a tool, which establishes a topography of power, and naming the "other' implies the maintenance of a hierarchy. I argue here that this applies also to subgroups and internal divisions within ethnic groups. In order to keep the political project alive a boundary separating the émigrés and the rest of the world needed to be established.

With the collapse of the Communist system, which meant the fulfillment of the political project, the situation became blurred. Freedom gained in 1989 and the symbolic "return" of the presidential insignia in 1990 undermined the foundations of Polish diaspora identity and created a situation where new forms of boundary maintenance had to be established. The previous pattern of "othering," however, had preserved its social function and the waves of newcomers, economic migrants, coming from Poland in search of bread filled the void left by the ideological enemy—the Communists—thus giving old structures a new, stronger meaning. Since it used the same tool—branding everything from Poland as "stained," "impure," and morally suspicious—it has been easily adopted by Odyssean refugees and their political discourse.

The othering also had to be communicated to outsiders since, for the majority of British society, Poles constitute a homogenous ethnic group. A stronger and more powerful boundary had to be constructed in order to reinforce generational differences and to communicate the status of the established community who were also valued for the prestige of World War II veterans—something equally appealing to British and Polish society. Unsurprisingly the diasporic community invests a lot of time and effort to keep this distinction alive. The self-definition of Polish émigrés has been even recognized by the Polish consular authorities and on the official papers from the embassy the group is referred to as Emigration of Independence (*emigracja niepodległościowa*) along with a group called *Polonia,* which basically means all other migrants plus second generation Poles.

Along with reinforcing their distinct Odyssean refugee identity, creating a degree of cultural, class, and educational difference with the newcomers helps also to legitimize their roles as holders of social and political capital not only vis-à-vis British society, but also in relation to the Polish government, which increasingly recognizes the importance of its worldwide diaspora. In fact, the Polish state's policy toward its diaspora is deliberately based on a exclusionist policy that emphasizes Polish exiles—living proof of Polish military grandeur—and deemphasizes the post-1989 migration from Poland—an uneasy indication of Poland's economic downturns and sometimes painful transformation process (Garapich 2006).

Boundary construction is visible in extreme cases where there is a threat of losing an important asset for any ethnic minority—reputation in the eyes of the host society. The darker side of the world of Polish migrants has been sometimes described as Hobbessian, a world where Poles denounce each other to the authorities, viciously competing and ruthlessly exploiting fellow compatriots (Duvell 2004; Jordan 2002). There are reports of Polish extortion gangs operating, for example, in the Slough area (Garapich 2006), a fact noted also by the British press (Ford 2004), or involvement in forging and selling passports. Potentially damaging for the image of the "community" as a whole, the established Polish diaspora seems to have two choices: either take action, thereby assuming a degree of commonality and responsibility, or do nothing that justifies a specific boundary construction in naming the migrants in need as "different" and "alien." Most of the diasporic institutions chose to distance themselves and do nothing. In fact, diasporic elites are very reluctant to address the social problems of more recent migrants and live in a state of denial about the challenges posed by their arrival. I have been all too often confronted with comments that the world of Polish new migrants is "not ours." As one leader of the Polish community told me, "They are different. We do not want to have anything to do with them." Members of the older generation sometimes express their fear that the "newcomers will ruin the reputation we have worked for all these decades." A common reference to newcomers is that they are "sovietized" (Siemaszko 2003), implying a step backward in their civic, behavioral, and moral competence compared with prewar Poland and is thus associated with the state of pollution of previously clean Polish character.[7]

Despite the United Kingdom being one of the main destinations for Polish migrants, the social safety net of assistance and advocacy from the diaspora toward the newcomers is rather poor. The Federation of Poles in Great Britain—which on its Web site presents itself as "an official representative of the Polish community"—is an exception, however. It has launched an information campaign for Poles who want to migrate, calling on them to be properly prepared. Yet, with a very limited budget and the absence of fresh ideas, the role of the federation is fairly modest. Their attitude toward the social needs of newcomers reflects the fact that they encourage people in need to return to Poland rather than provide active help.[8] This organization relies strongly on funding from the veteran associations and hence needs to constantly challenge more conservative segments of the elite.

Not that migrants are left to their own devices. The institutional void has been filled by a vast increase in commercial advice offices and, strongly connected with them, the ethnic media. Since the year 2000, and booming after EU enlargement in 2004, a specific migration "business" or "industry" (Cohen 1997; Hernandez-Leon 2005; Salt 2004) has emerged, which has facilitated the transnational movements, networking, and political orientations of Poles.

This development had important consequences since migrants, through legalization of their work and tax payments, began a process of integrating fully into the labor market and welfare state and hence extending their transnational citizenship based on social and political rights granted by EU legislation. The alienation and marginalization associated with illegal work (Osipowicz 2001) was gone, at least in theory, creating avenues for further advancement. Transnational citizenship was further enhanced by the emergence of ethnic media, specifically directed toward new immigrants, but also widely used through the Internet by migrants-to-be in Poland, hence creating a dense transnational media environment. In 2001 only one eight-page and very conservative paper, associated with the first generation of World War II veterans, the *Polish Daily and Soldiers Daily,* was in circulation. Today, in London alone, there are four weekly magazines, and one bimonthly; in these publications, the whole range of issues concerning newcomers are discussed and covered.

It is difficult to underestimate the role that these new forums have in forming common interests and a sense of common fate and identity among new migrants. They also stimulate various forms of participation in social networks and British society as a whole, like running an information campaign about social and political entitlements, actively encouraging participation in the trade union movement, or addressing sensitive issues of migrants' racism and relationships with other ethnic groups. The pluralization of discourses in the ethnic media have encompassed the voices of previously excluded segments of the diasporic public sphere and also helped newcomers to express their frustration about divisions within the Polish community and the privileged position of the established diaspora.[9] In the spring of 2006 a new association, "Poland Street," was formed to create a "counterbalance to the representation of old Polish community."[10] Initially the association was not interested in being included in the structure of the Federation of Poles in Great Britain. However, after a change of leadership it accepted the dominant role of the federation. In discussions with leaders the main arguments supporting this change were that "they have been here first" and the fact that "they are well known among the British." Tellingly one of the activities of the association has been to clean the graves of the Polish pilots at the Gunnersbury Cemetery. As one of the initiators of the event said, this was to "confront the negative stereotype about the newcomers" and show the established community that they also cherish values of patriotism and the nation.

Poland Street remains a marginal organization, something that reinforces the argument that we must look beyond the formal and institutional face of a group. Polish post-Accession migrants often contest and transcend nation-centric perspectives on citizenship by establishing a bilocal orientation and multiple senses of belonging. As users of social and political entitlements that accompany EU transnational citizenship, they are keen to take an active voice in their home communities by voting, signing petitions, debating political events in Poland on the Internet, and so on. The biggest public protest emphasizing the rights of transnational citizenship (the issue concerned a double taxation Polish fiscal policy that penalized migrants with attachments to two countries) has been organized by a coalition of the media, Web sites, companies in the business of facilitating remittances, and the Poland Street Association. It is quite obvious that the formal immigrant associational life of Poles in the United Kingdom is just a small fraction of the entire set of transnational networks that are being woven to support participation in the social and political life of both countries. One example is the booming popular music scene with bands shuttling back and forth between Poland and the United Kingdom. Their role has been recognized by the British trade union GMB, which decided that the best way to inform Polish migrants of their social and political rights would be by inviting Polish rock bands to play at the Glastonbury Festival. A further example is the role that British trade unions play in bringing Solidarity organizers to the United Kingdom or visiting job fairs in Poland.

By renegotiating and challenging the accepted national emigration ideology, the two social worlds of the Odyssean refugees and the new migrants reflect, in an extreme version, the two faces of Polish society since the collapse of Communism in 1989. The difference in vitality in the organizational structures that cater to each group is striking. The old diaspora is aging, their associations and newspapers are closing down, social clubs are being sold off, and members are dying. The old émigré symbolism and ideology, reflected in these organizations, are alien to newcomers who value a more positive attitude toward mobility, lead transnational lives, and do not see themselves as victims with a myth of return. Newcomers describe their differences with the older generation of émigrés in the following words:

> All the time I regard myself neither as an emigrant nor a member of Polonia . . . [Polish diaspora] I have a Polish passport and I am the citizen of the world . . . there are Polish in London who are not Polonia, it's as simple as that . . . Polonia is a closed unit that's it. (Personal Interview in London)

> Of course they deserve a lot of respect because they did a lot of important work . . . and we have to understand the specifics of people of certain age that at one stage of their life began to live deep in the past and build their everyday life around what was before. It is not that they are totally closed to others, to younger people to some changes . . . and to new issues . . . there is a huge difference between that generation and ours not only due to the age but because the attitude to life is different . . . the younger people have a consumerist attitude towards life . . . the older have . . . let's say they created an establishment for Poles living in Great Britain. (Personal Interview in London 2006)

Newcomers are driven by highly individualized attitudes, market orientated values, consumerism, and sense of the power of their own agency (Duvell 2004; Garapich 2006). Their transnational mobility and how they represent it contrasts with the older emigration ideology. For them, migration is not about trauma and loss, but rather is a continuation of their individual biographies, educational opportunity, as well as a *rite of passage* into adult life in a global city (Eade, Drinkwater, and Garapich 2007). Thus the migration experience has become individualized and the long cherished link between nationalism and emigration in Polish political discourse has been weakened. In a world of individualized and flexible identities, stimulated by a powerful belief in British meritocracy, there is little space for the "preservation" of a particular set of Polish émigré traditions and nationalistic political ideas that shaped the history of Polish diaspora. This involves not only a generation gap but also class and cultural divisions that run deep within Polish society. In fact, this division—between free-market enthusiasts, individualistic, mobile, urban, and middle-class aspiring Poles and traditional, antiliberal, more inward-looking Poles who explicitly rely on family and Christian values—is not only an embodiment of the liberal vs. communitarian debate but also a visible sign of certain conflicts and tensions in Polish society in general (Domański 2002).

POLITICS OF PARTICIPATION AND PARTICIPATION IN POLITICS

I have traced how different migratory experiences of members of one ethnic group and their discursive manifestations are being replayed and reinforced through particular state-centric and nationalistic discourses and behavior. I have also described the growth of a challenge to these traditional discourses as Polish post-Accession migrants formulate their sense of place and use their European transnational citizenship to acquire various social and legal entitlements. This of course is a recipe for intracommunity tensions as the state-centric, nationalistic ideology of emigration is confronted with a much more multifaceted and postmodern perspective on belonging and citizenship.

HOW DO THESE DIFFERENT PERSPECTIVES AFFECT
CIVIC AND POLITICAL ENGAGEMENT?

On the basis of the Maastricht Treaty of 1 May 2004, which established the concept of European citizenship, Polish migrants along with other nationals of new accession states were granted voting rights at the municipal, regional, and EU level. Although this form of citizenship has been described by scholars as quasicitizenship (Martiniello, 1994: 41; Castles and Davidson 2000: 98) without doubt it has empowered immigrants since it enfranchised at least a hundred thousand Polish nationals in the United Kingdom, mostly in London. This was probably the biggest act of democratization within the British political system since women gained the vote at the beginning of the twentieth century.

However, the "official" representatives of the Polish community kept silent about the political empowerment of their coethnics. For Patrick Ireland and many other political scientists, voting rights are the ultimate political opportunity structure—the goal of many struggles for inclusion by immigrants. Theoretically enfranchisement should be the goal of any immigrant population in the view of most political scientists. Yet no Polish established organization made any effort to educate or campaign in order to encourage people to use that right. "We are not a political organization" was the mantra I heard when asking about reasons for silence during the hotly contested elections for the mayor of London in which Polish citizens could take part for the first time as EU citizens. "No, I do not see a reason why we should," said the president of the Federation of Poles in Great Britain when asked why the organization was not running a campaign to encourage people to take an active part in the elections.[11] The president stressed that it is the business of British authorities, not his, to let people know their rights and that his organization has little to gain from migrants exercising their right to vote. More figuratively the Polish church leader who traditionally reads a letter from the Polish Episcopate before every election in Poland reminding people to fulfill their civic duty, when asked if he would do the same in the case of elections in London, responded: "No, why would we do that? These people belong to Poland and they should have their hearts there." Another leader of an umbrella association offered a perfect example of the tension between a traditional and exclusive nation-bound concept of citizenship, and emerging new possibilities: "Yes, we would encourage it if these were elections in Poland, but here . . . no, here everyone has to choose in private if he wants to go or not." The distinction between "private" and "public" in this statement suggests the idea that voting is essentially about state loyalty and there can be only one state in peoples' mind.

Less surprisingly the same response was given by representatives of the Polish state. The Polish ambassador said simply: "This would be interfering into the internal British affairs." Of course, the Polish state sees participation in elections of a foreign country as a potentially disloyal act, something that reduces control over its citizens. A similar position held by the earlier generation of émigrés shows how nationalistic and state-centric notions of citizenship are mutually reinforced by state policies and the exclusionist practices of Odyssean refugee institutions. Citizenship in both perspectives (that of state policies and that of the earlier generation of Polish émigrés) entails not plural attachment and individual rights but, rather, the monopoly of one state. It also entails the obligation of the individual towards the collective—one nation, one state—even from abroad, or maybe especially from abroad, considering that as a "moral issue" emigration ideology imposes specific obligations toward the citizen.

The explanation for the silence on voting rights and the refusal to civically educate the newcomers is that, as holders of considerable political, financial, and social capital, the first generation of Poles has monopolized the public sphere in which migrants might have operated in the United Kingdom. It would be counterproductive to raise civic awareness levels among new migrants, since it could mean undermining their position as the only public face of the Polish community. The cultural and social distance within the community helps to legitimize the existing power relations and dominant position of current Polish ethnic leaders. Constructed as a moral and sacred issue crucial for Polish nationalistic ideology, the Polish diaspora *has* to be political otherwise it would lose its power and legitimacy. The associational structures created by the established generation of émigrés, supported by a state-centric ideology, have become a mechanism for social exclusion and the reproduction of hierarchy.

If the politics of difference construction influences relations within a group, the whole perception of relations between different ethnic groups changes, too. Polish leaders assume that a natural, civic place for a Pole abroad (which in nationalistic discourse is an abnormality in itself—the only morally accepted one is as a political refugee) is only in the organizational structures of ethnic associations seen as separate from British public life. This, in turn, has its origins in people who view themselves as a distinct group in relation to other ethnic groups living in the United Kingdom. Many leaders and members of the first generation of emigrants refuse to be called members of an ethnic minority. In some cases using the term generates anger and protest and several times I have been warned not to use the phrase "ethnic minority" when referring to Poles in press articles, considering that—as one leader told me—it "puts us on the same level as Hindus and blacks." Polish diasporic leaders, therefore, deliberately choose not to participate in a political arena that is made possible through the ethnic claims making of British multiculturalism (Statham 1999). Historically Poles in the United Kingdom were well connected to the Conservative Party and successfully used their white, middle-class, proempire, promonarchy, and anti-Communist status to gain access to power. Emphasizing ethnicity too much would mean having to share the multicultural pie with others on an equal footing.

However, considering that diasporas are increasingly becoming a field of "contested constituency" (Adamson 2004) where different agents try to attract attention and monopolize migrants' home-oriented emotions, Polish elites and the state strongly reactivate the emigration ideology of victimhood, trauma, and "sedentary metaphysics." This, in turn, acts as a brake on civic education, political incorporation, and the self-awareness of migrants as social actors. Tellingly the only high-ranking Pole who addressed migrants on the issue of using their political rights as EU citizens was the vice president of the European Parliament when he visited a Polish community of new migrants in Scotland.

### CONCLUSION

The study of recent developments within the world of the Polish migrant diaspora in the United Kingdom is essentially a study of social change where an established elite is challenged by waves of new migrants who are a potential threat to the existing social hierarchy. The rise in the economic position of newcomers that has resulted from the enlargement of the European Union has led to an entrenchment on the part of those of earlier migration waves. Individuals of the earlier waves reinforce old divisions in order to maintain their position. This leads to further closure, reinforcement of the exclusiveness of old structures, and denial of the needs and problems faced by the newcomers. Any strong action toward a coethnic would assume commonality, responsibility, and mutual fate—something that would open existing power structures to contestation. Reinforcing distinctiveness helps to maintain hierarchy based on political ideology instead of commonality based on ethnicity. The division is even more striking since these waves are strongly connected not only in the context of belonging to the same migration chain but also financially, socially, and culturally. After all, established émigrés and the second generation, like mainstream British society, benefit hugely from cheap builders and affordable nannies. Last but not least, they are also viewed by the British public as one "community."

As we debate the channels of participation and civic awareness of immigrants, it is important to remember that the politics of difference construction within one immigrant group, its infrapolitical dynamics can determine the process of inclusion sometimes more powerfully than the institutions or attitudes of the host society. The limitations of Ireland's "political opportunities structures" approach are that it concentrates on *what* tools are available, not *why* they are used by some people and not by others. In responding to these theoretical limitations an anthropological perspective that focuses on what people actually do and say (or even what they do not say for that matter) in everyday interaction is paramount. A perspective that treats ethnic and national identities as relational and dynamically and situationally constructed is also of crucial importance. It enables us to rediscover the political functions of symbols, myths, nationalistic narratives, and dialectics of inclusion and exclusion associated with the emergence of transnational citizenship. Additionally the Polish migration experience described here offers a powerful critique of the multicultural corporatist approach, which sees ethnic groups as bounded, homogenous, and essentialized entities acting with one voice in a national context.

Finally, in relation to the ongoing development of European transnational citizenship, the case presented here offers a reminder that the tensions between the old style exclusive national citizenship and emerging forms of postnational citizenship are not limited to negotiations between a host society or host state and immigrant groups. It can also play out within ethnic groups themselves, where contradictory notions of citizenship and belonging are also being negotiated and formulated. Assuming the homogeneity of an ethnic group is not only a methodological error, but also a serious underestimation of the fact that state-centered ideologies and nationalisms have a particular interest in mobilizing diasporas, which very often use their position of power to exclude any dissident voice.

## ACKNOWLEDGMENTS

This article would not have been possible without the support of several institutions and funders. Hereby I would like to thank the European

Commission and its Marie-Curie Fellowship program, which allowed me to participate at the AAA annual conference in Washington in 2005, where an earlier version of this chapter was delivered. I thank the Economic and Social Research Council in the United Kingdom, which permitted me to carry out research (RES-000–22–1294) on Polish migrants conducted at the Center for Research on Nationalism, Ethnicity and Multiculturalism (CRONEM) at the University of Surrey and the University of Roehampton. I also want to express my gratitude to people who shared valuable comments on the chapter and expressed a patient and understanding approach to my clumsy English: Caroline B. Brettell, John Eade, David Garbin, and Deborah Reed-Danahay.

NOTES

1. This is popular among political scientists; see for instance Statham (1999).
2. In a mass survey of Polish households (Diagnoza Spoleczna 2005), 22 percent of Poles expressed their desire to migrate abroad with a quarter pointing to the United Kingdom as the favorite destination.
3. The extreme case of an anti-EU and antiimmigration UKIP party leader, caught employing Polish builders, added to the general attitude of acceptance toward Polish migrants in the United Kingdom, considering that it highlighted the fact that economic migrants benefit from the overall economy and fill labor shortages—something that even nationalists had to accept on their doorstep.
4. Survey conducted by the Center for Research on Nationalism, Ethnicity and Multiculturalism at University of Surrey and Roehampton. Avaliable at: http://www.surrey.ac.uk/Arts/CRONEM/index.htm.
5. The national anthem includes the motive of reemigration; repeating words "March, March—from Italian land to Polish." It was written in Italy by the Polish legions serving under the Napoleon during the wars of the early nineteenth century.
6. This is where Polish prewar anti-Semitism came in handy; pointing to the fact that Jews were omnipresent in the Polish Communist party and the regime police apparatus.
7. In June 2003, working at the time for the *Polish Daily*, I reported a case of an advertisement in a shop window ten meters from the biggest center of the Polish diaspora in Hammersmith, London. The ad explicitly offered in Polish a passport forgery "service." In a newspaper commentary I criticized the tendency of Polish community leaders to ignore the problems at their doorstep and to view the world of new migrants as totally separate from their own. In a typical response, one of the leaders of the community withdrew his yearly donation to the newspaper and I have been told by the editor not to mention the issue any more. The international press has noted this tension as well. In October of 2005, the *International Herald Tribune*, in an article about the newest wave of Polish migrants to the United Kingdom published the following: "There is some ambivalence in Britain about the arrival of the East Europeans. Some of the loudest complaints have come from the older generation of Poles, who moved to Britain during World War II and now gripe about the brusque manners of the newcomers" (International Herald Tribune 21 October 2005).
8. Interview with the president of Federation of Poles, June 2004.

9. One notable example in the new media is the reports of life of the Polish gay community in the United Kingdom—an impossibility in the conservative *Polish Daily*. The very recent press discussion on the financial difficulties of the émigré newspaper *Polish Daily*, or criticism of the event offer of the Polish Social-Cultural Center in London, are notable examples of improved relations between both groups. It would have been impossible a few years back.

10. Interview with the president of Poland Street, 2 June 2006.

11. Interview with the president of Federation of Poles, June 2004.

CHAPTER 7

# Origin Myths, Conspiracy Theories, and Antiracist Mobilizations in France

*Robert Gibb*

OVER THE PAST twenty-five years, associations have been an important vehicle for the political mobilization of immigrants and their descendants in France. The principle of freedom of association is enshrined in a specific provision of the French Common Law known as the "1 July 1901 Law" (*Journal Officiel de la République Française* 1901). This defines an association as "the agreement by which two or more persons combine their knowledge or act together for a purpose other than that of profit-sharing" (Article 1). The right of French citizens to form such associations freely, without the need for government authorization or a preliminary declaration, is a cornerstone of the 1901 Law (Article 2).[1] Foreign nationals were granted the freedom of association in 1981, and since then associative activity has represented a significant form of civic participation and engagement for both French citizens and foreign nationals resident in France.

Through an examination of competing accounts of the circumstances surrounding the creation in the mid-1980s of SOS-Racisme, a French antiracist association, this chapter explores the way in which origin myths and conspiracy theories can fulfill important de-legitimating functions for social agents engaged in processes of political mobilization and claims making around issues of citizenship, civic participation, and belonging. In so doing, it highlights the fact that symbolic struggles to define the meaning of previous mobilizations are an important part of the history of antiracist and immigration politics in France. The chapter begins by describing forms of political mobilization and associative activity by young (French) people of

immigrant/colonial origin in France during the early 1980s, before focusing on the emergence within the field of antiracist politics of a new association called SOS-Racisme. As the 2005 wave of urban unrest in France
revealed, there is a kind of "collective amnesia" about these events among
both social scientists and young working-class people of immigrant origin
living in the suburbs (Bazin et al. 2006; Beaud and Masclet 2006). The
present chapter attempts to recover part of this history through an analysis
of different interventions by social agents involved in the field of antiracism
at an earlier stage of its development.

In addition to providing insights into debates about the circumstances
surrounding the creation of the French antiracist organization SOS-Racisme,
the chapter draws attention to two general theoretical points. The first is that
myths and rituals fulfill important functions for political (and other) organizations. As the political anthropologist David Kertzer has explained: "In
order to have members, or even adherents, an organization must have some
way of representing itself, and it carves out a distinct identity through both
mythic and ritual means. Organizations propagate myths regarding their origin and purpose, while members engage in symbolic practices that serve to
mark them off from nonmembers. These myths often assert the group's superiority" (Kertzer 1988: 17–18). Ritual practices and symbolic representations,
in other words, play a key role in both creating and maintaining distinctive
organizational identities. The material discussed here provides an illustration
from the French antiracist movement of this aspect of processes of political
mobilization, civic participation, and claims making.

The chapter also highlights a second theoretical point that is the importance of analyzing the political field, in the words of the French sociologist
and anthropologist Pierre Bourdieu, not only as a "field of forces" but also
as a "field of struggles which tends to conserve or transform this field of
forces" (1998: 381). Although Bourdieu is writing here about the literary or
artistic field, his comments apply equally to the political field: "the history
of the field is the history of the struggle for the monopoly of the imposi-
tion of legitimate categories of perception and appreciation; it is the very
*struggle* which makes the history of the field" (Bourdieu 1998: 261, italics
in original). As Bourdieu explains, this struggle expresses itself in the different, and often conflicting, "position takings" [*prises de position*] by social
agents involved in the field (1998: 379). The origin myths and conspiracy
theories about the creation of SOS-Racisme examined in this chapter can
be viewed in this light as examples of political position takings by social
agents (individuals and organizations) involved in struggles to define the
nature and meaning of national belonging, antiracist politics, and modes of
civic engagement in France.

## ASSOCIATIONS, PARTY POLITICS, AND
## ANTIRACIST MOBILIZATIONS IN FRANCE

The origins of SOS-Racisme can be traced back to the victory of the Socialist Party (PS) candidate François Mitterrand in the May 1981 presidential election in France. The left-wing government, which was subsequently formed under Prime Minister Pierre Mauroy, quickly introduced several pieces of legislation intended to signal its determination to break with the repressive immigration policies of the previous center-right administration. One of these new, and symbolically important, measures was the law of 9 October 1981, which granted foreigners the right of association. Previously foreigners had been required to obtain prior authorization from the interior minister before forming an association and stringent conditions were attached. The new Socialist legislation removed these restrictions and resulted in a significant increase in the political mobilization of North Africans (Wihtol de Wenden 1991: 320–21).[2]

The associations formed by young people of immigrant/colonial origin in the suburbs of cities such as Paris and Lyons after 1981 were initially designed to promote their self-organization and participation in local life. However, several events occurred over the next two years that radicalized the activity of many of these groups and focused them on issues of racism, equal rights, unemployment, and police violence. The summers of 1982 and 1983 witnessed a series of racist incidents in which young people, predominantly of North African origin, were shot and killed either by police officers or by other (white) inhabitants of their housing estates. In the intervening period, a group of Franco-Maghrebis living in the Lyons high-rise estate Les Minguettes staged a twelve-day hunger strike to protest against poor housing conditions. The leader of the hunger strikers, Toumi Djaïdja, was himself later shot and nearly killed by a police officer in June 1983. The fact that the perpetrators of such crimes were frequently either acquitted or given light sentences by the courts only served to increase the sense of injustice experienced by young people of immigrant/colonial origin. The success of the far-right Front national in the September 1983 municipal by-election in Dreux (sixty kilometers west of Paris) further fueled their fears about racism in French society (Jazouli 1992: 43–52).

In response to these events, Toumi Djaïdja and other young people living in Les Minguettes decided to organize a nation-wide march, as a form of nonviolent protest to the racism, police brutality, and poverty with which they were confronted. Assisted by a Catholic priest, Christian Delorme, they prepared the "March for Equality and against Racism" (*Marche pour l'égalité et contre le racisme*),[3] which left Marseille in October 1983 almost unnoticed by politicians and the (Parisian) media alike. When the march finally arrived in Paris on 3 December 1983, however, the demonstrators numbered 100,000 and a delegation was received by President Mitterrand in the glare of the national media. Mitterrand used the occasion to announce the creation of a single residence and work permit (valid for ten years and automatically renewable) for foreigners (Bouamama 1994).

The 1983 march brought the existence of the so-called second generation to public attention. It also represented a key stage in the political mobilization of young people of immigrant/colonial origin in France. Nevertheless, the subsequent attempt, in June 1984, to create a national structure for the movement revealed significant divisions between the Parisian- and Lyons-based collectives that had been formed after the march. In particular, a split emerged between those who favored the construction of an autonomous "Maghrebi" movement and those committed to working closely with French antiracist and other organizations. This led to the disintegration of the Parisian collective, but a group of its former members launched an appeal in July 1984 for a second march that came to be known as Convergence 84. The organizers aimed to highlight the culturally and ethnically mixed nature of French society and also the importance of strategic cooperation between Franco-Maghrebi and traditional antiracist associations. However, the unfolding of Convergence 84 served instead to underline the gulf between French antiracist activists and young people of immigrant/colonial origin and the march ended in Paris in an atmosphere of disillusionment and recriminations (Jazouli 1992: 81–94; Bouamama 1994: 89–107).

It was at the final Parisian rally of Convergence 84 that members of SOS-Racisme made their first public appearance, selling a badge bearing the slogan "Hands off my pal" (*Touche pas à mon pote*). The association had been founded several months previously by a group of Paris-based students and political activists opposed to racist violence and the rise of the FN (see Juhem 2001). The badge proved extremely popular with young people (from a range of different backgrounds) and by the end of March 1985 over 300,000 had been sold (*Libération* 25 March 1985). In the intervening period, SOS-Racisme's articulate and charismatic president, Harlem Désir (the French-born son of a West Indian father and an Alsatian mother), appeared on a current affairs television program and generated valuable publicity for the new association.[4] Thereafter its profile was further raised by prominent intellectuals, entertainers, media figures, and politicians who agreed to wear the badge publicly and act as sponsors (*parrains*). All of these factors contributed to a highly successful first six months for SOS-Racisme that culminated in the organization of a free concert at the Place de la Concorde in Paris on 15 June 1985, which was attended by an estimated 300,000 people (Désir 1985; Hargreaves 1991).

The rapid rise of SOS-Racisme did, however, generate a significant amount of controversy. The Franco-Maghrebi associations that had participated in the 1983 march and Convergence 84, for example, accused SOS-Racisme of attempting to marginalize their movement (most of the founders of the association had not been involved in either of these events) and of substituting a moral(istic) denunciation of racism for their specific demands for equal rights. The presence of members of the Jewish students' organization UEJF (*Union des étudiants juifs de France*) and the perceived underrepresentation and limited influence of Franco-Maghrebis within the leadership of SOS-Racisme also caused concern (*Le Monde*, 10 May 1985; Kettane 1985: 33). Moreover Harlem Désir's repeated insistence that SOS-Racisme was an independent and apolitical movement against racism and the FN increasingly came to be questioned. Critics on both the political Left and Right claimed that the PS was manipulating SOS-Racisme in order to mobilize young people for the forthcoming legislative elections (*Le Figaro* 28 March 1985; *Le Monde* 21 September 1985).

In this section I have presented a brief historical account of the main events leading up to the creation of the French antiracist association SOS-Racisme in 1984. As I have indicated, the circumstances surrounding its emergence and the nature of its links with the French Socialist Party quickly became topics of widespread public and political debate. The remainder of the chapter will present a more detailed analysis of a range of prominent, and conflicting, accounts of SOS-Racisme's origins and development. I will suggest that these can be understood as forms of political myth mobilized in ongoing struggles about organizational identities, political participation, and antiracist politics.

## POLITICAL MYTHS, ORGANIZATIONAL IDENTITIES, AND ANTIRACIST POLITICS

Political myths are an important aspect of the political imagination in most, if not all, human societies. This has been particularly true historically in France, where "political upheavals have constantly been accompanied by an amazing mythological effervescence" in the period since the 1789 Revolution (Girardet 1986: 11). Conspiracy myths and ideas of a Golden Age, for example, have emerged at regular intervals and offered ways of making sense of complex events and processes such as revolutions or industrialization (see Girardet 1986). At a much more mundane level, but no less significantly, a number of radically different "mythological" narratives about SOS-Racisme's origins and function have developed in the years since its creation in 1984. These accounts provide competing explanations of the association's early success and popularity, and remain important reference points in current debates about antiracist and immigration politics. In the following sections, I examine the contested history of SOS-Racisme, drawing on both published sources and material from field research which I conducted in 1993–94.

## Origin Myths

The production of myths about SOS-Racisme's origins and the definition of its identity were crucial tasks for the association's founders, especially in the first few months of its existence. In a series of interviews with journalists, Harlem Désir and Julien Dray (the association's first president and vice president respectively) repeatedly emphasized the new association's originality and distinctiveness with respect to existing antiracist and immigrant organizations and provided accounts of its creation. Both men subsequently published books in which they developed these "myths" in more detail. I intend to focus here on Désir's and Dray's books and to show how they present a particular construction of SOS-Racisme's history and identity.

The first to be published was *Touche pas à mon pote* by Harlem Désir (1985). The book covers the initial twelve months of SOS-Racisme's existence and also contains a brief autobiographical portrait. (It was later translated into several other European languages.) In the second chapter, a series of events is described which Désir himself refers to, without further elaboration, as "the foundation myth of the association" (1985: 148). One evening in October 1984, Désir recounts, he and a group of student friends had arranged to meet together for a pizza. A member of the group, a Senegalese man called Diégo, arrived late and visibly upset. Diégo then explained that on his way to join them a woman in the same metro carriage had cried out that her purse had been stolen. He had been the only black person in the carriage and all the other passengers had turned and looked suspiciously in his direction. Although the woman had subsequently found her purse, Diégo had been so angered by this example of "everyday racism" (*racisme ordinaire*) that he had resolved to return to Senegal. Désir claims that Diégo's experience convinced the other members of the group that they had to "react" (*réagir*), and that the decision to create a new association called SOS-Racisme was made in the days that followed (see Désir 1985: 23–25).

The other chapters of *Touche pas à mon pote* outline the ways in which the association's founders secured the support of celebrity sponsors (*parrains*), succeeded in attracting media attention and organized a series of demonstrations, concerts, and other initiatives. Désir is concerned throughout to highlight SOS-Racisme's originality and distinctiveness with regard not only to established antiracist and immigrant associations but also to political parties. Antiracist and human rights organizations such as the Human Rights League (LDH), International League against Racism and Anti-Semitism (LICRA), and the Movement against Racism and for Friendship between Peoples (MRAP), for example, are criticized for their failure to prevent the rise of racism and are dismissed as "too official, too unwieldy, too bureaucratic" (26). SOS-Racisme, on the other hand, is presented as a dynamic, youthful rejection of racism and intolerance (145). The various associations which participated in the 1983 and 1984 marches against racism and for equality (the so-called Beur movement) are portrayed, for their part, as "the expression of the particular demands of a specific community," i.e., North Africans in France. According to Désir, the founders of SOS-Racisme deliberately set out, in contrast, "to ignore the traditional divisions between communities" and to build "intercommunity solidarity" (*une solidarité intercommunautaire*) (103, 33).

In addition, Désir emphasizes the nonpartisan and moral nature of SOS-Racisme's approach, as well as its difference from traditional political organizations. The association's spokespeople made the first of these points frequently over the course of 1985, in response to allegations that SOS-Racisme was closely linked to the Socialist Party. Thus, in a newspaper interview before the June 1985 concert in Paris, Désir stated: "First of all, our orientation is a moral orientation. Our positions are based on a certain number of principles, which are neither partisan nor political" (quoted in *Libération*, 13 June 1985; see also Désir 1985: 145–46). The second point is developed in *Touche pas à mon pote*, where Désir insists that SOS-Racisme has nothing in common with the "quiet, dusty respectability" (*pignon poussiéreux sur rue tranquille*) of traditional organizations, which do little more, he implies, than turn out for the annual May Day demonstration (145). Désir argues that the association's media-oriented strategy (with its reliance on concerts and badges) is more appealing to young people than conventional forms of political activism involving regular committee meetings and the distribution of leaflets (145; see also Désir's comments quoted in *Libération*, 25 March 1985).

In most respects, the section of Julien Dray's book *SOS Génération* (1987) devoted to SOS-Racisme is very similar to Désir's earlier account in its presentation of the association's history and identity. Dray writes, for example, that SOS-Racisme was created by a "group of friends" in response to the emergence of the National Front and a rise in racist attacks (Dray 1987: 204). He too emphasizes that "SOS-Racisme is independent. Totally" (216). Like Désir, he argues that SOS-Racisme differs from "Beur" associations in being "a generational movement" rather than one based on a specific ethnic or religious identity (214). Dray is also concerned, finally, to highlight the originality and effectiveness of SOS-Racisme's use of concerts and other media-oriented events to involve young people in the fight against racism (208–9).

An important difference, however, is that the "foundation myth" involving the Senegalese student Diégo does not appear in Dray's book. It is replaced by an origin myth or narrative of a more explicitly political nature. Whereas Désir had included relatively little on the previous activist experiences of the founder members, Dray situates the creation of SOS-Racisme in relation to his and other members' break with "leftism" (*gauchisme*) and the "minority action" of Trotskyist groups such as the Revolutionary Communist League (Dray 1987: 193, 185). He states that: "At the start, we thought: let's take the opposite approach to the tiny [leftist] splinter groups and play the media card, completely and unashamedly" (205). The origins of SOS-Racisme are thus traced back by Dray to his and others' dissatisfaction with the perceived sectarian and marginal nature of far-left politics, presented as completely divorced from the interests and preoccupations of the mass of the population (183).

A review of these two books, along with the numerous interviews with Dray and Désir which were published in newspapers and magazines in 1985 and 1986, provides valuable insights into the ways in which the founders of SOS-Racisme sought to construct not only a distinctive identity for the new association but also a particular view (or views) of its origins.[5] As I have shown here, Désir and Dray actively sought, both in interviews and in their own books, to promote particular myths about the origins of SOS-Racisme as well as to identify the association's distinctiveness and assert its superiority over other antiracist or immigrant organizations. The image of SOS-Racisme that emerged from these accounts was, however, rejected by many activists in the antiracist and human rights movements as well as by external commentators. Almost immediately a number of alternative narratives—or myths—about the circumstances surrounding the association's creation and about its political function began to circulate in activist circles and in the national press. These included several types of conspiracy theories.

### Conspiracy Theories

For at least the past two centuries, conspiracy theories have occupied a central place in the political imagination of European countries such as France (and elsewhere). As Girardet has noted, the "spectre" of Jewish, Jesuit, and Masonic plots to seize political power and achieve global domination has continuously "haunted" French society over this period (Girardet 1986: 32). In his study of anti-Jesuit conspiracy theories in nineteenth-century France, Geoffrey Cubitt has sought to explain the appeal of such forms of political analysis. He suggests that: "conspiracy theories do three things: explain what happens as the intended product of conscious human volition; establish the division of humanity into two opposed camps; and affirm a discrepancy between the surface appearance and the hidden reality of human affairs. For convenience, these may be called the 'intentionalist,' the 'dualist,' and the 'occultist' functions of conspiracy theory" (Cubitt 1993: 296–97). In other words, a conspiracy theory is a way of "imagining" politics that asserts that a given event or series of events is the direct result of the deliberate action of a particular conspiratorial group; that there is a sharp contrast between this minority and the vast majority of the society's population; and that a radical difference exists between the outward appearance of the world and its true nature or reality (see also Cubitt 1989: 13–18).

According to Cubitt, an analytical distinction can be drawn between two "rhetorical styles" found in conspiracy theories. The first, which he describes as the "conspirator-centered" style, is mainly concerned to identify the particular individuals involved in a conspiracy and to trace the links between them. As Cubitt notes, this style of conspiracy theory tends to be characterized by "[t]he strong odour of card-index" (1989: 20). The "plan-centered" style, on the other hand, focuses less on cataloging individuals than on revealing "a sinister pattern" between apparently unconnected events. Cubitt argues that both of these styles are present in most conspiracy theories, although one or the other may predominate (1993: 296).

Over the past twenty years, a number of conspiracy theories involving allegations of political manipulation have been put forward to account for the creation and early success of SOS-Racisme (see, for example, Pfister 1988: 71–72; Closets 1990: 254–88). Perhaps the most well-known and controversial of these is contained in Serge Malik's *Histoire secrète de SOS-Racisme* (1990). An active member of SOS-Racisme from February 1985 until April 1986, Malik contests the "official" versions of the association's origins and purpose provided by Désir and Dray. He sets out to expose the "secret history" that, he claims, the leadership has concealed both from ordinary members of SOS-Racisme and from the general public. Describing the creation of the association as "a manipulation carried out by professionals" (*[u]ne manip de pros*), he challenges in turn the leadership's depiction of SOS-Racisme's nature, function, and achievements (Malik 1990: 40).

First, Malik alleges that SOS-Racisme was not the politically neutral or independent association that its founders pretended. He suggests, on the contrary, that there was a very close, even organic, relationship between SOS-Racisme (or at least its leadership) and the Socialist Party (PS). On the one hand, he emphasizes repeatedly that Dray and other leading figures were all members of the Socialist Party, and that many had been active previously in student or far-left politics. On the other, he claims that two members of Mitterrand's presidential staff, Jean-Louis Bianco and Jacques Attali, were heavily involved, with Désir and Dray, in both the launch of the association and its subsequent development. The political neutrality of SOS-Racisme, he concludes, was more "apparent" than "real' (79–82).

Secondly, Malik implies that the primary motivation of those who founded SOS-Racisme—Julien Dray in particular—was to further their own political careers and ambitions and that the creation of a movement against racism and the rise of the National Front (FN) was simply a means to this end rather than a reflection of a more deep-seated commitment to the antiracist struggle. He suggests again that appearances are deceptive and that "SOS-Racisme is in reality only a phantom movement. Its real function is to be the public relations office and personal pressure group of Julien Dray" (174). In Malik's view, Dray deliberately used SOS-Racisme to build up a network of influential contacts and increase his individual standing within the Socialist Party, with the aim of eventually becoming a deputy. The ordinary people who joined SOS-Racisme to combat racism, he states bluntly, were "used, abused, manipulated in the exclusive service of Dray's career and the political line of the PS" (159).

According to Malik, Dray's calculation at the outset was that the launch of an antiracist youth movement was likely to be the most effective means of assuring his own promotion within the Socialist Party. The PS had not been able to forge lasting links with the Franco-Maghrebi associations involved in the 1983–84 marches and was relatively absent from the field of anti-racism. Having identified this "niche" (*créneau*) (39), Dray then proceeded to develop the idea of SOS-Racisme and to enlist the support of key figures in the Socialist Party. As far as the Socialists were concerned, Malik asserts, the creation of SOS-Racisme appeared to offer a welcome way of capitalizing on the "Beur" movement and mobilizing young potential voters in the run-up to the 1986 legislative and 1988 presidential elections. Malik continues that SOS-Racisme's subsequent success and the role it was perceived to have played in securing Mitterrand's reelection as president in 1988 ensured that Dray was rewarded with a nomination as the PS candidate for a relatively safe seat in the Essonne *département* to the south of Paris in the legislative elections held a few months later (158).

Finally, Malik provides an assessment of SOS-Racisme's achievements that differs significantly from that of the association's leadership. He states that "SOS has certainly succeeded in pushing back the rising tide of Beur demands, but definitely not that of racism, nor the influence of Le Pen" (154). In his view, the local-level, grassroots action and the concrete policy proposals developed by Franco-Maghrebi associations in the early 1980s were effectively "annihilated" by the emergence of SOS-Racisme and its emphasis on a media-oriented form of antiracism (154). He criticizes SOS-Racisme for its reliance on slogans and concerts and its resulting invisibility "on the ground" (*sur le terrain*), in housing estates and workplaces where acts of racism and discrimination occur on a daily basis (175). Indeed, Malik even claims that SOS-Racisme's leaders have contributed to a "trivialization" (*banalisation*) of racism by their frequent (ab)use of the term "racist" as a way of stigmatizing their opponents or for other, purely polemical reasons (167). Rather than preventing the expansion of Le Pen's National Front, he concludes, SOS-Racisme has in fact been "the red carpet used by the far right in France to emerge from the shadows into the light" (175).

The publication of Malik's *Histoire secrète de SOS-Racisme* in the summer of 1990 attracted a significant amount of press coverage, although this was heavily determined by the general political orientation of the newspapers concerned. The right-wing daily press, for example, seized on the book as convincing proof of the association's links with and support for Mitterrand and the Socialist Party (*Le Quotidien de Paris*, 1 June 1990; *Le Figaro*, 2 June 1990). The weekly paper of the National Front, for its part, carried long extracts from the book, claiming that it showed that the association had been controlled by "Zionists" from the Jewish students' organization UEJF (*National Hebdo*, 14–20 June 1990; see also *Aspects de la France*, 12 July 1990). The left-leaning weekly magazine *Le Nouvel Observateur*, however, chose to publish an interview with Harlem Désir in which he dismissed Malik's account as "pseudo-revelations" and "a falsified re-writing of history" (*Le Nouvel Observateur*, 7–13 June 1990). Other center-left daily and weekly publications played down the importance of the book, describing it as a fairly predictable "settling of scores" on the part of a former member of SOS-Racisme with his erstwhile fellow activists and its allegations as "not really new" (*Politis*, 7–13 June 1990; *Le Monde*, 15–16 June 1990).

It is not my intention here to assess the truth or falsity of the various assertions that Malik makes in the course of his book. As I indicate in the next part of this chapter, the exact nature of the circumstances surrounding SOS-Racisme's creation continued to be the subject of claim and counterclaim throughout the period of my fieldwork and it remains difficult to draw firm conclusions even today. The point I want to emphasize is, rather, that Malik's account can be analyzed as a type of conspiracy theory in which the "conspirator-centered" style predominates. As an "explanation" of the emergence of SOS-Racisme, I would argue, it performs the three functions (intentionalist, dualist, and occultist) that Cubitt suggests are characteristic of conspiracy theories.

First, the association's rise is presented as the result of a deliberate strategy on the part of Dray and influential figures in the Socialist Party. Secondly, the small "conspiratorial group" around Dray is sharply distinguished from the majority of activists and members of the public who, the implication is, are unaware of the "manipulation" that is taking place. Finally, the "official" image of SOS-Racisme—as an apolitical, spontaneous response to racism and the National Front—is contrasted with the underlying "reality"—the association was created in order to further Dray's political ambitions by serving as an electoral tool for the Socialist Party. The emphasis throughout is on identifying the connections between, on the one hand, Dray and (to a lesser extent) Désir, and, on the other, senior figures in the Socialist Party, including Mitterrand himself. In this sense, the book adopts a conspirator-centered rather than a plan-centered style of argument.

An interpretation of SOS-Racisme's history in terms of political manipulation or conspiracy, however, is problematic for several reasons. As Cubitt has pointed out, one of the weaknesses of conspiracy theories is that they deny "the improvisational element in human affairs and the intentional openness of historical outcomes" (Cubitt 1993: 314) by presenting everything as the intended outcome of conscious human action. Malik implies, for example, that SOS-Racisme's success was inevitable, after the decision had been made to launch the association. Although it is true that SOS-Racisme had the considerable advantage of massive state funding (for its first concert and similar initiatives) and relatively easy access to the media, there was no guarantee that the association would attract widespread public support. This is a point that a member of SOS-Racisme made to me in an interview. While acknowledging that the association's creation was "a real political decision" on the part of a group around Dray, he added that: "What was spontaneous was people's reaction. . . . It wasn't written in stone though, even though there had been a decision to [launch the association]. People have decided to create other movements in the past but . . . [The success of SOS-Racisme] even exceeded, I think, at a certain point, initial expectations" (Interview, 3 October 1994). The association's popularity, in other words, could not simply be planned or "decided" in advance by Dray and the other founder members. It is a recognition of this element of historical unpredictability that is absent from Malik's account. Instead, the rise of SOS-Racisme is treated as an inevitable, continuous process, consciously planned and realized from beginning to end by a small group of conspirators.

The distinction that Malik draws between a "conspiratorial" minority and a "non-conspiratorial" majority raises a second problem. As Cubitt has shown, this kind of dualism is a characteristic feature of conspiracy theories. In the case of Malik's analysis of SOS-Racisme, however, it leads to a depiction of the association's grassroots activists and supporters as mere pawns in the political games of Dray (to advance his career) and the Socialist Party hierarchy (to ensure Mitterrand's reelection as president in 1988). Represented as an undifferentiated mass, "[t]he activists" (1990: 159) are viewed by Malik only as the unwitting victims of a political manipulation and not as actors and strategists in their own right. Malik completely ignores the fact that the existence of a range of sources of information combined with a relatively high level of general education means that citizens in contemporary Western democracies such as France are not easily manipulated by political or other elites (see Charlot 1994: 131).

Thus there is no attempt in the book to explore the reasons for the continuing involvement of many people—including Malik himself (see *Politis*, 7–13 June 1990)—even after allegations that the Socialist Party was attempting a "take-over" (*récupération*) of SOS-Racisme had appeared in the national press during the spring of 1985 (*Le Figaro*, 28 March 1985; *Le Quotidien de Paris*, 28 March 1985). This is an issue that I have attempted to address elsewhere (Gibb 2001b), through a detailed examination of an incident in which pressure from grassroots activists forced the association's leadership to abandon plans for an electoral agreement with a prominent politician. The material discussed there highlights the fact that grassroots members of SOS-Racisme have highly developed political perspectives and strategies of their own and are not just puppets of their leaders. This is a very different view of SOS-Racisme's ordinary members to the one that emerges from Malik's account.

*An Ongoing Controversy*

The origin myths and conspiracy theories considered above can be regarded as political "position-takings" (to use Bourdieu's terminology) in a struggle to define the dominant forms and meanings of antiracism in France during the late 1980s. The circumstances surrounding the creation of SOS-Racisme in 1984 remained the subject of controversy well into the next decade, however, as I discovered when I conducted field research in Paris in the mid-1990s. In the final part of this chapter I examine a number of further accounts of the association's history published in 1993 and 1994, which appeared to confirm earlier versions of events. I also discuss material taken from interviews that I conducted during this same period with representatives of other antiracist or immigrant organizations. What the interview extracts highlight is the importance of ongoing struggles in the present over the nature and significance of past mobilizations.

In 1993, the former special adviser to President Mitterrand, Jacques Attali, published the first volume of his political memoirs. It contained the following entry, dated Monday 1 April 1985: "Harlem Désir launches 'SOS Racisme.' The original idea came from Jean-Loup Salzmann and Julien Dray, and Jean-Louis Bianco [the General Secretary of Mitterrand's Elysée staff] organized everything else" (Attali 1993: 793). There is no elaboration of this comment, however, and the actual steps supposedly taken by Bianco to set up SOS-Racisme are left unspecified. Nevertheless, Bianco himself was interviewed on this subject in April 1994 by three journalists undertaking an investigation of Mitterrand's alleged links with members of the far right. When the book (Faux, Legrand, and Perez 1994) was published six months later it contained a long extract from this interview. In response to a direct question about the role he played in the creation of SOS-Racisme, Bianco states: "Personally, I tried to help them [the association's founders] to obtain funding from government ministries" (quoted in Faux, Legrand, and Perez 1994: 30). He also admits to putting Dray and the others in contact with Mitterrand's communications and marketing advisers.

On the basis of this and other material, the authors of the book suggest that the promotion of SOS-Racisme was in fact the second prong of a twofold electoral strategy pursued by Mitterrand in the early 1980s. The first was to facilitate the emergence of Le Pen and the National Front, in order to foster divisions within the mainstream right and split the right-wing vote. "[O]peration SOS-Racisme," on the other hand, was intended to remobilize a left-wing electorate (and the Socialist Party) around antiracism in the context of falling opinion poll ratings. This argument is, however, rejected by Julien Dray, who is also quoted in the book. Dray denies that SOS-Racisme was the result of a "Machiavellian calculation" on the part of Mitterrand and insists that "the PS saw [the arrival] of SOS as a divine surprise as it did not know how to respond to the FN" (quoted in Faux, Legrand, and Perez 1994: 31).

During my fieldwork in 1993 and 1994, therefore, the history of SOS-Racisme remained the subject of claim and counterclaim among high-ranking politicians, journalists, and members of the association. Within the broader antiracist movement at this time, the origins and role of SOS-Racisme also continued to generate heated debate. Many argued that the development of SOS-Racisme had been encouraged by the Socialist administration in the mid-1980s in a deliberate attempt to depoliticize the antiracist struggle and to undermine the "Beur" movement. One of the organizers of the 1983 March, who later joined SOS-Racisme for a short period, stated in an interview published in December 1993: "I think that the Beur movement failed because of political manipulation. The Socialist Party wanted a moral type of anti-racist movement: with 'Touche pas à mon pote' it was no longer a question of the struggle for equality. I, personally, allowed myself to be taken in" (Titouss

1993: 45). A similar argument was put forward by a former General Secretary of the antiracist association MRAP when I interviewed him in 1994:

> Everything was done in order to get this mass of young people with them [i.e., SOS-Racisme], but on a vague basis. That is: by definition, a festival [such as the massive free concert SOS-Racisme organized in June 1985] is the vaguest type of political event there can be. There's no analysis, it's more emotional. The slogan "Touche pas à mon pote," too, is an emotional and not a political slogan. Thus, a political analysis of what racism is, what its causes are, and how to combat it was removed. It was replaced by this idea of what was called "the moral generation." So that forms part of the operation as well: to depoliticize the antiracist movement and create an apolitical anti-racist movement. (Interview, 17 November 1994)

The suggestion here is that the "moral" type of antiracism promoted by SOS-Racisme was attractive to the incumbent Socialist administration because it turned attention away not only from the specific demands for equal rights formulated by Franco-Maghrebi activists but also from a socioeconomic analysis of the underlying causes of racism.

The related idea that SOS-Racisme had been launched by the authorities to prevent the further development of an autonomous Franco-Maghrebi movement was also current in activist circles during the period of my fieldwork. When I myself interviewed several activists who had participated in the "Beur" movement and then founded another association (the Comité national contre la double peine), one of them stated: "As we see it, the authorities tried to set up those associations—such as SOS-Racisme or France-Plus—because they saw that they were going to face a movement of young Arabs. It was *inconceivable*, as far as they were concerned, that there could be a movement originating from immigrants. . . . For the government, that couldn't be tolerated; it was out of the question" (Interview, 8 December 1994). Adding that he himself "hated" SOS-Racisme, the same activist went on to provide the following assessment of SOS-Racisme's achievements: "At a certain point, there was a movement of young people who were protesting against all the inequalities and all the discrimination they were facing. What is the most serious aspect is that [SOS-Racisme] has set back the movements associated with immigrants and their descendants immeasurably, by creating a cloud of smoke. They have set people back, and they have discredited the movements associated with immigrants and their descendants. And I resent them a lot for that. They have done a lot of damage politically." For this activist, then, the emergence of SOS-Racisme undermined the action initiated by Franco-Maghrebi activists in the early 1980s against racism and in favor of equal rights, thereby arresting the development of an autonomous Franco-Maghrebi section of the wider antiracist movement.

A negative assessment of SOS-Racisme's contribution to the struggle against racism was also provided by a representative of a council of immigrant organizations (Conseil des associations immigrées en France) whom I interviewed at this time:

> After a dozen years of the existence of SOS-Racisme, nothing has changed. The simple reason for this is that SOS-Racisme has remained . . . The committees, if you look at SOS-Racisme's committees, where do you find them? You find them in the universities, in the big cities, in Paris for example. You are not going to find a committee in, for example, Mantes-la-Jolie [a town in the Paris suburbs], where there's trouble. You don't find a committee of SOS-Racisme there. Yet, racism exists there on a day-to-day basis, segregation on a day-to-day basis. Why? Because young people there do not believe in [SOS-Racisme]. . . . They think that those people [involved in SOS-Racisme] . . . are not people who are close to them: they are people who are in it for something else. (Interview, 5 December 1994)

According to this activist, SOS-Racisme had failed to establish itself in the housing estates around cities such as Paris and was thus unable effectively to address the racism and discrimination experienced by the people living there on a daily basis. The association lacked credibility in the eyes of young people on these estates, who suspected its involvement in the antiracist struggle to be merely a means to other political ends.

These extracts from interviews with members of a number of immigrant and antiracist organizations highlight some of the tensions concerning SOS-Racisme and its position in the French antiracist movement that existed during the period of my fieldwork in the mid-1990s. To a large extent these date back to the association's emergence in 1984 and its subsequent impact on antiracist and immigrant mobilizing and claims making in France. Together with the other material discussed in this chapter, the interviews draw attention to the way in which the meaning of past political mobilizations is a key stake in ongoing debates between members of different antiracist and immigrant organizations.

## CONCLUSION

As the other chapters in this section also demonstrate, processes of political mobilization and claims making by immigrants and other social agents involve symbolic (and material) struggles over organizational identities, modes of civic engagement, and issues of citizenship and belonging.

This chapter has examined conflicting accounts of the circumstances surrounding the creation of the French antiracist association SOS-Racisme in the mid-1980s, arguing that these can be analyzed as examples of two different types of political myth: origin myths and conspiracy theories. It has also explored the different ways in which the forms of political and civic engagement promoted by SOS-Racisme, and its relationship to political parties and the state, were viewed by its founder members and by representatives of Franco-Maghrebi and other antiracist organizations. The negative impact of the rise of SOS-Racisme, closely linked to the governing Socialist Party, on more "autonomous" (and politically challenging) immigrant and antiracist organizations emerges as a key theme in the interviews discussed in the final part of the chapter. Although the concept of "political opportunity structure" is problematic, as the chapters by Però and Garapich in this section rightly emphasize, the material discussed here does illustrate how the political activism of immigrants and their descendants can be shaped in important ways by the structure of the wider political field and the configuration of (party) political power.

ACKNOWLEDGMENTS

I am very grateful to Caroline B. Brettell and Deborah Reed-Danahay, and to my colleagues Bridget Fowler, Justin Kenrick, Andrew Smith, and Satnam Virdee, for their comments on earlier versions of this chapter. I bear sole responsibility, of course, for any errors or weaknesses that it may contain. All translations from the French are my own. The original research on which the chapter is based was funded by the Economic and Social Research Council of Great Britain (Award Number: R00429234105).

NOTES

1. See Debbasch and Bourdon (1997: 116–25) and also Barthélemy (2000: 11–57) for an account of the historical background to the 1901 Law.
2. Viet (1998: 428) notes that between 1981 and 1993 the number of associations increased from 600 to 4,000.
3. The media subsequently labeled it "The March of the *Beurs*," this being the backslang (*verlan*) term used primarily (but not exclusively) by young people of North African origin in the Parisian suburbs to define themselves. Here, however, I will retain the original title "The March for Equality and against Racism" for two main reasons. First, the term "*beur*" originated and was employed chiefly in the housing estates around Paris; young people of North African origin in the suburbs of Marseille and Lyons, where the idea of the march was conceived, did not generally refer to themselves as "beurs" but rather as "*maghrébins*" (Wihtol de Wenden 1991: 330). The media's subsequent adoption and often indiscriminate use of the category "beur" has increasingly led to its rejection by young people even in Paris (Barbara 1992). Secondly, the label "The March of the Beurs" gives the impression that only people of North African origin were

involved, whereas marchers with other backgrounds were also present, albeit in lesser numbers (Bouamama 1994: 68–70). In the light of the above points, I will refer throughout this chapter to young people of North African origin as *Franco-Maghrebis* and avoid the term "beur" as far as possible.

4. As Negrouche (1992: 49) has indicated, Harlem Désir became "a sort of Robin Hood of antiracism, highly prized by journalists."

5. Nevertheless, as the Italian sociologist Alberto Melucci has argued, the process of collective identity formation involves an interaction and negotiation between the various levels of an organization or movement; an analysis of "leaders' discourse" and the "top" of collective action alone is not sufficient (Melucci 1995: 52). For an analysis of the public statements of the association's leaders combined with an investigation of the local level of action and the perspectives of ordinary members see Gibb (2001b).

CHAPTER 8

# "Call Us Vote People"

## CITIZENSHIP, MIGRATION, AND TRANSNATIONAL POLITICS IN HAITIAN AND MEXICAN LOCATIONS

*Karen E. Richman*

TWENTY-FIVE YEARS after the debarkation of boatloads of poor Haitians in South Florida, Haitian immigrants are becoming citizens and voting Haitian American politicians into local and statewide government offices. Meanwhile, these citizens are wooed by Haitians running in the Haitian presidential elections. They are targets of vigorous transnational campaigning even though they may not participate in the political process.

This chapter analyzes Haitians' transborder citizenship in light of the growing scholarly literature on migrants' political transnationalism, in particular, the case of Mexico's deterritorialized political space and the tenacious campaigning of the politician known as the Tomato King. Like Mexico, the Haitian state has fashioned itself as a transterritorial entity, yet Haiti has neither established a mechanism for migrants to cast votes in elections nor recognized dual citizenship. This disparity was magnified in the recent debate over whether a Haitian American businessman and frozen food magnate in the United States should have been allowed to run as a candidate in Haiti's 2005–6 presidential elections. Even as migrants' remittances constitute the largest source of external funding for their home economies, migrants' aspirations both to incorporate into their new setting and to be politically involved in their home state are as yet unfulfilled.

Sources for this discussion include interviews with activists, leaders, and observers of transmigrant and immigrant politics who are citizens of Haiti and Mexico and Haitian-born and Mexican-born citizens of the United States. Haitian and Mexican news media, including radio broadcasts, are also resources for the chapter. The analysis draws especially upon my ongoing ethnography of Haitian transnational migration in Haiti, South Florida, and Chicago and my study of the rise of transnationalist discourse in Haitian politics (Richman 1992, 2001, and 2005). The comparative discussion engages the growing literature in sociology, anthropology, and political science on Mexican transborder political agency and civic participation.

## HAITIAN POLITICAL PROCESSES IN SOUTH FLORIDA

In Florida, six Haitian Americans have been elected to local offices. One Haitian American was voted into a statewide office. When "the gentleman from Haiti" was introduced by the speaker to the state legislature on its first day of business after the election, Philip Brutus received a standing ovation. Brutus says he was inspired by Marie St. Fleur's reelection to the state legislature of Massachusetts, where she is now joined by Linda Dorsina, another Democrat and Haitian American woman, married to an Irish American from a prominent political family. St. Fleur and Dorsina were elected in multiethnic, working-class districts where 10 percent of eligible voters are Haitians.[1] Brutus, a Democrat, faced better odds in a district where 20 percent of the eligible voters are Haitian Americans. But, as he recounted to Haitian American journalist Marjorie Valbrun, the decision to court other ethnic groups, especially African Americans, helped him in his second attempt to get elected. Brutus told Valbrun, "I stood there representing the Haitian nation, all black people, all immigrants, all poor people . . . who dreamed of the day." He acknowledged the perception of Haitian supporters whose votes helped carry him to the State House. "They see me as a guy who can represent everyone, but who they can still call 'our guy'" (Valbrun 2001).

"I don't think they're going to call us 'boat people' anymore," a Haitian immigrant told the same reporter, "They're going to call us 'vote people.' We're voters." Haitian immigrants' shift to voting citizens surged in the late 1990s, along with other United States immigrants, in response to punitive amendments to a 1996 welfare reform bill denying worker and other benefits to noncitizens. These new Haitian-born U.S. citizens had in fact been singled out for training to operate the voting equipment. Philip Brutus, while running for election to the Florida legislature, appeared on Creole public access television programs to demonstrate how to vote. He had attributed his narrow loss (by only fifty-one votes) in the previous election to the disqualification of double-voted ballots cast by new Haitian citizens and successfully remedied the deficit (Valbrun 2001). Joe Celestin, recently elected mayor of North Miami after two campaign runs, regularly attends naturalization ceremonies to congratulate Haitians who have become new

U.S. citizens and distributes voter registration forms to them.[2] "Politics is a science," he told Valbrun with a smile. His rational approach to politics, which is recounted in detail in Valbrun's report, included a study of the demography of Haitian settlements in Dade County, which determined where to launch a campaign. His methods also included a strategic shift to the Republican Party after two unsuccessful tries to get elected as a Democrat.

### "(Don't) Vote for Me"

At the same time as these new Haitian citizens were helping to elect coethnic citizens to local and state office in the United States, they were receiving campaign visits from Haitian politicians running for office in Haiti. Indeed because of the dangers of being in public in Haiti, the campaign might have been more visible outside than inside the nation-state. The campaign for the Haitian presidency in the United States saw candidates adopting U.S. campaign styles, including holding the first three-party debates in front of Haitian audiences in Boston (Bracken 2005). Dany Toussaint, a notorious strongman, launched his campaign with a huge billboard along Interstate 85 bearing his image, decorated in the red, white, and blue colors of the Haitian flag, with the text, "Dany Toussaint, Haiti's Next President! Ensuring Security, Health, Tourism, Education & Agriculture" (Charles 2005).

The presidential candidates' transnational political strategy took a page from Aristide's first campaign play book, which took place outside as much as inside Haiti. His Lavalas (Deluge) campaign had a branch called "Lavalas Pou Lakay" (Lavalas for Home), as well as a "Lavalas Lakay" (Lavalas at Home) (Richman 1992). During his presidential campaign, Aristide broke new ground by validating the diaspora and reformulating their experience in positive, vivid Creole idioms and metaphors. He promised inclusion, in stark contrast to previous Haitian regimes variously feared, ignored, and rejected by exiles. Significantly, Aristide directed his first major postvictory speech to Haitians outside. His New Year's Eve speech, entitled "Message to the Diaspora," concluded with this comforting vow:

> Sisters and brothers spread throughout the four cardinal points of the diaspora, even if we don't meet face to face, remember that you have a country that looks you in the eye so that you can look it in the eye, so that this face to face makes you want to throw yourself into its arms. Its arms are outstretched to welcome you, to kiss you, to embrace you as a child who did not leave to go away forever, but who left in order to return.
>
> Sè m a frè m k ap viv . . . nan 4 kwen dyaspora a, menm si nou pa wè fas a fas, sonje ke nou genyen yon peyi k ap gade ou nan je pou ou menm ou ka

gade l nan je, pou fas a fas sa a fè ou vin lage kò ou nan bra l. De bra l ouvè pou akeyi ou, pou bo ou, pou anbrase ou kòm pitit ki pat ale pou ale nèt, men ki te ale pou retounen bò isit.

What did Aristide mean by "return"? He explained during the same "Message to the Diaspora." Some Haitian migrants should return home to invest in businesses and create jobs, but the majority should continue straddling national boundaries. The Haitian state would now make it easier for them to do so. He said:

> You who are thirsty to return home, it doesn't mean you have to give up residence elsewhere. What we want is for you to be able to return home whenever you want and for you to be able to return where you are working now whenever you like. I am not asking you to return permanently and forsake the other place completely.

> Nou menm ki swaf retounen . . . lè ou rive, ou pa oblije rive nèt san ou pa ka retounen kote ou sòti a . . . Sa nou vle se ke ou kapab retounen lakay ou lè ou vle e retounen kote ou ap travay kounyè a lè ou vle tou. M pa mande ou vini isit nèt pou ou bliye lòt bò nèt.

Shortly after taking office in February 1991, Aristide announced the formation of a Dixième Department, modeled on the internal nine departments with cabinet-level representation, which would "govern" Haitians no matter where they resided. The arbitrary application of the department model to Haitians outside doomed it to fail, and many now laugh at the use of the words "the tenth," but Aristide's creation of a ministry to represent Haitians abroad was widely supported. This model continued after his exile in 2003, though the leadership post was demoted to secretary of state. President Aristide's vision of migrants as "the bank of the diaspora" (bank de dyaspora a) was hardly transformed in the discourse of the secretary of state for Haitians abroad who came to Chicago in 2004. He was addressing an audience of Haitians gathered at a Chicago hotel to discuss migrants' role in economic development in Haiti and to hobnob with the head of the U.S. State Department's Aid for International Development for Latin America.

Rhetorical and representational strategies play an important role in appropriating the dual loyalty of migrants. In neither his first nor his second terms, both of which were cut short by coups d'état, did President Aristide realize the first necessary step to guarantee migrants' rights as transborder citizens: recognition of dual citizenship for Haitians. This measure would have required a change in the Haitian constitution, which, as Nina Glick

Schiller and Georges Fouron (2001: 244) point out, a president was power-less to enact. In 2003, the 47th Haitian legislature considered a bill lifting restrictions on dual citizenship law, but it was not brought to a vote. Some blame the political chaos and violence that soon dissolved the government; others point to President Aristide's failure to press for passage of the legis-lation. In response to my query about why the political empowerment of the diaspora was not achieved, a Haitian man who has not emigrated said, "Aristide didn't care. It was all talk. He wasn't going to do anything to ad-vance the migrants' interests. The legislature [throughout the 1990s] was majority Lavalas [Aristide's party]. Why didn't they act?"

Rhetorical and representational strategies thus play an important role in appropriating the dual loyalty of migrants. In his chapter in this volume, Michal Garapich argues that the "politicization" of the migration experi-ence is a typical tool in nationalist discourse. In the case of Polish rhetoric of the state, migration is constructed as a traumatic experience of loss, thus creating a myth of return.

In his examination of the case of Guanajuato's United States-bound migrants during the last decade, Michael Smith (2003b) concludes that management of the discourse of "the migrant" is a key lever in the Partido Acción Nacional (PAN) state's and elites' efforts to co-opt migrants' local pride and translocal networks and practices. President Vicente Fox, who was governor of the state from 1991–2000, played a key role in the state's effort to constitute "a transnational Guanajuatense political subject" (Smith 2003b: 494).

In order to co-opt migrants, elites and the state reconfigure the mean-ings of "migrant," "region" and "citizen." Deployment of such reified terms extracts them from meaningful contexts, in which national and transna-tional structures and relations of differential power play key roles. The mi-grant is imagined as an abstract individual "freed" of a social context. That individual is nonetheless imagined as endowed with certain concrete char-acteristics: it is a male who became a man by passing through the rite of mi-gration into manhood. The establishment of this modern rite of passage has repeatedly been documented by ethnographers of contemporary Mexican-U.S. migration (Grimes 1998; Hondagneu-Sotelo 1994; Hirsch 2003).

Visual images do their part in turn to overdetermine this patriotic symbolic politics by fixing the relationship of migration to these dominant notions of gender and family (Smith 2003b: 497). In case anyone in Gua-najuato might have missed the masculine inflection of the Spanish term for "the migrant," visual images reinforced the masculinity of the migrant in relation to the femininity of those at home. Posters and statues in town squares depicted the heroic male migrant, with wife and children positioned

behind him in a relation of *respeto* (deference). Whether appearing on plac-
ards or off, and side by side with Governor Fox on television, the "poster
migrant" of Guanajuato during the 1990s was Angel Calderón, a migrant
whose collaboration with the state resulted in a concrete instance of the sort
of local development needed to stem the tide of out-migration: an assembly
plant. The promotion of this heroic migrant narrative masked how, by employing a low-paid female labor force, the factory reproduced the structure
of male emigration. Through such modes, states and elites present the il-
lusion of supporting migrants while actually doing little to promote their
political agency.

In the 1990 presidential campaign, Aristide's political rivals included
Marc Bazin, the U.S. favorite, who ultimately garnered only 11 percent of
the vote compared to Aristide's 67 percent. While Bazin barely acknowledged a role for the diaspora in his campaign for the 1990 presidential
election, in 2005 he was a zealous supporter of migrants' transnational
political empowerment. Significantly, his transnationalist political speech
writer (and campaign manager) was Leslie Voltaire, the former minister
of Haitians living abroad in the Aristide government. Reporting on a Bazin campaign stop in New York, Amy Bracken related how, in his effort
to show his transnationalist credentials, Bazin told the ninety or so New
York audience members that he had lived in Washington for eighteen years
on the staff of the World Bank. "And so I'll say to you, Haitians abroad,
Diaspora, with Bazin as president, you will have the right to vote," he
said. "With Bazin as president, you will have dual nationality." Bracken
comments that the audience silenced him with "wild applause." But, as she
reports in the insightful piece entitled "(Don't) Vote for Me," few would
be able to return to Haiti to vote in person. Absentee voting is not yet an
option for Haitians abroad.[3] Despite Haitian immigrants' inability to participate in the upcoming elections, the candidates continued to campaign
actively among them.

An American politician who represents a constituency that includes
Haitians has stepped in to address this void. On 25 January 2005, Florida
Democratic Representative Kendrick Meek, who could well be challenged
in the next election by a Haitian American candidate from his district,[4]
wrote letters to the Interim Prime Minister Latortue, President Bush, and
UN Secretary General Kofi Annan arguing for the establishment of means
that would allow Haitians to vote in the upcoming elections. In his letter,
cited below, Representative Meek lists other nation-states, and "even Iraq,"
that allow migrants to cast ballots in the United States and challenges Haiti
to do the same. He also calls upon his familiarity with Latortue and Latortue's understanding of the situation of Haitians in the United States.

Dear Prime Minister Latortue,

I write to request that your government take whatever actions are necessary to allow Haitian citizens living in the United States to vote in Haiti's upcoming national elections at a consulate or other appropriate location in the United States. While some Haitians undoubtedly would want to return home to vote, it is also likely that, for reasons of cost, family or work, others would greatly benefit from having the option of casting their ballots in the United States.

In our conversations, you have often spoken about the importance of free elections in Haiti to establish a permanent government and have those elections conducted this year. As you know, there are over a quarter million Haitians who are U.S. legal residents living in the United States. At present, voters must all return to Haiti to cast their ballots.

I am certain that you agree with me about the importance of ensuring the widest possible participation in the elections. Haiti has just celebrated the 200th anniversary of its independence from France. It is the second democracy in our hemisphere, with a long and proud history. However, the present voting requirement works against full voter participation by placing a heavy burden on Haitians living in the United States. Surely, Haiti can join other democracies in the world, including France, Ukraine, the Philippines, and even Iraq.

I am enclosing a copy of a letter I wrote to President Bush, urging him to provide Haiti with the funding and administrative assistance necessary to allow Haitians living in this country to vote in your elections. I am also enclosing a copy of a letter I wrote to United Nations Secretary-General Kofi Annan requesting his support and assistance.

However, the key is the willingness of your government to permit this change in the interests of making possible the widest possible voter participation in Haiti's elections.

In the interest of full democratic participation by your citizens, I urge you to do whatever is necessary to permit Haitians living in the United States to vote in the United States, rather than having to return to Haiti.

Thank you for your consideration of this important matter.
Sincerely yours,

KENDRICK B. MEEK
Member of Congress

*Citizenship and Candidates*

The Haitian constitution does not yet recognize the citizenship of Haitian nationals who became citizens elsewhere. To Dumarsais (Dumas)

Mécène Siméus, a U.S. citizen and a powerful mogul in the U.S. processed food industry, this law was just one more obstacle to be overcome in a long and successful business career whose 2005 declared goal was being elected to the presidency of Haiti.

Dumarsais Siméus represented himself as the Haitian Horatio Alger, whose rags to riches story uniquely qualified him to be president of Haiti. His campaign used the catchy tone of American-style political ads. Siméus described himself as the son of rural peasants, one of twelve children who grew up in a two-room hut in Pont Sondé, outside the town of Gonaïves. Siméus recounted dreaming of sailing for a new life in America. He attended a parochial high school in Port-au-Prince, later earning admission to Florida A&M University in Tallahassee. Siméus said he worked his way through school with menial jobs at factories and restaurants, eventually graduating from Howard University and the University of Chicago business school. Siméus climbed the corporate ladder at companies including Atari, Inc. and Rockwell International, eventually rising to the top ranks of Beatrice, a $2 billion multinational corporation. In 1996, he founded a fast food manufacturing company in Mansfield, Texas, with $160 million in annual sales, whose clients include Burger King, T.G.I. Fridays, and Denny's. The Web site for Siméus Foods International, Inc. (SFI) is an ode to the concept of progress: technological prowess, efficiency, speed, and precision. The site features a photographic image of a machine spitting out frozen, breaded meat patties. A woman, dressed in a white lab coat and yellow hard hat, minds the machine in this frozen, sanitized environment.

Siméus' narrative explained his late entry into politics last spring as a spontaneous response to the pleas of Haitian leaders. "Delegations of key Haitian business, civic and charitable leaders called on the global businessman, asking him to consider running for President and leading the land of his birth in a bold new direction" (http://www.simeus06.com). According to his press releases, he responded as if to a moral calling. He did not plan to enter politics, but rather was compelled to do so upon witnessing the relentless misery of Haiti. As a no-nonsense American who made it to the top of the corporate world, he knew what needed to be done. Excerpts from a campaign speech tout his technocratic, business know-how: "We will bring real business know-how from the outside world here to Haiti. And we will stand tall for all that is fair and good and true so that every child can grow up to achieve the Haitian dream."

Siméus further suggested that as an outsider and a respected citizen of the United States, he was not tainted by the corruption and cronyism "inside."

We have a chance right now to bring the light of democracy, transparency and freedom, to lift Haiti from the crushing weight of despair, and it is slipping away by the second. The choice is clear and it is in all of our hands. Do we continue the same old failed politics that has beggared our beloved country or do we bring real change to our nation, with strong new leadership that has actually created real jobs, built businesses in the real world, brought health care and clean water to the people of Haiti, and put food on the table for thousands of people around the planet? This is our chance to sweep away the failed, corrupt politics of the past and join hands to build a bold new vision of unity, prosperity and success. (http:// www.simeus06.com)

To fend off suspicions that this U.S. citizen was no longer a real Haitian, Siméus offered his peasant roots in Pont Sondé and evidence of competence in the vernacular: "There is no one in the political elite who speaks Creole [the language of Haiti's majority] as well as I do" (Lakshmanan 2005). (Such boasting was a measure of Aristide's influence on the valorization of Creole as a respectable idiom for political discourse.) As proof of his commitment to help rescue his poor relatives, he stated that he brought forty of them to the United States. But to stave off criticism of his residence outside, he insisted, "I have been coming back always" (2005). A campaign announcement read, "As required by the Constitution, he is a Haitian citizen of Haitian origin, owns property in Haiti and has been a continuous and visible presence there throughout his life, personally and through his foundation, which supplies clean water and health care to the people of Haiti." His campaign stated that the Siméus Foundation, a nonprofit charitable organization, was founded in 1999.

The campaign had also begun referring to their candidate as a "Haitian-Born Reformer Nominated by a Broad Coalition of Political Parties." In fact, he was the nominee of the party known as *Tèt Ansanm*, "All Together," a broad-based prodemocracy reform coalition with thirty senatorial candidates and ninety-nine candidates for deputy in the Haitian Congress. The branding of Siméus as a reformer strained credulity. The Haitian weekly *Haïti Progrés* viewed Siméus as the Bush administration's "own candidate" (2005). They reported that Siméus' campaign was "run by Rob Allyn, a Republican political consultant and hit-man for Bush's 2004 re-election campaign. Allyn falsely announced that Venezuelan President Hugo Chavez had lost the referendum for his recall in 2004 and was the architect of President Vicente Fox's 2000 election victory in Mexico."

Was this transborder citizen really challenging the political elite and the status quo? Having reached the upper ranks of transnational corporate capital,

if he had been elected, would he have promoted popular democratic participation? Siméus' campaign style was certainly "legible" to a U.S. electorate
through its discourse of hostility to the state, business know-how, humble
roots, and a meritorious reward of the American Dream. How credible it
was to Haitians is more questionable, since they have a very sensitive nose for
smelling out opportunistic, "house boy" and "prostitute" politicians, as Aristide once called the candidates running in 1989, many of whom ran again. It
seems unlikely that a plurality of the Haitian electorate who went on to elect
Aristide's populist successor, René Préval, would have recognized Siméus's
claims to legitimacy. The host of a Creole language news program, broadcast
on radio in Washington, D.C., dismissed Siméus in a conversation with me
as a "vakabon," a con man. Siméus is accused of paying judges on the Haitian
Supreme Court to take the unprecedented step of issuing a ruling bypassing
the decree of the Electoral Council that barred citizens of other nation-states
from running for election. Another political operator, a Florida republican,
told me during the Haitian presidential election that Siméus exaggerated the
impact of his influence in Gonaïves and the importance of "the little clinic"
he built there. A Haitian physician who is resident of Haiti concurred, adding that the little clinic is a "very small" contribution for a man of such great
wealth, and besides, he probably gets a tax deduction for his donation.

The Haitian physician further explained after the election that his initial
reaction to Siméus's transnational candidacy had been positive. Siméus was
initially attractive because, as an outsider, he was removed from the corrupt
world of Haitian politics. He was too rich to want to get into politics to use
the office to enrich himself. And because he became rich outside Haiti, he
could not easily be accused of corrupt business practices. As a can-do executive, he offered the promise of fixing problems that no Haitian had yet been
able to solve. But he dismissed the candidate once he heard the rumor about
Siméus's tactics for getting his name onto the presidential ballot. Siméus's
insistence that Haitian law did not apply to him did not bode well for his
commitment to respecting laws he did not approve of in the future. Another
Haitian man, who is a citizen of the United States, expressed the same critique when he exclaimed in a disgusted tone that Siméus said that the Haitian
constitution was just a worthless piece of paper.

Siméus's engagement in migrant political transnationalism was not
unique. Nor was his specific effort, as a U.S. citizen, to try to circumvent
his home state's naturalization and electoral laws, in order to enter the political fray. His personal myth and campaign rhetoric, as well as his home
state's shifting response to his campaign, most closely echoed the story of
another transmigrant who made it rich in the food industry in the United
States: *El Rey del Tomate* (The Tomato King), Andrés Bermúdez.

There are obvious differences between the "home" nation-states of the two food magnates. Zacatecas, an important "sending" state in Mexico, is three times larger than Haiti, with about 20 percent of Haiti's population, and Zacatecas's particular politics and laws figured prominently in the evolution of Bermúdez's political campaign whereas local politics in Gonaïves hardly interfered in the Haitian frozen food king's situation. Yet the structural similarities between the two cases are significant, beginning with the proximity of the two nation-states to the United States and the high degree of influence the northern power wields over these peripheral economies. The transformation of Zacatecan and Haitian agrarian economies into producers of migrants for export culminated in the transnationalist orientation of their societies. Both states' belated and near simultaneous recognition of these trends led to the promotion of "state-led" transnationalism (Goldring 2002) and the counter movements of Zacatecan and Haitian migrant transnational political organizations to influence political change in both home and host states.

As Matt Bakker and Michael Peter Smith (2003) recount, Andrés Bermúdez worked his way up from a migrant farm worker to a labor contractor, grower, and inventor of a tomato transplanting machine. Like Siméus, the Tomato King offered his expertise as a successful business leader to straighten out the corrupt and pitiable government of his home country. And like Siméus, he claimed not to seek political reward but rather to respond to a calling to rescue his native state. Seeing the relentless misery in Zacatecas during return trips, he realized he had "to do something" (68). This narrative propelled the Tomato King's easy election to the post of county president of the city of Jerez. But it was instantly disputed in the legal system, and despite Bermúdez's successful defense of his victory in the lower court, the federal court's subsequent ruling in a suit brought by a rival candidate prevented him from taking office.

After Bermúdez's election was overturned by the federal supreme court, he condemned President Fox for his failure to intervene. Fox, a former governor of Guanajuato, was known before the presidential campaign as a strong promoter of migrants' transnationalism and for state-migrant collaborations in economic development. Bermúdez charged, "On the one hand, he says he is going to push for legal reforms regarding the right to vote of Mexicans abroad, and on the other, he denies us full political rights" (8). The high court reaffirmed Mexico's dual citizenship law, passed in 1998, when it decided that this new U.S. citizen was indeed also a Mexican citizen. (Mexicans who were naturalized elsewhere before 1998 indeed have to apply to recoup their Mexican citizenship. But those who became citizens of another state after 1998 are not assumed to have given up their

Mexican nationality.) The high court, however, upheld the second charge in the suit that Andrés Bermúdez did not maintain "effective and uninterrupted residency" in Zacatecas during the year prior to the elections. The minimum residency period for candidates running in local and state elections in Zacatecas is one year. (National elections in Mexico require candidates to maintain a five-year effective residence.)

The Tomato King's supporters among Zacatecan migrant transnational political organizations mobilized to reelect their migrant candidate. To do so, they lobbied to achieve state-level election reforms (Smith and Bakker 2005: 139). Their success resulted in a reduction of the residency period for local elections to six months. The statute is known as *la ley migrante.* Miguel Moctezuma (2004: 1), who was involved in authoring and promoting the law, regards the passage of the law as a partial victory—"a progressive law but a very limited one" (*una ley avanzada . . . y muy limitada*) for transnational migrant political empowerment. As he wrote in *"Votar Aquí, O Votar Allá"* (To Vote Here or to Vote over There), the law unequivocally recognizes the transborder life of Zacatecan citizens, but it limits migrants' representation, for example, by preventing them from running in gubernatorial elections. The migrants' victory nonetheless enabled their candidate not only to assume the mayorship of Jerez but also to advance an electoral campaign at the federal level three years later. In 2006, the Tomato King was elected representative of Zacatecas and now represents Zacatecans inside and outside the state and the nation-state in the federal legislature. A leader of a Zacatecan transnational political organization based in California, Efrain Jimenez, and a member of the "council of twenty," whom I interviewed, unequivocally views the Tomato King's political victories as a victory for "the migrants" and a clear step in demonstrating migrants' growing assertion of political clout.

## MIGRANT TRANSNATIONAL POLITICS FOCUSED ON IMMIGRANT POLITICAL INCORPORATION

Migrant hometown associations' strategies for increasing their clout in home states are closely linked to increasing their legitimacy in the United States. Fox (2006: 35) ) and others have documented the increasing "civic binationality" of Mexican home town associations whose members started out focused exclusively on aiding their home societies but came to the realization that success here leads to success abroad. A recent sign of that realization is the role leaders of Mexican migrant transnational associations played in organizing a mass, national mobilization to protest antiimmigrant legislation in the U.S. Congress. The mobilization was sparked by the March 2006 demonstration organized by the Coalition against HR4437 (the number of the antiimmigrant bill sponsored by Representative John Sensenbrenner) in Chicago, an alliance between old and new immigrant groups, unions, and religious organizations. The coleader of the organization was the head of the local Michoacán home town association.

Haitian immigrants in the United States have meanwhile come to the realization that greater involvement in local civic and political life in the United States might increase their clout in Haiti. Pierre-Louis asserts in his review of the activities of Haitian hometown associations based in New York that "by becoming United States citizens and maintaining contact with Haiti through the hometown associations, they can encourage their local politicians to keep Haiti at the center of their lives" (Pierre-Louis 2006: 133). This message could not have been made clearer to Haitians in Chicago in August 2006, at the opening of the local and statewide election season. The Haitian Consulate of Chicago circulated an invitation to a reception hosted by the Haitian American Voter Participation Organization for all candidates on the Democratic ticket from the governor to local offices to the estimated 15,000 Haitian and Haitian Americans in Chicago. The flyer stated, "Compatriots, Join us when we meet the candidates in the 2006 November Election . . . They are coming to get the endorsement of the Haitian-American community. You must be there to make a difference . . . The time has come again for us to stand up and to get involved on the American political scene as Haitian-Americans [sic]." The same week that the flyer was disseminated, Jean André Gérard Bingué, the founder of the organization, spoke on a Haitian radio show, which is broadcast for two hours each Saturday on a Chicago public radio station. The host of the two-hour Creole show exhorted the audience to show up at the event in large numbers to demonstrate their presence, adding, "If we don't get involved, we don't have a voice, and without a voice, we have no power." The guest, in turn, asserted that the more political clout Haitians have here, the more they can influence events back in Haiti. If something is going on in Haiti that Haitian Americans don't like, they can do something about it through the U.S. political system. He also suggested that Haitians follow the example of Jews in their relation to Israel. Jews, he said admiringly, are among the most powerful groups in the United States.

Bingué has been an active campaigner for Democratic candidates in several local and statewide elections (Valbrun 2002). In my interview with Bingué, he explained his strategy for influencing affairs in Haiti through political networking in Chicago. As he spoke, the nature of those politics— clientelism—emerged. "I could have gone to Haiti. When Aristide was in power, I was asked to run for representative of my district. I didn't go. I can help my country more by being here." To illustrate, he said that the

Sanitation Department of Chicago is going to donate twelve garbage trucks to Haiti. "I could never have done that for my country if I were there."

### A Transnational Migrant Political Coup?

Chicago is home to a relatively small Haitian diaspora community in the United States, ranked after Florida, New York, Boston, New Jersey, Connecticut, and Washington, D.C.[5] While the caché of political favors inside the Chicago political machine might help eliminate the waste festering in the streets of Port-au-Prince, the stakes of political clientelism for Florida Haitians can result in a much cleaner sweep of the Caribbean country. In fact, the interim government of Haiti between 2003 and 2006 was informally called the Boca Raton government of Haiti.

The ascendancy of the "Boca Raton government" in Haiti marks the rise of a small and influential group of Haitian immigrants in Florida. Haitian Republicans of Florida was formed around 1990 at a moment when the Democrats' status as the majority party in Florida was in decline. According to a founder of the organization (who asked to remain anonymous), he and a handful of Haitians decided that they could play a greater role in the ascending Republican Party. Their primary goal has been to gain legitimacy in the United States in order to influence affairs 700 miles across the Caribbean in the politics and economy of Haiti. Republican candidate Jeb Bush rejected the group's overtures during his first unsuccessful campaign for governor. Chastened by the loss, he reached out to the Haitian Republicans during his second campaign. The governor's Haiti Advisory Group, whose stated mission is to influence the development and affairs of Haiti, is composed of members of this organization. (Dumarsais Siméus is also a member. Elected Haitian American officials in Florida are invited to participate in their meetings as well). In 2004, Jeb Bush became the first Florida governor to visit Haiti.

Through a combination of strategy, luck (including that their governor was the son of a former president and the brother of the current president) and the brazen intervention in the home state by the host state's military, Haitian Republicans of Florida realized their transnationalist mission. Their strong imprint on Haiti at present is no more obvious than in the current "Boca Raton government" of Haiti. Their engagement in political transnationalism has "succeeded" in a way that more legitimate efforts of migrants barred by the conflicting citizenship laws and transnational rhetoric of the Haitian state have not.

After the U.S.-led coup d'état and exile of Jean-Bertrand Aristide in 2003, a "council of wise men" met to determine the new leadership of the Haitian state. They chose Gérard Latortue as prime minister. Latortue was born in 1934 in Haiti, where he became a lawyer and an economist. He nonetheless lived most of his adult life outside the country. According to the official biographical narrative, Latortue fled the Duvalier regime in Haiti in 1963 and worked in Africa and Europe for the United Nations for more than two decades. He returned briefly to Haiti during the 1980s to serve in an ephemeral, interim government. In 1994, he settled in Boca Raton and established himself in the real estate business and as a Haitian radio and television talk show host. He was also a member of the small group of Haitian Republicans who were clients and patrons of Jeb Bush.

The Latortue government's purpose was "to pacify the country . . . by cracking down on Aristide supporters" and to "prepare for new presidential and parliamentary elections," according to Alex Dupuy (2006: 132). The objective of the election was to "bring to power a government that would respect the rules of the political game dictated by the major capitalist powers and the international financial institutions and restore the balance of power between the government and the bourgeoisie through the traditional pact of domination favorable to the latter" (132–33). As a man who claimed to wield all of the resources for rising to the top of the corporate world—from social and cultural capital to political and economic capital—Siméus would have seemed to have represented the Boca Raton government's ideal candidate. The U.S. State Department certainly saw Siméus as the man for the job and seems not to have anticipated the clash between a patron and a client of the same powerful "uncle," one a model U.S. corporate citizen and the other a model "colonial" administrator.

U.S. Secretary of State Condoleeza Rice traveled to Port-au-Prince on the eve of the scheduled elections. Contrived photographs of Rice's visit with Interim Prime Minister Gérard Latortue demonstrated the intimate and steadfast relationship between the Texas and Florida governments of the United States and the Boca Raton government of Haiti. Nonetheless, Rice's public pronouncement criticized the electoral council's decision to respect the constitution and to bar the candidacy of a benefactor of George Herbert, George Walker, and Jeb Bush. Standing at a press conference with Latortue, Rice urged the de facto Boca Raton government of Haiti to ensure "open, fair and inclusive presidential elections." "This is going to be an election in which there will be broad representation. And as I said, I think anyone who wants to run in these elections should be allowed to run in these elections because there is no reason to fear any candidacy in a free and open election. And the most important issue here is that the elections be free and open and inclusive" (Secretary Condoleeza Rice, Remarks with Haitian Prime Minister Gérard Latortue: U.S. Department of State, 27 September 2005. Available at: http://www.state.gov/secretary/rm/2005/54059.htm.). Thus did the secretary of state pressure the de facto government preparing for allegedly democratic elections to circumvent its own (antimigrant) laws. Their refusal to do so suggests that the elites' roles in mass democratic politics is not fixed.

A revealing acknowledgement of the ambivalent and liminal position of transborder citizens surfaced during the press conference. The interim prime minister of the Boca Raton government of Haiti was responding to Rice's rejoinder to a journalist's queries about the possibility of President Aristide's return to Haiti and the disparate treatment of Cuban and Haitian refugees. Latortue seized the opportunity to talk about the deportation of criminals and the unnamed United States citizen's efforts to run for president of Haiti. He said:

> I am in total agreement with Madame Secretary of State on her response, but I would like to add two things. First of all concerning the deportation, I have raised the question several times with the embassy because we discovered that there is a link between deportations and security in Port-au-Prince. We saw that several cases of kidnappings and auto theft have been perpetrated by individuals who were deported. Sometimes they were people who didn't even know Haiti, who had been raised in the United States, committed crimes in the United States, and after having served their sentences there were sent back to Haiti. I asked for at least a moratorium for the electoral period and this would be the contribution of the United States to security in Haiti for this period. We talked about it. We were unable to agree on this point but we continue to talk about it.
>
> My second point concerns the elections. All political parties are able to participate in the elections. Any exclusions are due to constitutional or legal reasons. Proof of that is that out of the fifty-four candidates who presented themselves, thirty-two have been accepted and perhaps there will be two or three more. There was one who was not accepted, for example, because he is no longer a Haitian citizen. We have proof that on the 12th of February 2005, he came with an American passport to Haiti, signed the sheet saying that he was a U.S. citizen. And anyone can understand that he's not allowed to take part in the elections. There were also legal objections that have to do with the fact that some candidates might have managed government funds, and in these cases you need to get special authorization after an audit of your administration proving that you did not steal government funds.

In his comment, the prime minister juxtaposed two ideally marginal types of stateless persons. Significantly these rejected "citizens" occupy the polar ends of the social hierarchy. One is at the top rung, a member of the corporate, capitalist class. The other is an effective untouchable at the bottom—a convicted criminal. Despite the vast social and economic gulf separating the powerful magnate and the pariah, they are equally marginal with respect to a Haitian state that is itself peripheral and weak. Indeed the exclusion of the elite business leader is intensified by being rhetorically linked to the criminal. The disparaging stereotype of the immoral or criminal migrant is commonly reproduced in Haiti and other sites of mobile labor production and wage remittance consumption. *Dyaspora* (diaspora), like *pocho* in Mexican Spanish, a word denoting the discolored skin of rotting fruit, is frequently a derogatory term (Villareal 1989; Danticat 2001; Richman 1992 and 2005; Glick Schiller and Fouron 2001). The implication that any migrant is or can be a *dyaspora* or a *pocho* threatens all persons struggling for belonging and representation in the two (or more) states they inhabit. The precarious position that many migrants experience is echoed in the cases reported in other chapters in this section. Robert Gibb describes how racism directed toward Africans in France rose to a level that prompted the formation of the antiracist organization SOS-Racisme.

## CONCLUSION

The political aspirations of Dumas Siméus stumbled over the contradictory rhetoric and practices of an ambivalently transnational nation-state. Despite Haiti's transnationalist rhetoric, which continues despite Aristide's exit from the political stage, the Haitian state demonstrated that it is still not ready to open up the Haitian political system to the electoral participation of migrants whose money keeps the home state afloat, even, or especially, if that heroic migrant is the most successful of them all.

The declaration by President Aristide of Haiti's Tenth Province coincided in 1990 with Mexican President Ernesto Zedillo's explicit reference to his country as "a trans-territorial Mexican nation." While the Mexican government at federal and state levels has belatedly established political mechanisms for migrants' political participation at home, the Haitian state has yet to do so. Dual citizenship for Haitian migrants remains the unfulfilled promise of a government that rivaled, if not surpassed, Mexico's in its professed zeal for the transborder incorporation of migrants.

As for voting rights, while Haitians may not vote from "outside," Mexico's migrants are the equivocal beneficiaries of a recent law that, to borrow from Moctezuma's assessment of the Zacatecan migrant law, is both "progressive and very limited." The rules established by the Mexican legislature in 2005 for procuring and submitting mail-in-ballots are so cumbersome that they almost seem designed to discourage the practice. In order to register to vote, Mexican citizens abroad must have a valid voter registration card. Anyone lacking a card must return to Mexico to apply for one and wait up to two weeks for it to be issued. The cynical strategy recalls that of commercial companies that boldly advertise product rebates to encourage purchases, anticipating that only the most dogged consumers will go through the cost in time and money to receive the free gift. In the recent elections of July 2006, only about 56,749 of the estimated 4.2 million Mexican citizens living in the United States successfully registered to vote (Rivera-Salgado 2006: 33). A survey conducted among Mexican migrants five months before the elections by the Pew Hispanic Center further revealed that few were aware of how to register and only 55 percent knew that a presidential election in which migrants could register to vote was taking place (cited by Rivera-Salgado 2006: 33).

These measures would seem to support Luis Guarnizo, Alejando Portes, and William Haller's (2003: 1211) argument that "although a stable and significant transnational field of political action connecting immigrants with their polities of origin does indeed exist, migrants' habitual transnational political engagement is far from being as extensive, socially unbounded, 'deterritorialized' and liberatory as previously argued." The cases of the two migrants who rose to be "kings" in the agribusiness industry demonstrate that nationalist barriers to transborder citizenship in relatively weak home states remain tough. Neither magnate succeeded in throwing enough of his weight around in the home state to rise unchallenged to political office. While the frozen food magnate who inhabited the highest corporate social sphere garnered little support for his cause among the Haitian masses inside or outside Haiti, the Tomato King's populism was perceived as genuine enough to inspire savvy members of a grassroots, transnational organization to mobilize to change the Zacatecan election laws. Though more powerful forces managed to limit the migrant law to a partial victory, the Zacatecan migrants claimed the win as theirs. Andrés Bermúdez's recent election to the Mexican legislature is their vindication. Like their Mexican counterparts, Haitian migrants are recognizing that opportunities to affect change in Haiti lie in greater immersion in U.S. politics. But that route is not confined to electing Haitian Americans to office. Those migrants who have succeeded in affecting politics in Haiti have done so through clientelist relations with politically powerful U.S. elites. They have succeeded in ways that more legitimate efforts of migrants barred by the conflicting citizenship laws and transnational rhetoric of the Haitian state have not.

NOTES

1. Marie St. Fleur's political ascendance appeared to be fixed with her assumption of the role of chairperson of the Ways and Means Committee of the Massachusetts House of Representatives and her invitation to be the running mate of

Attorney General Tom Reilly in the 2006 gubernatorial election. Her rise was suddenly halted in early 2006 when an inquiry into her finances revealed that she had failed to pay her taxes. St. Fleur immediately withdrew her candidacy for lieutenant governor (http://www.boston.com/news/local/massachusetts/articles/2006/02/01/st_fleur_withdraws_as_reillys_running_mate/).

2. Alex Stepick, Carol Dutton Stepick, and Philip Kretsedemas (2001: 9) report that Joe Celestin was quoted in the Miami Herald as claiming, "North Miami belongs to Haitians." He later disavowed the quote, arguing that he really said, "If Haitians are going to continue moving into North Miami at the same rate as they are moving now, based on the question I was asked by the reporter, in 10 years North Miami could be for Haitians what Hialeah is for Hispanics."

3. Castles and Davidson's 2000 analysis raises questions about the United States' tacit encouragement of the Haitian presidential campaign on U.S. territory. Is the host state's agenda for enabling the transnational political participation of migrants part of a strategy to ensure democratic-looking elections that will legitimize the United States' undemocratic agenda for the nation? Could it also be intended to discourage migrants from becoming part of U.S. society and encourage their self-selected removal? Could it further help undermine class and panethnic alliances that threaten the capitalist-state system (as Glick Schiller found in the state's encouragement of a Haitian ethnic identity in New York in the 1970's)?

4. Schonwald (2005) reports in an article titled "The Meek Better Look Out" that a Haitian American plans to run against the U.S. representative in the upcoming election.

5. Relative to larger Haitian diaspora populations on the East Coast of the United States, in New York, Boston, and South Florida, Haitians in Chicago have been characterized as less organized and less influential. Valbrun reports that "While Haitian immigrants in Florida are fast becoming part of the mainstream political machine, those in the Midwest continue to lag behind, failing to even articulate a set of political priorities" (2002: 1). The Florida political machine to which Valbrun refers includes the eight elected local and statewide officials. There are now two Haitian American officials in greater Chicago, an alderman in Evanston, and a state senator who took Barak Obama's state senate seat when Obama was elected to the U.S. Senate.

# PART III

# New Spaces of Citizenship

KAREN RICHMAN'S CHAPTER in the previous section addresses several aspects of transnational citizenship practice. The three chapters in this final section explore new spaces for the practice of citizenship, addressing in particular the relationship between globalization and citizenship. They demonstrate new forms of empowerment in these new spaces, and they broaden our understanding of citizenship by focusing on cultural, social, and political dimensions. Most importantly these chapters underscore the limitations of a narrow focus on legal citizenship as the basis of citizenship practice.

The chapter by Bernard Wong addresses how local citizenship practices among Chinese entrepreneurs in Silicon Valley are shaped by the global economic context of their work. Globalization, he argues, enhances localization—it enriches the practice of local citizenship. The Chinese of Silicon Valley have actively promoted voter registration drives, built local coalitions with other ethnic groups to get candidates elected, and engaged in organizations that facilitate their ability to "give back" to their country of adoption once they have established themselves on sound economic footing. Indeed such organizations are among the most important new spaces of local citizenship (Brettell and Reed-Danahay 2008). The Silicon Valley Chinese are, in Wong's view, committed rather than flexible citizens who, despite employment in a transnational arena, often intend to remain in the United States and are eager, therefore, to be "good" U.S. citizens. Their transnational lives foster rather than hinder their involvement in the U.S. political arena. They do not view their cultural citizenship, their desire to retain some aspects of being Chinese, in any way precluding being social and political citizens of the United States as well.

Nina Glick Schiller and Ayse Caglar, through a comparison of two cases, one in Halle in East Germany and the other in Manchester, New Hampshire, also explore the relationship between the local and the global, but their emphasis is on the role of religion (in the form of Evangelical Christianity) in creating a space for citizenship practice and the construction of an identity that transcends state borders. They engage in a critical assessment of the meaning of social citizenship, which they define as the process whereby individuals assert rights to citizenship substantively through social practice rather than formally through law. Through a close ethnographic analysis of several born-again Christian communities in Germany and the United States, Glick Schiller and Caglar demonstrate how migrants make claims to belonging not based on a politics of difference, human rights regimes, or legal citizenship but as part of a global Christian project. They further argue that by emphasizing the vertical relationships between individuals and the state in their discussions of citizenship, scholars ignore the significant and substantive horizontal relationships forged between migrants and "fellow" citizens. Glick Schiller and Caglar conclude their discussion by focusing on the politicoreligious character of late twentieth- and early twenty-first-century U.S. politics. Fundamentalist Christians have indeed reenergized politics in the United States, for both the native born and the foreign born. In this new world, as these authors so astutely point out, the U.S. flag is not a symbol of Americanization but rather of the global Christian political project.

In the final chapter, Caroline Brettell explores the Internet as a new space of political mobilization for a group of deterritorialized individuals who have no official citizenship status in the United States but who are nevertheless powerfully engaged in citizenship practices. She describes how a group of immigrants, most of them green card holders but not U.S. citizens, become civically educated, civically engaged, and politically incorporated through their involvement an Internet organization (unitefamilies.org) founded to lobby Congress to change a particular immigration law. The forum provided by the Internet allows members to build a virtual coalition, to teach one another about the political process, and to express their frustrations about what rights are or are not accorded to them as legal residents of the United States. Clearly the Internet is one of the new public spheres for the expression of citizenship, be it local, national, or global.

CHAPTER 9

# Globalization and Citizenship

## THE CHINESE IN SILICON VALLEY

*Bernard P. Wong*

MANY SCHOLARS have suggested that globalization diminishes citizen attachment and participation in local and national institutions and will create a rootless society of transnationals who have severed their ties with family and nation states (Appadurai 1995 and 1996; Hannerz 1990, 1993, and 1996; Hannerz and Lofgen 1994) and become noncommittal flexible citizens (Ong 1999; Ong and Nonini 1996; Soysal 1994; Jacobson 1996). The present chapter will argue that this expectation is far from the truth. The data obtained from this study shows that the Chinese in Silicon Valley have made extraordinary efforts in grounding themselves economically and politically in their new land. The process of establishing themselves locally includes the use of cultural and economic resources to find lucrative employment in the United States and overseas and to develop global and local entrepreneurship. Transnationalism through the use of social and economic resources in two or more countries is now common place. However, the use of these resources does not preclude civic engagement, participating in local politics, and experimenting with a form of cultural citizenship and incorporating oneself in one's local community. Further global economic transactions require linkages between the transnational migrants with the host and home communities. Globalization, as will be demonstrated later in this chapter, propels citizenship making rather than creating rootless existence among the Chinese in Silicon Valley. Globalization intensifies the use of cultural resources and social connections to help the transnational migrants to establish themselves in the community.

## A TRANSNATIONAL COMMUNITY

The Chinese community in Silicon Valley is a transnational community with members participating intensively in the global economy. To begin with, the Chinese there are immigrants from different parts of the world, Taiwan, Hong Kong, the People's Republic of China, Southeast Asia, Europe, Canada, and South America (Wong 2006). By far, Taiwan and Mainland China are the two main sources of the Chinese immigrants. Many of these immigrants are transnational workers who straddle two or more cultures. Further, even the children of first-generation immigrants who are employed in Silicon Valley commute to different parts of the world. In both cases, these individuals serve as trouble-shooters in order to solve problems for their companies in various areas of their operation, from technology, investment, sales, production, and personnel management to research. Most of these international itinerants are concerned with establishing roots in the United States, but they attempt to achieve their American Dream via participation in the global economy. Their return trips to Asia are vehicles for them to establish themselves in the United States. The multifaceted aspects of the existence of these transnational migrants show that it is difficult to have a monolithic categorization of these globe trotters simply as transnationals or flexible citizens (Soysal 1994)). The Chinese community in Silicon Valley shows that one can be a transnational (Basch, Glick Schiller, and Blanc 1994) and at the same time a committed citizen with a cultural heritage. They are experimenting with a form of "multicultural citizenship" (Rosaldo 1989) with feet in two cultures but citizenship rooted in one national state (Wong 2006).

### AN JU LE YE: ESTABLISHING HOME AND BUSINESS

Starting a company in Silicon Valley requires money, time, and commitment. It is done not just for financial gain, but also for an indication that one wants to settle in the community permanently. This is particularly so among new immigrants. After they have been in Silicon Valley for a while, and if they plan to stay in the United States, they will take certain decisive steps like purchasing a house, establishing a business, or continuing their employment in the United States. To have a comfortable home and a satisfying enterprise (*an ju le ye*) is their goal. "Enterprise" means either a career or a business. One informant told me that to be really successful and to be respected in the United States one should own a business:

> I worked for a number of years for a big company after I got my PhD. From working and living in America, I learned that I could teach in a university and publish a number of books. It would be a comfortable life

for me. But this will not earn me much respect in society. I would be known among my colleagues and in the university circle. I will not be respected by my fellow men and American society. I notice that if you are a Ford, a Rockefeller, or a successful entrepreneur, and if you have a business and contribute employment to the community, you will be somebody. Since I left China, I wanted to be successful in the United States. I decided that I need to start a company. After I have a successful business and contributed to society by producing a useful product, hiring employees and giving much to charity, I would be respected by the community. (Personal interview)

Another Chinese CEO echoed this sentiment. He said that having a successful company that provided others with employment would earn him respect in U.S. society. This desire for respect is related to an idea of being a committed U.S. citizen. He said he started first as an engineer and then later became an entrepreneur. With his financial success, he was able to contribute much to the community. He became an important member of the Board of Regents of the University of California system. Thus entrepreneurship helped him to establish a position in the community. He is totally rooted in the United States. For immigrants, one's business is thus a means to establish roots (Wong 2001, 2006).

David Lam of Lam Research told me that there are more first-generation Chinese than U.S.-born Chinese interested in becoming entrepreneurs: "There are three groups of Chinese: Hong Kong, Taiwan, and Mainland Chinese. Among those who run start-up companies, the foreign-born Chinese are more numerous than the local-born Chinese. Entrepreneurship requires risk-taking. Immigrants work hard and are willing to take more risk. Chinese immigrants also want to achieve social mobility through the accumulation of wealth by establishing businesses" (Dr. David Lam, personal interview).

Another reason for starting a firm is to fight the glass ceiling. Many of my informants as well as other researchers insist that the glass ceiling exists because Chinese immigrant engineers are often bypassed for promotion. Discrimination also exists in another form: receiving less pay for doing the same job. Anna Lee Saxenian (1999) has found similar practices. But the glass ceiling phenomenon was more prevalent in the 1990s than it is in the 2000s. This is due presumably to a better understanding of the Chinese as well as to the recognition that it is not good business practice to discriminate against people on the basis of race or ethnicity. This is particularly the case in Silicon Valley where a performance meritocracy has now become the norm. By doing otherwise, a good company may lose its most talented workers. Mr. Chun Xia is an example. "After I graduated from the University of Illinois, I started to work for a company. The salary was quite good. However, as a foreign-born, you always feel the glass ceiling. After working for a while, I thought about opening my own company" (Zhang 2000). When people become their own boss, they feel that they do not have to put up with prejudice. One informant told me that it made no sense to him when he had to train someone who was inferior to him and who would be promoted above him. Such practices create a serious morale problem. Furthermore, in Silicon Valley it is difficult to obtain and keep the best talent. And it is costly for a company to hire head hunters to replace continuously departing workers. The point here is clear: discrimination and a glass ceiling forced some of the Chinese in Silicon Valley to resort to starting their own businesses or look for another job.

### GLOBALIZATION AND NEW ECONOMIC OPPORTUNITIES

When economic spheres extend beyond traditional national boundaries, economic opportunities become enlarged as well. Not only do Chinese engineers of Silicon Valley return to the other side of the Pacific, but an excess of talent in China will come to fill market gaps or shortage areas in Silicon Valley. Globalization can assist employment in both the United States and China, enlarging investment opportunities.

Why do these Chinese return to work in Asia? One of the reasons is that globalization has created employment opportunities for Chinese Americans (Alsop 200; *South China Morning Post* 1995; Wong 2006). Another reason was the slow job market during the recent recessions in the United States (*South China Morning Post* 2002; *The Economist* 2003; Wong 2006). A third reason is the glass ceiling of U.S. corporations that prohibits the upward mobility of the Chinese in Silicon Valley (Wong 2001 and 2006). The movement of these former immigrants does not follow the direction prescribed by globalization theorists like Andre Frank (1967) and Immanuel Wallerstein (1980). Both suggested the dependency of the "periphery" (the underdeveloped economy) on the core (the developed economy). The flows of local goods and migrants are from the periphery to the industrialized nations and to the benefits of the latter. People and goods, as indicated in this chapter, flow in either a bidirectional or circular way (Rouse 1996; Wong 2006).

When the U.S. economic downturn was hitting hard in 2001, many cities and provinces in Mainland China attempted to seize the advantage and lure high-tech professionals from Silicon Valley. On 28 November 2001, at a job fair in Silicon Valley, more than one hundred representatives from seventeen provinces and the national government of China sought candidates for eight hundred positions (Wong 2006). Because China had just been admitted to the World Trade Organization (WTO) and was positioned to develop a global economy, employers wanted to meet potential employees and vice versa. The occasion was festive and attendance was good. Despite poor weather, thousands of job seekers participated.

Silicon Valley Chinese who have *"guanxi"* (connections) in China have an added advantage when launching new businesses in China. Mr. Wing Han is one example. He left China in 1986 to study in the United States. After receiving his PhD in biomedical science he worked at several California pharmaceutical companies. He married, became a U.S. citizen, and made his home in Silicon Valley. His salary in 2000 exceeded $100,000 a year. However, Mr. Han knew that he would never make more than $150,000 to $200,000 a year in the United States because of the glass ceiling. As it turned out, a businessman approached him when he attended a conference in China. This Chinese businessman said to Mr. Han, "I want to invest in your company. I'll give you a $1 million a year." After some deliberation and with the help of a colleague whose mother was the vice mayor of technology in Shanghai, Mr. Han accepted the offer to set up shop in China. Thanks to good connections (*guanxi*), Mr. Han was able to raise $3.4 million from Chinese government venture capitalists. His colleague's mother from Shanghai quickly used her own *guanxi* to arrange meetings with more than twenty government-backed agencies to sort through paperwork and financial details. In early 2001, Mr. Han left his company in south San Francisco and began commuting to Shanghai. Mr. Han returns to the United States every other month to visit his wife, two sons, and his parents in Silicon Valley.

My data obtained from fieldwork indicated that the engineers who are willing to go to Asia are often younger. They have U.S. citizenship, green cards, or permanent residency in the United States. If they have not yet acquired these, however, they prefer to wait until they have obtained them before they seek employment in Asia. Many keep their purchased properties or apartments in the United States even if they are gone to work in Asia (Wong 2006). For those who have families, the wage earners will leave their spouse and children behind in the United States when they fly to work in Asia; they leave home to work. This is just another indication that they are interested in returning to the United States.

Their base is still the United States and Asia is only a place in which to find work or to start a company. This differs from the Chinese immigrants of the nineteenth century who came to the United States to make money and who planned to return home to lead a life of elegant retirement. As I said earlier, some Silicon Valley Chinese professionals feel that because of the level of prejudice in the United States, their opportunities for promotion will be limited if they work in companies run by non-Chinese Americans. Some feel that there is and will always be a glass ceiling. However, I use the word *some*, because not *all* the Chinese feel that way. To avoid this predicament, there are several adaptive strategies. One is for a Chinese engineer to start his or her own business (as discussed earlier in this chapter). Another is to find other job opportunities in China, Taiwan, and Hong Kong. This is what causes "return migration." But I must qualify the use of this phrase for it often is not necessarily a return since it is not permanent. These workers return temporarily to work or to be entrepreneurs in Asia, always with the notion of one day returning to the United States permanently. Dovelyn R. Agunias and Kathleen Newland (2007) called these returnees circular migrants. I call this movement "temporary reverse migration" (Wong 2006).

Commonly the husband returns to Asia but the wife stays in the United States. This is also a reversal of nineteenth-century Chinese immigration patterns in which the men left for the United States and their women stayed in China. Modern-day Chinese returnees still believe that their children will have a better chance of getting into universities in the United States and they themselves prefer the physical environment of the United States. There is also a concern about political stability in Taiwan, Hong Kong, and China. This practice of temporarily returning to the land of one's origins or to another overseas location in order to seek employment and other economic opportunities was quite common in the U.S. recessions of the early 1990s and the return migration phenomenon was not unnoticed by the U.S. media (*New York Times* 1995; *Time Magazine* 1994). The *San Jose Mercury News* (1993) estimated that 30 percent of the Taiwanese immigrant engineers who formerly worked in Silicon Valley had returned to Taiwan in search of better opportunities. My informants estimated that during this time at least a fourth of the valley's Hong Kong immigrant professionals returned to their land of origin as well. Census data taken from the San Francisco Bay Area in 1990 indicate that Chinese immigrants did tend to receive lower salaries when compared to the white population and this data has been confirmed by the research of Analee Saxenian (1999). Those engineers who felt that they were being discriminated against were not hesitant to leave their jobs in the United States to return to Asia. Returning to Asia was an adaptive strategy that Chinese engineers used to fight discrimination.

There were additional factors that motivated the temporary return of high-tech Chinese personnel to Asia. During the early 1990s, the Taiwanese government made deliberate efforts to recruit Chinese high-tech engineers and companies and to secure their return to Taiwan. A counterpart to Silicon

Valley, the Hsinchu Scientific Campus, was set up in Taiwan with subsidies from the government. On the Hsinchu Scientific Campus near Taipei there are research facilities, condominiums for families and bachelors, restaurants, business and factory sites, and tennis courts and other recreation facilities, all created with funding from the government. Accordingly some Taiwanese engineers returned and became vice presidents or presidents of new companies. Others arrived on the new campus to work in research and development offices sponsored by the government. By early 2000 the tide had changed and ever more Chinese were returning or going to China to assume employment or to start new businesses. As implied above, two factors fueled this exodus: (1) the recession of 2001; and (2) the preferential treatment given these returning workers by the government of China. Taxes, for example, were low, and the workers were given such benefits as housing subsidies and transportation assistance. Not least of these perks was the respect accorded to the returned Chinese engineers. Scientist and engineers are highly respected in China and those who have higher degrees from overseas are particularly valued: they are said to be "gold-plated." Many informants told me that when they worked in U.S. high-tech companies, they were considered nothing more than run-of-the-mill employees or *"gao ji hua gong"* (high-class laborers). But when they returned to China, they were treated as special and valuable talent, or *"gao ji zhi shi fan zhi"* (high-class intellectuals). They told me that in China they have higher positions and enjoy more prestige from when doing the same job in the United States.

After they have accumulated enough savings, they would return to the United States. Some are able to start global businesses with branches in the United States and in China. This is called *"liang di tou zi"* (investment in two places). Or they might organize a research and development office in the United States, but have their sales and production facilities in China. Thus the Chinese returnees do use their connections, bilingual abilities, and bicultural backgrounds to conduct a transnational business, but they treat the United States as their permanent home. Thus there is no divided loyalty. They are committed to the United States. It is only out of practicality and for the sake of their economic survival that they may have to go back to China or Taiwan. Chinese American engineers can be adamant about the fact that mainstream U.S. society often suspects the Chinese of divided loyalties. One Chinese engineer told me the following story:

> My friend is a German American. He lived and worked in Germany for seven years for an American company. He speaks German and his family even moved there living in a huge mansion. No one called him unpatriotic. But when a Chinese American returns to do the same, he will mostly

be suspected by the immigration official as unpatriotic. My friends, who
have to travel back and forth between Taiwan and the United States, were
often questioned by immigration officials for spending too much time
overseas. This is unfair! Some people have to travel overseas to do business. They have to make a living! (Personal interview)

### GLOBALIZATION AND ECONOMIC BRAIN-DRAIN

When social scientists decry an economic brain-drain as the result of
immigration, they are in fact making the assumption that when migrants
leave their home country for a new country, they will never return home
and that their movement is nonreversible and permanent. When migrants
move permanently to a new country, their departure implies, according
to these social scientists, a loss of talent for the country of origin. Hence
the concept of what is known as brain-drain. In the case of Chinese engineers moving to the United States, their movement implies a brain-drain
in China. Similarly when Chinese Americans engineers from Silicon Valley
move back to Asia, some will assume that this is a loss of talent for America.
In reality the departure of an oversupply of manpower can be a blessing in
disguise. A glut of engineers can depress wages and profits for certain industries. Several engineers who recently arrived from China have told me that
there are many unemployed software engineers in China looking for opportunities to go overseas. The fact that certain talent leaves one place to go to
another should not be seen as a permanent or a one-way process. From my
research I found this assumption to be invalid. As actors and decision makers, human beings can redirect or modify the direction of their migratory
movement. I have seen engineers who pursue a circular migration route,
sometimes working here in Silicon Valley and sometimes in Singapore or
China before returning to the United States again. In this modern world,
traversing national borders is a new mode of human existence. The modern
employee or entrepreneur often needs to travel to make a living. They have
to make their rounds in order to be successful. It is not appropriate therefore
to use the term "brain-drain." Rather we should consider it a circulation of
brainpower or a globalization of brainpower. Synergy of talent around the
globe is now a reality.

The global itinerants who take part in this circulation of brainpower
may be divided into three groups. The first group is made up of the owner/
entrepreneurs of transnational corporations. As we have seen, a company
can be localized and globalized simultaneously. One entrepreneur, Wang
Zhidong, has in fact used the concept "glocal"—an abbreviation for
global and local to describe his company, Sina.com. This Internet company serves Chinese communities worldwide by offering e-commerce and

community services in the Chinese language to four localized Web sites targeting China, Hong Kong, Taiwan, and overseas Chinese in North America (Wong 2001 and 2006).

The second group of high-tech migrants who travel frequently between continents spreading brainpower is made up of company-sent people assigned to places like China, Singapore, London, Hong Kong, or Taiwan. This included Americans working for U.S. companies who have been assigned to a foreign country for a number of years and then return to the United States (Wong 2006).

Problems-solvers or trouble-shooters, who are truly traveling brainpower, define the third group. These technicians are on assignment to deal with certain issues or technical problems of a company in different parts of the world. They are individuals who travel with a special agenda and on a prearranged schedule. Some Chinese engineers have told me that after they arrive in a foreign country, they are immediately wined and dined and then driven to their living quarters or hotel. They are then told about their schedules and specific responsibilities. After receiving their instructions, they set to work right away on the tasks assigned to them. There is not much free time or possibilities to rearrange itineraries. Their life is quite regimented. Upon finishing their assigned tasks, they return to their headquarters, which is often in Silicon Valley (Wong 2001 and 2006).

In the recession of the 1990s, there were more Taiwanese returning to Taiwan to work, but during the 2001 recession there were more Mainland Chinese returning to China for employment. This was due to the need for high-tech personnel in those localities. In the 1990s most of the Chinese high-tech engineers in Silicon Valley were from Taiwan. There were few Mainland Chinese then. Then as today, all of these returnees are either U.S. citizens or permanent residents of the United States. In fact, they are the people who can afford to return to China or Taiwan. Then, if anything happens, they have a place to return to. For whatever reason (economic, political, or educational), many of these high-tech Chinese made their decision a long time ago to stay in the United States permanently. After they have made a fortune, they will return to the United States. Thus they cross national borders back and forth to make a living. This circulatory movement of contemporary migrants differs from those in the past. Oscar Handlin (1972), Milton Gordon (1964), Herbert Gans (1962), and other immigration scholars have not studied this kind of immigration movement. This is due to the fact that today's economy is globalized. Achieving the American Dream sometimes requires multiple departures from the United States and work overseas.

Some want to take advantage of the booming economy in China. People told me that *now* is the time to do business in China because China's recent entry into the WTO is thought to be advantageous for entrepreneurs in the high-tech businesses. These people believe that there is a huge Chinese market waiting for U.S. goods such as computers and other high-tech products. They also believe that the tariffs for U.S. products in China will be lower because of China's admission into the WTO. Many Mainland Chinese are anxious to seize this opportunity to open up a firm and to return to China to participate in the new economic era. Again this group of entrepreneurs has no intention of returning to China permanently. The globalization in this case is for the sake of localization!

## GROWING ROOTS IN SILICON VALLEY: CLIMBING THE SOCIAL LADDER AND OBTAINING CULTURAL CITIZENSHIP

Contrary to the popular perception that the Chinese are foreigners who are not committed to their host country, I found that many of the Chinese are firmly grounded in the United States. Of the one hundred entrepreneurs for whom I have biographical data, most are seriously interested in community affairs. Many are highly dedicated to community activities and civic and local affairs. For instance, Leonard Liu is California Motion Pictures Commissioner, David Lee is a regent of the University of California system, and Stanley Wang is a member of the Board of Trustees of the California State University system. Some Chinese are activists who participate in U.S. politics through community involvement by running for political office or by supporting other Asian politicians and politicians who are sympathetic to Chinese American or Asian American concerns. They also participate in the valley's many professional and community organizations. When I interviewed them about their commitment, the majority told me that they wanted to establish roots in America. Their professed ideology is "*luo di sheng gen*" (establishing roots). Some even said, "If we don't stay in America, where shall we go?" or "We have lived in this country for such a long time. We work here and our children were born here. Our work is here and our family is here. Whether we like it or not, we are going to stay permanently in this country."

Occasionally there are other voices; "Taiwan is very similar to the United States now. Whatever we have in the United States, Taiwan has also. The differences between the two are becoming less and less. I may go back to Taiwan to lead my life of retirement but it does not mean that I do not like America. If I do go back there it is because of my parents and my relatives." Others said, "Even if I want to go back to Taiwan, my children may not want to live there permanently. They were born and raised here in America. This is their country. For this reason, I will stay here." Several informants did tell me that they would return to Taiwan to stay there for good. However, an overwhelming majority of the Taiwanese Chinese prefer to stay in the United States permanently.

The majority of the Hong Kong Chinese and Mainland Chinese immigrants whom I interviewed told me that they also wanted to stay in this country permanently. Many applied for citizenship as soon as they qualified for it. An overwhelming majority of the Chinese have only one passport. As compared to Europeans from Germany, United Kingdom, Italy, France, and Spain, the Chinese immigrants are the ones who want to be naturalized citizens as soon as they are allowed legally. Among the Europeans whom I interviewed in Silicon Valley, they prefer to keep their original citizenships and are contented with having their green cards (permanent residency). The Chinese are eager to be U.S. citizens. Some of them even bring their newly acquired passports to show their friends in their offices. They are also anxious to purchase homes in Silicon Valley. To this end, Chinese engineers, especially those who are married, are concerned about accumulating enough money for the down payment on their future home. On weekends, many Chinese families go to open houses to visit homes that are for sale. From 1999 to 2000 when the high-tech business was at its peak, one would see Chinese buyers camping out overnight in front of new houses in order to be the first to purchase them. Once they have homes, their concerns then shift to mortgage payments and an education fund for their children. Many banks in Silicon Valley are familiar with the consumption patterns of Chinese Americans and have invented special banking products just for them. After working for hours, these Chinese spend much of their free time on their homes, their families, and the education of their children. These are root-planting activities. In Chinese, one is said to be working to "*an ju le ye*" (to have a comfortable home and a satisfactory enterprise). In order to save money for their children's education, the Chinese are frugal about furniture, appliances, and automobiles. They do not change their cars frequently. Nor do they spend exorbitant amounts of money for household goods. They only purchase what they deem to be practical and durable. From visiting the homes of many engineers, I have noticed that the furniture they purchase tends to be quite modest. For those who are interested in entrepreneurship, they also save money for their future start-up company. Some may use part of their savings to purchase stock in the hope of accumulating money in the stock market. From these consumption patterns, it is easy to recognize that Chinese American engineers and entrepreneurs are planning for permanent settlement in the United States. They want to be established in Silicon Valley, especially in the communities that are known for their excellent schools, such as Cupertino and Los Alto Hills. Some of the younger engineers from Mainland China told me that the price of housing in the valley is beyond their reach, with an average home easily selling for $600,000 in Cupertino and $1 million in Los Alto Hills. They said to me that after they have accumulated sufficient savings and when they are ready, they may purchase homes elsewhere in the United States where housing is more affordable. But they do plan to stay in America! They definitely have accepted the ideology of *"luo di sheng gen"* (literally means: when one reaches the destination, one must grow root).

## POLITICAL PARTICIPATION AND THE
## CIVIC ACTIVITIES OF THE CHINESE

It is common knowledge that in order to fully participate in the larger society, ethnic groups need to have political representation. Knowing the importance of having elected officials to fight for their interest, the Chinese in Silicon Valley have sought to participate in local and national politics through (1) registering Chinese voters, (2) competing for political office at all levels, city and county, and (3) forming coalitions with other ethnic groups so as to elect politicians who are sympathetic to their concerns.

Globalization activities have not deterred the commitment of the Chinese to the United States. In San Jose, the registrar of Voter Registration Programs indicated that more and more Asians, including the Chinese, are voting. Former mayor Michael Chang of Cupertino told me that the Chinese are participating in local politics in increasing numbers. They normally start with school boards and move to city council elections. He said that the Silicon Valley Chinese are sympathetic to Chinese candidates in general. They also encourage and support both local and national Chinese politicians. Many Chinese politicians from out-of-state come to do fundraising among the Chinese of Silicon Valley, including Gary Locke (during his run for governor of the state of Washington) and S. B. Wu (lieutenant governor of Delaware).

Chinese Americans are adamant in the fight for their rights. News about discrimination in business practices spreads quickly via e-mail in the valley. Racial slurs of white salesmen and other discriminatory practices are reported instantly. Supportive of the cause of Wen Ho Lee, many valley Chinese donated money for his legal defense. The experience of Dr. Wen Ho Lee touched many Chinese in Silicon Valley. They believed that he was wrongly accused of being a spy and unfairly imprisoned. In a sense, his life echoes the lives of many Taiwanese Chinese. Wen Ho Lee was born in 1939 to a poor peasant family in Taiwan. He was one of ten children in the Lee family. When he graduated from middle school he was able to pass a competitive university exam and was admitted to Cheng Kung University. After he finished, he came to the United States to study at Texas A&M. He got his MS in 1965 and his PhD in physics in 1969.

Wen Ho Lee has two grown children, one a software engineer and the other a computer technician. Wen Ho is a family man who likes to cook and do housework. His hobbies are fishing, gardening, listening to music, and reading. But in December of 1999 he was accused by the U.S. government of being a spy. Then in September of 2000 he was cleared of fifty-nine charges derived from that accusation and he pleaded guilty to a lesser felony count of "knowingly violating security rules in downloading classified nuclear data" (*San Francisco Chronicle* 2000).

The high-tech Chinese are familiar with the case of Wen Ho Lee. Many feel that Dr. Lee was targeted due to his race. Some Chinese were disappointed and others angry with Dr. Lee's decision to accept the plea-bargain deal because they did not think he was guilty of any of the allegations of espionage that cost him his job and caused him the pain and suffering he had to endure. Because of the Wen Ho Lee case, some U.S. politicians demanded close scrutiny of ethnic Chinese businesses in the scientific community and tighter controls of U.S. high-tech transfers and export. Some of the Chinese believe that these politicians were unfairly stirring up hatred against Chinese American high-tech personnel and their businesses. Their beliefs were a result of the conviction Chinese Americans feel that U.S. society has a habit of distrusting and treating the Chinese as scapegoats since the California Gold Rush in the 1840s. Today in the popular press in the United States, the stereotype that Chinese cannot be loyal citizens is still being perpetuated. To combat this unfair depiction, as will be demonstrated later in this chapter, many Chinese Americans in Silicon Valley are determined to correct this image through their political and civil participation in the United States.

Many Chinese Americans believe that anti-Chinese racism still exists in the United States. Were Dr. Lee not a Chinese American, many Chinese argue that he would not have been singled out for investigation. Although Chinese Americans have served this country and fought for it, they still feel that they have been singled out for unusual and unfair treatment (*San Francisco Chronicle* 2001). Despite such fears, some Silicon Valley Chinese believe that the best way to fight racism is through coalition building with other ethnic groups, and in this way to change the system by participating in it. They feel that more Chinese Americans must participate in the political system so as to give voice to the concerns and interests of the Chinese in Silicon Valley. Some, in fact, do run for electoral office and attempt to fight racism through the system.

In order to safeguard their business and professional interests, they organize interest groups and associations. The high-tech Chinese of Silicon Valley are decision makers, movers, and shapers of their destiny.

*Voter Registration*

The Chinese in Silicon Valley are gradually realizing the importance of participating in elections, and they have started to organize voter registration drives. Kansen Chu, a Taiwanese immigrant, David Lee of the San Francisco-based Chinese American Voters Education Committee, and Michael Chang, the former mayor of Cupertino, have made great efforts to register Asian voters. One informant said: "Asians are the fastest growing ethnic group in the county. They have no voice but they've reached critical mass. The conditions are ripe for greater representation."

In Santa Clara County, the heart of Silicon Valley, Asian Americans make up 23.4 percent of the county's population. However, not all of those eligible to vote have registered. Another informant said: "Although we have big numbers here in terms of population, we don't have a strong voice unless we register and participate. Unless we are registered, we are an invisible group of people, as far as politicians or community leaders are concerned." Realizing the importance of voter registration, Kansen Chu and David Lee asked for help from the Chinese ethnic press, the *Sing Tao Daily* and the *World Journal*, which have a combined daily readership of 230,000. Apparently their work was quite successful. For the March election of 2000 in Santa Clara, there were 23,244 registered Chinese voters who were immigrants from Taiwan, Hong Kong, and Mainland China. Among registered Chinese voters, 11,050 voted, giving a participation rate of 47.5 percent (Wong 2006).

*Elections*

Chinese immigrants in Silicon Valley have learned that they need to have elected officials who will represent their interests and so, many Chinese now run for political office. There were two Chinese candidates for the Cupertino Union School District in 1997 and both won. One was Julius Chiang who was a manager of two bank branches and a graduate with a bachelor's degree from the University of California, Berkeley. The other candidate was Ben Liao, a software engineer with Apple Computer, Taligent, and Hewlett Packard. He graduated with a master's in computer science from Texas A&M University. In 1999 Barry Chang, a civil engineer, was elected as a member of the Governing Board of Cupertino Union School District. Meanwhile in the Foothill/De Anza Community College District and the Fremont Union High School District, Chinese American candidates, Kathryn Ho, Hsing Kung, and Homer Tong have been active participants in school elections.

Previously the mayor of Milpitas was Henry Manayan, a Filipino Chinese. Michael S. Chang, the former mayor of Cupertino City, is now a city council member. For the Santa Clara election of 6 November 2001, there were six Chinese Americans running for various political offices. The brothers Paul Fong and Alan Fong ran for Foothill/De Anza Community College District and Orchard School District. Ben Liao and Pearl Cheng ran for the Cupertino School District. Patrick Kwok ran for the city council of Cupertino, and Wei Wong for the city council of Palo Alto (Wong 2006). Patrick Kwok, Ben Liao, Pearl Cheng, and Alan Fong won their elections. There are now three former Chinese American mayors in Silicon Valley. One of them is Aileen Kuo who won her mayoral election in 2004 in Saratoga. Otto Lee is the mayor of Sunnyvale and Kris Wang is currently the major of the city of Cupertino. All of these three mayors are immigrants. These political participations and public service indicate that Chinese Americans are determined to ground themselves in America. Their citizenship activities go beyond the acquisition of a green card or a passport. They are creating new political and social spaces in this valley community (Wong 2006; *Asian Week* 2007). Contrary to the stereotype image that Chinese Americans are incapable of being "good citizens" (*Daily Breeze* 2001), from my fieldwork data and written sources, the majority of the Chinese Americans, whether they are immigrants or U.S.-born, whether they are scientists or engineers, are highly engaged in citizenship-making activities. In addition to producing mayors, the Chinese in Silicon Valley have produced a large contingent of school board members and numerous social activists fighting for digital equality, human rights, and good government (*Asian Week* 2001, 2005, and 2007).

*Coalitions*

In order to make an impact on the larger society, the Chinese in Silicon Valley realize that it is important to build coalitions with other ethnic groups that have common interests and have had similar experiences in the United States. Coalition politics have proved to be successful in the United States. The NACCP, the Rainbow collation, La Raza, Hispanic American, and others have all found that there is strength in numbers. For Chinese Americans, this means forming a united front with Vietnamese Americans, Filipino Americans, Korean Americans, and Japanese Americans. (In official statistics, the Chinese and other ethnic groups are often lumped together as Asian Americans.) Some of the successful coalitions that have been formed with this in mind include (1) the Asian American Public Policy Institute of San Jose, (2) the Asian Americans for Community Involvement of San Jose, (3) the Asian Pacific American Consortium of San Jose, and (4) the Cross-Cultural Community Services Center of San Jose. Asian American coalition also leads to an expansion of ethnic identity. Thus one is Chinese but could be included at the same time as an Asian American organization.

In interviewing Chinese politicians in Silicon Valley, I learned that the Chinese American population alone is not large enough to assert any political influence but Asian Americans, numerically, could have a considerable influence. They could form a sizeable voting block to fight for more citizenship rights and equality. In addition to coalition building, the Chinese in Silicon Valley participated in two other important projects to gain inroads to U.S. political system: The Committee of 100 and the 80/20 projects.

The Committee of 100 is a national nonpartisan organization composed of U.S. citizens of Chinese descent. Members come from different walks of life but are generally successful citizens in the United States. The goal of the committee is to promote the interests of the Chinese in the United States by addressing important issues concerning the well-being of the Chinese community and issues affecting U.S.-China relations.

The Committee of 100 has some famous and highly accomplished Chinese Americans as members. Its membership includes well-known cellist Yo Yo Ma, celebrated architect I. M. Pei, and Chancellor Chang-lin Tien of the University of California, Berkeley. Quite a few Chinese American entrepreneurs from Silicon Valley are also members, including David Lam, George Koo, and Milton Chang. The committee aims to eradicate prejudices against and obstacles to the advancement of the Chinese in the United States. It has undertaken tasks such as helping to clear the name of Dr. Wen Ho Lee and it has given awards to journalists who are helpful to the Chinese community. The Committee of 100 in its 2001 annual meeting presented a Headliner Journalism Award to CBS correspondent Mike Wallace for an objective presentation of the case of Wen Ho Lee on *Sixty Minutes*. The committee recognizes the achievements of Chinese Americans as well as other Asian Americans. The achievements of Norman Mineta (Transportation Secretary), Elaine Chao (Secretary of Labor), and Mike Honda (Congressman from California) have been recognized by the committee, as have the accomplishments of Chancellor Chang-lin Tien and Jerry Yang of Yahoo!. The committee's work is an example of how Chinese Americans, including those in Silicon Valley, are anxious to establish roots in America.

The 80/20 is a national, nonpartisan project devised by a group of concerned Chinese Americans. It was originally an attempt to create a block-vote among all Asian Americans in order to influence the 2000 U.S. presidential election. The organization hoped to unite 80 percent of all Asian Pacific American voters in the support of one presidential candidate. Such a block would be attractive to any politician and it was hoped that the candidate who won the election with the support of this block would take an interest in the Asian community.

Silicon Valley Chinese are active in this organization. The 80/20, together with the Committee of 100, has sponsored the Flag Project, a movement to promote Asian Pacific American involvement in the patriotic flying of the flag on national holidays such as Memorial Day and Independence Day. The project is designed to show mainstream U.S. society that the Chinese are also Americans. It is a tool used to inform the larger society that the Chinese are part of the United States and that they are just as loyal as other citizens.

*Civic Duties and Voluntarism*

Silicon Valley Chinese realize the importance of contributing to the community and participating in civic activities. On 28 October 2001, in Sunnyvale's Chinese Cultural Center, a seminar focused on Chinese voluntarism. Seminar participants all agreed that it was meaningful and valuable to do voluntary civic work. In fact, the Taiwan-based Buddhist Compassion Relief Tzu-chi Foundation has shown the value and meaning of such civic involvement by being active in voluntary work. A spokesperson explained the foundation's position: "Our master reminds us quite frequently that we are newcomers to this country. We have gotten a lot from this society and we should therefore give back to this society. Since we want to establish roots in America, we have to contribute our talents and our resources. The service of Tzu-chi transcends politics, religion and ethnicity. We want to be part of the mainstream society and want to help the mainstream society and their problems" (Wong 2006: 124). Chinese immigrants in Silicon Valley also believe that there are other benefits for the Chinese community in their voluntary work. These include the elevation of the status of the Chinese community. Charitable work is an important tool for community or public relations. When the seminar on voluntarism was offered, the attendance was good with more than one hundred people from the Chinese community present. They were eager to find out what they could do to help the less fortunate among themselves and in the larger society.

The Committee of 100 and the 80/20 project are example how the Chinese in Silicon Valley are concerned about their civic responsibility and their interests in community services. This was particularly true in the 2001 election in which many Chinese city and school district officials were elected. As a further example of this concern, the Chinese in Cupertino decided to organize a Chinese buffet at Quinland Community Center to entertain the low-income and senior citizens of the community. Councilman Patrick Kwok, Councilman Michael Chang, Barry Chang of Cupertino Union School District, and other elected officials served this dinner to the attendees on 18 December 2001. Some cynics argued that paying back to the community is not the real motive. They argued that it is a strategy to convert their economic capital to social capital—to earn "respectability" and social prestige. Some may have this as a motive. However, analyzing the backgrounds of the public service people, one could quickly find out that most of the volunteers, donors of social services, and community activists are committed to helping their fellow citizens. Some feel that they have gained a lot from their community and want to pay back their community.

Professor Peter Lee of San Jose State University told me that the Chinese are learning how to organize voluntary services to help the less fortunate in the community. Chinese American students in local high schools are also looking for opportunities to help others by participating in peer tutoring and other community service projects. There were many fund raising activities to raise money to support the victims of the 9/11 incident. Thus, civic engagement is highly visible in this community.

MULTIPLE PASSPORT HOLDERS AND "FLEXIBLE CITIZENSHIP"

It is a myth that many Chinese immigrants are multiple passport holders. From my fieldwork, I found that majority of the Chinese immigrants do not have two passports, except for the very rich from Southeast Asia and Taiwan. Some extremely successful entrepreneurs from Hong Kong may have British and U.S. passports and some wealthy Chinese from Taiwan may have dual citizenship. Some Chinese criminals who engage in illegal activities like trafficking human beings (snake heads) and drug dealing have also multiple passports. However, a vast of majority of the Chinese simply could not be citizens of two or more countries. First, the law in China does not allow dual citizenship. Second, the PRC (the People's Republic of China) encourages the overseas Chinese to participate fully in their host societies (Wong 2006). When someone becomes a U.S. citizen, one has to give up the Chinese citizenship. Similarly in the case of Taiwan, when a naturalized Chinese American returns to Taiwan to seek public offices, one has to give up his or her U.S. passport (Wong 2006). In the case of the Hong Kong Chinese, a vast majority of them do not have the means to become naturalized citizens of the United Kingdom.

In contrast with some other immigrant populations (Europeans, for example), the Chinese in Silicon Valley are anxious to get green cards and eventually to become U.S. citizens. Why is this case? From my fieldwork, I learned that once the Chinese make up their mind to become immigrants, they want to be part of the United States and do not want to be treated as "foreigners." Second, the United States is one of the most desirable countries for them to settle. Educational opportunity and political stability are some of the reasons why they choose to come to the United States. Third, as mentioned above, current policies in PRC encourage the Chinese to assimilate into the host country and, in fact, give special treatment to Chinese with U.S. citizenship in investment, travel, and employment in China (Wong 2006). Fourth, they know that U.S. citizens are eligible for social and political benefits in the form of voting rights and government services. Finally, they want to be treated as the other citizens in the United States. This means being free of being scapegoated as spies and being free from discrimination in hiring, promotion, education, housing, and other aspects of social life.

Although Chinese immigrants are eager to become U.S. citizens, they also want to retain Chinese culture, including local culture. Expressions like "*Tai Mei Ren*" (Taiwanese American) and "*Meiji Hua Ren*" (U.S. citizens of Chinese descent) are being used to indicate the cultural differences. Regional cultural affiliations such as Hong Kong Chinese, Shanghai Chinese, and Beijing Chinese are also being used as markers of distinction. Local cultural identities—Beijing style Lion Dancers, Hong Kong styled music (Western rock music sung in Cantonese)—are often featured in community events or festivals in Silicon Valley and at Cinco De Mayo and Chinese New Year celebrations. These are all examples of the making of cultural citizenship. They are citizens of the United States with a separate cultural heritage. Increasingly the Saturday Chinese schools offer classes in local dialects such as Minanhua, Hakka, and Cantonese. The students are the second-generation Chinese in the United States. They are enculturated into their ancestral (regional) cultures. This form of multicultural citizenship is a new phenomenon even in Silicon Valley. Traditionally to be an American was to be "anglicized American." Today the trend is to be a multicultural citizen. In the local Chinese press, phrases like "Taiwanese American," "Chinese American," and "Hong Kong American" are being used to depict the different ethnic identity of the U.S. citizens of Chinese decent. To what extent this is the trend among other ethnic groups is an empirical question worthy of further investigation.

## CONCLUSION

The Chinese in Silicon Valley invest considerable energy in establishing themselves economically and politically in the United States. Their globalization efforts do not decrease their dependence on Silicon Valley. The transnational flow and cross-cultural networks and organizations they maintain do not diminish the importance of place or traditional culture. On the contrary, these transnational networks are used to assist new immigrants in grounding themselves economically in the United States. There is also a continued linkage with the national institutions of the United States: elections, coalitions, political parties, and special-interest groups. My findings here echo those of other globalization studies (Evans 1999; Escobar 2001).

"*Luo di sheng gen*" (establishing roots) and "*an ju le ye*" (having a comfortable home and a satisfying enterprise) are professed sentiments of the Chinese in Silicon Valley. This is also reflected in their interest and participation in local and national politics. The New York Times (2004) has noted the eagerness of the Chinese to be part of the United States and their success in making political inroads in Silicon Valley. To grow roots in a community requires journeys back to the ancestral land. This is an unusual kind of journey for new immigrants. They left their ancestral home to establish a new home. Now in order to fortify and enrich their new home in the United States, the immigrants have to return to their ancestral home once again. It is clear these new immigrants are actively engaged in shaping their destiny. This new way of searching for the American Dream is indeed novel to transnational migrants, but their activities are directed to building a new life in the United States.

This chapter has shown that certain aspects of globalization may be worthy topics for future research. How has globalization created opportunities for the transnational migrant's entrepreneurship and employment? How has globalization provided ways for the transnational migrant to fight racism and obtain personal dignity? Many nation-based scholars who look at the movement of people in terms of one-way migration will need to reexamine such concepts as brain-drain, assimilation, community, ethnic entrepreneurship, and citizenship. The present study has found that among Chinese transnational migrants, discussion of the circulation of talent, jobs, and wealth is more meaningful than a discussion of brain gain or brain loss. Similarly, amidst political assimilation, there is cultural pluralism. Many Silicon Valley Chinese participate in domestic and national politics while still valuing their culture. Thus political assimilation and maintenance of cultural and ethnic boundary go hand in hand. Furthermore the circulation of talent and the continuous back-and-forth movement of the Chinese transnationals do not necessarily mean that Chinese transnationals are not loyal citizens of America. In fact, data obtained from this research show that the majority of the Silicon Valley Chinese want to participate in U.S. democracy and want to be treated equally.

In conclusion, globalization and localization can coexist. Globalization does not imply political apathy or noncommitment to local culture, community, and nation-state. Rather multicultural citizenship can be useful for the establishment of roots and the protection of minorities in the context of globalization.

CHAPTER 10

# "And Ye Shall Possess It, and Dwell Therein"

## SOCIAL CITIZENSHIP, GLOBAL CHRISTIANITY, AND NONETHNIC IMMIGRANT INCORPORATION

*Nina Glick Schiller and Ayse Caglar*

THIS CHAPTER ARGUES that the theology, practices, and identities deployed by born-again Christian migrants constitutes a form of social citizenship that challenges established notions of rights to territory and belonging articulated within state-based concepts of citizenship. In so doing, migrants engage in nonethnic incorporation, a form of settlement and identification that dramatically differs from those generally discussed and debated by migration theorists and policy makers. Using our research among born-again Christians in Halle/Saale, Sachsen-Anhalt, Germany, and in Manchester, New Hampshire, from 2001 to 2005, we explore the ways migrants use evangelizing Christianity to facilitate claims to social citizenship in their countries of settlement.[1] We examine the ways in which born-again Christianity can bring migrants and natives into local and global political engagement. We also note that migrants' biblically based claims to territory and belonging articulate and reinforce the neoconservative global agenda. In this way, migrants and natives participate in a globe spanning imperial political project that extends far beyond the electoral politics of their locality and nation-state of settlement, while also becoming incorporated locally.

### CONCEPTUALIZING CITIZENSHIP

The word "citizen" is now generally understood as a person who is fully a member of a modern state and as such has all possible legal rights, including the right to vote, hold political office, and claim public benefits. Citizens of states also have certain responsibilities that vary from country to country

(Bauböck 1994; Shafir 1998). However, the clear-cut textbook-style definition gets very muddy in practice and in different states people practice and
conceive of citizenship somewhat differently. In fact, there is an increasing
disjuncture between the rights stemming from formal membership in a state
and the substantive rights of people residing in that state.

As scholars of citizenship have noted, not all people who are legal citizens
receive the same treatment from the state or are able to claim the same rights.
There are often categories of people who are legal citizens according to the
laws of a state, yet who face various forms of exclusions and denials of civil
rights because they are not considered to be truly part of the nation. These
categories include members of lower social classes–both rural and urban—and
persons who are racialized or gendered in ways that put them outside the body
politic (Hamilton and Hamilton 1997; Haney-Lopez 1998; Lister 1997; Marshall 1964; Yuval-Davis 1997a). These exclusions operate both within systems
of law and within civil society. In states such as Morocco, currently, or the
United States, for long periods of U.S. history, both men and women have
had legal citizenship but this status has accorded women fewer legal rights in
domains of family law or property rights (Jones and Jonasdottir 1988; Salih
2003). As was finally acknowledged in the 2005 urban uprising in France,
despite the fact that black immigrants from former colonies have been able to
become citizens of France, they face barriers in entering either professions or
politics; and black children are routed into vocations rather than university
tracks (Tagliabue 2002; Craig 2005). These examples draw attention to the
fact that the formal status of membership does not guarantee an array of civic
and socioeconomic rights to the citizens.

On the other hand, although legal citizens are often denied full civil
rights, many states grant a range of rights to those who reside legally in a state
but do not have legal citizenship and may even be ineligible to become citizens. As Yasemin Soysal (1994) has emphasized, although they lacked formal
membership in the host nation, migrants and their descendants often have
been accorded various social, economic, civil, and cultural rights. The access
accorded to these migrants has revealed the disjuncture of formal and substantive citizenship rights. Consequently in understanding the social dynamics
of participation in societies, scholars of citizenship increasingly have examined the practices and performance of citizenship rights, rather than only the
formal status of membership. Moreover, they have expanded the concept of
citizenship by decoupling formal and substantive citizenship rights and distinguishing between cultural and social citizenships.

Because citizenship in its actual practice has discrete legal, cultural, and
social aspects, separate literatures have developed to address these various dimensions. As defined by Renato Rosaldo and Juan Flores, cultural citizenship

refers to "the right to be different with respect to the norms of the dominant national community, without compromising one's right to belong" (1997: 57). This approach to citizenship was a product of struggles against cultural assimilationist or integrationist projects. Advocates of cultural citizenship called for changes in law and readings of national history, as well as for the legitimation of diverse cultural practices. Their goal was to insure that the multiple cultural heritages contained within a single nation-state would be recognized and respected; they wanted the practice of cultural difference to be accompanied by the assurance of equal opportunity (Kymlicka 1998).

The struggles to have the Spanish language accepted within a variety of legal, educational, and social settings in the United States, to wear a headscarf in public schools in France, or to obtain state licenses for Muslim butchers to practice their trade in Germany would be classified as struggles for the right to be different while being accorded equal opportunity. As such they are struggles for cultural citizenship because the state is asked to respect the right of people living within its territory to maintain diverse values, practices, and institutions, whether or not the claimants are legal citizens (Silvestrini 1997: 44). The concept of cultural citizenship can be seen as a demand that modern states acknowledge that they are in effect legally plural, containing within them institutions, norms, and codes of conduct that mandate and shape different and sometimes conflicting sets of behavior.

However, because the concept of cultural citizenship focuses on identities and the diversity of cultural practices, it does not address the way in which persons who are not citizens participate in the common social, economic, and political life of a specific state and claim rights in these multiple domains. In order to address these practices and claims, scholars have begun to speak of social citizenship. These incorporative forms of daily participation in the social life of a locality generate claims and assertions of belonging that move beyond the politics of difference and the cosmology of identity politics. They contribute to institutional practices and experiences of governance that contribute to the daily forms of state formation of nation-states.

Social citizenship differs from legal citizenship because of the lack of mesh between formal citizenship and the allocation of rights, benefits, and privileges. When people without official membership make claims to belong to a state through collectively organizing to protect themselves against discrimination, or when they receive rights and benefits from a state or make contributions to the development of a state and the life of people within it, they are said to be social citizens. Social citizens assert rights to citizenship substantively through social practice rather than law. Increasingly citizenship is coming to be understood not as "a bundle of formal rights, but the entire mode of incorporation of a particular individual or group into a society" (Shafir 1998:23). This approach to citizenship alerts us to what Gershon Shafir (1998: 23–24) argues is a "major feature of modern society: a simultaneous and interconnected struggle for membership or identity or both with the intention of accessing rights that are disbursed by the state" on the basis of social presence rather than formal law. This approach to citizenship, which is concerned with the moral and performative dimensions of membership beyond the domain of legal rights, defines the meaning and practices of participation and belonging as it is displayed within the public sphere (Holston and Appadurai 1999). Consequently, although legal citizenship is generally seen as the venue of an individual's participation in the political and social process of the nation-state, migrants who do not have legal standing may influence the political agenda and social life of a state in multiple ways. For example, U.S. legal permanent residents (green card holders) act as social citizens when they organize an Internet campaign to change U.S. immigration laws (see Brettell in this volume)

Often authors stress that despite persisting transnational identities, new migrants can become active and committed members of their nation-state of residence (see Wong in this volume). Much of the theorization of social citizenship has remained within the container of the nation-state, even though migrants and their descendants may live their lives across borders and claim various types of legal, cultural, or social rights in more than one country. Consequently we need to develop studies and concepts of citizenship that can extend beyond state borders, while remaining cognizant of the continuing ability of state based institutions to control various types of force, and police borders. There has been exploration and debate about the nature and significance of transnational or transborder citizenry in the form of dual citizenship or multiple memberships (Aleinikoff and Klusmeyer 2001; Bauböck 1994; Faist 2000; Caglar 2004; Glick Schiller 2005a; Soysal 1998). However, there is work still to be done in connecting transnational processes to the internal dimensions of citizenship. Studies of migrant practices of citizenship within social fields that extend within and across state borders can contribute to this process of theory building (Glick Schiller and Fouron 2001).[2]The study of migrant transnational social fields becomes part of a larger intellectual project of understanding how global networks of information, ideas, and discourses contribute to the development of the concept and practice of citizenship within particular states. In this project, migrants are useful to think with because their transnational networks are highlighted by the processes that label them as foreign.

Many people claim rights in a state and act within its institutional and governmental processes not only without formal citizenship but also while they reside in another state. Underlying their transborder practices is some type of claim to membership, rights, and voice in more than one state. Most of the research and discussion of multiple membership claims and transborder citizenship has focused on migrants social citizenship practices that connect a new land of settlement and a homeland. In these instances, migrants who become citizens of a new state, continue to influence their homeland, even if they have abandoned their legal citizenship rights (Benda-Beckmann 2001; Kearney 1991; Caglar 2002; Levitt 2001; Pessar 1995; Richman 1992; Basch, Glick Schiller, and Blanc 1994; Glick Schiller 1999, 2005b, and 2005c). Migrants who live their lives across borders may claim a voice in the public sphere and legal rights including tax concessions and property ownership in the state from which they migrated but in which they no longer hold full, legal citizenship. Or migrants who retain homeland legal citizenship and continue to be engaged in that homeland also act as social citizens in their new land of settlement. This form of practice becomes a topic of public debate when migrants who are not legal citizens seek to shape the foreign policy of their country of settlement toward their native land.

There is also a form of transborder citizenship in which claimants are less interested in membership within a territorial state than in the recognition of their rights to political voice. The Kurdish experience in Europe might provide an example of this form of social citizenship (Østergaard-Nielsen 2002). Persons embracing Kurdish identity have been able to insert themselves as claimants to political rights and voice within specific European states and the European Union. They have obtained political voice, recognition, and certain rights on the basis of a global human rights regime and a rights discourse instituted by international organizations and international treaties. The rights regime was an arbiter of Kurds' social citizenship in the countries in which they settled in Europe. Migrants who claimed Kurdish identity were able to obtain specific legal protection and expand the scope of their entitlements in Europe through the human rights regimes, not through claims of formal citizenship rights.

The human rights regime is not the only globe spanning network and ideological basis for social citizenship claims. Some migrants make these claims in the name of religion. In these instances migrants claim rights to residency in a state, social benefits, respect, and moral and political leadership on the basis of their membership in a global religious project and the social field created by its networks of organizations (Levitt 2003; Van Dijk 2004; Vasquez and Marquard 2003). Religious claims and networks can foster social citizenship. On the basis of what they see as their God-given rights, migrants whose religious networks constitute a transborder social field can act upon the institutional, legal, and societal processes of the state and locality in which they have settled. However, although the various global religions connect migrants to social networks and organizations that reach within and across nation-states, all religions are not equally positioned to facilitate the claims making of their adherents to rights within a particular state. There is a large and growing body of work on the global reach of Islam and its local manifestations in the lives of migrants and the states in which they have settled (Amiraux 2001; Allievi and Nielsen 2003; Schiffauer 1999; Foblets 2002). Rather than explore the religious claims to social citizenship, most of the research on Islam in Europe remains within the confines of a cultural citizenship framework or one that has underlined the impact of human rights regimes in migrants' claims-making processes. However, it is apparent that Muslims have faced considerable barriers in their efforts to use religious identities and networks to forge claims of substantive citizenship rights in Europe.[3]

Christianity offers a more welcoming pathway. We suggest that scholars of social citizenship must address migrants' use of global Christian theology and identities as forms of incorporation and transnational connection. In the remainder of this chapter we explore the ways born-again Christian migrants facilitate their social citizenship in the United States and Germany through participation in religious, transnational social fields. They claim belonging and rights to their new land without reference to the politics of difference, human rights regimes, or legal citizenship. Born-again Christianity as a form of claims-making positions migrants as missionaries in relationship both to their state of settlement and global Christian projects. Christian migrants regard their country of settlement as a terrain of evangelization where they have been sent by God to settle and establish Christian morality. Their narrative of settlement and claims to rights resonate with the U.S. neoconservative worldview and its imperial political project. Currently the U.S. neoconservative agenda has replaced the discourses of neoliberal economics with a rhetoric of Christian morality (Harvey 2005). Neoconservatives have claimed U.S. leadership for a reinvigorated Christian project of evangelization (Glick Schiller, Caglar, and Guldbrandsen 2006a; Urban 2006). When migrants base their claims to citizenship on a universalist Christian message of the sovereignty of Jesus, they participate in a political domain that both reaches into and extends far beyond the reaches of the electoral politics of a particular state.

## EXAMINING THE SOCIAL CITIZENSHIP OF BORN-AGAIN CHRISTIANS IN TWO SMALL-SCALE CITIES

To provide examples of migrants' use of a Christian social citizenship, we will draw on ethnographic research we conducted from 2001 to 2005 among born-again Christian migrants in two small-scale cities, Manchester, New Hampshire, and Halle/Saale, Sachsen-Anhalt, Germany.[4] In Halle we worked with two born-again congregations, one predominantly Congolese and the other predominantly Nigerian. But it is significant that the members of both congregations did not see themselves in ethnic terms—at least in the context of building their congregation. They were not building an ethnic church identified by the cultural or national identity of its members. Rather both churches in Halle situated themselves within a global Christian mission and in organizations that linked them not to homeland churches but to a Pentecostal movement now being organized throughout and Europe and globally (Glick Schiller, Caglar, and Guldbrandsen 2006b; Karagiannis and Glick Schiller 2006). This is central to these migrants' understanding of their right to be in Germany. While most have entered as asylum seekers and a few as students, these migrants do not use their personal histories or legal statuses to explain their presence or make claims on the state. They do not, for example, refer to either the right of asylum within the German Constitution or to the international human rights regime in explaining why they believe they have the right to be in Germany. Instead, they justify their presence and subsequent actions in terms of claiming Halle and Germany for Jesus.

For example, Pastor Mpenza, the Congolese pastor of the L'Esprit du Seigneur Church, explained his presence in Germany, as well as his insistence that his church be understood as Christian, and not Congolese, by saying, "No, no. It isn't a Congolese church. This is not the origin of the Word of God. I have told you about my origin. I have come from Congo where I met my Lord, where I worked for the Lord. And now I am here, in Germany, where I had the feeling that the inhabitants were in need of the same message. So I've clearly said that this church is not a Congolese church. I've clearly said it is a church of Jesus."

Both Pastor Mpenza and his congregants insisted that their right to live in Germany came from the Lord and was contained within scripture. The message of the Bible was clear: "Every place whereon the soles of your feet shall tread shall be yours" (Deuteronomy 11: 24). They were stakeholders in Germany because of God's promise to believers. "For ye shall pass over Jordan to go in to possess the land which the Lord your God giveth you, and ye shall possess it, and dwell therein" (Deuteronomy 11: 31). Pastor Joshua of the Miracle Healing Church and his congregants held the same beliefs based on their reading of scripture. Their place was in Germany because they had been sent by God. We were often told "It was not by accident that I came to this place."

The two congregations differed in their size, the networks of their pastors, the particular talents of their leaders, and the legal status of their members. Most of the members of L'Esprit du Seigneur remained asylum seekers with only temporary rights to stay, although the pastor and his wife had been granted refugee status with permanent residency. The congregation of only about thirty members was not totally African; there were a few German women. However, almost all the members were quite poor. Only a few of the African members spoke passable German. In contrast, the Miracle Church had approximately 150 members. A growing number of the migrant members had obtained permanent legal status through marrying Germans and could speak some German. The German partners, especially if they were women, became active members of the church. The congregation increasingly was able to recruit other Germans as members. By 2005 about 20 percent of the congregation was German.

Given their differences, the congregations differed in their methods of evangelization but they shared a commitment to this mission. Members of the L'Esprit du Seigneur decided that they could use music to bring the people of Halle, both migrants and nonmigrants, to God. They found that on various occasions they were welcome to sing choral music in various activities organized and funded by various public institutions and political foundations. To the pastor and his congregation, these concerts "took place within the frame of evangelization. There is evangelization by means of language and there is evangelization by means of music."

It is important to note that the local representatives of the institutions in Halle and the state of Sachsen-Anhalt, who sponsored or funded these musical performances, and the pastor and performers from the L'Esprit du Seigneur held very different views of the purpose and accomplishments of the concerts. Occasionally the sponsors and funders approached the migrants as asylum seekers who had rights to live in Halle because of universal principals of human rights. For example, when the leaders of the congregation decided to stage their own public performance in 2003, they were advised to hold the concert on the International Day of Human Rights. Under this guise, a foundation linked to the German Green Party assisted the church in renting instruments and publicizing the concert.

More often, German organizations approached the migrants as Africans who could give the city a facade of multiculturalism during particular public occasions and celebrations. Consequently gospel choirs in which church members were prominent were invited to perform during the Week of Foreigners, a yearly event held in many German cities, during "African Week," an annual event in Halle, and during summer folk festivals. Sometimes performers received small stipends for their participation. The church was also provided with space for Sunday prayer services in a meeting center for "Germans and Foreigners." During the Week of

Foreigners, city dignitaries and multicultural brokers attended the Sunday service of L'Esprit du Seigneur in this meeting center and joined in the singing.

Compared to Pastor Mpenza, Pastor Joshua, the leader of Miracle Healing Church of Halle, developed few ties to local nonreligious institutions and, although the church had a choir, its members did not participate in multicultural events. Instead the Miracle Healing Church evangelized by organizing healing services, promising that all those who accepted Jesus into their lives would be cured of diseases such as "cancer, blindness, and menstrual problems." These diseases, believers claimed, were brought on by demonic forces. Those healed were encouraged to testify so as to provide evidence that "Jesus is alive" that the "Holy Spirit moves in Halle."

The Miracle Church posted on the home page of its Web site two photos, one of the church building and one of Pastor Joshua praying with a blond, white young woman. The caption proclaimed that the church was "the place of miracles, signs, and wonders. There is Power in God's Word!! Here . . . the sick get healed, the blind see, and many are delivered from bondage of sin." By 2005 Pastor Joshua had began to hold healing services for German congregations in neighboring cities. The church produced video tapes of these services and sold them through their Web site and at church services. In 2005, the congregation held a five-day public healing conference in a sports arena in Halle. Two to three hundred people were in attendance on any evening, two-thirds of whom were German. Pastor Joshua and the spiritual warriors of the Miracle Church promised that as worshipers came forward and engaged in prayer, the demons of illness and failure would be forced from their body by the Holy Spirit and "the door of power" would be opened (Field Notes, Healing Conference 2005). When Pastor Joshua called on participants to come forward to be healed both migrants and natives came forward, prayed, and sometimes fell into a trance.

In staging the conference, the Miracle Church received significant assistance from two missionary organizations that were newly established in Halle, one a Mennonite group from the United States and a second led by an Egyptian-German man and his German wife. The two missionary organizations served as cosponsors of the conference, providing staff, speakers, security, prayer counselors, prayer warriors, and organizational experience. However, it was the migrants of the Miracle Healing Church and their religiosity that were central to the event. All participants acknowledged the migrants' religious and moral leadership and sensibilities, which set the spiritual tone and parameters of the event.

Most of the natives who attended and sought healing were already part of local Pentecostal churches; many had deep ties in local village life. There

were teachers, counselors, and the unemployed. Almost all had more economic resources than the migrants. Ranging in age from teenagers to pen-
sioners, they were brought to the healing conference and various healing
services by their search for spiritual passion and community. Many found
what they sought from the healing activities that the migrants organized
and orchestrated.

In staking their claims to Halle the born-again Christian migrants used
not only biblical authority but also their enmeshment in transnational born-
again networks. In calling the healing conference in Halle, members of the
Miracle Healing Church were responding to and implementing the message
of a pan-European Pentecostal conference held in a Berlin stadium in June
2003. The Berlin conference, attended by several members of the Miracle
Healing Church, called for a European-wide organization of Pentecostal
Churches to bring religious revival to Germany. Those who heeded the
preaching of the Miracle Church felt empowered by the strength of the
network ties as well as the belief system they were offered. They were also
modeling their activities after similar healing services that are being held
throughout the world, often led by African migrants and attended by thousands of believers.

The transnational network within which each congregation was situ-
ated became visible to congregants through the presence of visiting pastors.
Pastor Mpenza had ties to other churches in Belgium, France, Congo, and
Chad. Pastor Joshua, the Nigerian pastor, operated on a grander scale and
consequently the migrants who participated in the network of the Miracle
Healing Church found themselves part of more extensive networks that were
linked to other German cities and to the United States, South Korea, and
India. An Indian pastor, based in western Germany, had visited more than
once and convinced the church to support his missionary work in India by
sending funds on a regular basis. The Miracle Healing Church also participated in the Morris Cerullo World Evangelism Organization and sent funds
to Cerullo's efforts to convert Jews in Israel to born-again Christianity.

Through their pastors and their transnational ties, the congregants were
exposed to and experienced themselves as part of overlapping Christian
globe-spanning networks in ways that validated their faith and their presence in Halle. These ties also served as a form of social capital that could on
occasion be shrewdly manipulated. A previous pastor of the Miracle Church
used ties to Belgium to obtain asylum. The Miracle Church was also able to
spawn a new congregation in near-by Magdeburg, led by a Nigerian man
married to a German woman from that city. Becoming a pastor took no
formal training but only the recognition by others that you had a calling
from God.

Evidence of their connections to the Miracle Healing Church and through it to a global Christian social field directly assisted the asylum seekers in this congregation who were attempting to settle in Germany by marrying a German. Young German couples in the eastern part of Germany often do not get married. In this setting, church membership evolved as a form of courting. The migrants who were church members often were able to convince German partners of their good character, as well as the necessity of marriage, by involving the partner in church services. During these services, the potential spouses could see that while they might find the religious behavior of their partner strange, the congregation was part of a broader and powerful movement that had legitimacy in other parts of Germany and globally and one that had an increasing German as well as African leadership. They also learned that marriage was necessary to be a member of this church movement. The desire of their African partner to marry was presented not as a utilitarian effort to obtain a passport but as an act that promised both partners health, prosperity, and fulfillment with the assurance of divine assistance. In these marriages, migrants not only preached and practiced a Christian morality as the basis of their own local and global social citizenship but also shaped the citizenship practices and beliefs of native Germans.

Once married, migrants found that their spouse's family networks were sometimes welcoming. Although the German families were often poor, they could provide various types of direct assistance such as childcare and local knowledge about accessing governmental offices and benefits. This local knowledge enhanced the ability of migrants to claim rights as social citizens.

Any assessment of the impact of migrants' social citizenship must include the role played by migrants in expanding the social citizenship of natives. The engagement of Germans as congregants and spouses within the born-again religious networks introduced by African migrants in Halle makes that point clear. Scholars who debate the distinction between formal and substantive citizenship by focusing solely on the vertical relationships between the individual and the state miss a highly significant yet little noted aspect of social citizenship. They ignore the horizontal relationships forged by many migrants, which entail substantive ties to "fellow" citizens (Offe 1994). Christianity as a set of practices, networks and ideology provided the bases and discourses for such horizontal networks among the members of a born-again social field whose participants did not distinguish between a migrant and a native. By joining with migrants, natives who were active in the born-again churches obtained new possibilities of forging ties locally and transnationally. These natives, who came from socially and economically diverse backgrounds, contributed to the efforts to form a new Christian public morality and spirituality.

The significance of our findings in Halle Germany about migrants' use of born-again local, national, and transnational networks to become social citizens in their locality of settlement are strengthened by our similar findings in Manchester, New Hampshire. In Manchester, we worked with the Resurrection Crusade, a coalition of more than eighteen local born-again congregations.[5] The Resurrection Crusade was organized by Heaven's Gift, a Nigerian refugee, who had been living in Manchester for five years. He was able to obtain refugee status, at least in part, because of his membership in a global Christian network and he came to Manchester with these networks. The member churches of the Resurrection Crusade include migrants but most of the congregations were composed primarily of white natives of New Hampshire.

The conditions in Manchester and the United States made it possible for Heaven's Gift and the Crusade to extend their Christian network building into political and economic domains. Political and business leaders were receptive to public representations of immigrants as part of the life of the city, to public displays of religious fervor, and to the incorporation of migrants as cheap, unskilled labor. In this setting the Crusade built a social field that linked their network and the migrants in it to local and state-level Republican and Democratic politicians. The New Hampshire governor in 2004, who was a conservative Republican and strong Bush supporter, personally attended a prayer breakfast of the Resurrection Crusade. The Democratic mayor of Manchester attended the breakfasts from 2003–5 and developed an ongoing relationship to the Crusade. He welcomed members to city hall each year for the "National Day of Prayer," allowed the Crusade to pray in the Aldermanic Chambers in 2005, and made it possible for the Crusade to hold yearly prayer programs in a city park for which the city provided a band shell and speaker system.[6]

In his 2004 messages to the Crusade's prayer breakfast and annual conference, the mayor used a diversity narrative, one that reflected the view of migrants that predominated among Manchester's political and economic leadership. Speaking at the breakfast, the mayor emphasized the contributions of immigrants and refugees to the city through their hard work and diverse cultures. He praised the newcomers who, through their factory work, contributed to the strength of the city's economy. The mayor's letter to the prayer conference noted that by the beginning of the twenty-first century Manchester welcomed "new immigrants from Central America, South America, Asia, Africa, and Central Europe." He went on: "Manchester experienced an infusion of energy and vitality that has contributed to a sense of rebirth, where people from all ethnicities and religious backgrounds come together to form a new and exciting community. We celebrate the diversity of Manchester and embrace the fact that people from all over the world come to our wonderful city to find the freedom to practice the religion of their heritage."

It is important to note that the mayor eventually realized that he was preaching to the wrong choir. By 2005 he was tearfully reporting to the Crusade's prayer breakfast that his granddaughter had been miraculously healed after members of the group had prayed for her. His new narrative reflected his realization that the type of citizenship that Heaven's Gift and the migrants in his network were marshalling was Christian and not cultural. Rather than emphasizing their foreignness and diverse religious heritage, the migrants who participated in the prayer breakfasts and prayer conferences portrayed the city of Manchester as divided between those who sided with Jesus and those who stood with the devil. As did the African migrant pastors in Halle, Heaven's Gift stressed the need to rid the city of all demons and evil spirits and build a Christian community. He said that God had sent migrants as missionaries to bring true Christian morality to the city and declate that Jesus was in charge. All political leaders, whatever their party, were bound to make biblical scripture the law of the land. Clearly, without assertions of cultural difference, references to human rights regimes or invocations of formal citizenship in a nation-state, born-again Christianity provided the migrants, as well as the natives who joined them, with a form of membership. It gave them the means of claiming, participating in, and contributing morally and politically to the public sphere in Halle and Manchester.

Migrants and natives told us that they came to the events because of their concerns for religious unity, stronger families and churches, and the need to ensure Manchester was a Christian city. The white natives of New Hampshire who came to events sponsored by the Crusade had class backgrounds that ranged from manual labor to successful business people. Many had developed personal networks with migrants through such shared activities as prayer "intercessors" or other Christian projects in the city. For core activists, migrants and natives alike, the network of believers became their primary social field, if assessed by the density of their network ties. At the same time, migrant core activists built weak but significant bridging ties into other spheres of life including the political domain.

The ties were weak in Mark Granovetter's (1973) sense that the migrants' networks to political actors were not based on multiple mutual or dense connections. But the ties provided the migrants, who participated in the Crusade's social field, with social capital. They became connected to people who could and did provide resources: shop foreman who helped with hiring; middle-class house wives who furnished apartments for new comers or provided clothing and furniture for newborns; and public officials who provided network members with prestige, social acceptance, and access to public resources. The Crusade's social field enabled the establishment and the expansion of horizontal networks of trust that encompassed both migrants and natives. Migrants who are not activists in the Crusade but who attended churches, breakfasts, prayer conferences, and days of prayer linked to the Crusade had an entry way to this social field and its social capital.

The Crusade was more than an organizational nexus. It had its own individual activists who drew their family, friends, and coworkers into an expanding field of Christian activity and connection. From 2002 to 2005, migrants from all over the world increasingly joined this social field that was constructed and expanded by Heaven's Gift and his core activists. The number of migrants in the core also increased. About 20 percent of those who attended conferences, prayer breakfasts, and prayer events sponsored by the Crusade were migrants of African, Caribbean, Latin American, and Asian origin. Most of the congregations that joined the Crusade resembled Heaven's Gift's home church; they were composed primarily of white New Hampshire natives. Although there was a Spanish-speaking and an African American congregation within the Crusade network, these congregations stressed that their primary identity was not as ethnic churches but as true born-again Christians.

Among the public resources made available to Heaven's Gift through political networks was a weekly television show on local public access television in which Heaven's Gift was the featured preacher. This outlet gave him a broader public, which reinforced the ability of members of the Crusade to obtain access to political leaders and politicians. At the same time, the nonethnic base built by immigrants in the Crusade could open the door for their direct participation in electoral politics. In the course of our study, Manchester elected Dominican, Haitian, and Puerto Rican state representatives. The Haitian representative also had a religious cable television program and his connection to public access television provided him with an array of other influential city-wide networks. Although the Puerto Rican candidate received support from his Hispanic constituency, all three men could only be elected by having a strong base among immigrants of all nationalities, as well as voters who were native to New Hampshire. Their election provided an indication to migrants in the Crusade of the possibilities that may flow from exactly the kind of the political networks Heaven's Gift has developed for himself and members of the organization.

As did the Miracle Healing Church in Halle, the Resurrection Crusade belonged to a born-again Christian social field that extended around the world. It included a pastor of Nigerian background who lived in England and a husband and wife evangelical team from Texas who made yearly visits to Manchester in a circuit that took them around the world. They brought with them and infused into the prayers of the Manchester churches a militant language calling for "spiritual warfare" by "prayer warriors." The Texas couple headed the U.S. Prayer Center that produced books, videos, and DVDs and distributed them into dozens of countries. They were experts in "spiritual housecleaning," a process of prayer that claimed to remove demonic forces from a home. As did the pastors and members of the two churches in Halle and Heaven's Gift and members of the Crusade in Manchester, these Texas preachers portrayed world events and human sickness in terms of an ever present battle between God and Satan. The Crusade trained "prayer intercessors" in "strategic or city level spiritual warfare" against the devil who assigns his "territorial spirits. . . . to rule geographical territories and social networks" (Smith 1999: 23). In 2005 the Crusade established the Manchester Prayer Center in an office building in the business district of Manchester where Christians could come to pray or could call to speak to a spiritual counselor. All these activities legitimated the claims of the Resurrection Crusade, including its migrants, to not only being a part of the city but of providing it with spiritual leadership.

### SOCIAL CITIZENSHIP AND BORN-AGAIN INCORPORATION IN SMALL SCALE CITIES

In a city such as Manchester forming a Nigerian congregation would have been difficult considering there were only a handful of Nigerians in the city and they included both Catholics and Muslims. However, Heaven's Gift might have had success in using a panethnic African identity to form a church. There were several hundred African Protestants in Manchester and an African identity is becoming part of public discourse and these migrants' self-ascription. Instead Heaven's Gift joined a home church that was mostly white and working class but included in its ranks migrants from Ghana, Iraq, and Sudan. And he invested most of his energies in building a religious network that linked believers together on the basis of a born-again Christian rather than ethnic, national, or racial identity.[7] In Halle, there were enough migrants to organize Nigerian and Congolese churches based on their national identity and to link those congregations to homeland churches. Yet this form of settlement and ethnic religious identification was not taken.

The significance of the incorporative pathway of born-again Christianity as a means of exercising social citizenship in both Manchester and Halle, although followed by relatively few migrants, must be evaluated within the context of the minimal possibilities for either ethnic incorporation or social mobility on the basis of education that the two cities provided. In Manchester, as in Halle, cultural or social citizenship claims based on ethnic community formation were difficult to develop because the cities lacked the resources that encouraged ethnic organizing in gateway or global cities: a critical mass of migrants of a single nationality, an ethnic niche economy or market, and social and philanthropic support for ethnic organizations.[8] In Manchester, unlike larger-scale cities such as New York or Boston, very few public or private agencies provided migrants with opportunities to develop careers as culture brokers who represent the needs or interests of particular ethnicities. Those few migrants who obtained positions in social service agencies generally have not occupied managerial positions and there has been little social mobility for migrants or the possibility for them to become incorporated into city life as representatives of ethnic groups. In settings in which there seem to be fewer supports for ethnically-based incorporation, nonethnic religion allowed some migrants in both cities to exercise a form of social citizenship that linked them to both their new city of residence and globally (Glick Schiller, Caglar, and Guldbrandsen 2006a and 2006b).

While, on the one hand, ethnic community formation as a form of social or cultural citizenship may be less feasible in small-scale cities, incorporation through Christian congregations that preach global Christianity may be more possible and more salient in these locations.[9] In these cities, a religion such as Christianity, especially in its born-again or Pentecostal varieties, offered connections to people ranging from international preachers to political leaders who are important in local, national, and global arenas. Such forms of connection and the social capital that its weak ties provided were certainly visible in both cities.[10]

Both Manchester and Halle were not only small in size but also in scale—that is to say they have no hubs of finance, commerce, culture, or media that would provide a cosmopolitan context for migrant settlement. In both cities, migrants were cast simultaneously as dangerous or exotic others and as useful colorful bodies that represent a necessary component for marketing the city as a global actor. Migrants, especially African migrants, were highly visible, despite their small numbers. Migrants tend to bring a more cosmopolitan aura to these cities and to the extent that city officials and business leaders sought to market their cities as localities of multicultural difference, they looked to the migrants.[11] The migrants who joined the nonethnic churches sought a place of worship that did not highlight their public differentiation and brought them together with the natives on terms other than cultural difference. They welcomed the Christian born-again churches, such as those in the Resurrection Crusade network or the Pentecostal churches of Halle, because they divided the world between the saved and unsaved. This categorization allowed migrants to be among the saved, allocating them legitimacy and including them among the saviors of the city.

It is interesting to note that both the U.S. Prayer Center and the *Bund freikirchlicher Pfingstgemeinden* (Organization of Free Churches) specifically encouraged identification with the local city. The global evangelizing networks to which the congregations we studied belonged all made reference in their literature and their Web sites to the need to wage spiritual warfare in order to root out the evil within each locality. By choosing to emphasize a Christian universalism rather than an ethnic particularism, the migrants who joined this religious movement sought ways to become incorporated as local and global actors on their own terms. They obtained political voice, as well as access to various kinds of social and economic resources not on the basis of legal citizenship, cultural difference, or human rights but on biblical scripture.

## CHRISTIAN SOCIAL CITIZENSHIP AS AN IMPERIAL PROJECT

The Christian social citizenship claims of the migrants in our study reflected and resonated with the current political project of the leadership of the United States and its efforts to influence political outcomes not only in the United States, but worldwide. The connections between current U.S. foreign policy and fundamentalist Christians we observed were both ideological and organizational. Rather than repudiating states or political activism, these fundamentalist Christians supported special roles for certain states in the battle against evil. The United States was seen as a redeemer nation and the modern state of Israel was taken as evidence of God's plan coming to fruition. Support for the United States in both Afghanistan and Iraq could be heard from both the Nigerian pastor and core migrant members of the Miracle Church in Halle and from the Nigerian head of the Resurrection Crusade in Manchester and his members.

Among fundamentalist Christians, the role of the United States in the world is linked to biblical prophecy. Multilateralism including the United Nations is understood as part of a current conjunction of evil, a war of Armageddon, disease, immorality, and natural disaster that the Bible foretells (Oldfield 2004). If multilateralism is the work of the devil, than U.S. unilateralism can be justified as the work of God. It is important to note that there is no single born-again movement but a series of overlapping organizations, each of which has their own priorities but all of which have been loosely united in support of U.S. actions around the world.

Key makers of U.S. foreign policy and the president of the United States are members of this transnational social field. President George W. Bush is himself a fervent born-again Christian and belongs to religious networks that hold these beliefs. However, it is not just Bush's personal beliefs that have connected U.S. foreign policy to a fundamentalist form of Christianity. Grassroots networks of fundamentalist Christians have become directly engaged in political solicitation for candidates and policies of the Republican Party and in support of U.S. imperialist projects in the Middle East and elsewhere. The Christian Coalition, founded in 1989 by preacher Pat Robinson with the goal of "defending America's Godly heritage by getting Christians involved in their government again," was at first seen as a stronghold of the far right (Christian Coalition 2005). By 2004 the Coalition had become a mainstream player in the Republican Party and in the White House. Its ability to turn out the vote was made clear by the results of the Republican congressional victories in 1994 and directly contributed to Bush's ability to take the White House in 2000 and 2004. This activity and influence became widely acknowledged by both scholars and the press, especially after the religious vote proved to be significant in the 2004 presidential elections.[12]

The efforts of neoconservative theorists to actually recruit a religious migrant constituency have been less widely remarked upon. Paralleling the recruitment of anti-Communist Hungarian, Cuban, Czech, Polish, and Vietnamese refugees during the Cold War, the neoconservatives have been using U.S. refugee policy to select born-again Christians who are encouraged to espouse and propagate their religious fundamentalism throughout the United States. Often these refugees come from areas of interest to U.S. foreign policy. Of central interest seems to be refugees from an array of countries linked to the U.S. goal of dominating the world's oil supplies. The United States has accepted Christian asylum seekers and supported political leaders and movements from such countries as Sudan, Indonesia, and Nigeria. Many of these countries are characterized by tensions between Christians and Muslims.[13]

The U.S. Prayer Center, the fundamentalist Christian network to which Heaven's Gift and his Resurrection Crusade organization belong, has distributed President Bush's biography in return for a financial pledge to their organization. The center, recruiting worldwide under the slogan of "Disciplining the Nations," boasted that its members include 4,000 pastors. These disciples were encouraged to identify with the United States, which was portrayed on the Web site, during the year before the 2004 elections, as "God's right hand under President Bush," who speaks directly with the Lord. Readers were informed that the United States was founded in order to institute a Christian mission and were encouraged to use their vote to make sure that the nation once again embraced this cause.

Through such messages, people within fundamentalist Christian networks such as the one organized by Heaven's Gift were encouraged to identify with the United States, even as they espoused a Christian identity. Heaven's Gift insisted that divisions over doctrine were the work of the devil and the goal of Christian organizing was unity. Part of that unity must be expressed by praying for President Bush because Bush had declared he was intent on obeying God's commands. Here it is important to note that identification with the United States was not a simple identification with a nation-state. This allegiance was given on the basis of a form of born-again ideology that portrayed the United States under Bush as leading the struggle against satanic forces and for the establishment of the kingdom of the Lord.

For these Christians, the U.S. flag did not symbolize Americanization, the assimilation of immigrants into a U.S. identity that precludes identification with the rest of the world. Instead the U.S. flag, which decorated the U.S. Prayer Center's Web site, was waved for the United States in its role of defending Christians globally and combating evil around the world. Distinctions between immigrants and foreigners lost importance vis-à-vis the more significant born-again Christian identity. What mattered was the acceptance of Jesus. Only those who believed would be saved.

Similar beliefs and perspectives were present in the migrant churches in Halle. As we have noted, Joshua, the Nigerian pastor of the Miracle Healing Church, maintained ongoing ties to and collected money for the Morris Cerullo World Evangelical Ministry, which was based in the United States and espoused the politics of U.S. fundamentalist Christians. Cerullo circled the world holding evangelical gatherings of tens of thousands of people and met with third world leaders (Cerullo 2005). It is important to note that Heaven's Gift was also a great fan of Cerullo, had attended one of his conferences, and had filled the Crusade's bookshelves with his books. Through the Cerullo ministry, the Miracle Healing Church in Halle supported evangelical work in Israel.

Ruby, a Nigerian woman who served as treasurer of the Miracle Healing Church, summarized her understanding of the God-Israel–Iraq-U.S. nexus as follows: To be "on the side of Israel is to be on the side of God. The U.S. is on the side of Israel." She also declared that the "United States must be doing the work of God in Iraq because it is a country with so many strong Christians and because it is a friend of Israel's." Through a network of networks the Miracle Church and the Resurrection Crusade were linked in their common support for Israel and its protector and major foreign donor, the United States.

It is widely acknowledged that in the past, missionaries served as ideological agents of imperial rule, legitimating the right of colonial states to transform the belief systems of the colonized and impose the values, standards, laws, and interests of the colonizers (Comaroff and Comaroff 1991). Christian missions also had a profound impact on the shaping of notions of race, gender, nation, and citizen in the colonizing countries, although this aspect of the global expansion of Christianity is less studied. Today the evangelizing organizations and networks of fundamentalist Christians follow a similar process globally by legitimating the exercise of imperial power. They provide the missionary zeal and the call for spiritual and moral revival. In their quest to claim membership in their new land, migrants to Europe and the Unites States from these regions become organizationally and ideologically linked to Christian fundamentalism, claiming the entire world as a U.S. domain. Their support for global evangelization is an aspect of their local role in their place of settlement. Their missionary activity often includes sending money and missionaries abroad as well as asserting spiritual leadership in their new home.

In their incorporation into municipalities, states, and into the United States as a whole, born-again Christian migrants find themselves quite at home. Their deeply held beliefs resonate with the dominant U.S. political project. The critique they make of the culture around them is reinforced and celebrated by those in power. The networks that may have brought them to the United States, or those they join, connect them not only to a welcoming rhetoric but also to powerful local and national political actors. Even without legal citizenship they find themselves welcomed into the processes of building political and cultural constituencies that affirm the dominant political project. They are esteemed as part of this project. The centrality of New Hampshire as a focus of presidential politics gives Christian migrants there a particularly high profile role.

Although the situation of born-again Christian migrants in Germany seems to be of a different nature, the evangelizing and expanding Christian networks and their capacity to access powerful people and legitimate their presence in Germany on similar grounds. While the majority of the population of the former West Germany holds official membership in a recognized church and pays taxes collected by the state to support church activities, born-again churches are seen by most of the population as sects rather than legitimate congregations. Furthermore, in the states of the former East Germany, most people do not belong to any church. Ironically, however, as in many other places in Europe, fundamentalist Christianity is growing rapidly in Germany. In this context, migrants who assert a belonging to the city by bringing Christian morality to the place find a kind of legitimacy that would not be accorded to other religious groups and leaders. Moreover, for the local Germans in eastern cities such as Halle who are faced with massive unemployment, the fact that African migrants can mediate connections to institutions of power through their globe spanning Christian networks can legitimate their local settlement. At the same time, the born-again migrants—connected as they are though Christian networks to the U.S. imperial project—feel that both heavenly and earthly powers grant them to right to speak and to belong wherever they have settled.

CONCLUSION

If we examined the two born-again congregations formed by migrants in Halle from the point of view of legal citizenship, we could easily conclude, as do many of the scholars in Germany, that such migrants are not part of German society. The recent changes in German citizenship laws that will now allow a handful of members of the two congregations to obtain citizenship are not changing the view of these scholars, who deploy an ethnic lens when they look at congregations such as the ones we studied. Prepared to see segregation and cultural difference, that is what they find. Yet the migrant members of these congregations developed pathways of incorporation. They began to speak and act in the name of the city despite their varying legal status. The born-again activities included: asserting rights to be in Halle and in Germany as God's missionaries, insisting on maintaining a presence in Germany, and obtaining state benefits and services despite the persistent efforts of the German state to force them to leave; participating in public activities that promote and celebrate the city; providing Germans access to transnational born-again networks; and providing public activities that promise healing to the general population. Thus, despite the nonreligious nature of the former GDR (German Democratic Republic), born-again Christian activities located the migrants (though ambiguously) into the city's social and political landscape.

The New Hampshire case is even more striking. Migrants, some of whom were not legal citizens and did not have the right to vote, were courted by city and state politicians because they organized a religious network that contained persons who were not only eligible to vote but consistently voted. Furthermore born-again Christian migrants in New Hampshire facilitate the incorporation of the natives into the city, nationally, and transnationally through their influential Christian networks and through the "healing" they provide.

In short, migrants, who hold a range of legal statuses including permanent resident, refugee, asylum seeker, and the undocumented, may make claims on the state in which they are living, despite their missing legal citizenship. Furthermore they may become social actors within that state influencing its policies, procedures, discourses, and foreign relations. However, it is important to note that the particular access to social citizenship through born-again Christian networks takes on much of its force from the particular historical conjuncture in which the United States holds the dominant position in the world and uses the neoconservative Christian project as a crucial part of its claim to legitimacy. Catholicism, Islam, and Buddhism also provide transnational networks and universalist claims that can offer its practitioners a claim to rights within a locality. The intermediate role claimed by Muslim organizations brought to France from Pakistan to missionize to North African migrants and then utilized by the French state in the midst of the fall 2005 urban uprisings is an instance of one form Islamic social citizenship. However, the various religious networks and narratives lead migrants to different sets of positioning and claims on states.

As we have shown in this chapter, discussions of citizenship cannot be grounded only in the legal system and cannot be confined to membership in a single nation-state. Migrants' access to overlapping networks that provide status, resources, and legitimation offer venues for their participation as social citizens within a nation-state of settlement and also can give them influence in other nation-states into which these networks extend. The transnational networks of born-again Christian migrants with their global claims to universal moral values can have an impact on the positioning of migrants within a particular locality and nation-state. The experiences of the born-again Christians in Manchester and Halle remind us that discussions of citizenship can not be reduced to legal citizenship, enfranchisement, and participation in the electoral system of a state. On the other hand, the types of social citizenship that migrants may assert can have an impact on the political process including the electoral system. Finally, as they assert their social citizenship locally, migrants may contribute to the wielding and legitimation of power, including imperial power, globally.

ACKNOWLEDGMENTS

A version of this chapter was delivered at the American Anthropological Association Session: Immigrants and the Practice of "Citizenship": Perspectives from Europe and the U.S., December 2005. The chapter builds on an analysis of citizenship in Glick Schiller (2005a), on migrants use of global Christianity in local settlement (Karagiannis and Glick Schiller 2006), on imperialism and transnational social fields (Glick Schiller 2005c), on nonethnic forms of migrant incorporation (Glick Schiller, Caglar, and Guldbrandsen 2006b), on social citizenship (Glick Schiller 2005d), and on city scale and migrant incorporation (Caglar and Glick Schiller 2006). Funding was provided by the Max Planck Institute for Social Anthropology, the McArthur Foundation (Program on Global Security and Human Sustainability), the Sidore Fellowship of the University of New Hampshire, the Center for Humanities of the University of New Hampshire and the Willy Brandt Guest Professorship, IMER, Malmö University. Special thanks to Gunther Schlee, Bert Feintuch, Caroline B. Brettell, Maja Pourzanovic

Frykmah, and the pastors and congregants for their encouragement. We have changed the name of all respondents in keeping with the commitments we made to them.

NOTES

1. The research team in Manchester consisted of Nina Glick Schiller, Thaddeus Guldbrandsen, and Peter Buchannan and in Halle, Nina Glick Schiller, Evangelis Karagiannis, Martin Seiber, Markus Rao, and Julia Wenzel and student assistants from the Department of Ethnology of Martin Luther University, Halle.
2. Building on concepts developed by the Manchester school of anthropologists (Epstein 1967; Mitchell 1969) and by Bourdieu, we define social field as a network of networks.
3. See, for example, research on Alevi and other Islamic networks in Europe in which migrants shape their religious claims within citizenship discourses and identity politics. Their claim making processes develop in interplay with the opportunity structures provided by various states, the EU, and human rights regimes.
4. Our broader study explores multiple pathways of local and transnational incorporation. Our ethnography included interviews with city leaders and more than sixty interviews with migrants in each city. In addition, we participated in events and activities of migrant religious organizations and interviewed core activists in both cities.
5. There are ethnic congregations in Manchester but if we configure our research by focusing only on ethnonationalist churches or transnational communities that build such churches we miss important transborder processes.
6. The National Day of Prayer was taken over by born-again Christians and used in their spiritual warfare campaigns.
7. Manchester did have some Protestant churches that were Spanish in language but Christian in identity and several Korean Protestant congregations seem to have promoted their ethnic distinctiveness.
8. For a discussion of the concept of scale see Brenner (1998, 1999a, 1999b, 2004) and Caglar and Glick Schiller 2006; for a plea to consider the context of the city see Brettell (2003)
9. This may be true for other religions as well.
10. The differences between the cities are addressed in another paper. See Glick Schiller, Caglar, and Guldbrandsen (2006b).
11. This occurred more in Manchester than in Halle, which has tried to emphasize its history rather than its diversity in recent marketing campaigns
12. Although by 2006 there was some disarray in the coalition, the grassroots believers did not doubt the righteousness of the project and continued to see war in the Middle East as evidence of "end times."
13. Eliot Abrahms, who became a member of the National Security Council under George W. Bush, previously wrote about religious freedom and then served as chair of the commission established by the U.S. International Religious Freedom Act of 1998.

CHAPTER 11

# Immigrants as Netizens

## POLITICAL MOBILIZATION IN CYBERSPACE

*Caroline B. Brettell*

A NUMBER OF SCHOLARS have begun to look at the Internet as a mechanism for organizing immigrant populations, creating community, and constructing identity (Clarke 2004; Gibb 2002; Graham and Khosravi 2002; Lee and Wong 2003; Miller and Slater 2000; Mitra 2000; Panagakos 2003; Rai 1995; Sokefeld 2002; Thompson 2002). In particular they have emphasized how the Internet works to link dispersed populations to their homelands. Daniel Miller and Don Slater, for example, observe that Trinidadians who live in London, New York, Toronto, or Miami use the Internet to keep in touch with family and friends in Trinidad as well as to "reconstitute or enact 'trini-ness' on line" (2000: 27). Writing about Haitians, Angel Adams Parham uses the concept of the "diasporic public sphere" to draw attention to how Internet forums "help marginal actors strengthen their own networks and gain needed attention from civil society actors during community struggles" (2004: 202). He further suggests that while Internet forums are places where people distanced by space can express their opinions to a broad audience, the more challenging goal is to "foster networks among these others that one can mobilize around specific issues or projects" (203).

The process of mobilization alluded to by Parham has not been thoroughly examined for immigrant populations despite its apparent effectiveness in the broader population, evidenced in particular by the Howard Dean presidential campaign, as well as by such organizations as MoveOn.org. Indeed, as recently as 2002, in an article published in *Political Geography*, Lynn Staeheli et al. noted that there was no sign of immigrant mobilization on the net. "The political spaces seem to be informational spaces in which the politics are not easily or directly read" (2002: 989). These authors ask whether the Internet can become a political space "in which issues related to the incorporation of immigrants can be debated or whether it is a space that fosters a more fractionalized politics unlikely to lead to greater political incorporation of immigrants" (991). Their interests parallel a broader debate in the literature about whether or not the Internet "mobilizes or demobilizes citizens" (Weber, Loumakis, and Bergman 2003: 26). Staeheli et al. conclude that the Internet is "far more effective at providing information than it is in mobilization" and that "the frequently heralded potential of the Internet as a space for politics is not being met" (2002: 1005). And yet others have suggested that the speed and connectivity of the Internet offer a powerful foundation for the organization of political and social movements (Castells 2001; Cohen and Rai 2000; Gurak 1997).

In this chapter, and as a contribution to the anthropology of online communities (Wilson and Peterson 2002), I document a case of Internet political mobilization among a group of immigrants who have been working since early 2004 to lobby Congress on immigration policy and legislation.[1] I explore the process of civic education and engagement that this Internet group represents, as well as how it illustrates one mechanism of political incorporation for new immigrants in the United States. The group is called Unitefamilies.org. The majority of active members are legal permanent residents of the United States (green card holders) who have found themselves in a bind. This bind is best represented by two stories:

Nori [a pseudonym], a Japanese citizen, has been a lawful permanent resident of the United States since the early 1990s. He earned an MBA from Northern Arizona University. He "fell in love" with the United States and has made many friends. He does volunteer work and pays his taxes. In 2003 he met a Japanese woman, Midori, who worked in the Chicago area where he was then living. Before she left for Japan, when her visa expired, he proposed to her. She accepted and they "were in heaven for just a moment." Then they realized that if Nori, as a legal permanent resident, married her, it would take six years before Midori would be granted a visa to enter the United States to be with him. During this waiting period, Midori would not even be allowed to enter the United States as a visitor. "We are suffering from separation, and frustrated by this inhumanity. Don't I deserve a right to live with my loved one? She is highly educated, likes to help others, and I'm sure she will contribute to this country in many ways."

Amit [a pseudonym], a citizen of India, is living in the United States and has a green card. A few years ago he married Priya [a pseudonym] who was in the United States on an H-1B visa, working for a big telecommunications company. When Priya became pregnant they started to worry about what they were going to do. If Priya stopped working after the baby was born she would go "out of status" and would have to leave the country within ten days, probably taking her U.S. citizen baby—who would require a visa to enter India—with her. If she stayed she would face deportation and the impossibility of ever returning. If she continued to work the baby would have to be in day care although they could bring Priya's mother to the United States for as much as six months [if they could arrange a tourist visa for her—harder after 9/11] to care for the baby at home. If she continued to work but was laid off, they would again face the possibility of separation and waiting for several years before the family could be reunited.

Nori and Amit, both of whom are active members of Unitefamilies, may not be U.S. citizens but they are netizens. A netizen has been defined as "a person actively involved in online communities" (http://en.wikipedia.org/wiki/Netizen), or, more broadly speaking, as a citizen of the Net. Mark Poster (2001:7) is somewhat more precise, using "netizen" to refer to a political subject constituted in cyberspace. While his emphasis is on the deterritorialized netizen who "shares allegiance to the nation with allegiance to the net and to the planetary political spaces it inaugurates," I use the term here to describe a group of individuals who are using the Internet to create a civically engaged community of practice (Lave and Wegner 1991) online.

By the spring of 2006, the netizens of Unitefamilies were about 700 in number from around the United States and even abroad[2] who had come together online to raise awareness in Washington and around the United States about what they saw as an inequity in immigration policy and something that contradicts the family values posited by the Bush administration. If an individual who has entered the United States on a student visa (F1) or on a temporary work visa (H1B), or some other temporary work visa (B1, L1, etc.), returns to the home country to marry, he/she can bring the new spouse into the United States almost immediately (although the accompanying spouse is not permitted to work). The same applies to a U.S. citizen. An individual with a green card (i.e., someone who is lawfully in the United States and is a contributing member of society in terms of working and paying taxes) who returns to the home country to marry has the right to apply for legal immigrant status for his or her spouse (and minor children should they eventually arrive). But, statutory numerical limitations on available visas, coupled with immigration backlogs, generally result in waiting times of five years or more.[3] During this long wait, the foreign resident spouse (and young children) are not permitted to enter the United States. They cannot apply for visitor visas or any other visa (for example, a student visa) because this would be viewed as contradictory to the application for legal residence status. Furthermore, while they wait for the I–130 (a petition for a relative) to be approved and for a visa number to be issued, the LPR spouse must reside predominantly in the United States or lose green card status. Families are consequently divided.

The main goal of Unitefamilies.org has been to garner support in the U.S. Congress for bill HR 1823, a new version of bill 3701 that was sponsored in 2004 by two Democrats—Sheila Jackson-Lee and Robert Andrews—that would amend provisions of the V-visa—a temporary, non-immigrant visa—and remove the current restrictions on that visa. The V visa was enacted by the 106th Congress as part of the LIFE Act of 2000 and allowed family members to coreside while immigrant visa petitions were in process. But this law, which only applied to those who were married before 2000, expired in December of 2003. By 2006, an entirely new population of legal permanent residents had been caught and, like Nori and Amit, were living apart from their spouses and sometimes their minor children.

The data for this chapter derived from my role as both participant and observer in the activities of Unitefamilies.org, beginning in the spring of 2004 and extending through the summer of 2006. As an observer I monitored the Internet exchanges of the group; as a participant, I helped with media coverage in the Dallas area, wrote letters to my congresspersons and senators on their behalf, and accompanied two members on a visit to the local Dallas office of Senator John Cornyn. I have also made a monetary contribution to their efforts.

## Getting Started

Unitefamilies.org was founded in 2004. During the first year emphasis was placed on increasing visibility, and on passage of bill 3701.[4] One writer noted in April of 2004 that the group membership had increased significantly and that the bill itself was being discussed on another online Web forum hosted by an immigration attorney whom they later contacted and who became active with Unitefamilies as well.

Much of the discussion focused on developing an organized set of activities. "We need fresh ideas and to determine the best strategies," wrote one participant. Others observed that they needed to gather some statistics on how many individuals were affected. The members considered hiring a lobby group but recognized that this would take money. "How many people are aware of our site? How many are ready to give $10? How many 100$?" one writer asked. He continued, "If we have 10 interested people who are not millionaires, then there is almost nothing we can do, but if we

have tens of thousands." Members equally pondered how to give their issue
visibility. "If each interested [party] will get 1–2 friends to write exactly the
same letter to a senator will it really help to raise awareness?"

In the summer and fall of 2004, with the advice of someone who was
learning the ways of Washington, there was an active effort to raise funds
for a breakfast meeting with a U.S. senator who has been active on immigration issues. The group was told that they needed $11,000—"a contribu-
tion" to the senator (something that shocked, should I even say appalled,
this anthropologist but that the members of Unitefamilies sanguinely accepted as just part of the process and the way things work in the United
States). The fund raising effort was challenging because it involved the
development of trust in the faceless sphere of Cyberspace. How do you
convince contributors that their money is being used for the purpose intended by people they do not know?[5] These concerns were expressed most
eloquently by one writer: "Is it possible to see information about how contributions are planned to use or being used? The only problem keeping
me (and probably many others) from giving significant contributions is
absence of clarity of its spending. Here I'm not talking about 10$ contri-
bution which is easy to give away even for nothing, but I'm talking about
amounts like 200$–1000$."

The group was able to set up a mechanism for contributions and during the fall they raised $8,000. Since the sum was insufficient, the breakfast
with the U.S. senator was put on hold. During late spring and early summer 2005 they tried again and by the end of June they had raised close to
$12,000 from seventy-one members. By this time the breakfast idea had
been abandoned in favor of letter writing campaigns to those senators and
congresspersons who were active and visible on aspects of immigration
reform[6] and it was decided that the funds should be redirected to hiring
a public relations firm to help make their case on Capitol Hill and in the
media. The group tried to impart a sense of urgency—"Time is not on our
side. Before we know it H.R. 1823 might come to an end." Throughout
the summer repeated e-mails asking for contributions were sent out—the
goal was $50,000. The account manager wrote "If you can donate $500 to
our group, please do so. If you cannot for whatever reason, please consider
donating 2 days of your gross pay. I would think only 2 days of your gross
pay is a fair amount for ALL OF US." One member offered 60,000 American Airlines miles to a raffle for those who contributed during the late
summer and through September 30. In October 2005 the group moved to
hire an identified PR firm for three months—what they could afford. In
the spring and summer of 2006 they directed the new funds they had raised
toward hiring a lobbyist who appeared to be working quite effectively.

The discussion of money generated some other creative ideas that were shared with the group, all of which indicate immigrant perspectives on U.S. values and culture. For example, in June 2004 one writer suggested a system of "premium processing." He wanted a poll to find out how many people would be willing to pay twenty thousand dollars to save seven years of living apart; or ten thousand dollars. He suggested that individuals often spend this kind of money to travel home to see the spouse. Another member, in response to this communication, suggested that this is "the American way: you can buy your way into the country . . . and it is cheaper than the 'founding a business' greencard (which requires you to start a business with 20+ employees and over $100K–$1M in the bank)." He and the original poster speculated on how much money premium processing would generate for the salaries of immigration officers. But concerns about unfairness—for poor immigrants—were equally expressed. And while the original poster suggested that this kind of program would eliminate some antiimmigrant sentiments among those who think immigrants take money from U.S. citizens, the other member noted that Americans are patriots and would not want to "sell" their country. "Just as we wouldn't!" he added.

At the end of 2004, one member offered his own assessment of what they had accomplished and where they needed to go. He noted that they were in the process of assembling a list of representatives and senators likely to support their issue, judging them based on their past voting records and media statements. Several had been contacted. He wrote:

A lot of ideas were debated during the course of 2004. We concluded that we should all aim for just one idea rather than disperse all over. We felt that HR 3701 has the greatest chance of passing since the V-visa had already been enacted once before and the bill does not create any new immigrant visas. National security is not compromised. Unfortunately, we didn't raise our voices loud enough to be heard. We really need to fix that. . . . Congresspeople and aides that I have spoken to have repeatedly said that we need people in Republican constituencies to appeal to their Congressmen/women. Many Republicans are moderate in their views on legal immigration and support family unity.

He then turned to an assessment of areas that needed more work. The group, he thought had to overcome a sense of hopelessness, suggesting that their work required commitment, perseverance, and patience; they had to keep their eye on the ball and "row in the same direction"; they had to find a dynamic leader with time to devote to the cause; and they had to identify people in Republican constituencies who would write to their congresspersons. What this posting suggests is that the first year of activity and organization had resulted both in progressive civic education and in the formulation of a concrete political strategy. It is to these two issues that I now turn.

## A PROCESS OF CIVIC EDUCATION

In the spring of 2004, one member who had clearly informed himself of the political process shared with others the steps by which an immigration bill becomes law in the United States.[7] He observed that passing a bill "is an arduous process. Most bills die in the immigration subcommittee. Every subcommittee and committee is chaired by a Republican and the chairperson controls the (sub)committee agenda. The House subcommittee chair should not be expected to look at a bill until at least 50 Representatives sign on to the bill (3701 has 4)." He offered a final comment: "The current anti-immigrant climate, the fact that the immigration subcommittee chairs are anti-immigrant, the fact that H.R. 3701 was introduced by a Democrat, and the fact that Democrats are divided as to which measure to support are not helping."

The failure to make any progress with HR 3701 in 2004 contributed to an increasing awareness that to be successful they had to have bipartisan support. Thus, in early May of 2005, one participant warned that if they had too many Democrats and no Republicans "our bill will be looked upon as a Democrats bill and then it will become an automatic refusal case for Republicans. My suggestion would be to work on Republicans at least for the next couple of weeks."

Someone explained the difference between gaining cosponsorship for a bill—what they would prefer; gaining support—that the politician would vote yes—; and absence. A general strategy based on this lesson was finally outlined as one member asked for confirmation. "So our aim is: (a) First get Republican Reps co-sponsorship; (b) Add as many as Demo Reps support; (c) Once we get one Republican co-sponsorship, we will get more Republicans support. But I am not aware/clear of when this bill comes on the floor for voting. What are next steps involved? How much time they do get [sic] for voting after introduction?"

Sometimes the education was very basic. When one member wrote that Susan Davis was a Republican another corrected it, telling his Internet colleague that "when you see Rep in front of someone's name it means 'representative' not Republican." This was followed by giving the address of a Web site to visit to find out the party affiliation of various members of the U.S. House and Senate. Another shared what he had learned about how to write an effective petition from research online. He wrote, "While we are investigating the best way to host an online petition, I think we should also focus on the text of the petition. I have read a few petitions on http://petitiononline.com and come up with the following. I would request those who are good at this to wordsmith it for greater impact. According to the experts, the most important reasons why some petitions are more successful than others are: They raise awareness among the most people; their petition text compels action."

Another member made these suggestions.

(1) While representing the group, make sure that the person writing to the legislator is from the legislator's constituency. Legislators ignore letters from those outside their constituencies; (2) Lobby day. Go as a group to Washington and talk to various legislators. If you can't meet the legislators themselves, talk to their policy aides. This will get the message across. They can't ignore you if you are talking to them face-to-face; (3) Even though family unification may not be that controversial, frequently such bills get tacked on to other controversial provisions, and this results in the bill never passing. That might be why other bills have received lukewarm reception; (4) There may not be much point in talking to the anti-immigrant.

Some members worked to become well informed about pending legislation and to share their knowledge online. In late spring of 2005 there were extensive online discussions of the Kennedy-McCain bill and the absence in it of anything relevant to their concerns. One writer, who had called both offices and received polite but lukewarm responses, had this to say at one point: "It looks like their bill, just like all other immigration bills, is mainly about illegal immigrants. Getting them to address our issue too in their upcoming bill is our aim."

The members of Unitefamilies quickly learned that they needed to use their network to create localized groups to work on their own representatives. "We need to mobilize across the country so particular people are dealing with their own Senators and Congressmen—this is how DC works." Particular attention was given to bringing Bobby Jindal, a freshman congressman from Louisiana and an Indian American on board; one member went so far as to try to identify people at Louisiana universities who were immigrants of one status or another.[8] Those with Internet savvy did research online. They identified laws in other countries that were "more friendly" to people in their situation, as well as the bills that had been proposed by various members of the House, the sponsors and cosponsors, and their outcomes. This was a mechanism for learning where particular politicians stood on immigration issues and who might be sympathetic to their cause.

The group had the good fortune in the spring of 2005 to receive the pro bono assistance of a corporate attorney who had a good deal of legislative experience. They did not find her; she found them, taking an interest,

she said, because she had a Japanese friend affected by the laws currently
in place. She directed the attention of the group to a legislative strategy
document that she had composed after a telephone conversation with some
members of the group. She wrote: "If you want to conduct an effective
legislative campaign that is designed to get your legislation passed, then you
will read my legislative strategy and try to follow it as best you can. I hope
you realize that it will be very hard to get this legislation passed if the only
people who support it are from India—Congress likes to help the broadest
range of people possible." This attorney suggested that they needed to provide their congressional supporters with as much information as possible,
anticipating questions that might arise from the opposition during debate
and providing responses. "Politicians, just as we all do, hate surprises during
a debate or argument. A lawmaker who has made up his/her mind to support us will support us even if there are one or two good arguments against
our bill. But they need to be prepared to answer opposing arguments."

### DEVELOPING A POLITICAL STRATEGY

In the early spring of 2005 the most active members came up with a
systematic division of labor and a plan of action. People were assigned to
different tasks (and interestingly enough, by this time many were no longer
anonymous and were using their personal e-mails rather than posting to the
Yahoo! group site, indicating an extension beyond the impersonality of Cy-
berspace]. Among the tasks were media contacts and membership outreach;
coordinating with USINPAC (a Washington, D.C., lobbying group focusing on U.S.-India issues); monitoring specific lawmakers; revamping the
Web site; and raising funds. The poster asked other members to volunteer
for particular activities and suggested that work should begin immediately
since there was no time to waste. He ended with the following: "All members, regardless of the group, are requested to spread the word. Start a chain
mail, bring in new members, print a new t-shirt or do something. We des-
perately need people from various communities such as Hispanic, Philip-
pino [sic], Chinese, European, etc. Please step forward and identify yourself.
Most importantly, keep up your spirits and shed the negative thoughts. . . .
Let us stay on and put up a good fight. I can, for sure, tell you that if we
stand together and work together, we will definitely win."

During the spring of 2005 members of Unitefamilies actively lobbied
members of Congress and reported their results online. Members were informed of the times when local congressmen would be in their districts
and encouraged to make personal contact at that time. Sometimes members
were scolded for their lack of responsiveness. To broaden the base some
members worked on getting the site advertised on Google, focusing on a

host of key words that would catch people's attention and lead them to the Web site. New template letters were posted and individuals shared the responses they received with others.

An Internet Petition was finalized and pretty quickly had more than 400 signatures. By the end of September of 2005 it had more than 1,000. During this process some members raised a number of broader issues that they thought might be included. "Should we include President Bush's 2000 promise to unite families in our petition? Should we mention any of the following:—family unity is the cornerstone of the American immigration system—separating a husband and wife or a parent from a child is counter to the heart of American values? Should we tie it in with economics—how much money is leaving the country to support family abroad? I think that we need some numbers for the petition to be taken seriously. We need an estimate of the number of people affected." For a while the group also debated online about involving churches—as a way to spread their cause and gain support within mainstream U.S. society from institutions that clearly were on the side of family values. Wrote one member "I know some illegal immigrants got support from Church or some other organizations, why we cannot [*sic*]?"

In early June of 2005 members of the group had a teleconference that lasted for one hour and subsequently a very impressive e-mail of action items and justifications was distributed. A list of talking points to help members who met with their own representatives was circulated. During the summer of 2005, in addition to executing the action items (which focused largely on contacting specific senators—especially those on the immigration subcommittee of the 108th and 109th Congress, broadening the base of those who became involved in making contacts with their representatives and encouraging employers to express concern about their problem), the group made efforts to reach out to Hispanics and Koreans. They had their petition translated into Spanish. They explored the idea of having someone participate in the "Ask the White House" interactive forum. They also decided to continue raising awareness and this meant a better-developed media strategy. In early August 2005 a delegation met with Representative Charles Fishman in Washington and shared their minutes of the meeting online. They recognized the need to keep working on securing solid Republican cosponsorship so that HR 1823 would not be viewed as a Democrat's bill. These efforts continued into the fall of 2005. In October of 2005 one member shared with the group the letter he had received from Senator Richard Lugar—it was read as a positive step since Lugar indicated knowledge of HR 3701 and stated that if the new legislation came to the floor of the Senate he would keep the views of the letter-writer in mind.

## Tackling the Media

Some members had attempted to capture some media attention during the fall of 2004 by carrying banners at election rallies and by contacting CNN after the Lou Dobbs series on immigration ran. Others wanted to point out to the CNN staff that by only covering illegal immigrant issues they were not dealing with all aspects of immigration. However, only in the spring of 2005 did the group begin to consider a more concerted media strategy. In January of 2005 one member wrote:

> It is time we get serious about making some noise in the media. . . . We are probably not going to be able to get big guys like CNN and Fox to cover our stories. But, we definitely stand a good chance with local news-papers. First let us do the groundwork. Do some research on internet and come up with names, organizations and contact info of reporters who in the past have written on immigration related issues. At this point in time, it doesn't matter if the article was pro or anti immigration. It doesn't mat-ter if the reporter or his organization is some big-shot or not.

Another member observed that a few good print articles would draw broader attention in the electronic media. He suggested that they make things personal because "reporters like to talk to people who have prob-lems." The group developed a press release and indeed had some success with coverage during the spring, summer, and early fall of 2005, includ-ing some stories in Indian newspapers in India and one in a Taiwanese online newspaper.[9] Among the media objectives settled on in June of 2005 were: greater involvement of the mainstream media, including news mag-azines, which they thought would increase Republican interest in their cause; using a PR firm to help increase the membership; creating a press kit for journalists and congressional members; writing op-ed articles for mainstream newspapers; and providing their stories to "affluent" maga-zines—*Vanity Fair*, *GQ*, *Vogue*.

During the spring of 2006 the group took full advantage of the fact that the country itself was focused on immigration reform. They had sev-eral media successes, including a program on legal immigration on Na-tional Public Radio. Members were encouraged to call in with their stories and comments during the airing. Similarly several local reporters across the country indicated an interest in having personal stories and many members complied. Messages such as the following appeared frequently: "Folks, I just talked to Deepti Hajela from the Associated Press in New York City. She wants to talk to affected LPRs (Legal Permanent Residents) from New York City. So, members in that area, please contact her as soon as you can by email. Thanks." The consultant they had hired also landed two full pages for articles on *News India U.S.A.* and members were asked to submit wedding and family photos. He also sent out explicit instructions for composing good and succinct letters to the editor, encouraging the group to write in response to an op-ed they had succeeded in placing in the *Washington Post*. In the summer of 2006 the Associated Press picked up their cause and an article appeared in a number of newspapers across the country.[10]

## NOT WITHOUT FRUSTRATION

Maintaining the momentum did not occur without moments of frustration and impatience expressed by members of the group—frustration with each other and particularly with those who did not participate and do their bit; impatience with political officials who were nonresponsive; frustration directed at U.S. society; and impatience at the slowness of the political process. But these sentiments were reigned in by others, who reminded everyone about Internet etiquette as well as offered good political advice about keeping one's eye on the target.

Time was of the essence for many. As one member put it—"the approach we have taken now is good if we have all the time in the world. People, by the time your spouse joins you, you will have reached middle age and all the charm about being married is gone . . . fast action is what we need." Another member offered this: "What is really upsetting is that there are many affected people who are doing nothing. Several people feel that their letters/petitions will not get any attention and this is a lost cause. If we can fight this apathy and get our act together, I think we can convince Congress to pass this bill." Some even contextualized their problem in broader cultural terms. Thus one Indian member observed: "In the Indian system of arranged marriages, permanent residency is an automatic black mark. A friend of mine had to break his engagement because of this." Presumably this occurred because Indian parents know it may mean years of separation.

A Ukrainian member wrote that in his country, a group such as this would "set tents next to Congress stairway and demand what we really want: that is—to be united with our loved ones. They would not leave until some politician would come out and make a statement. But well, we are in a democratic country. Trying to lobby anything through senators or a PR campaign is the most ineffective way to fight for the simple human right. Most of you guys with oriental mentality think that you can get it by lubricating the system. Good luck."

More generally, a few members took it upon themselves to boost morale whenever frustration took over. One writer mentioned having a Chinese friend who flies back to China for two weeks to be with his wife and then returns to work who had resigned himself to the fact that this was just the status quo and how he had convinced him to join the group to fight for their rights. Collectively, this writer suggested, they could be a powerful voice. Another wrote: "What we are engaged in is called a 'grass roots' effort. That means that it starts at the ground level and works its way up the chain as more and more regular people come together to support the need for legislative reform. As you are beginning to realize the more we stick together and sing the same song, the more likely our voice will be heard. . . . Grass roots efforts can work and have worked. But we need to be consistent, persistent, and unified. Then everyone wins."

The "cheerleading" did not always stem criticism of the U.S. immigration system. One member wrote: "Current immigration law practically requires spouse of US GC holder to be as bright as himself in order to get to U.S., otherwise—no way except 7 year waiting [sic]." He saw a system that "makes all H-1B people suffer from unemployment, all students suffer from instability while letting illegal aliens stay. . . . U.S. immigration system give more chances to those who commit fraud and violate laws rather than for to those who try to work hard and earn the right to be American." When one member equated immigration with slavery, another member responded with: "I do understand that your outbursts . . . are results of the pain and misery you have been put through by our immigration system. However, I have to say that we should NOT stoop down to the level of America/American bashing. Let us stay focused on our issue and let us fight for family reunification. Let us not get into the wider pro or anti immigration arguments. . . . We do not want to agitate anybody—inside or outside this group. I expect each of you to be responsible and careful in what you say and post to the group."

The summer of 2005 brought more optimism as Unitefamilies members saw some of their efforts yielding results and the support for HR 1823 growing. As one member wrote, noting the "awesome" progress with congress people, "Maybe we should become SHOCK jocks, just like Howard Stern!" And another, who signed himself as "the eternal optimist" observed that the statistics on petition signatures, Web site visits, and group membership were encouraging and simply wrote "Don't give up, don't ever give up."

But there were also notes of caution with one member astutely advising that what they needed to do is attach their bill to a larger bill. This, he suggested, required research on what bills have the greatest chance of passing and on the procedure for attaching one bill to another in the context of bipartisan politics.

During the spring of 2006, as Unitefamilies members followed the debates on immigration reform, frustrations (and the sense of injustice) increased because so much of the emphasis was on illegal immigration. In early June 2006, one member observed: "I write to you in SHAME that senate considered CROOKS people who did everything legally. I have been away from my wife for 5 years now and still you and the senate thought that given Amnesty to ILLEGAL BORDER JUMPERS was a priority but my poor wife should CONTINUE TO SUFFER. Why should my taxes go to teach a child of an illegal immigrant when I am not even given the liberty to be with my wife and start planning a family?"

There was also a good deal of discussion about mounting a lawsuit and some members went online to investigate (and then share with the group) precedent cases where the government was sued. One member wrote the following with a degree of optimism: "We have good chances of winning the lawsuit. What do we have to loose [sic] . . . US government can't punish us for this . . . If illegals can come and demand legalization then we can also demand justice. Believe in yourself and in your demand and in your rights. All we need is a smart lawyer, and some signatures for CLASS–ACTION LAWSUIT. Worst case, if we don't have money, we can file the lawsuit ourselves."

Others responded with more caution, questioning whether there were sufficient grounds for a suit and posing the question of what rights noncitizens really had. For a day or two there was a debate about whether or nor immigration was a privilege.

### Engaging in the Larger Debate: Immigration and Antiimmigration

Some of this discussion generated useful comments about how to engage the broader U.S. public—their friends and colleagues in the workplace in their issue and in broader immigration issues. It also revealed a powerful sense of rights—indeed this was a group making a rights-based argument. One member said that he recognized how important it was to get mainstream Americans to sign the petition but said that he was having some difficulty doing this.

The reason is that I feel some level of shame trying to ask my close friends to support our bill and also [I am] afraid to shade my relationship if he doesn't support it. When I ask for it I can't answer simple questions and this is my problem . . . Here is my conversation with one of my coworker-citizens who I expected to sign up, but it didn't happen: (1) I explain my problem that I suffer and here is the solution; (2) He says that he understands it but America can not support everybody in the world; (3) I say immigrants are helping economy, hard working; (4) He asks then why shouldn't we open all US borders and let everybody in?; (5) At this point I don't know what to say. If I say yes, he will laugh at me, if I say no then no. . . . Any ideas how to make him sign a petition?

Another member replied in this way: "Nobody is asking America to support everybody in the world. Neither are we asking America to go to Uganda and help unite families there. We are asking OUR government (yes, it is our government too, because they use our money to function) to permit us live with our spouses. If the government can't do it, then the government should stop inviting people over to immigrate."

During the spring of 2005 there was also an interchange about how U.S. immigration policy (as it affected them) was shaped by the potential for marriage fraud. Observed one member: "If our opponent is going to argue that [the] V-visa encourages marriage fraud, then he/she will need to give us some kind of proof. How many fraud cases were there on V-visa? Probably none. Most of the marriage fraud cases involve US citizens, not LPRs." Another member added: "I want all of you to stop being afraid of opposition to our bill from anti-immigrant lobbies. As I said in one of my previous e-mails, our opponents will never oppose us publicly. Even staunch anti-immigrant advocates such as Representative Tom Tacredo, when asked on TV, was quick to say 'I am not against legal immigration, I'm against illegal immigration.'"

One individual, writing in early June of 2006 noted that his home city was planning to hold a hearing on immigration and he wanted to take the collective feedback of the group to it. He wanted to know about how the situation infringed on their productivity and what they thought local governments might do to improve the situation. "Cities do have an interest. For example, divided families have well documented ill affects on children that lead to risky behavior and increased local social issues. City tax revenues are lost by the inability of H1B visa holders to start a business or to move to higher paying jobs."

## CONCLUSION

Research on Internet communities and culture has begun to attract the attention of scholars, including anthropologists. A good portion of this work has focused on how the Internet can be used to mobilize people around global issues (forms of global citizenship?) such as the environment or human rights or the antiglobalization movement itself (Capling and Nossal 2001; Ribeiro 1998). Some scholars of immigration have begun to explore how the Internet sustains transnational connections or fosters hybrid identities. However, there is much less research on how immigrants are using the Internet to organize and mobilize to achieve specific political goals (Wilson and Peterson 2002), and the significance of such activities for the process of political incorporation.

In this chapter I have analyzed how the Internet has facilitated the creation of a virtual coalition of immigrants who have been empowered by their online contacts to formulate a political strategy to effect change in immigration policy. As Gustavo Lins Ribeiro has pointed out, computer networks provide "a swift and inexpensive means of communication, . . . a data availability that multiplies the opportunities for individuals and groups to denounce, articulate, and campaign" (1998: 342). The members of Unitefamilies are involved in all these activities and while separated by distance they have managed to accomplish a good deal in a short period of time. And their work continues.

This coalition of individuals may or they may not be successful, but they are nevertheless exemplary "citizens" who have already demonstrated very active civic engagement and participation and, despite the fact that they cannot vote (often *the* measure of political incorporation in broad national surveys), these individuals demonstrate a high level of political incorporation—higher than many U.S. citizens. They are using the political process to fight for their rights and they are using the Internet as a tool to mobilize this fight. And yet many of them recognize that it is just that—a tool—and that more conventional methods—writing letters, making appointments, attending rallies, getting stories in the press—are also equally important to their cause. Ribeiro has written that "cybercultural politics can be divided into two different, but interrelated, realms. One is defined by the political activity within the Internet itself; the other by the relationship between computer networks and political activism in the real world" (1998: 332).

What is perhaps most interesting to watch is the fluidity of leadership, if one can even call it that, in the group. Although there is a "core group," specific individuals seem to fade in and fade out of the Internet dialogue. When one individual steps down from the motivating and coordinating role, someone else seems to step in. New members come online all the time and there are apparently many "hoverers" who are reading, and learning, and occasionally engaged, offering advice, observation, or comment. These may be some of the same characteristics of offline grassroots political "groups" as well. As the following posting in the spring of 2006 suggests, some of them feel that in the process of working to unite families they had become part of a cyberspace family: "I just want to thank you the people who donate some money to hire Paul. We have to keep this thing rolling to get more cover from news and media. . . . Send letters to local newspapers. . . . Please don't forget to save some money from lunch and dinner. We might need to donate again. Friends, we don't have any one here. However we became family in here . . . Network and help is the main thing we need now."[11]

Many people initially become civically engaged because some issue or problem touches them personally and they want to participate in effecting change. The majority of Unitefamilies members are indeed personally affected by what appears to them, and to me, a harsh reality of one aspect of U.S. immigration law. On 5 October 2005 one member wrote "I am in Fremont, CA. My spouse is in Bombay, India waiting for her green card since last 3 years and her priority date is still 14 months away." The underlying sadness and frustration of his circumstances and of this communication were patently apparent. It is my hope that by drawing attention to their activities as netizens, I will also draw attention to the cause of the members of Unitefamilies, and to consideration of their particular problem in the context of the broader issue of immigration reform.

NOTES

1. I was introduced to this group early in 2004 by a young man whom I was interviewing as part of an NSF-funded project on new immigrants in the Dallas-Fort Worth metroplex (BCS #003938). Afterward I began to track the work of this group as a member and semiactive participant. Parham (2004) is critical of previous studies of Internet communities because they take a snapshot, short term approach. As a result they cannot reveal changes over time. Considering that I have monitored the work of this particular group for more than eighteen months what I emphasize here is precisely how political strategies have developed and altered. Unitefamilies is one example of these kinds of Internet groups. Others that came to my attention in the spring of 2006 were ImmigrationVoice.org (which has been lobbying to ease backlogs in employment immigration) and American Families United which has been lobbying for relief for U.S. citizen families. See Kalita (2006). Any opinions, findings, and conclusions or recommendations expressed in this chapter are those of the author and do not necessarily reflect the views of the National Science Foundation.

2. Individuals in various situations are part of this group: those who live in the United States and are separated from spouses who are in the home country but with no minor children; those who live in the United States and are separated from spouses in the home country who are caring for their minor children there; those who live in the United States with minor children while the spouse lives in the home country; those who are single but unable to proceed with a marriage because they are green card holders; those who married a person already in the United States who was on a nonimmigrant (student, temporary worker) visa at the time of the marriage and who might have to return to the home country when this visa expires; those who support the activities of the group although they are not affected by the legal restrictions that the group is working to change (including this author).

3. The arbitrariness of this law is evident in the fact that if a person gets married just a day before receiving his/her greencard he/she is permitted to bring his/her spouse to the United States immediately on a dependent visa but one day

after and the spouse faces a waiting period of five years or more before being able to enter the United States.

4. H.R. 3701 (108th congress) was a bill "to amend the Immigration and Nationality Act to extend the provisions governing nonimmigrant status for spouses and children of permanent resident aliens awaiting the availability of an immigrant visa, and for other purposes."

5. Many of the members are from India, a country where there is little trust in politicians and where bribes are common.

6. These can be found at http://unitefamilies.org/action/w_sample1.html and http://unitefamilies.org/action/w_sample2.html.

7. He wrote: "1. The bill is introduced in either the House or the Senate; 2. The bill is referred to the immigration subcommittee of the chamber where it was introduced; 3. The immigration subcommittee has to approve the bill; 4. It then goes to the judiciary committee of that chamber; 5. The judiciary committee has to approve the bill; 6. The bill then goes to the full chamber; 7. The full chamber must approve the bill; 8. A bill of identical text must be approved by the immigration subcommittee, judiciary committee, and full membership of the other chamber; 9. The bill then goes to the President who must approve it. It is then law."

8. Congressman Jindal did meet with several members of the group.

9. See for example www.wireh.com/News/General_News/group_seeks_to_reunite_separated-Immigrant.

10. See for example www.dallasnews.com/sharedcontent/APStories/stories/D8IE CEH01.html.

11. Paul was a lobbyist that the group hired during the spring of 2006 who was able to help them quite significantly with public exposure.

# Afterword

## SOME CONCLUDING REFLECTIONS

### *Nancy Foner*

THE CHAPTERS IN THIS VOLUME offer important insights and rich data that push forward our understanding of citizenship and civic and political participation among immigrants in the United States and Western Europe. These topics are of growing interest in the immigration field and anthropologists have much to contribute to them. In this afterword, I offer reflections on several themes that come out in the chapters, including the benefits of an ethnographic approach and the effects of transnational ties on civic and political engagement. I also consider some questions that arise in beginning to think more systematically about a theme or approach that is implicit in the organization of the book: cross-national comparisons.

### ETHNOGRAPHIC APPROACH AND TRANSNATIONAL TIES

One contribution of the volume is its ethnographic approach. In general, ethnographic research is able to provide up-close, in-depth knowledge of the day-to-day lives of individuals and bring people—their perspectives, social relations, and problems—to life (Foner 2003a). Because ethnographers study on-the-ground social relations, they can shed light on the complex ways that migrants, in their everyday lives, are affected by and, at the same time, respond to, and sometimes seek to influence or change, state policies. This goes beyond policies concerning naturalization and legal citizenship, as many of the chapters make clear. Most migrants, after all, are not legal citizens of the countries where they live; yet as social citizens, as Glick Schiller and Caglar emphasize, they participate in, and may claim rights in, the social, economic, and political life of the state. Through participant observation, ethnographers are well positioned to illuminate migrants' perceptions, ideas, and values—and their sense of belonging or exclusion—as these both reflect and affect their relation to political, legal, economic, and social institutions and policies in the receiving society.

In analyzing immigrant civic and political participation, ethnographic research can reveal, as Garapich argues, dynamics within ethnic groups that are relevant to group mobilization, including which group members decide to participate in public life and why, which individuals assume leadership roles, and why members of a group choose particular discourses—for example, ethnic or class-based—in claims making. Given that ethnographic research typically extends over a considerable time period and involves long-term contact with individuals, it is able to show, as Peró notes in his discussion of Latin Americans in London, how patterns of mobilization within a group change over time—even in the context of a single and stable institutional environment. In a similar vein, Brettell's analysis brings out how political strategies were developed and altered among online immigrant "netizens" in the course of her two-year, participant-observer study.

Given anthropologists' sensitivity to the links that migrants maintain with their countries of origin, it is not surprising that many chapters discuss transnational ties as they relate to civic and political engagement in the "host" as well as "home" society. The argument that transnational practices and political incorporation in the new society go hand in hand receives support in the volume, most notably in the essays by Richman and Wong and the editors' introduction. The "high-tech" Chinese immigrants in Silicon Valley who travel back and forth between California and China, according to Wong, are eager to become U.S. citizens and use transnational networks and opportunities to ground themselves in and establish roots in the United States.

To be sure, transnational ties sometimes slow the acquisition of new loyalties and identities in the new society. However, a growing body of research on immigrants in the United States indicates that this is generally not the case. Rather than detracting from involvements in the United States, engagement in home-country-based politics and organizations can actually accelerate the process of political integration.

A number of studies show that transnational political participation strengthens migrants' ability to mobilize a base of support for political issues and elections in the United States and reinforces or encourages an interest in U.S. politics (see Foner 2007a). The skills learned in one context frequently travel well to others—so that the experience gained in founding hometown committees or participating in other kinds of transnational political activities can be transferred and usefully applied to campaigns to advance migrants' interests in U.S. cities and towns (Guarnizo, Sanchez, and

Roach 1999; Portes and Rumbaut 2006: 138–39). Immigrants who participate actively in U.S. political life are often the most likely to be involved in
transnational activities (Itzigsohn and Giorguli-Saucedo 2005). In a recent
study, Afro-Caribbean New Yorkers with high levels of involvement in
home-country civic and political activities were more likely than others to
vote in the United States—as well as to engage in other forms of political
participation beyond voting such as raising money for New York politicians
or becoming active in Democratic political clubs (Rogers 2006).

Despite widespread fears that dual nationality will blur immigrant loyalties and undermine commitment to the United States, evidence indicates
that dual nationality may, in fact, encourage immigrants to naturalize. Although the United States naturalization oath requires renunciation of other
citizenships, U.S. law has evolved in the direction of increased ambiguity
or outright tolerance in favor of dual nationality—what has been called a
"don't ask, don't tell" policy. The big change, however, is that a growing
number of states of origin permit their citizens to retain nationality despite naturalization elsewhere—with Haiti, China, South Korea, and Cuba
among the few major sending-country exceptions. A study of Latin American immigrants reveals that immigrants from countries recognizing dual
nationality are more likely to seek U.S. citizenship than those from countries that do not recognize it. Becoming a U.S. citizen is an easier decision
when it does not entail losing privileges in, or renouncing allegiance to,
one's native land or the possibility of being viewed as a "defector" there
(Jones-Correa 2001).

## COMPARISONS OF THE UNITED STATES AND EUROPE

A strength of the book is that it groups together case studies from the
United States and Western Europe as a way to understand political and civic
engagement across national borders. It thus lends itself to further questions
about parallels and contrasts in the immigrant experience in Europe and the
United States—and how these are linked to social, political, and economic
institutions and structures in each national context as well as the particu-
larities of immigrant flows there. In the comments that follow, I consider a
few topics that can benefit from comparative analysis and that are suggested
by or have relevance for issues touched on in the volume.

Let me start with the subject of legal citizenship. Much has been written, particularly in the political science literature, about citizenship policies
in the United States and Western Europe, including the acquisition of citizenship, naturalization policy, dual nationality, and the political and social
rights of immigrants. The United States, of course, stands out in its unqual-
ified—and long-term—attribution of citizenship to those born on U.S. soil

(*jus soli*) in contrast to the tradition of citizenship by descent from one or both parents who are nationals (*jus sanguinis*) in continental Europe. Many scholars have argued that the massive postwar immigration in Europe—and common need to integrate immigrants—have led to a convergence process as continental European countries have moved in an American direction to make it easier for long-settled immigrants and their children to acquire citizenship (e.g., Weil 2001). Relative convergence is a better term (Howard 2005). Despite the liberalization of citizenship policies in a number of European countries, national differences remain. Based on his analysis of policies in the fifteen "older" member states of the European Union, Marc Howard (2005: 715–16) notes that Western European countries with longer traditions of immigration and citizenship by birth have the most liberal citizenship policies (with regard to citizenship by birth and residency requirements for naturalization) and are the most tolerant of dual citizenship; the Nordic and Germanic countries are still generally less liberal and less tolerant of dual citizenship; and the southern European countries are generally in-between.

Legal citizenship is associated with particular political and economic benefits or advantages in every country, but it also affects immigrants' identities and sense of membership or belonging. And this leads to the general issue of inclusion and exclusion that is at the heart of many chapters in this volume—and other historically rooted institutional differences in the United States and Western Europe (apart from citizenship policies) that have a powerful affect on immigrants and their children.

One of the most glaring contrasts has to do with race. The U.S. legacy of slavery and segregation makes the U.S. experience with immigration strikingly different from Europe's. Since its formation the United States has had a large, subordinated black population inside its territorial boundaries. About 12 percent of the nation's population is African American and the proportion is much higher in many major cities.

Race, especially the black-white divide, has long been a significant—some would say *the* significant—social division in the United States. African Americans are a classic case of legal citizens, mentioned by Glick Schiller and Caglar, who face exclusion and denials of their civil rights because they are racialized. They are, in truth, the quintessentially racialized Americans with a history of massive oppression and stigmatization—and they remain more residentially segregated and less likely to marry outside their group than other racial minorities. Indeed the special position of blacks has been an essential element in how ethnic or racial groups of immigrant origin have defined themselves and their position in U.S. society (Foner and Fredrickson 2004). Relations between immigrants and

African Americans—distancing and competition as well as instances of cooperation and coalition-building—is a topic of pressing scholarly and political importance.

In continental Western Europe immigrants are more likely to be stigmatized on the basis of culture than of color-coded race. Skin color does play a role in racialization in Europe, as several of the chapters in this volume make clear, yet cultural differences, especially those associated with religion, loom larger than in the United States. The quintessentially racialized group in most of Western Europe is Muslims, who represent a high proportion of immigrant minorities and a growing share of the population.

Anti-Muslim sentiment in Europe has sometimes been characterized as "cultural racism," in which culture or religion is essentialized to the point that they become the functional equivalent of biological racism and groups are seen as inherently inferior on the basis of their culture or religion (see Foner 2005: 217–18). Scholars have written that "Muslimophobia is at the heart of contemporary British and European cultural racism" (Modood 2005: 37); of "European Muslimania" as a "third major artery in the historical articulation of racial eurology" (Goldberg 2006: 362); and of racialized perceptions of Islam and the racial dimensions of Islam (Cesari 2004: 32, 24). To be sure, there is anti-Muslim prejudice and discrimination in the United States, especially in the wake of September 11, but they are much less of an issue than in Europe. Partly this is because Muslims are a much smaller proportion of the immigrant population in the United States—according to estimates, less than 5 percent of the foreign born and their children. Unlike in Europe, where Muslims live in poor neighborhoods and have high rates of unemployment, they have done relatively well economically and educationally in the United States. Moreover, Islam has been added to the existing "rainbow coalition" of religions in the United States, whereas in Europe, as Jytte Klausen notes, "religious pluralism is a new social fact that yet has to be fitted into legal frameworks and public practices" (2005: 107).

The racialization of people of African ancestry in the United States creates particular dilemmas for immigrants defined as black, like the Haitians discussed by Richman, yet the presence of a huge African American population has also been advantageous in some ways for immigrant and second generation people of color. In the wake of the civil rights movement, a series of laws and programs have been instituted that were originally justified as a response to the caste-like status of African Americans and later extended to other groups, especially Latinos, to promote greater representation of ethnoracial minorities. For example, there have been affirmative action and other programs to improve racial minorities' access to higher education as well as bilingual and English as a second language (ESL) programs and, in the political sphere, legislation creating voting districts where minorities are at least competitive. Black immigrants have benefited from the presence of a huge African American population in other ways, including the ability to unite with African Americans in a large "black" vote in cities like New York and access to resources for upward mobility through the existence of a growing African American middle class and its "middle-class minority culture of mobility" (Foner 2005:118–20). In Western Europe, immigrants are generally confronted, in neighborhoods and at work, with native white (and Christian) working-class communities and structures whereas for black and Latino immigrants in the United States, their African American and native-born Latino "proximal hosts" may provide a warmer (although, of course, not unproblematic) and more helpful welcome and sense of belonging.

A sense of belonging or membership is also affected by institutional arrangements concerning religion—which differ significantly in Europe and the United States. In the United States, the Constitution's First Amendment dictates the separation of church and state, the principle of equal protection or application of laws is enshrined in the Fourteenth Amendment, and religious pluralism is widely accepted (Klausen 2005: 164–65). The fact that most immigrants in the United States share a religious orientation—Christianity—with the majority of long-established Americans has also helped them to feel a part of American society, as compared to Western Europe where a high proportion of immigrants are Muslims living in overwhelmingly Christian societies. In addition, the United States is a more religiously committed nation and thus more accepting of immigrants' religious involvement. Asserting a religious identity, whether Protestant, Catholic, Buddhist, or Hindu, is an acceptable way to be American and different at the same time, and religious institutions are places where immigrants can lay claims to inclusion in U.S. society.

In contrast, in Western Europe, Muslim immigrants confront, on the one hand, secular Europeans who are suspicious of claims based on religion and its requirements and, on the other, historically rooted societal institutions and national identities that remain anchored to an important extent in Christianity and do not make room for Islam (Alba and Foner 2005).

The institutionalization, special privileges, and public support of Christianity in Western Europe have played a role in the sense of marginalization and exclusion felt by many Muslim immigrants and their children (Alba and Foner 2005). In France, despite the official ideology of *laïcité*—the exclusion of religion from the affairs of state—the state owns and maintains most Christian churches. The same law that permitted this arrangement prevents the state from building new ones—so that the country's 4–5 million Muslims do not enjoy the same privileges as Christians. Most French mosques are, as a result, ad hoc structures, not very different from storefront churches.

In Britain and France the state provides financial support for religious schools as long as they teach the national secular curriculum. Inevitably, these arrangements, while seemingly fair to all religions, favor the most established ones. As of 2005, the French state had yet to fund a Muslim school in France. In Britain (where senior Anglican bishops sit in the House of Lords by right as part of the Anglican "establishment") the government funds nearly 7,000 Church of England and Catholic schools but only five Islamic schools in a nation of 1.6 million Muslims. In the Netherlands the majority of children go to state-supported religious schools, nearly all Protestant and Catholic, while the country's estimated one million Muslims have only about thirty-five of their own publicly funded primary schools (Alba and Foner 2005). In Germany, the Protestant and Catholic churches, as well as Judaism, but not Islam, the third-largest faith, are entitled to federally collected church taxes and the right to run state-subsidized religious social services and hospitals (Klausen 2005).

Yet another important topic related to issues of citizenship and civic and political engagement is the nature and impact of the welfare state. Western European countries have much stronger welfare states than the United States and more generous health, housing, and financial benefits for social as well as legal citizens. Indeed the United States stands out among rich democracies as the only country without "universal coverage for medical care based on principles of social right and shared risk" (Wilensky 2002: 582); in 2002, an astounding one in three immigrants (compared to 13 percent of the native-born) were without health insurance (Migration Policy Institute 2004).

Most scholars, and no doubt the authors in this volume, would agree that it is better for society as a whole to have a strong welfare state, but an issue is whether there may be some negative unintended consequences for immigrants. Western European welfare states have tended to provide a high level of legal protection and rights for workers, and some scholars argue that this has contributed to a deep insider-outsider cleavage, with immigrants and their adult children displaying high levels of unemployment and low rates of labor force participation and being resented for taking advantage of liberal welfare state provisions as "free riders." Immigrants in the United States, by contrast, come to a society with highly flexible labor markets where they find entry-level jobs fairly easily, although large

numbers are stuck earning low pay without the kinds of government social supports, including healthcare, child care, and housing assistance, that
are more widely available in Europe. In fact, there is more inducement to
take and remain in low-level jobs in the United State because government
benefits are so scarce.

A full-scale comparison of the immigrant experience in the United States
and Western Europe related to issues of citizenship and civic and political
incorporation would have to explore a host of other topics—including immigrant participation and success in electoral politics, government policies
emphasizing common civic values involved in citizenship, and the impact
of national integration models, paradigms, and discourses (Alba and Foner
n.d.). My comments, moreover, have focused on the nation-state level, and
obviously many variations and complexities would emerge if the focus were
on particular cities or regions. My own writings have highlighted the way
that New York City stands out in the U.S. context, including its history of
immigration, political structure and culture, and large and extraordinarily
diverse immigrant population (Foner 2005, 2006, 2007b). In what ways
might the analyses in this volume by Reed-Danahay of Vietnamese in the
Dallas-Fort Worth region, Smith of asylum seekers in Dublin, and Silverstein of Algerians in Paris—to mention just three chapters—be different if
these groups were considered in other cities and metropolitan areas in the
same country? Glick Schiller and Caglar also raise questions about certain
small-scale cities as compared to major gateway destinations; they argue
that the small city of Manchester, New Hampshire, provides immigrants
with few resources for ethnically based incorporation, such as a critical mass
of a single nationality, an ethnic niche economy or market, and social and
philanthropic support for ethnic organizations, that are found in places like
New York City.

It is a measure of this volume's value that it suggests so many questions.
In the past few decades, immigration has been changing the face of Western Europe and the United States, and these anthropological case studies
offer valuable ethnographic data and analyses that help to illuminate the
structures in which immigrants operate and the state policies that shape
their options as well as the way they interact and mobilize in response. The
essays not only contribute to understanding the dynamics of immigration,
citizenship, and political behavior but also, no doubt, will stimulate and
influence additional work on these topics in the future.

# References

Accession Monitoring Report. 2004, 2005, 2006, 2007. Home Office, London. Available at: http://www.ind.homeoffice.gov.uk/aboutus/reports/accession_monitoring_report.

Adams, David W. 1995. *Education for Extinction: American Indians and the Boarding School Experience, 1875–1928*. Lawrence: University of Kansas Press.

Adamson, Fiona B. 2004. "Contested Constituencies. Political Entreprenuers and the Mobilization of Immigrant Population in France (1954–1962) and Germany (1984–2000). Paper presented at the 14th Biennial Conference of Europeanists, Palmer House Hilton, Chicago, 11–13 March.

Agunias, Dovelyn R., and Kathleen Newland. 2007. Circular Migration and Development. *Migration Policy Institute Policy Brief* (April):1–19.

Aïchoune, Farid. 1985. *La Beur Génération*. Paris: Sans Frontière/Arcantère.

Alba, Richard, and Nancy Foner. 2005. Can It Happen Here? *The Nation* (October 17): 20–22.

———. N.d. Entering the Precincts of Power: Do National Differences Matter for Immigrant-Minority Political Representation? Unpublished paper.

Aleinikoff, Alexander, and Douglas B. Klusmeyer, eds. 2001. *Citizenship Today: Global Perspectives and Practices*. Carnegie Endowment for International Peace.

Allievi, Stefano, and Joergen S. Nielsen, eds. 2003. *Muslim networks and Transnational Communities in and across Europe*. Leiden, the Netherlands: Brill.

Al-Shahi, Ahmed, and Richard Lawless. 2005. *Middle East and North African Immigrants in Europe*. London and New York: Routledge.

Alsop, Ronald. 2007. Chinese Business Grads Feel Mainland Lure. *Wall Street Journal*. 13, 27 March.

Amiraux, Valérie. 2001. *Acteurs de l'islam entre Allemagne et Turquie: Parcours militants et experiences religieuses*. Paris: L'Harmattan.

Amit, Vered. 2002. Reconceptualizing Community. In *Realizing Community: Concepts, Social Relationships and Sentiments*, ed. Vered Amit, 1–20. London: Routledge.

———, ed. 2002. *Realizing Community: Concepts, Social Relationships and Sentiments*. London: Routledge.

Anderson, Benedict. 1983. *Imagined Communities: Reflections on the Origin and Spread of Nationalism*. London: Verso.

———. 1991. *Imagined Communities: Reflections on the Origin and Spread of Nationalism*. Rev. ed. London: Verso.

———. 1992. *Long-Distance Nationalism: World Capitalism and the Rise of Identity Politics*. The Wertheim Lecture. Amsterdam: CASA.

Anderson, Wanni W., and Robert G. Lee. 2005. Asian American Displacements. In *Displacements and Diasporas: Asians in the Americas*, ed. Wanni W. Anderson and Robert G. Lee, 3–22. New Brunswick, NJ: Rutgers University Press.

Angel-Ajani, Asale. 2000. Italy's Racial Cauldron: Immigration, Criminalization and the Cultural Politics of Race. *Cultural Dynamics* 12 (3):331–52.

Anthias, Floya, and Gabriella Lazaridis, eds. 2000. *Gender and Migration in Southern Europe: Women on the Move*. Oxford: Berg Publishers.

Appadurai, Arjun. 1991. Global Ethnoscapes: Notes and Queries for a Transnational Anthropology. In *Recapturing Anthropology*, ed. Richard G. Fox, 191–210. Santa Fe, NM: School of American Research.

———. 1995. The Production of Locality. In *Counterworks: Managing the Diversity of Knowledge*, ed. Richard Fardon, 205–25. London: Routledge.

———. 1996. *Modernity at Large: Cultural Dimensions of Globalization*. Minneapolis: University of Minnesota Press.

Aristide, Jean-Bertrand. 1990. Mesaj Aristide pou Dyaspora a. *Haïti Progrès*. 31 December.

*Asian Week*. 2001. A Lifetime of Activism. February 23. Bay Area Section, 1.

———. 2005. Asian Power in the Golden State. December 2. Bay Area Section, 1.

———. 2007. Mayors Talk About Running Their Cities. March 30. Bay Area Section, 1.

Attali, Jacques. 1993. *Verbatim: Tome 1: Chronique des années 1981–1986*. Paris: Fayard.

Austin, J. L. 1962. *How To Do Things With Words*. Cambridge, MA: Harvard University Press.

Back, Les et al. 2002. New Labour's White Hart: Politics, Multiculturalism and the Return of Assimilationism. *Political Quarterly* 74 (4):445–54.

Bakker, Matt, and Michael Peter Smith. 2003. El Rey del Tomate: Migrant Political Transnationalism and Democratization in Mexico. *Migraciones Internacionales* 2, no. 1 (January–June):59–83.

———. 2005. The Transnational Politics of the Tomato King: Meaning and Impact. *Global Networks* 5 (2):129–46.

Balibar, Étienne. 1988. Propositions on Citizenship. *Ethics* 98 (4):723–30.

———. 1989. Is There a "Neo-Racism"? In *Race, Nation, Class: Ambiguous Identities*, ed. Étienne Balibar and Immanuel Wallerstein, 17–28. London: Verso.

———. 2002. *Politics and the Other Scene*. London: Verso.

———. 2004. *We, the People of Europe? Reflections on Transnational Citizenship*. Trans. James Swenson. Princeton, NJ: Princeton University Press.

Bancel, Nicolas, Pascal Blanchard, and Françoise Vergès. 2003. *La République coloniale: Essai sur une utopie*. Paris: Albin Michel.

Barbara, Augustin. 1992. "Beur," de l'emblème au stigmate. *Hommes et Migrations* 1154:26–27.

Barjaba K., Dervishi Z., and Perrone L. 1992. L'Emigrazione albanese: spazi, tempi e cause. *Studi Emigrazione* 29, (107): 525–39.

Barker, Martin. 1981. *The New Racism*. London: Junction Books Ltd.

Barth, Frederic. 1969. *Ethnic Groups and Boundaries*. Boston: Little Brown & Co.

Barthélemy, Martine. 2000. *Associations: Un nouvel âge de la participation?* Paris: Presses de la Fondation Nationale de Sciences Politiques.

Basch, Linda, Nina Glick Schiller, and Cristina Szanton Blanc. 1994. Nations Unbound: Transnational Projects, Postcolonial Predicaments, and Deterritorialized Nation-States. Amsterdam: Gordon and Breach.

Battegay, Alain, and Ahmed Boubekeur. 1993. *Les images publiques de l'immigration*. Paris: CIEMI/Harmattan.

Bauböck, Rainer. 1994. *Transnational Citizenship: Membership and Rights in International Migration*. Aldershot, England: Edward Elgar Publishing.

Bauman, Gerd. 1996. *Contesting Culture: Discourses of Identity in Multi-Ethnic London*. Cambridge: Cambridge University Press.

Bauman, Zygmunt. 1997. The Making and Unmaking of Strangers. In *Debating Cultural Hybridity: Multicultural Identities and the Politics of Anti-Racism*, ed. Pnina Werbner and Tariq Modood, 46–57. London and Atlantic Highlands, NJ: Zed Books.

Bazin, Hughes. 1995. *La Culture hip-hop*. Paris: Desclée de Brouwer.

Bazin, Laurent, Robert Gibb, Catherine Neveu, and Monique Selim. 2006. The Broken Myth: Popular Unrest and the "Republican Model of Integration" in France. *Anthropology Today* 22:16–17.

BBC. 2004. Ireland Votes to End Birth Right. BBC News, 13 June. Available at: http://news.bbc.co.uk/2/hi/europe/3801839.stm.

Bean, Philip A. 1989. Fascism and Italian-America Identity: A Case Study: Utica New York. *Journal of Ethnic Studies* 17:101–119.

Beaud, Stéphane, and Olivier Masclet. 2006. Des "marcheurs" de 1983 aux "émeutiers" de 2005: Deux générations sociales d'enfants d'immigrés. *Annales: Histoire, Sciences sociales* 61:809–43.

Bellah, Robert, Richard Madsen, William Sullivan, Ann Swidler, and Steven Tipton. 1985. *Habits of the Heart: Individualism and Commitment in American Life*. New York: Harper and Row.

Benda-Beckmann, Keebet von. 2001. Transnational Dimensions of Legal Pluralism. In *Begegnung und Konflikt. Eine Kulturanthropologische Bestandsaufnahme*, ed. Wolfgang Fijentscher, 34–48. München: Verlag der Bayerischen Akademie der Wissenschaften.

Benhabib, Seyla, ed. 1996. *Democracy and Difference: Contesting the Boundaries of the Political*. Princeton, NJ: Princeton University Press.

Bermudez Torres, Anastasia. 2003. *ICAR Navigation Guide. Refugee Populations in the UK: Colombians*. London: Information Centre for Asylum and Refugees.

Blion, Reynald. 1996. De La Cote-D'Ivoire a L'Italie. Practique migratoires des Burkinabe et logiques d'etats. *Studi Emigrazione/Etudes Migrations* 33 (121):47–69.

Bloemraad, Irene. 2005. The Limits of de Tocqueville: How Government Facilitates Organizational Capacity in Newcomer Communities. *Journal of Ethnic and Migration Studies* 31 (5): 865–87.

———. 2006. *Becoming a Citizen: Incorporating Immigrants and Refugees in the United States and Canada*. Berkeley: University of California Press.

Bocca, Giorgio. 1998. *Gli italiani sono razzisti?* Italy: Garanzi Editore.

Borgé, Jacques, and Nicolas Viasnoff. 1995. *Archives de l'Algérie*. Milan: Editions Michèle Trinckvel.

Bouamama, Saïd. 1994. *Dix ans de marche des Beurs: Chronique d'un mouvement avorté*. Paris: Desclée de Brouwer.

Bouamama, Saïd, Hadjila Sad-Saoud, and Mokhtar Djerdoubi. 1994. *Contribution à la mémoire des banlieues*. Paris: Editions du Volga.

Boubeker, Ahmed, and Mogniss H. Abdallah. 1993. *Douce France: La saga du mouvement Beur*. Paris: Im'media.

Bourdieu, Pierre. 1986. The Forms of Capital. In *Handbook of Theory and Research for the Sociology of Education*, ed. John G. Richardson and trans. Richard Nice, 241–58. New York: Greenwood Press.

————. 1992. Rites as Acts of Institution. In *Honor and Grace in Anthropology*, ed. John G. Peristiany and Julian Pitt-Rivers and trans. Peter Just, 79–89. Cambridge: Cambridge University Press.

————. 1998. *Les règles de l'art: Genèse et structure du champ littéraire*. Rev. ed. Paris: Seuil (Collection: Points Essais).

Bousetta, Hassan. 2000. Institutional Theories of Immigrant Ethnic Mobilisation: Relevance and Limitations. *Journal of Ethnic and Migration Studies* 26 (2): 229–45.

Bousquet, Gisèle L. 1991. *Behind the Bamboo Hedge: The Impact of Homeland Politics in a Parisian Vietnamese Community*. Ann Arbor: The University of Michigan Press.

Bowen, John. 2006. *Why the French Hate Headscarves*. Princeton, NJ: Princeton University Press.

Bracken, Ali. 2005. Asylum families kept apart. *Irish Times*, 24 June. Available at: http://www.ireland.com/newspaper/features/2005/0624/1119394873883.html.

Bracken, Amy. 2005. (Don't) Vote for Me. News and Opinion on Situation in Haiti. 11 July. Available at: http://www.williambowles.info/haiti-news/2005/haiti_vote_071105.html.

Brah, Avtar. 1996. *Cartographies of Diaspora*. London and New York: Routledge.

Brandes, Stanley. 1975. *Migration, Kinship and Community: Tradition and Transition in a Spanish Village*. New York: Academic Press.

Brenner, Neil. 1998. Between Fixity and Motion: Accumulation, Territorial Organization and the Historical Geography of Spatial Scales, *Environment and Planning D: Society and Space* 16 (5):459–81.

————. 1999a. Beyond State-centrism? Space, Territoriality and Geographical Scale in Globalization Studies. *Theory and Society* 28 (2):39–78.

————. 1999b. Globalization as Reterritorialisation: The Rescaling of Urban Governance in the European Union. *Urban Studies* 36 (3):431–51.

————. 2004. *New State Spaces: Urban Governance and the Rescaling of Statehood*. New York: Oxford University Press.

Brennock, Mark. 2004a. McDowell Changes Argument on Referendum: Constitutional Referendum: Background. *Irish Times*, 9 April. Available at: http://www.ireland.com/newspaper/ireland/2004/0409/1079399172867.html.

————. 2004b. Labour Says Citizenship Proposal "Deeply Flawed." *Irish Times*, 28 May. Avaliable at: http://www.ireland.com/newspaper/ireland/2004/0528/1084325414420.html.

Breton, Raymond. 1964. Institutional completeness of ethnic communities and the personal relations of immigrants. *American Journal of Sociology* 70 (2):193–205.

Brettell, Caroline B. 2000. Theorizing Migration in Anthropology. In *Migration Theory: Talking Across Disciplines*, ed. Caroline B. Brettell and James Hollifield, 97–135. New York and London: Routledge.

————. 2003. Bringing the City Back In: Cities as Contexts for Immigrant Incorporation. In *American Arrivals: Anthropology Engages the New Immigration*, ed. Nancy Foner, 163–195. Sante Fe: School of American Research.

————. 2005. Voluntary Associations, Social Capital, and the Social Incorporation of Asian Indian Immigrants in the Dallas-Fort Worth Metroplex. *Anthropological Quarterly* 78 (4):853–83.

————. 2006. Political Belonging and Cultural Belonging: Immigration Status, Citizenship, and Identity among Four Immigrant Populations in a Southwestern City. *American Behavioral Scientist* 50:70–99.

Brettell, Caroline B., and Deborah Reed-Danahay. 2008. "Communities of Practice" for Civic and Political Engagement: A Comparison of Asian Indian and Vietnamese Immigrant Organizations in a Southwestern Metropolis. In *Civic Roots and Political Realities: Community Organizations and Political Engagement among Immigrants in the United States and Abroad*, ed. S. Kartick Ramakrishnan and Irene Bloemraad. New York: Russell Sage Press.

Brown, John Seely, and Paul Duguid. 2000. *The Social Life of Information*. Boston: Harvard Business School Press.

Brubaker, William Rogers, ed. 1989. *Immigration and the Politics of Citizenship in Europe and North America*. Lanham, MD, New York, and London: University Press of America and the German Marshall Fund of the United States.

———. 1992. *Citizenship and Nationhood in France and Germany*. Cambridge, MA: Harvard University Press.

Buijs, Gina, ed. 1993. *Migrant Women: Crossing Boundaries and Changing Identities*. Oxford: Berg Press.

Burrell, Kathy. 2004. Homeland Memories and the Polish Community in Leister. In *The Poles in Britain 1940–2000*, ed. Peter D. Stachura, 69–85. London and Portland, OR: Franck Cas.

Butler, Judith. 1990. *Gender Trouble: Feminism and the Subversion of Identity*. New York: Routledge.

CADIC Amnesty International. 2005. Amnesty International Coalition against the Deportation of Irish Children. Available at: http://www.amnesty.ie/user/content/view/full/3211.

Caglar, Ayse. 2002. *Encountering the State in Migration-Driven Transnational Social Fields: Turkish Immigrants in Europe*. Habilitationsschrifft: Free University of Berlin.

———. 2004. "Citizenship Light": Transnational Ties, Multiple Rules of membership and the "Pink Card." In *Worlds on the Move*, ed. Jonathan Friedman and Shalini Randeria, 273–92. London: I. B. Tauris.

Cannon, Steve. 1997. Paname City Rapping: B-Boys in the Banlieues and Beyond. In *Post-Colonial Cultures in France*, ed. Alec G. Hargreaves and Mark McKinney. London: Routledge.

Capling, Ann, and Kim Richard Nossal. 2001. Death of Distance or Tyranny of Distance? The Internet, Deterritorialization, and the Anti-globalization Movement in Australia. *Pacific Review* 14: 443–65.

Carter, Donald Martin. 1997. *States of Grace: Senegalese in Italy and the New European Immigration*. Minneapolis: University of Minnesota Press.

Cassidy, Luke. 2003. Non-EU Parents of Irish-Born Children Facing Deportation. *Irish Times*, 23 January. Avaliable at: http://www.ireland.com/newspaper/breaking/2003/0123/breaking2.htm.

Castells, Manuel. 2001. *The Internet Galaxy: Reflections on the Internet, Business, and Society*. Oxford: Oxford University Press.

Castles, Stephen. 2000. *Ethnicity and Globalization*. Thousand Oaks, CA: Sage Publications.

Castles, Stephen, and Alastair Davidson. 2000. *Citizenship and Migration: Globalization and the Politics of Belonging*. New York: Routledge.

Castles, Stephen, and Mark J. Miller. 2003. *The Age of Migration*. 3rd ed. New York: The Guilford Press.

Caussé, Bruno. 2006. Zinédine Zidane, la legende térnie. *Le Monde*, 11 July.

Certeau, Michel de. 1988[1984]. *The Practice of Everyday Life*. Trans. Steven F. Rendall. Berkeley: University of California Press.

Cerullo, Morris. 2005. World Evangelism. Available at: http://www.mcwe.com.

Cesarani, David, and Mary Fulbrook, eds. 1996. *Citizenship, Nationality and Migration in Europe.* London: Routledge.

Cesari, Jocelyne. 2004. *When Islam and Democracy Meet: Muslims in Europe and inthe United States.* New York: Palgrave Macmillan.

Chaker, Salem. 1998. *Berbères aujourd'hui.* 2nd ed. Paris: Haramattan.

Charles, Jacqueline. 2005. Haiti's Presidential Election: Toussaint ad campaign turns motorists' heads. *Miami Herald.* 12 November, 1B.

Charlot, Jean. 1994. *La politique en France.* Paris: Fallois/Livre de poche.

Chavez, Leo R. 1991. Outside the Imagined Community: Undocumented Settlers and Experiences of Incorporation. *American Ethnologist* 18 (2):257–78.

———. 2001. *Covering Immigration: Popular Images and the Politics of Nation.* Berkeley: University of California Press.

Cheong, Pauline et al. 2005. *Immigration, Social Cohesion and Social Capital: A Critical Review.* Paper presented at the 'Whither Social Capital?' Conference, London. 7 April.

Christian Coalition. 2005. Roberta Combs: A Message from Our President. Available at: http://www.cc.org/about.cfm.

Clarke, Kamari. 2004. *Mapping Yoruba Networks: Power and Agency in the Making of Transnational Communities.* Durham, NC: Duke University Press.

Clarkin, Allison. 2005. *Claiming Place and Legibility in the Republic: The Making of Berber Citizens in France.* Ph.D. Dissertation. Department of Anthropology, New School University.

Clifford, James. 1994. Diasporas. *Cultural Anthropology* 9 (3):302–38.

Closets, François de. 1990. *La grande manip.* Paris: Seuil.

Cohen, Abner. 1974. *Two-Dimensional Man: An Essay on the Anthropology of Power and Symbolism in Complex Society.* Berkeley: University of California Press.

Cohen, Anthony P. 1985. *The Symbolic Construction of Community.* London: Tavistock Publications, Ltd.

Cohen, Robin. 1997. *Global Diasporas: An Introduction.* London: University College London Press.

Cohen, Robin, and Shirin M. Rai, eds. 2000. *Global Social Movements.* London: The Athlone Press.

Cole, Jeffrey. 1997. *The New Racism in Europe: A Sicilian Ethnography.* Cambridge: Cambridge University Press.

Comaroff, Jean, and John Comaroff. 1991. *Of Revelation and Revolution, Volume One: Christianity, Colonialism, and Consciousness in South Africa.* Chicago: University of Chicago Press.

Cotesta, Mauro, and Simone De Angelis. 1999. Mass media, immigrazione e conflitti etnici in Italia: analisi quantitativa dell'informazione sull'immigrazione. *Studi Emigrazione/Migration Studies* 36 (135):395–413.

Coutin, Susan Bibler. 1998. From Refugees to Immigrants: The Legalization Strategies of Salvadoran Immigrants and Activists. *International Migration Review* 32:901–25.

———. 2003a. *Legalizing Moves; Salvadoran Immigrants' Struggle for US Residency.* Ann Arbor: University of Michigan Press.

———. 2003b. Cultural Logics of Belonging and Movement: Transnationalism, Naturalization, and U.S. Immigration Politics. *American Anthropologist* 30:508–26.

Creed, Gerald W., ed. 2006. *The Seductions of Community: Emancipations, Oppressions, Quandaries.* Santa Fe: School of American Research Press.

Crowley, Ethel, and James MacLaughlin. 1997. *Under the Belly of the Celtic Tiger: Class, Race, Identity and Culture in the Global Ireland*. Dublin: Irish Reporter.

Cruickshank, Barbara. 1996. Revolutions within: self-government and self-esteem. In *Foucault and Political Reason: Liberalism, neo-liberalism and rationalities of government*, ed. Andrew Barry, Thomas Osborne and Nikolas Rose, 231–52. Chicago: University of Chicago Press.

Cubitt, Geoffrey. 1989. Conspiracy Myths and Conspiracy Theories. *Journal of the Anthropological Society of Oxford* 20:12–26.

———. 1993. *The Jesuit Myth: Conspiracy Theory and Politics in Nineteenth-Century France*. Oxford: Clarendon.

*Daily Breeze*. 2001. Spy Hysteria Fuels View of Asians. 13 August, B5.

Danticat, Edwige. 2001. *The Butterfly's Way: Voices from the Haitian Diaspora in the United States*. New York: Soho Press.

Debbasch, Charles, and Jacques Bourdon. 1997. *Les associations*. 6th ed. Paris: Presses Universitaires de France (Coll.: Que sais-je?).

Deegan, Gordon. 2003. We Pray the Minister Will Show Some Mercy. *Irish Times*, 27 January. Available at: http://www.ireland.com/newspaper/ireland/2003/0127/1042461618271.html.

De Genova, Nicholas. 2005. *Working the Boundaries: Race, Space, and "Illegality" in Mexican Chicago*. Durham: Duke University Press.

Delerm, Philippe. 2006. Le Brésilien. *Le Figaro*, 3 July, 15.

Department of Justice. 2005. Minister Announces Details of Revised Arrangements for Residency. 14 January. Available at: http://www.justice.ie/80256E01003A02CF/vWeb/pcJUSQ68MNEK-en.

———. 2006. Minister McDowell Publishes Outcome Details of Irish Born Children Scheme 2005. 1 May. Avaliable at: http://www.justice.ie/80256E01003A02CF/vWeb/pcJUSQ6PLE7P-en.

Derderian, Richard L. 2004. *North Africans in Contemporary France: Becoming Visible*. New York: Palgrave Macmillan.

Désir, Harlem. 1985. *Touche pas à mon pote*. Paris: Grasset.

Diagnoza Społeczna. 2005. Survey results available at: http://www.diagnoza.com/.

Do, Hien Duc. 1999. *The Vietnamese Americans*. Wesport, CT: Greenwood Press.

Domański, Henryk. 2002. *Polska klasa średnia*. Wroclaw, Poland: Uniwersytet Wrocławski.

Donald, James. and Ali Rattansi. 1992. Introduction. In *Race, Culture and Difference*, ed. James Donald and Ali Rattansi 1–10. London: Sage Publications, Ltd.

Dorais, Louis-Jacques. 1998. Vietnamese Communities in Canada, France, and Denmark. *Journal of Refugee Studies* 11 (2):107–25.

Dray, Julien. 1987. *SOS Génération: Histoire de l'intérieur du mouvement des jeunes de novembre–décembre 1986*. Paris: Ramsay.

Droussent, Claude. 2006. L'Edito. *L'Equipe*, 10 July, 1.

Dummett, Michael. 2001. *On Immigration and Refugees*. London: Routledge.

Dunn, Ashley. 1995. Skilled Asians Leaving U.S. For High-Tech Jobs at Homes. *New York Times*. 21 February, A1.

Dupuy, Alex. 2006. Haiti Election 2006: A Pyrrhic Victory for René Préval. *Latin American Perspectives* 148 (33):132–41.

Durand, Alain-Philippe, ed. 2002. *Black, Blanc, Beur: Rap Music and Hip-Hop Culture in the Francophone World*. Lanham, MD: Scarecrow Press.

Duret, Pascal. 1996. *Anthropologie de la fraternité dans les cités*. Paris: Presses Universitaires de France.

Duvell, Franck. 2004. *Highly Skilled, Self-Employed and Illegal Immigrants from Poland in United Kingdom*. Working Paper. Warsaw: Center for Migration Studies.

Eade, John. 1989. *The Politics of Community: The Bangladeshi Community in East London*. Aldershot: Avebury.

Eade, John, Isabelle Fremeaux, and David Garbin. 2002. The Political Construction of Diasporic Communities in the Global City. In *Imagined Londons*, ed. Pamela K. Gilbert, 159–76. Albany, NY: State University of New York Press.

Eade, John, Stephen Drinkwater, and Michal P. Garapich. 2007. Class and Ethnicity: Polish migrants in London. ESRC report available at: www.surrey.ac.uk/arts/cronem.

*The Economist*. 2003. Business: Chinese Entrepreneurs on Their Way Back. 8 November, 71.

ECRE. 2006. European Council on Refugees and Exiles, Factsheet on Asylum in Europe. Available at: http://www.ecre.org/factfile/facts.shtml.

Edelman, Marc. 2001. Social Movements: Changing Paradigms and Forms of Politics. *Annual Review of Anthropology* 30:285–317.

Elias, Norbert. 1987. *The Society of Individuals*. Trans. Edmund Jephcott. Cambridge, MA: Basil Blackwell.

Elias, Norbert, and George Scotson. 1994. *The Established and the Outsiders*. London: Sage.

Epstein, Arnold Leonard, ed. 1967. *The Craft of Social Anthropology*. London: Tavistock.

Erdmans, Mary Patrice. 1992. The Social Construction of Emigration as a Moral Issue. *Polish American Studies* 49 (1):5–25.

———. 1995. Immigrants and Ethnics: Conflict and Identity in Polish Chicago. *The Sociological Quarterly* 36 (1):175–95.

———. 1998. *Opposite Poles: Immigrants and Ethnics in Polish Chicago, 1976–1990*. University Park, PA: Pennsylvania State University Press.

Escobar, Arturo. 1992. Culture, Practice and Politics: Anthropology and the Study of Social Movements. *Critique of Anthropology* 12:395–432.

———. 2001. Culture Sits in Places: Reflections on Globalism and Subaltern Strategies of Localization. *Political Geography* 20 (2):139–74.

Escobar, Cristina. 2004. Dual Citizenship and Political Participation: Migrants in the Interplay of United States and Colombian Politics. *Latino Studies* 2:45–69.

European Commission. 2004. *Asylum: Offering Protection for the Most Vulnerable. Information and Communication Unit*. Brussels: Directorate-General for Justice, Freedom and Security, B-1049.

Evans, Peter. 1999. Fighting Marginalization with Transnational Networks: Counter-Hegemonic Globalization. *Contemporary Sociology* 29 (1):230–41.

Faist, Thomas. 2000. Transnationalization in International Migration: Implications for the Study of Citizenship and Culture. *Ethnic and Racial Studies* 23 (2):189–222.

Fanning, Bryan. 2002. *Racism and Social Change in the Republic of Ireland*. Manchester: Manchester University Press.

Fassin, Didier, and Eric Fassin. 2006. *De la question sociale à la question raciale? Représenter la société française*. Paris: Harmattan.

Faux, Emmanuel, Thomas Legrand, and Gilles Perez. 1994. *La main droite de Dieu: Enquête sur François Mitterrand et l'extrême droite*. Paris: Seuil.

Feldblum, Miriam. 1999. *Reconstructing Citizenship: The Politics of Nationality Reform and Immigration in Contemporary France*. Albany, NY: State University of New York Press.

Fennema, Meindert and Jean Tillie. 1999. Political Participation and Political Trust in Amsterdam: Civic Communities and Ethnic Networks. *Journal of Ethnic and Migration Studies* 25:703–26.

Flores, William V. 1997. Citizens vs. Citizenry: Undocumented Immigrants and Latino Cultural Citizenship. In *Latino Cultural Citizenship: Claiming Identity, Space and Politics*, ed. William V. Flores and Rina Benmayor, 255–77. Boston: Beacon Press.

Flores, William V., and Rina Benmayor, eds. 2000. *Latino Cultural Citizenship: Claiming Identity, Space, and Rights.* Tempe, AZ: Bilingual Review Press.

Foblets, Marie-Claire. 2002. Muslims, a new transnational minority in Europe? Cultural pluralism, fundamental liberties and inconsistencies in the law. Paper delivered at the conference *Mobile People, Mobile Law: Expanding Legal Relations in a Contracting World.* Max Planck Institute for Social Anthropology, Halle, Germany. 7–9 November.

Foner, Nancy. 2001. Immigrant Commitment to America, Then and Now: Myths and Realities. *Citizenship Studies* 5 (1):27–40.

———. 2003a. Anthropology and Contemporary Immigration: Where We Have Been and Where We Are Going. In Nancy Foner, ed., 2003c, 3–44.

———. 2003b. Anthropology and the Study of Immigration. In *Immigration Research for a New Century*, ed. Nancy Foner, Ruben G. Rumbaut, and Steven J. Gold, 49–53. New York: Russell Sage Foundation.

———, ed. 2003c. *American Arrivals: Anthropology Engages the New Immigration.* Santa Fe, NM: School of American Research Press.

———. 2005. *In a New Land: A Comparative View of Immigration.* New York: New York University Press.

———. 2006. Immigrants at Home. *New York Times*, 26 November, City Section.

———. 2007a. Engagements across National Borders, Then and Now. *Fordham Law Review* 75:2483–92.

———. 2007b. How Exceptional is New York? Migration and Multiculturalism in the Empire City. *Ethnic and Racial Studies* 30:999–1023.

Foner, Nancy, and George Fredrickson. 2004. "Immigration, Race, and Ethnicity in the United States: Social Constructions and Social Relations in Historical and Comparative Perspectives." In *Not Just Black and White*, ed. Nancy Foner and George Fredrickson, 1–19. New York: Russell Sage Foundation.

Foner, Nancy, Rubin Rumbaut, and Herbert Gold. 2000. *Immigration Research for a New Century: Multidisciplinary Perspectives.* New York: Russell Sage Foundation.

Forcari, Christophe. 2006. L'extrême droit célèbre la défaite de Bleus trop noirs. *Libération.* 12 July, 10.

Ford, Robert. 2004. Polish Conmen, Preying on Immigrants. *Saturday Times*, 27 June, 14.

Fordham, Signathia. 1996. *Blacked Out: Dilemmas of Race, Identity, and Success at Capital High.* Chicago: University of Chicago Press.

Foster, Robert. 1991. Making National Cultures in the Global Ecumene. *Annual Review of Anthropology* 20:235–60.

Fox, Jonathan. 2006. Introduction. In *Invisible No More: Mexican Migrant Civic Participation in the United States*, ed. Xóchitl Bada, Jonathan Fox, and Andrew Selee, 1–4. Washington, DC: Woodrow Wilson International Center for Scholars.

Frank, Andre. 1967. *Capitalism and Underdevelopment in Latin America.* New York: Monthly Review Press.

Frank, Geyla. 1997. Jews, Multiculturalism and Boasian Anthropology. *American Anthropologist* 99 (4):731–45.

Fraser, Ursula. 2003. Two-tier citizenship–The Lobe and Osayande Case. Paper presented at conference Women's Movement: Migrant Women Transforming Ireland held at Trinity College Dublin, 20–21 March.

Freeman, James M. 1989. *Hearts of Sorrow: Vietnamese-American Lives*. Stanford, CA: Stanford University Press.

————. 1995. *Changing Identities: Vietnamese Americans, 1975–1995*. Boston: Allyn and Bacon.

Freedman, Jane, and Carrie Tarr, eds. 2000. *Women, Immigration and Identities in France*. New York: Berg Publishers.

Friedman, Marilyn. 2005. *Women and Citizenship*. New York: Oxford University Press.

Fuglerud, Øivind. 1999. *Life on the Outside: The Tamil Diaspora and Long Distance Nationalism*. London: Pluto.

Gans, Herbert. 1962. *Urban Villagers: Group and Class in the Life of Italian-Americans*. New York: Free Press.

Garapich, Michal. 2006. My nie mamy z tym nic wspólnego—czyli polska diaspora w Wielkiej Brytanii na skrzyżowaniu między lokalizmem a globalizacją. *Przegląd Polonijny* 2:69–88.

Garbaye, Romaine. 2000. Ethnic Minorities, Cities and Institutions: A Comparison of the Modes of Management of Ethnic Diversity of a French and British City. In *Challenging Immigration and Ethnic Relations Politics*, ed. Ruud Koopmans and Paul Statham, 283–311. Oxford: Oxford University Press.

Gardner, Martha. 2005. *The Qualities of a Citizen: Women, Immigration and Citizenship, 1870–1965*. Princeton, NJ: Princeton University Press.

Geddes, Andrew. 2003. *The Politics of Migration and Integration in Europe*. London, Thousand Oaks, and New Delhi: Sage Publications.

Gellner, Ernest. 1983. *Nations and Nationalism*. Ithaca, NY: Cornell University Press.

Germany Info. 2001–6. Background Paper: Citizenship Reform and Germany's Foreign Residents. German Embassy, Washington, DC. Available at: http://www.germany.info/relaunch/info/archives/background/citizenship.html.

Gibb, Camilla. 2002. Deterritorialized People in Hyperspace: Creating and Debating Harari Identity over the Internet. *Anthropologica* 44:55–67.

Gibb, Robert. 2001a. Toward an Anthropology of Social Movements. *Journal des Anthropologues* 85–86:233–53.

————. 2001b. Leadership, Political Opportunities and Organisational Identity in the French Anti-Racist Movement. In *Leadership and Social Movements*, ed. Colin Barker, Alan Johnson, and Michael Lavalette, 60–76. Manchester: Manchester University Press.

Gibson, Margaret A. 1989. *Accommodation without Assimilation: Sikh Immigrants in an American High School*. Ithaca, NY: Cornell University Press.

Giddens, Anthony. 1991. *Modernity and Self-Identity*. Cambridge: Polity Press.

Gilbertson, Greta, and Audrey Singer. 2003. The Emergence of Protective Citizenship in the USA: Naturalization among Dominican Immigrants in the post 1996 Welfare Reform Era. *Ethnic and Racial Studies* 26:25–51.

Gilroy, Paul. 1991. *There Ain't No Black in the Union Jack: The Cultural Politics of "Race" and Nation*. Chicago: University of Chicago Press.

Girardet, Raoul. 1986. *Mythes et mythologies politiques*. Paris: Seuil.

Glick Schiller, Nina. 1999. Transmigrants and Nation-States: Something Old and Something New in the U.S. Immigrant Experience. In *The Handbook of International*

*Migration: The American Experience*, ed. Charles Hirschman, Philip Kasinitz, and Josh DeWind, 94–119. New York: Russell Sage.

———. 2005a. Transnational Social Fields and Imperialism: Bringing a Theory of Power to Transnational Studies. *Anthropological Theory* 5 (4):439–61.

———. 2005b. Long Distance Nationalism. In *Encyclopedia of Diasporas: Immigrant and Refugee Cultures Around the World. Volume One*, ed. Melvin Ember, Carol R. Ember, and Ian Skoggard, 70–80. New York: Kluwer Academic/Plenum Publishers.

———. 2005c. Transnationality. In *A Companion to the Anthropology of Politics*, ed. David Nugent and Joan Vincent, 448–67. Malden, MA: Blackwell.

———. 2005d. Transborder Citizenship: Legal Pluralism within a Transnational Social Field. In *Mobile People, Mobile Law: Expanding Legal Relations in a Contracting World*, ed. Franz von Benda-Beckmann, Keebit von Benda-Beckmann, and Anne Griffiths, 27–50. London: Ashgate.

Glick Schiller, Nina, Ayse Caglar, and Thaddeus C. Guldbrandsen. 2006a. Jenseits der "etnischen Gruppe" als Object des Wissens: Lokalität, Globalität und Inkorporationsmuster von Migranten. In *Die Macht des Lokalen in einer Welt ohne Grenzen*, ed. Helmut Berking, 105–44. Frankfurt and Main: Campus Verlag.

———. 2006b. Beyond the Ethnic Lens: Locality, Globality, and Born-Again Incorporation. *American Ethnologist* 33 (4):612–33.

Glick Schiller, Nina, and Georges E. Fouron. 2001. *Georges Woke Up Laughing: Long-Distance Nationalism and the Search for Home*. Durham, NC: Duke University Press.

Glick Schiller, Nina, Linda Basch, and Cristina Szanton Blanc. 1995. From immigrant to transmigrant: theorizing transnational migration. *Anthropological Quarterly* 68 (1):48–63.

Gold, Steven J. 1992. *Refugee Communities: A Comparative Field Study*. Newbury Park and London: Sage.

Goldberg, David Theo. 2006. Racial Europeanization. *Ethnic and Racial Studies* 29:331–364.

Goldring, Luin. 1998. The Power of Status in Transnational Social Fields. In *Transnationalism from Below*, ed. Michael Smith and Luis Guarnizo, 165–95. New Brunswick, NJ: Transaction Publishers.

———. 2001. The Gender and Geography of Citizenship in Mexico-U.S. Transnational Spaces. *Identities* 7 (4):501–37.

———. 2002. The Mexican State and Transmigrant Organizations: Negotiating the Boundaries of Membership and Participation. *Latin American Research Review* 37 (3):55–99.

———. 2003. Gender, Status, and the State in Transnational Spaces: The Gendering of Political Participation and Mexican Hometown Associations. In *Gender and U.S. Immigration: Contemporary Trends*, ed. Pierrette Hondagneu-Sotelo, 341–58. Berkeley: University of California Press.

Goodhart, David. 2004. Too Diverse? *Prospect Magazine*, February, 30–37.

Gopnik, Adam. 2006. Rules of the Game: Can We Forgive Him? *New Yorker*, 24 July, 22–23.

Gordon, Milton. 1964. *Assimilation of American Life: The Role of Race, Religion, and National Origins*. New York: Oxford University Press.

Górny, Agata, and George Kolankiewicz. 2002. Reemigracja z Wielkiej Brytanii—poszukiwanie „nowego" czy kontynuacja „starego." In *Migracje powrotne Polaków*, ed. Krystyna Iglicka, 122–60. Warsaw: Instytut Spraw Publicznych.

Graham, Mark, and Shahram Khosravi. 2002. Reordering Public and Private in Iranian Cyberspace: Identity, Politics and Mobilization. *Identities: Global Studies in Culture and Power* 9:219–46.

Graham, Pamela M. 1998. The Politics of Incorporation: Dominicans in New York City. *Latino Studies Journal* 9 (3):39–64.

Granovetter, Mark. 1973. The Strength of Weak Ties. *American Journal of Sociology* 78 (6):1360–80.

Grillo, Ralph. 1985. *Ideologies and Institutions in Urban France: The Representation of Immigrants*. Cambridge: Cambridge University Press.

———. 2005. Backlash Against Diversity? Identity and Cultural Politics in European Cities. *COMPAS Working Paper No. 14*. Oxford: Centre on Migration Policy and Society.

Grimes, Kimberly. 1998. *Crossing Borders: Changing Social Identities in Southern Mexico*. Tucson: University of Arizona Press.

Grosfoguel, Ramon. 1997. Introduction: "Cultural Racism" and Colonial Caribbean Migrants in Core Zones of the Capitalist World-Economy. *Review* 22 (4):409–34.

Guarnizo, Luis, Alejandro Portes, and William Haller. 2003. Assimilation and Transnationalism: Determinants of Transnational Political Action among Contemporary Migrants. *American Journal of Sociology* 108:1211–48.

Guarnizo, Luis Eduardo, Arturo Ignacio Sanchez, and Elizabeth Roach. 1999. Mistrust, Fragmented Solidarity, and Transnational Migration: Colombians in New York City and Los Angeles. *Ethnic and Racial Studies* 22:367–96.

Guarnizo, Luis, and Michael Peter Smith. 1998. The Locations of Transnationalism. In *Transnationalism from Below*, ed. Michael Smith and Luis Guarnizo, 3–34. New Brunswick, NJ: Transaction Publishers.

Gupta, Akhil, and James Ferguson. 1992. Beyond Culture: Space, Identity and the Politics of Difference. *Cultural Anthropology* 7 (1):6–23.

———. 1997. Beyond "Culture": Space, Identity and the Politics of Difference. In *Culture, Power, Place: Explorations in Critical Anthropology*, ed. A. Gupta and J. Ferguson. Durham, NC: Duke University Press.

Gurak, Laura J. 1997. *Persuasion and Privacy in Cyberspace: The Online Protest over Lotus Marketplace and the Clipper Chip*. New Haven, CT: Yale University Press.

Gustafson, Per. 2002. Globalisation, Multiculturalism and Individualism: The Swedish Debate on Dual Citizenship. *Journal of Ethnic and Migration Studies* 28 (3):463–81.

Hagan, Jacqueline Maria. 1994. *Deciding to Be Legal: A Maya Community in Houston*. Philadelphia: Temple University Press.

Hage, Ghassan. 2000. *White Nation: Fantasies of White Supremacy in a Multicultural Society*. New York: Routledge.

Hahn, Carole L. 1998. *Becoming Political: Comparative Perspectives on Citizenship Education*. Albany: State University of New York Press.

Haïti Progrés. 2005. This Week in Haiti. 31 August–6 Septebmer. Vol. 23 (25).

Hakken, David. 1999. *Cyborgs @ Cyberspace/An Ethnographer Looks to the Future*. New York: Routledge.

Hall, Kathleen D. 2002. *Lives in Translation: Sikh Youth as British Citizens*. Philadelphia: University of Pennsylvania Press.

Hamidi, Camille. 2003. Voluntary Associations of Migrants and Politics: The Case of North African Immigrants in France. *Immigrants and Minorities* 22 (2–3):317–32.

Hamilton, Dona, and Charles Hamilton. 1997. *The Dual Agenda: The African-American Struggle for Civil and Economic Equality*. New York: Columbia University Press.

Hammar, Tomas. 1990. *Democracy and the Nation State: Aliens, Denizens, and Citizens in a World of International Migration*. Aldershot: Avebury.

Handlin, Oscar. 1972. *Uprooted: The Epic Story of the Great Migrations that Made the American People*. 2nd ed. Boston: Little, Brown.

Haney-López, Ian. 1998. *White By Law: The Legal Construction of Race*. New York: New York University Press.

Hannerz, Ulf. 1990. Cosmopolitans and Locals in World Culture. *Theory, Culture and Society* 7 (2–3):237–51.

———. 1993. The Withering Away of the Nation? *Ethnos* 58 (3–4):377–91.

———. 1996. *Transnational Connections: Culture, People, Places*. New York: Routledge.

———. 1997. Scenarios for Peripheral Cultures. In *Culture, Globalization and the World System: Contemporary Conditions for the Representation of Identity*, ed. Anthony D. King, 107–28. Minneapolis: University of Minnesota Press.

Hannerz, Ulf, and Orvar Lofgen. 1994. The Nation in the Global Village. *Cultural Studies* 8 (2):198–207.

Hardy-Fanta, Carol. 1993. *Latina Politics, Latino Politics: Gender, Culture and Political Participation in Boston*. Philadelphia: Temple University Press.

Hargreaves, Alec G. 1991. The Political Mobilization of the North African Community in France. *Ethnic and Racial Studies* 14:350–67.

Hart, David. 1999. Right and Left in the Atlas Mountains: Dual Symbolic Classifications among the Moroccan Berbers. *The Journal of North African Studies* 4 (3):30–44.

Harvey, David. 2005. *The New Imperialism*. New York: Oxford University Press.

Healy, Alison. 2003. Racism "alive and well" in Tramore, says councilor. Irish Times, 16 August. Available at: http://www.ireland.com/newspaper/ireland/2003/0816/1060901585257.html.

———. 2005. Rights Body Points to Irish Abuses. Irish Times, 26 May. Available at: http://www.ireland.com/newspaper/world/2005/0526/1116889038752.html.

Hein, Jeremy. 1995. *From Vietnam, Laos, and Cambodia: A Refugee Experience in the United States*. New York: Twayne Publishers.

Heller, Thomas. 1997. Modernity, Membership and Multiculturalism. *Stanford Humanities Review* 5:2–6.

Hernandez-Leon, Ruben. 2005. The Migration Industry in the Mexico-U.S. Migratory System. California Center for Population Research On-Line Working Paper Series. Available at: http://www.ccpr.ucla.edu/ccprwpseries/ccpr_049_05.pdf.

Herzfeld, Michael. 1987. *Anthropology Through the Looking Glass: Critical Ethnography in the Margins of Europe*. Cambridge: Cambridge University Press.

———. 2003. *The Body Impolitic: Artisans and Artifice in the Global Hierarchy of Value*. Chicago: University of Chicago Press.

———. 2005. *Cultural Intimacy: Social Poetics in the Nation-State*. 2nd ed. New York: Routledge.

High Court of Ireland. 1990. *Fajujonu vs. Minister for Justice, Equality and Law Reform*. [1987] IEHC 2, [1990] 2IR 151.

Hirsch, Jennifer. 2003. *A Courtship after Marriage: Sexuality and Love in Mexican Transnational Families*. Berkeley: University of California Press.

Hobsbawm, Eric. 1959. *Primitive Rebels*. New York: Praeger.

———. 1983. Introduction: Inventing Traditions. In *The Invention of Tradition*, ed. Eric Hobsbawm and Terence Ranger, 1–14. Cambridge: Cambridge University Press.

———. 2000[1969]. *Bandits*. New York: New Press.

Holland, Kitty. 2004a. Abortion and Isolation: Crisis Pregnancies among Non-Nationals Increasing. *Irish Times*, 9 July. Available at: http://www.ireland.com/newspaper/ireland/2004/0709/1086274535009.html.

———. 2004b. Action urged on 'abusive treatment' of refugees. *Irish Times*, 20 July. Available at: http://www.ireland.com/newspaper/ireland/2004/0720/1089856822654.html.

———. 2005. Stuck in Ireland's hidden villages. *Irish Times*, 9 April. Availabe at: http://www.ireland.com/newspaper/newsfeatures/2005/0409/1112397331824.html.

Holston, James, and Arjun Appadurai. 1999. Introduction: Cities and Citizenship. In *Cities and Citizenship*, ed. James Holston, 1–20. Durham, NC: Duke University Press.

Hondagneu-Sotelo, Pierrette. 1994. *Gendered Transitions: Mexican Experiences of Immigration*. Berkeley: University of California Press.

Hondagneu-Sotelo, Pierrette, and Cristina Riegos. 1997. Sin organizacion no hay solucion: Latina Domestic Workers and Non-traditional Labor Organizing. *Latino Studies Journal* 8:54–81.

Howard, Marc Morje. 2005. "Variation in Dual Citizenship Policies in the Countries of the EU." *International Migration Review* 39:697–720.

Hutchinson, John, and Anthony Smith, eds. 1994. *Nationalism*. Oxford: Oxford University Press.

IRC. 2002. Information Note on Asylum Seekers and Accommodation Centres. *Social Policy Information Note No. 1*. Dublin: Irish Refugee Council.

———. 2004. Information Note on Asylum Seekers and Accommodation Centres. *Social Policy Information Note No. 1*. Dublin: Irish Refugee Council.

Ireland, Patrick. 1994. *The Policy Challenge of Ethnic Diversity: Immigrant Politics in France and Switzerland*. Cambridge, MA: Harvard University Press.

Irish Refugee Council. 2004. The Citizenship Referendum—Why the Irish Refugee Council Says No. 21 May. Avaliable at: http://www.irishrefugeecouncil.ie/press04/pr21-5-04.html.

Irish Statute Book. 2004. Irish Nationality and Citizenship Act, 2004. Government of Ireland, Houses of Oireachtas. Available at: http://www.irishstatutebook.ie/ZZA38Y2004.html.

*Irish Times*. 2004. Citizenship Referendum 2004: Path to the Poll. Available at: http://www.ireland.com/focus/referendum2004/pathtopoll/.

Itzigsohn, Jose, and Silvia Giorguli-Saucedo. 2005. "Incorporation, Transnationalism, and Gender: Immigrant Incorporation and Transnational Participation as Gendered Processes," *International Migration Review* 39:895–920.

Jacobson, David. 1996. *Rights across Borders: Immigration and the Decline of Citizenship*. Baltimore: Johns Hopkins University Press.

James-Johnson, Alva. 2004. Haitian Protesters Call for the Ouster of President Aristide in Fort Lauderdale. *Moun*. 24 January. Available at: http://www.moun.com/Articles/jan2004/1-25-3.htm.

Janowski, Monica. 2004. *Imagined Polands: notions of identity among the "first wave" of Polish migrants in the UK*. Paper presented at the conference Imagining Diasporas: Space, Identity and Social Change, held at the University of Windsor, Canada, 14–16 May.

Jaxel-Truer, Pierre. 2006. Mais qu'a bien pu dire Materazzi à Zidane. *Le Monde*. 12 July, 10.

Jazouli, Adil. 1986. *L'action collective des jeunes maghrébins de France*. Paris: CIEM/Editions l'Harmattan.

————. 1992. *Les années banlieues*. Paris: Seuil.

Jaźwińska, Ewa, and Marek Okólski, eds. 2001. *Ludzie na huśtawce. Migracje między peryferiami Polski a Zachodu.* Warsaw: Scholar.

Jenkins, Richard. 1997. *Rethinking Ethnicity.* London: Sage.

Joly, Daniele. 2002. Odyssean and Rubicon Refugees: Towards a Typology of Refugees in the Land of Exile. *International Migration* 40 (6):3–23.

Jones, Kathleen B., and Anna G. Jonasdottir. 1988. *The Political Interests of Gender: Developing Theory and Research with a Feminist Face.* London:Sage.

Jones-Correa, Michael. 1998. *Between Two Nations: The Political Predicament of Latinos in New York City.* Ithaca, NY: Cornell University Press.

————. 2001. Under Two Flags: Dual Nationality in Latin America and Its Consequences for the United States. *International Migration Review* 35:997–1029.

Joppke, Christian. 1999a. *Challenges to the Nation-State: Immigration in Western Europe and the United States.* Oxford: Oxford University Press.

————. 1999b. How Immigration is Changing Citizenship: A Comparative View. *Ethnic and Racial Studies* 22 (4):629–52.

Joppke, Christian, and Ewa Morawska. 2003a. Integrating Immigrants in Liberal Nation-States: Policies and Practices. In Christian Joppke and Ewa Morawska, ed., 2003b, 1–36.

————, eds. 2003b. *Toward Assimilation and Citizenship: Immigrants in Liberal Nation-States.* New York: Palgrave Macmillan.

Jordan, Bill. 2002. *Migrant Polish workers in London. Mobility, Labour Markets and Prospects for Democratic Development.* Paper presented on conference "Beyond Transition, Development Perspectives and Dilemmas," Warsaw, 12–13 April.

Jordan, Bill, and Frank Duvell. 2002. *Irregular Migration–the Dilemmas of Transnational Mobility.* Cheltenham, England: Edward Elgar.

Journal Officiel de la République Française. 1901. Loi du 1er juillet 1901 (relative au contrat d'association). *JO*, 2 July.

————. 2006. Loi n 2006–911 du 24 juillet 2006. *JO*, 25 July. Avaliable at: http://www.journal-officiel.gouv.fr/frameset.html.

Juhem, Philippe. 2001. Entreprendre en politique de l'extrême gauche au PS: La professionnalisation politique des fondateurs de SOS-Racisme. *Revue française de science politique* 51:131–53.

Kalita, S. Mitra. 2006. Skilled Immigrants Turn to K Street High-Tech Workers Awaiting Green Cards Hire Lobbyists, Hit the Hill. *Washington Post*, 26 April, D01.

Karagiannis, Evangelos, and Nina Glick Schiller. 2006. Contesting Claims to the Land: Pentecostalism as a Challenge to Migration Theory and Policy. *Sociologus.* 56 (2):137–71.

Karpathakis, Anna. 1999. Home Society Politics and Immigrant Political Incorporation: The Case of Greek Immigrants in New York City. *International Migration Review* 33:55–84.

Kastoryano, Riva. 2000. Settlement, Transnational Communities and Citizenship. *International Social Science Journal* 52:307–12.

Kearney, Michael. 1991. Borders and Boundaries of the State and Self at the End of Empire. *Journal of Historical Sociology* 4 (1):52–74.

Keaton, Trica. 2006. *Muslim Girls and the Other France: Race, Identity Politics, and Social Exclusion.* Bloomington: Indiana University Press.

Kelley, Robin D. G. 1996. Kickin' Reality, Kickin' Ballistics: Gangsta Rap and Postindustrial Los Angeles. In *Droppin' Science: Critical Essays on Rap Music and Hip-Hop Culture*, ed. William Eric Perkins, 117–58. Philadelphia: Temple University Press.

Kerber, Linda. 1997. The Meanings of Citizenship. *Journal of American History* 84 (3):833–54.

Kertzer, David. 1988. *Ritual, Politics and Power*. New Haven, CT: Yale University Press.

Kettane, Nacer. 1985. Beur: C'est un badge sur son visage! *Sans frontière* 92–93:31–34.

Khandelwal, Madhulika S. 2002. *Becoming American, Being Indian: An Immigrant Community in New York City*. Ithaca, NY: Cornell University Press.

Khellil, Mohand. 1984. *La Kabylie ou l'Ancêtre sacrifié*. Paris: Harmattan.

Kiang, Peter Nien-Chu. 2000. Asian Pacific American Youth: Pathways for Political Participation. In *Asian Americans and Politics: Perspectives, Experiences, Prospects*, ed. Gordon H. Chang, 230–57. Stanford, CA: Stanford University Press and Washington, DC: Woodrow Wilson Center Press.

King, Russell, and Krysia Rybaczuk. 1993. Southern Europe and the International Division of Labour: From Emigration to Immigration. In *The New Geography of European Migrations*, ed. Russell King, 175–206. London and New York: Belhaven Press.

Kelly, Gail P. 1977. *From Vietnam to America: A Chronicle of the Vietnamese Immigration to the United States*. Boulder, CO: Westview Press.

Kessous, Mustapha. 2006. Zidane, héros lointain et décevant de la Castellane. *Le Monde*. 11 July, 10.

Kibria, Nazli. 1993. *Family Tightrope: The Changing Lives of Vietnamese Americans*. Princeton, NJ: Princeton University Press.

Klausen, Jytte. 2005. *The Islamic Challenge: Politics and Religion in Western Europe*. New York: Oxford University Press.

Kloosterman, Robert, and Jan Rath, eds. 2003. *Immigrant Entrepreneurs*. Oxford: Berg.

Kofman, Eleonore. 2000. *Gender and International Migration in Europe: Employment, Welfare and Politics*. London and New York: Routledge.

Koopmans, Ruud, and Paul Statham. 2000. Migration and Ethnic Relations as field of Political Contention: An Opportunity Structure Approach. In *Challenging Immigration and Ethnic Relations Politics*, ed. Ruud Koopmans and Paul Statham, 13–56. Oxford: Oxford University Press.

Koslowski, Rey. 2000. *Migrants and Citizens: Demographic Change in the European State System*. Ithaca, NY: Cornell University Press.

Kostakopoulou, Theodora. 2001. *Citizenship, Identity and Immigration in the European Union*. Manchester: Manchester University Press.

Krause, Elizabeth L. 2001. Empty Cradles and the Quiet Revolution: Demographic Discourse and Cultural Struggles of Gender, Race and Class in Italy. *Cultural Anthropology* 16 (4):576–611.

Kymlicka, Will. 1995. *Multicultural Citizenship: A Liberal Theory of Minority Rights*. Oxford: Oxford University Press.

———. 1998. Multicultural Citizenship. In *The Citizenship Debates: A Reader*, ed. Gershon Shafir, 167–88. Minneapolis: University of Minnesota Press.

Kymlicka, Will, and Wayne Norman. 1994. Return of the Citizen: A Survey of Recent Work on Citizenship Theory. *Ethics* 104:352–81.

Lagnado, Jacob. 2004. *The London Service Sector and Migrant Labour in the 1990s: Colombians in Contract Cleaning*. Unpublished MSc dissertation. Milton Keynes: Open University.

Laguerre, Michel S. 1998. *Diasporic Citizenship: Haitian Americans in Transnational America.* New York: St. Martin's Press.

Lahire, Bernard. 1998. *L'homme pluriel.* Paris: Nathan.

Lakshmanan, Indira. 2005. In Struggling Haiti, Some Long for Ex-Dictator. *Boston Globe.* 27 October.

Lave, Jean, and Etienne Wegner. 1991. *Situated Learning: Legitimate Peripheral Participation.* Cambridge: Cambridge University Press.

Lebovics, Herman. 1992. *True France: The Wars over Cultural Identity, 1900–1945.* Ithaca, NY: Cornell University Press.

Lee, Rachel C., and Sau-ling Cynthia Wong, eds. 2003. *AsianAmerica.net: Ethnicity, Nationalism, and Cyberspace.* New York: Routledge.

Le Gouaziou, Véronique, and Laurent Mucchielli, eds. 2006. *Quand les banlieues brûlent . . . Retour sur les émeutes de novembre 2005.* Paris: La Découverte.

Lentin, Ronit. 2003. Pregnant Silence: (En)Gendering Ireland's Asylum Space. *Patterns of Prejudice* 37 (3):301–22.

Lentin, Ronit, and Robbie McVeigh, eds. 2002. *Racism and Anti-Racism in Ireland.* Belfast: Beyond the Pale Publications.

Levin, Michael. 1997. The New Nigeria: Displacement and the Nation. *Journal of Asian and African Studies* 32 (1–2):1–11.

Lévi-Strauss, Claude. 1963. Do Dual Organizations Exist? *Structural Anthropology*, vol. 1. New York: Basic Books.

Levitt, Peggy. 2001. *The Transnational Villagers.* Berkeley: University of California Press.

———. 2003. You know, Abraham was Really the First Immigrant: Religion and Transnational Migration. *International Migration Review* 37 (143):847–74.

Lewenstein, Dan. 2006. *The Invisible Community: Counting London's Latin Americans and Responding to their Needs.* London: Indoamerican Refugee and Migrant Organization.

Lin, Jan. 1998. *Reconstructing Chinatown: Ethnic Enclave, Global Change.* Minneapolis: University of Minnesota Press.

Lister, Ruth. 1997. Citizenship: Towards a Feminist Synthesis. *Feminist Review* 57:28–48.

Lucassen, Leo. 2005. *The Immigrant Threat: The Integration of Old and New Migrants in Western Europe since 1850.* Urbana: University of Illinois Press.

Mach, Zdzislaw. 1994. *Symbols, Conflict, Identity.* Albany: State University of New York Press.

———. 1998. *Niechciane miasta. Migracja i tożsamość społeczna.* Universitas Kraków.

———. 2005. Polish Diaspora. In *Immigration and Asylum: From 1900 to the present, Volume Two,* ed. Matthew J. Gibney and Randall Hanson, 477–81. Santa Barbara, CA: ABC Clio.

Macilwaine, Cathy. 2005. *Coping Practices Among Colombian Migrants in London.* London: Queen Mary, University of London.

MacSharry, Ray, and Padraic White. 2000. *The Making of the Celtic Tiger: The Inside Story of Ireland's Boom Economy.* Dublin: Mercier Press.

Mai, Nicola. 2002. Myths and Moral Panics: Italian Identity and the Media Representation of Albanian Immigration. In *The Politics of Recognizing Difference: Multiculturalism in Italy,* ed. Ralph Grillo and Jeff Pratt, 77–94. Aldershot, England, and Burlington, VT: Ashgate.

Maira, Sunaina. 2004. Youth Culture, Citizenship and Globalization: South Asian Muslim Youth in the United States after September 11th. *Comparative Studies of South Asian, Africa and the Middle East* 24:18–30.

Malik, Serge. 1990. *Histoire secrète de SOS Racisme*. Paris: Albin Michel.

Malkki, Liisa H. 1997. National Geographic: The Rooting of Peoples and the Territorialization of National Identity among Scholars and Refugees. In *Culture, Power, Place: Explorations in Critical Anthropology*, ed. Akhil Gupta and James Ferguson, 52–74. Durham, NC: Duke University Press.

Mamdani, Mahmood. 1996. *Citizen and Subject: Contemporary Africa and the Legacy of Late Colonialism*. Princeton, NJ: Princeton University Press.

Marfleet, Phil. 1999. Europe's Civilising Mission. In *New Ethnicities, Old Racisms*, ed. Phil Cohen, 19–36. New York: Zed Books. Ltd.

Marshall, Thomas Humphrey. 1964. *Class, Citizenship, and Social Class: Essays by T.H. Marshall*. Garden City, NY: Doubleday and Co.

Martinez, Luis. 1998. *La Guerre civile en Algérie*. Paris: Karthala.

Martiniello, Marco. 1994. Citizenship of the European Union: A Critical View. In *From Aliens to Citizens*, ed. Rainer Bauböck, 29–47. Aldershot: Avebury.

———. 2005. The Political Participation, Mobilization and Representation of Immigrants and their Offspring in Europe. In *Migration and Citizenship: Legal Status, Rights and Political Participation*, ed. Rainer Bauböck, 52–64. IMISCOE Report. Amsterdam: IMISCOE.

Marx-Scouras, Danielle. 2005. *La France de Zebda, 1981–2004: Faire de la musique un acte politique*. Paris: Autrement.

McConnell, Daniel. 2004. Government criticised for deportation. *Irish Times*, 12 July. Available at: http://www.ireland.com/newspaper/ireland/2004/0712/108627453919.html.

McIntosh, Peggy. 2003[1989]. White Privilege: Unpacking the Invisible Knapsack. In *Applying Anthropology*, 6th ed., ed. Aaron Podolefsky and Peter Brown, 210–13. Mountain View, CA: Mayfield Publishing Company.

Meek, Kendrick. 2005. Letter to Gerard Latortue, Interim Prime Minister and George W. Bush, President. 25 January. Available at: http://kendrickmeek.house.gov/press/2005.01.26.shtml.

Melucci, Alberto. 1985. The Symbolic Challenge of Contemporary Movements. *Social Research* 52:17–40.

———. 1995. The Process of Collective Identity. In *Social Movements and Culture*, ed. Hank Johnston and Bert Klandermans, 41–63. London: UCL.

Merrifield, Juliet. 2002. *Learning Citizenship*. IDS Working Paper 158. Brighton, UK: Institute of Development Studies.

Meunz, Rainer. 2006. Europe: Population and Migration in 2005. Migration Policy Institute. Available at: http://www.migrationinformation.org/Feature/display.cfm?id=402.

Migration Policy Institute. 2004. Health Insurance Coverage of the Foreign Born in the United States: Numbers and Trends. Available at: http://www.migrationpolicy.org/pubs/eight.

Miller, Daniel, and Don Slater. 2000. *The Internet: An Ethnographic Approach*. Oxford and New York: Berg Publications.

Miller, Mark. 1989. Political Participation and Representation of Noncitizens. In *Immigration and the Politics of Citizenship in Europe and North America*, ed. Rogers Brubaker, 129–43. Lanham, MD: University Press of America.

Mitchell, J. Clyde. 1969. *Social Networks in Urban Situations, Analyses of Personal Relationships in Central African Towns*, ed. J. Clyde Mitchell, 77–116. Manchester: Manchester University Press.

Mitra, Ananda. 2000. Virtual Commonality: Looking for India on the Internet. In *The Cybercultures Reader*, ed. David Bell and Barbara M. Kennedy, 676–94. London and New York: Routledge.

Moctezuma, Miguel. 2004. Votar Aquí o Votar Allá. *Masiosare 317*. 18 January. Official Web site of Dumarsais Siméus. Available at: http://www.simeus06.com/.

Modood, Tariq. 2005. *Multicultural Politics: Racism, Ethnicity and Muslims in Britain*. Minneapolis: University of Minnesota Press.

Modood, Tariq, and Pnina Werbner, eds. 1997. *The Politics of Multiculturalism in the New Europe: Racism, Identity and Community*. New York: Palgrave Macmillan.

Morawska, Ewa. 2001. Immigrants, Transnationalism, and Ethnicization: A Comparison of this Great Wave and the Last. In *E Pluribus Unum? Contemporary and Historical Perspectives on Immigrant Political Incoporation*, ed. Gary Gerstle and John Mollenkopf, 175–212. New York: Russell Sage Foundation Press.

Morokvasic, Mirjana. 1992. Une migration pendulaie: les Polanais en Allemagne. *Hommes et Migrations [Men and Migrations]* 1155:31–36.

Morris Cerullo World Evangelism. 2005. Available at: http://www.mcwe.com.

Mucha, Janusz. 1996. *Everyday Life and Festivity in a Local Ethnic Community: Polish-Americans in South Bend, Indiana*. East European Monographs. New York: Columbia University Press.

Muñoz, Carlos, Jr. 1989. *Youth, Identity, Power: The Chicano Movement*. London: Verso.

Mura, Loredana. 1995. Italy: Enduring a General Crisis. In *New Xenophobia in Europe*, eds. Bernd Baumgartl and Adrian Favell, 206-217. London: Kluwer Law International.

Murphy, Kara. 2006. France's New Law: Control Immigration Flows, Court the Highly Skilled. Migration Policy Institute. Available at: http://www.migrationpolicy.org/pubs/Backgrounder2_France.php.

Nash, Catherine. 1997. Embodied Irishness: Gender, sexuality and Irish identities. In *In Search of Ireland: A Cultural Geography*, ed. Brian J. Graham, 108–27. London: Routledge Press.

Nash, J. Madelein. 1994. Tigers in the Lab. *Time Magazine*, 21 November, 86.

Nash, June. 2005. Introduction: Social Movements and Global Processes. In *Social Movements: An Anthropological Reader*, ed. June Nash, 1–26. Oxford: Blackwell.

NCCRI. 2002. *NCCRI Progress Report 2002*. Dublin: National Consultative Committee on Racism and Interculturalism.

Ndiaye, Pap. 2005. Pour une histoire des populations noires en France: Préalables théoriques. *Le Mouvement Social* 213:91–108.

Negrouche, Nasser. 1992. L'échec des associations franco-maghrébines issues de l'immigration (1980–1990). *Esprit* 178:41–52.

Neveu, Catherine. 1995. *Nations, Frontières, et Immigration en Europe*. Paris: L'Harmattan.

———. 2000. European Citizenship, Citizens of Europe and European Citizens. In *The Anthropology of the European Union*, ed. Irene Béllier and Thomas M. Wilson, 119–36. Oxford and New York: Berg Publishers.

*New York Times*. 1995. Skilled Asians Leaving U.S. for High-Tech Jobs at Homes. 21 February, A1.

———. 2004. In One Suburb, Asian-Americans Gain a Firm Political Foothold. 3 January, A9.

Noiriel, Gérard. 1996[1988]. *The French Melting Pot: Immigration, Citizenship and National Identity*. Trans. Geoffrey de LaForcade. Minneapolis: University of Minnesota Press.

Odmalm, Pontus. 2004. Civil Society, Migrant Organizations and Political Parties: Theoretical Linkages and Applications to the Swedish Context. *Journal of Ethnic and Migration Studies* 30 (3):471–89.

Offe, Klaus. 1994. How Can We Trust our fellow Citizens? In *Democracy and Trust*, ed. Mark Warren, 42–88. Cambridge: Cambridge University Press.

O'Halloran, Marie. 2004. Citizenship system "being abused." *Irish Times*, 31 March, Available at: http://www.ireland.com/newspaper/ireland/2004/0331/1079399157 369.html.

Oldfield, Duane. 2004. The Evangelical Roots of US Unilateralism Foreign Policy in Focus. Available at: http://www.atimes.com.

Ong, Aihwa. 1996a. A Better Tomorrow? The Struggle for Global Visibility. *Sojourn* 12 (2):192–225.

———. 1996b. Cultural Citizenship as Subject-Making: Immigrants Negotiate Racial and Cultural Boundaries in the United States. *Current Anthropology* 37:737–62.

———. 1999. *Flexible Citizenship: The Cultural Logics of Transnationality*. Durham, NC: Duke University Press.

———. 2003. *Buddha Is Hiding: Refugees, Citizenship, and the New America*. Berkeley: University of California Press.

Ong, Aihwa, and Donald Nonini. 1996. *Ungrounded Empires*. London: Routledge.

Ong, Nhu-Ngoc T., and David S. Meyer. 2004. Protest and Political Incorporation: Vietnamese American Protest 1975–2001. Center for the Study of Democracy. University of California, Irvine. Available at: http://repositories.cdlib.org/csd/04–08.

ORAC. 2004. *Monthly Statistics, September 2004*. Dublin: Office of the Refugee Applications Commissioner.

Osipowicz, Dorota. 2001. Marginalizacja społeczna migrantów. In *Ludzie na huśtawce. Migracje między peryferiami Polski a Zachodu*, ed. Ewa Jaźwińska and Marek Okólski, 382–408. Warsaw: Scholar.

Østergaard-Nielsen, Eva. 2002. *Transnational Politics: The Case of Turks and Kurds in Germany*. London and New York: Routledge.

———. 2003 The Politics of Migrants' Transnational Political Practices. *International Migration Review* 37:760–86.

Page, Helan E. 1997. "Black" Images, African American Identities: Corporate Cultural Projection in the "Songs of My People." *Identities* 3 (4):557–603.

Panagakos, Anastasia N. 2003. Downloading New Identities: Ethnicity, Technology, and Media in the Global Greek Village. *Identities: Global Studies in Culture and Power* 10:201–19.

Parham, Angel Adams. 2004. Diaspora, community and communication: Internet use in transnational Haiti. *Global Networks* 4:1470–2266.

Park, Robert. 1969. Human Migration and the Marginal Man. In *Classic Essays on the Culture of Cities*, ed. Richard Sennet, 131–42. New York: Appleton-Century-Crofts.

Parsons, Craig A., and Timothy M. Smeeding, eds. 2006. *Immigration and the Transformation of Europe*. Cambridge: Cambridge University Press.

Patterson, Sheila. 1964. Polish London. In *London: Aspects of Change*, ed. R. Glass. London.

———. 1977. The Poles: an Exile Community in Britain. In *Between Two Cultures*, ed. James L. Watson, 210–55. Oxford: Oxford University Press.

Peabody, Susan, and Tyler Stovall, eds. 2003. *The Color of Liberty: Histories of Race in France*. Durham, NC: Duke University Press.

Perlmutter, Ted. 1998. The Politics of Proximity: The Italian Response to the Albanian Crisis. *International Migration Review* 32 (1):203.

Però, Davide. 2005a. *Immigrants and the Politics of Governance in Barcelona.* COMPAS Working paper no. 19. Oxford: Centre on Migration Policy and Society.

————. 2005b. Left-Wing Politics, Civil Society and Immigration in Italy: The Case of Bologna. *Ethnic and Racial Studies* 28 (5):832–58.

————. 2007a. *Latino Migrants' Mobilization and the British Integration Debate.* Paper presented at the IMISCOE B3 Workshop, Warsaw, 24 April 2007. European Network of Excellence on International Migration, Integration and Social Cohesion. Available at: http://www.imiscoe.org/.

————. 2007b. *Inclusionary Rhetoric/Exclusionary Practices: Left-wing Politics and Migrants in Italy.* New York and Oxford: Berghahn.

Pessar, Patricia. 1995. *A Visa for a Dream: Dominicans in the United States.* Boston: Allyn and Bacon.

Pessar, Patricia R., and Pamela M. Graham. 2001. Dominicans: Transnational Identities and Local Politics. In *New Immigrants in New York,* ed. Nancy Foner, 251–74. New York: Columbia University Press.

Pfister, Thierry. 1988. *Lettre ouverte à la génération Mitterrand qui marche à côté de ses pompes.* Paris: Albin Michel.

Phillips, Frank. 2006. St. Fleur Withdraws as Reilly's Running Mate. *Boston Globe,* 1 February. Available at: http://www.boston.com/news/local/massachusetts/articles/2006/02/01/st_fleur_withdraws_as_reillys_running_mate/.

Pierre-Louis, François. 2006. *Haitians in New York City: Transnationalism and Hometown Associations.* Gainesville: University of Florida Press.

Pi-Sunyer, Oriole. 1992. Perspectives on Marginality in Barcelona Schools. *Research Report 27.* Department of Anthropology: University of Massachusetts Amherst.

Portes, Alejandro, and Ruben Rumbaut. 2006. *Immigrant America: A Portrait.* 3rd ed. Berkeley: University of California Press.

Portes, Alejandro, and Josh DeWind, eds. 2007. *Rethinking Migration: New Theoretical and Empirical Perspectives.* New York and Oxford: Berghahn Books.

Poster, Mark. 2001. Citizens, Digital Media and Globalization. *Mot Pluriels* 18:1–10. Avalable at: http//www.arts.uwa.edu.au/MotsPluriels/MP1801mp.html.

Prévos, André J. M. 1996. The Evolution of French Rap Music and Hip Hop Culture in the 1980s and 1990s. *The French Review* 69 (5):713–25.

Pujadas, David, and Ahmed Salam. 1995. *La tentation du Jihad.* Paris: J.C. Lattès.

Putnam, Robert D. 2000. *Bowling Alone: The Collapse and Revival of American Community.* New York: Simon and Schuster.

Putnam, Robert D., Robert Leonardi, and Rafaella Y. Nanetti. 1993. *Making Democracy Work: Civic Traditions in Modern Italy.* Princeton, NJ: Princeton University Press.

Quandt, William B. 1998. *Between Ballots and Bullets: Algeria's Transition from Authoritarianism.* Washington, DC: Brookings Institution Press.

Rai, Amit S. 1995. Indian On-line: Electronic Bulletin Boards and the Construction of a Diasporic Hindu Identity. *Diaspora* 4:31–57.

Rangaswamy, Padma. 2000. *Namasté America: Indian Immigrants in an American Metropolis.* University Park: The Pennsylvania University Press.

Reed-Danahay, Deborah. 1996. *Education and Identity in Rural France: The Politics of Schooling.* Cambridge: Cambridge University Press.

————. 2003. Europeanization and French Primary Education: Local Implications of Supranational Policies. In *Local Meanings, Global Schooling: Anthropology and World Culture Theory*, ed. Kathryn M. Anderson-Levitt, 201–18. New York: Palgrave Macmillan.

————. 2006. The Vietnamese American Community: Exploring the Meanings of Cộng Đồng and other Concepts of Sociation among Vietnamese in the North-Central Texas, Unpublished Paper delivered at the Annual Meeting of the Canadian Association of Social and Cultural Anthropology (CASCA), Montreal, May.

————. 2007. Citizenship Education in the "New Europe": Who Belongs? In *Reimagining Civic Education: How Diverse Societies Form Democratic* Citizens, ed. E. Doyle Stevick and Bradley A. U. Levinson, 197–215. Lanham, MD: Rowman and Littlefield Publishers, Inc.

Reyhner, Jon A., and Jeanne M. Oyawin Eder. 2004. *American Indian Education: A History*. Norman: University of Oklahoma Press.

Ribeiro, Gustavo Lins. 1998. Cybercultural Politics: Political Activism at a Distance in a Transnational World. In *Cultures of Politics, Politics of Cultures: RE-visioning Latin American Social Movements*, ed. Sonia E. Alvarez, Evelina Dagnino, and Arturo Escobar, 325–52. Boulder, CO: Westview Press.

Richman, Karen. 1992. "A *Lavalas* at Home/A *Lavalas* for Home": Inflections of Transnationalism in the Discourse of Haitian President Aristide. In *Towards a Transnational Perspective on Migration: Race, Class, Ethnicity and Nationalism Reconsidered*, ed. Linda Basch, Nina Glick Schiller, and Cristina Blanc-Szanton, 189–200. New York: Academy of the Sciences.

————. 2005. *Migration and Vodou*. New World Diasporas Series. Gainesville: University of Florida Press.

Richman, Karen, and William Balan-Gaubert. 2001. A Democracy of Words: Political Performance in Haiti's Tenth Province. *Journal of the Haitian Studies Association* 7 (1):90–103.

Rivera-Salgado, Gaspar. 2006. Mexican Migrants and the Mexican Political System. In *Invisible No More: Mexican Migrant Civic Participation in the United States*, ed. Jonathan Fox, Xóchitl Bada, and Andrew Selee, 31–33. Washington, DC: Woodrow Wilson International Center for Scholars.

Roberts, Hugh. 2003. *The Battlefield Algeria, 1988–2002: Studies in a Broken Polity*. London: Verso.

Rodriguez, Olga. 2005. Mexico Mayor Eager to Escape Politics. *Associated Press*. 14 September. Avaliable at: http://www.globalgoodnews.com.

Rogers, Reuel. 2006. *Afro-Caribbean Immigrants and the Politics of Incorporation*. Cambridge: Cambridge University Press.

Rosaldo, Renato. 1989. *Culture and Truth*. Boston: Beacon Press.

————. 1994. Social Justice and the Crisis of National Communities. In *Colonial Discourse/Postcolonial Theory*, ed. Francis Barker, Peter Hulme, and Margaret Iverson, 239–52. Manchester: Manchester University Press.

————. 1997. Cultural Citizenship, Inequality and Multiculturalism. In *Latino Cultural Citizenship: Claiming Identity, Space and Politics*, ed. William V. Flores and Rina Benmayor, 27–53. Boston: Beacon Press.

————, ed. 2003. *Cultural Citizenship in Island Southeast Asia: Nation and Belonging in the Hinterlands*. Berkeley: University of California Press.

Rosaldo, Renato, and William V. Flores. 1997. Identity, Conflict, and Evolving Latino Communities: Cultural Citizenship in San Jose, California. In *Latino Cultural Citizenship: Claiming Identity, Space and Politics*, ed. William V. Flores and Rina Benmayor, 57–96. Boston: Beacon Press.

Rouse, Roger. 1996. Mexican Migration and Social Science Space of Postmodernism. *Diaspora* 1(1):8–23.

———. 1995. Thinking through Transnationalism: Notes on the Cultural Politics of Class Relations in the Contemporary United States. *Public Culture* 7:353–402.

Ruedy, John. 1992. *Modern Algeria: The Origins and Development of a Nation.* Bloomington: Indiana University Press.

Rutledge, Paul. 1992. *The Vietnamese Experience in America.* Bloomington: Indiana University Press.

Ryan, Aisling. 2005. Reform Issues in Irish Law and Practice. *Conference on Migrant Workers and Human Rights Law,* 1–14. Dublin: The Law Society of Ireland.

Saada, Emmanuelle. 2002. Race and Sociological Reason in the Republic: Inquiries on the Métis in the French Empire (1908–1937). *International Sociology* 17 (3):361–91.

Salih, Ruba. 2003. *Gender in Transnationalism: Home, Longing, and Belonging Among Moroccan Migrant Women.* London: Routledge.

Salt, John. 2004. New era of migration. Introduction paper for the 2nd EAPS conference. *Migrations in Europe: New trends, new methods of analysis.* Rome 24–27 November.

*San Francisco Chronicle.* 2000. Wen Ho Lee Admits Felony, Finds Justice. 12 September. A25.

———. 2001. Spy Hysteria Fuels View of Asians. 13 August. B5. *San Jose Mercury News.* 1993. Tide of Opportunities Turns for Taiwanese Engineers. 22 August. A1.

Sassen, Saskia. 1999. *Guests and aliens.* New York: New Press.

Saxenian, AnaLee. 1999. *Silicon Valley's New Immigrant Entrepreneurs.* San Francisco: Public Policy Institute of California.

Sayad, Abdelmalek. 2004. *The Suffering of the Immigrant.* Cambridge: Polity Press.

Schiffauer, Werner. 1999. *Islamism in the Diaspora. The Fascination of Political Islam among Second Generation German Turks.* University of Oxford, Transnational Communities Programme Working Paper WPT-99–06. Electronic document. Available at: http//: www.transcomm.ox.ac.uk/workimgpapers/Schiffauer_islamism.PDF.

Schnapper, Dominique. 1998. *Community of Citizens: On the Modern Idea of Nationality.* Trans. Sévérine Rosée. New Brunswick, NJ: Transaction Publishers.

Schneider, Jane. 1995. Introduction: The Dynamics of Neo-Orientalism in Italy (1848–1995). In *Italy's "Southern Question": Orientalism in One Country,* ed. Jane Schneider, 1–23. Oxford: Berg.

Schneider, Jo Anne. 1990. Defining Boundaries, Creating Contacts: Puerto Rican and Polish Presentation of Group Identity through Ethnic Parades. *Journal of Ethnic Studies* 18 (1):33–57.

Schonwald, Josh. 2005. The Meek Better Look Out: A Haitian-American candidate for the nation's most Haitian district. *Miami New Times.* 15 December.

Schonwalder, Karen. 1996. Migration, Refugees and Ethnic Plurality as Issues of Public and Private Debates in (West) Germany. In *Citizenship, Nationality and Migration in Europe,* ed. David Cesarani and Mary Fulbrook, 159–78. London: Routledge.

Scott, James. 1990. *Domination and the Arts of Resistance: Hidden Transcripts.* New Haven, CT: Yale University Press.

Scruton, Roger. 1982. *A Dictionary of Political Thought.* London: Pan Books.

Shafir, Gershon. 1998. The Evolving Tradition of Citizenship. In *The Citizenship Debates: A Reader,* ed. Gershon Shafir, 1–28. Minneapolis: University of Minnesota Press.

Shepard, Todd. 2006. *The Invention of Decolonization: The Algerian War and the Remaking of France.* Ithaca, NY: Cornell University Press.

Shiao, Jiannbin Lee. 2002. The Political and Philanthropic Contexts for Incorporating Asian American Communities. In *Contemporary Asian American Communities: Intersections and Divergences*, ed. Linda Trinh Võ and Rick Bonus, 216–28. Philadelphia: Temple University Press.

Shore, Cris. 2000. *Building Europe: The Cultural Politics of European Integration*. London: Routledge.

Shore, Cris, and Susan Wright. 1997. Policy: A New Field of Anthropology. In *Anthropology of Policy: Critical Perspectives on Governance and Power*, ed. Cris Shore and Susan Wright, 3–39. London: Routledge.

Siemaszko, Zbigniew. 2003. *Polacy w drugiej wojnie światowej*. Polska Fundacja Kulturalna: Londyn.

Silverstein, Paul A. 2000. Sporting Faith: Islam, Soccer, and the French Nation-State. *Social Text* 65/18 (4):25–53.

———. 2003. Martyrs and Patriots: Ethnic, National, and Transnational Dimensions of Kabyle Politics. *Journal of North African Studies* 8 (1):87–111.

———. 2004a. *Algeria in France: Transpolitics, Race, and Nation*. Bloomington: Indiana University Press.

———. 2004b. Headscarves and the French Tricolor. *Middle East Report Online*. 29 January. Available at: www.merip.org.

———. 2005. Immigrant Racialization and the New Savage Slot: Race, Migration, and Immigration in the New Europe. *Annual Review of Anthropology* 34:363–84.

Silverstein, Paul, and Chantal Tetreault. 2005. Urban Violence in France. *Middle East Report Online*. December. www.merip.org.

Silvestrini, Blanca. 1997. The World We Enter When Claiming Rights: Latinos and Their Quest for Culture. In *Latino Cultural Citizenship: Claiming Identity, Space and Rights*, ed. William Flores and Rina Benmayor, 39–54. Boston: Beacon Press.

Simon, Rita James and Caroline Brettell. 1986. *International Migration: The Female Perspective*. Totowa, NJ: Rowman and Allanheld.

Skrbiš, Zlatko. 1999. *Long Distance Nationalism: Diasporas, Homelands and Identities*. Aldershot, England: Ashgate.

Smith, Alice. 1999. *Dispelling the Darkness: How to Deal with Demonic Rulers*. Houston: U.S. Prayer Center.

Smith, Craig. 2005. Immigrant Rioting Flares in France for Ninth Night. *New York Times*, 5 Nov.

Smith, Craig, and Ariane Bernard. 2005. Angry Immigrants Embroil France in Wider Riots. *New York Times*, 5 November, Late Edition—Final, A1, column 2.

Smith, Michael Peter. 2003a. Transnationalism and Citizenship. In *Approaching Transnationalisms: Studies in Transnational Societies, Multicultural Contacts and Imaginings of Home*, ed. Brenda S. A. Yeoh, Michael W. Charney, and Tong Chee Kiong, 15–38. Norwell, MA: Kluwer.

———. 2003b. Transnationalism, the State and the Extraterritorial Citizen. *Politics and Society* 31 (4):467–502.

Smith, Robert. 1993. Los Ausentes Siempre Presentes: the Imagining, Making and Politics of a Transnational Community between New York City and Ticuani, Puebla. *Papers on Latin American and Iberian Studies*. New York: Columbia University.

———. 1997. Transnational Migration, Assimilation, and Political Community. In *The City and the World: New York's Global Future*, ed. Margaret E. Crahan and Alberto Vourvoulias-Bush, 110–32. New York: Council on Foreign Relations.

————. 2001. Mexicans: Social, Educational, Economic and Political Problems and Prospects in New York. In *New Immigrants in New York*, ed. Nancy Foner, 275–300. New York: Columbia University Press.

————. 2006. *Mexican, New York: Transnational Lives of New Immigrants*. Berkeley: University of California Press.

Smith, Sidonie, and Gisela Brinker-Gabler. 1997. Introduction: Gender, Nation and Immigration in the New Europe. In *Writing New Identities: Gender, Nation and Immigration in Contemporary Europe*, ed. Gisela Brinker-Gabler and Sidonie Smith, 1–30. Minneapolis: University of Minnesota Press.

Sokefeld, Martin. 2002. Alevism Online: Re-Imagining a Community in Virtual Space. *Diaspora* 11:35–73.

*South China Morning Post*. 1995. Asian Americans Return to Their Roots. 13 April, 7.

————. 2002. Fortune-Seekers Return. 16 January, 1.

Soysal, Yasemin Nuhoglu. 1994. *Limits of Citizenship: Migrants and Postnational Membership in Europe*. Chicago: University of Chicago Press.

————. 1998. Towards a Postnational Model of Membership. In *The Citizenship Debates: A Reader*, ed. Gershon Shafir, 189–217. Minneapolis: University of Minnesota Press.

Spencer, Jonathan. 1997. Post-Colonialism and the Political Imagination. *Journal of the Royal Anthropological Institute* 3:1–19.

Spring, Joel, ed. 2003. *Deculturalization and the Struggle for Equality: A Brief History of the Education of Dominated Cultures in the United States*. 4th ed. Boston: McGraw-Hill.

Staeheli, Lynn A., Valeri Ledwith, Meghann Ormond, Katie Reed, Amy Sumpter, and Daniel Trudeau. 2002. Immigration, the Internet and Spaces of Politics. *Political Geography* 21:989–1012.

Statham, Paul. 1999. Political Mobilisation by Minorities in Britain: A Negative Feedback of "Race Relations"? *Journal of Ethnic and Migration Studies* 25 (4):597–626.

Steele, Janis. 1997. *Constitutive Contradictions and "Belonging" in Montreal: Cultural Mediaries and Anthropological Theory*. Ph.D. Dissertation, UMass Amherst.

Stepick, Alex, and Carol Dutton Stepick. 2002. Becoming American, Constructing Ethnicity: Immigrant Youth and Civic Engagement. *Applied Developmental Science* 6 (4):246–57.

Stepick, Alex, Carol Dutton Stepick, and Philip Kretsedemas. 2001. Civic Engagement of Haitian Immigrants and Haitian Americans in Miami-Dade County. *Report of the Immigration and Ethnicity Institute*. Florida International University.

Stepick, Alex, Guillermo Grenier, Max Castro, and Marvin Dunn. 2003. *This Land is Our Land: Immigrants and Power in Miami*. Berkeley: University of California Press.

Stewart, Angus. 1995. Two Conceptions of Citizenship. *British Journal of Sociology* 46 (1):63–78.

Stoler, Ann Laura. 1997. Sexual Affronts and Racial Frontiers: European Identities and the Cultural Politics of Exclusion in Colonial Southeast Asia. In *Tensions of Empire: Colonial Cultures in a Bourgeois World*, ed. Frederick Cooper and Ann Laura Stoler, 198–237. Berkeley: University of California Press.

————. 2002. *Carnal Knowledge and Imperial Rule: Race and the Intimate in Colonial Rule*. Berkeley: University of California Press.

Stolke, Verena. 1995. Talking Culture: New Boundaries, New Rhetorics of Exclusion in Europe. *Current Anthropology* 36 (1):1–24.

Stora, Benjamin. 2001. *Algeria, 1830–2000: A Short History*. Ithaca, NY: Cornell University Press.

Supreme Court of Ireland. 2003. *Lobe and Osayande vs. Minister for Justice, Equality and Law Reform.* [2003] IESC 3.

Swinford, Steven. 2006. How many more can we squeeze in? *Sunday Times.* 27 August. Available at: http://www.timesonline.co.uk/article/0,,2087-2330273,00.html.

Sword, Keith. 1996. *Identity in Flux: The Polish Community in Britain.* Loughborough.

Tagliabue, John. 2002. Working to Put Blacks on France's Agenda. *New York Times.* 15 October, Late Edition—Final, A3, column 1.

Thomas, Dominic. 2007. *Black France: Colonialism, Immigration, and Transnationalism.* Bloomington: Indiana University Press.

Thompson, Kenneth. 2002. Border Crossings and Diasporic Identities: Media Use and Leisure Practices of an Ethnic Minority. *Qualitative Sociology* 25:409–18.

Tillie, Jean. 2004. Social Capital of Organizations and Their Members: Explaining the Political Integration of Immigrants in Amsterdam. *Journal of Ethnic and Migration Studies* 30:529–41.

*Time Magazine.* 1994. Tigers in the Lab. 21 November, 86.

Titouss, Kaïssa. 1993. J'ai claqué la porte de SOS-Racisme. In *Douce France: La Saga du Mouvement Beur (1983–1993),* Special edition of *Quo Vadis: La revue de l'agence IM'média* (Autumn–Winter):44–47.

Touraine, Alain. 1971. *The Post-Industrial Society: Tomorrow's Social History: Classes, Conflicts and Culture in the Programmed Society.* London: Wildwood House.

Triandafyllidou, Anna. 2001. *Immigrants and National Identity in Europe.* London and New York: Routledge.

———. 2006. *Contemporary Polish Migration in Europe. The Insiders' Story.* European University Institute. Ceredigion, Wales and Washington, DC: The Edwin Mellen Press.

Tsuda, Takejuki, ed. 2006. *Local Citizenship in Recent Countries of Immigration: Japan in Comparative Perspective.* Lanham, MD: Lexington Books.

TUC. 2004. Propping up rural and small town Britain: Migrant workers and the new Europe. Trade Unions Congress Report. Avaliable at: http://www.tuc.org.uk/extras/migrantNewEurope.pdf.

U.S. Census. 2006. People: Origins and Language. Available at: http://factfinder.census.gov/jsp/saff/SAFFInfo.jsp?_pageId=tp7_origins_language.

U.S. Census Bureau. 2002. American Community Service Profile. Fort Worth-Arlington, TX PMSA. Available at: http://www.census.gov/acs/www/Products/Profiles/Single/2002/ACS/Tabular/385/38500US192228001.htm.

U.S. Department of State. 2005. Secretary Condoleeza Rice, Remarks with Haitian Prime Minister Gerard Latortue. Available at: http://www.state.gov/secretary/rm/2005/54059.htm.

UNHCR. 2004. *UN Refugee Agency Report on Migration Europe.* Geneva: United Nations High Commissioner for Refugees.

Urban, Hugh. 2006. Bush, the Neoconservatives, and Evangelical Christian Fiction. *Journal of Religion and Society.* Available at: http://moses.creighton.edu/JRS/2006/2006-2.html.

USCR. 2003. *World Refugee Survey 2003: Ireland.* Washington: US Committee for Refugees.

Uwazurike, P. Chudi, and Michael C. Mbabuike. 2004. Nigeria's Perennial Crisis of Nationhood, Democracy and Development on the Wages of Social Negative Capital. *Dialectical Anthropology* 28:203–31.

Valbrun, Marjorie. 2001. Haitian-Americans: Their Search for Identity in South Florida. *Alicia Patterson Foundation* 20 (1). Available at: http://www.aliciapatterson.org/APF2001/Valbrun/Valbrun.html/.

———. 2002. Haitian-American Politics in Chicago. *Alicia Patterson Foundation* 20 (2). Available at: http://www.aliciapatterson.org/APF2001/Valbrun/Valbrun.html.

Van Dijk, Eijk. 2004. Negotiating Marriage: Questions of Morality and Legitimacy in the Ghanaian Pentacostal Doaspora. *Journal of Religion in Africa* 34 (4):438–67.

Van Dijk, Teun A. 2001. Multidisciplinary CDA: A Plea for Diversity. In *Methods of Critical Discourse Analysis*, ed. Ruth Wodak and Michael Meyer, 95–120. London: Sage Publications.

Vasquez, Manuel A., and Marie Friedmann Marquard. 2003. *Globalizing the Sacred: Religion across the Americas*. New Brunswick, NJ: Rutgers University Press.

Verdery, Katherine. 1996. Transnationalism, Nationalism, Citizenship and Property: Eastern Europe since 1989. *American Ethnologist* 25 (2):291–306.

Vertovec, Steven. 1996. Multiculturalism, culturalism and public incorporation. *Ethnic and Racial Studies* 19 (1):49–68.

———. 2006. *The Emergence of Super-Diversity in Britain*. COMPAS Working Paper no. 25. Oxford: Centre on Migration Policy and Society.

Vertovec, Steven, and Suzanne Wessendorf. 2005. *Migration and Cultural, Religious and Linguistic Diversity in Europe: An Overview of Issues and Trends*. COMPAS Working Paper no. 18. Oxford: Centre on Migration Policy and Society.

Viet, Vincent. 1998. *La France immigrée: Construction d'une politique, 1914–1997*. Paris: Fayard.

Villareal, José Antonio. 1989[1959]. *Pocho*. New York: Random House.

Walaszek, Adam. 2001. Polska diaspora. In *Diaspory. Migracje i społeczeństwo*, vol. 6, ed. J. E. Zamojski., 8–29. Warsaw: Neriton.

Wallerstein, Immanuel. 1974. *The Modern World-System*. New York: Academic Press.

———. 1980. *The Modern World-System II: Mercantilism and the Consolidation of the European Economy 1600–1750*. New York: Academic Press.

Walsh, Jimmy. 2004. O'Meara appalled by back-street abortions. *Irish Times*, 9 July. Available at: http://www.ireland.com/newspaper/ireland/2004/0709/1086274534692.html.

Weber, Lori M, Alysha Loumakis, and James Bergman. 2003. Who Participates and Why? An Analysis of Citizens on the Internet and the Mass Public. *Social Science Computer Review* 21:26–42.

Weil, Patrick. 2001. Access to Citizenship: A Comparison of Twenty-Five Nationality Laws. In *Citizenship Today: Global Perspectives and Practices*, ed. T. Alexander Aleinikoff and Douglas Klusmeyer, 17–35. Washington, DC: Carnegie Endowment for International Peace.

Wegner, Etienne. 1998. *Communities of Practice: Learning, Meaning, and Identity*. Cambridge: Cambridge University Press.

Werbner, Pnina, and Nira Yuval-Davis, eds. 1999. *Women, Citizenship and Difference (Postcolonial Encounters)*. London: Zed Books, Ltd.

Wihtol de Wenden, Catherine. 1991. North African Immigration and the French Political Imaginary. In *Race, Discourse and Power in France*, ed. Maxim Silverman. Brookfield, VT: Grower Publishing Co.

———. 1991. Immigration policy and the issue of nationality. *Ethnic and Racial Studies* 14:319–32.

Wilder, Gary. 2005. *The French Imperial Nation-State: Négritude and Colonial Humanism between the Two World Wars*. Chicago: University of Chicago Press.

Wilensky, Harold L. 2002. *Rich Democracies: Political Economy, Public Policy, and Performance*. Berkeley: University of California Press.

Williams, Raymond. 1983[1976]. *Keywords: A Vocabulary of Culture and Society*. Rev. ed. New York: Oxford University Press.

Wilson, Samuel M., and Leighton C. Peterson. 2002. The Anthropology of Online Communities. *Annual Review of Anthropology* 31:449–67.

Wimmer, Andreas, and Nina Glick Schiller. 2002. Methodological nationalism and beyond: nation-state building, migration and the social sciences. *Global Networks* 2 (4):301–34.

Wong, Bernard P. 2001. From Enclave Small Businesses to High-Tech Industries: The Chinese in the San Francisco Bay Area. In *Manifest Destinies: Americanizing Immigrants and Internationalizing Americans*, ed. David Haines and Carol A. Mortland, 111–37. Wesport, CT.: Praeger.

———. 2006. *The Chinese in Silicon Valley: Globalization, Social Networks, and Ethnic Identity*. Lanham, MD: Rowman & Littlefield Publishers.

Young, Iris M. 1990. *Justice and the Politics of Difference*. Princeton, NJ: Princeton University Press.

Yurdakul, Gökçe. 2006. State, Political Parties, and Immigrant Elites: Turkish Immigrant Associations in Berlin. *Journal of Ethnic and Migration Studies* 32 (3):435–53.

Yuval-Davis, Nira. 1997a Women, Citizenship and Difference. *Feminist Review* 57 (Autumn):4–27.

———. 1997b. *Gender & Nation*. Thousand Oaks, CA: Sage Publications.

Yuval-Davis, Nira, and Floya Anthias, eds. 1989. *Woman-nation-state*. New York: St. Martin's Press.

Zhang, Wei Tian. 2000. *Silicon Valley's Red Guards [Jeh Gu Hung Wei Bin]*. Taipei: Bookzone.

Zincone, Giovanna. 1999. Illegality, Enlightenment and Ambiguity: A Hot Italian Recipe. In *Immigrants and the Informal Economy in Southern Europe*, ed. Martin Baldwin-Edwards and Joaquin Arango, 43–82. London and Portland, OR: Frank Cass.

Zlolniski, Christian. 2006. *Janitors, Street Vendors, and Activists: The Lives of Mexican Immigrants in Silicon Valley*. Berkeley: University of California Press.

Zontini, Elisabetta. 2002. Resisting Fortress Europe. The everyday politics of Moroccan and Filipino Women in Bologna and Barcelona. Paper Presented and the 7th conference of the European Association of Social Anthropologists, Copenhagen 14–17 July.

Zubrzycki, Jerzy. 1956. *Polish Immigrant in Britain: A Study of Adjustment*. Oxford: Oxford University Press.

———. 1988. *Soldiers and Peasants: The Sociology of Polish Migration*. The Second M. B. Grabowski Memorial Lecture. London: Orbis Books.

# CONTRIBUTORS

CAROLINE B. BRETTELL is Dedman Family distinguished professor in the department of anthropology at Southern Methodist University and is currently serving as dean ad interim of Dedman College. Brettell is an internationally-known specialist on immigration and the anthropology of gender. She is the author of *Men Who Migrate, Women Who Wait: Population and History in a Portuguese Parish* (1986), *We Have Already Cried Many Tears: The Stories of Three Portuguese Migrant Women* (1982, 1995), *Writing Against the Wind: A Mother's Life History* (1999) and *Anthropology and Migration: Essays on Transnationalism, Ethnicity and Identity* (2003); co-author with Richard Brettell of *Painters and Peasants in the 19th Century* (1983); editor of *When They Read What We Write: The Politics of Ethnography* (1993), and *Crossing Borders/Constructing Boundaries: Race, Ethnicity and Immigration* (2007); co-editor of *International Migration: The Female Experience* (1986), *Gender in Cross-Cultural Perspective* (1993, 1997, 2001, 2005), *Gender and Health: An International Perspective* (1996), and *Migration Theory: Talking Across Disciplines* (2000, 2007). She is also the author of numerous book chapters and articles.

AYSE CAGLAR is professor and has been the head of the sociology and social anthropology department at the Central European University in Budapest since 2003. She received her M.A. and Ph.D. in anthropology from McGill University, Montreal, Canada, and was assistant professor at the Free University of Berlin, Institute of Ethnology, where she has received her Habilitation both in sociology and anthropology, prior to her appointment in Budapest. She was a *Jean Monnet* fellow at Robert Schumann Center for Advanced Study, Florence. Her research focus has been on transnational migration and its entanglements with the states; globalization, the rescaling of cities, neoliberalism and migrant incorporation; European citizenship, dual citizenship; transnational media and minority cultural productions, and European cultural policies. She is the author of numerous journal articles and book chapters and background reports on these topics, which have appeared in *Journal of Ethnic and Migration Studies, Journal of Ethnic and Racial Studies, Global Networks, Cultural Dynamics, Journal of Material Culture, New German Critique, Sociologu,* and *American Ethnologist.* She is the co-editor (with Levent Soysal) of a special issue of *New Perspectives on Turkey* (2004) on "Turkish Migration to Germany: Issues, Reflections and Futures."

NANCY FONER is distinguished professor of sociology at Hunter College and the Graduate Center of the City University of New York. She has studied Jamaicans in their home society as well as in New York and London, nursing home workers in New York, and has written widely on immigration to New York City. She is particularly interested in the comparative study of immigration—comparing immigration today with earlier periods in the United States, the immigrant experience in various American gateway cities, and immigrant minorities in the United States and Europe. Her thirteen books include *In a New Land: A Comparative View of Immigration* (2005), *From Ellis Island to JFK: New York's Two Great Waves of Immigration* (2000 and recipient of the Theodore Saloutos Award of the Immigration and Ethnic History Society), *Not Just Black and White: Historical and Contemporary Perspectives on Immigration, Race, and Ethnicity in the United States* (2004, with George Fredrickson) and *Islands in the City: West Indian Migrants in New York* (2001).

MICHAL P. GARAPICH is a social anthropologist working at the Center for Research on Nationalism, Ethnicity and Multiculturalism at Roehampton and Surrey Universities, London. He completed his Ph.D. on *Migration, Civil Society and Power—Anthropological Perspectives on Polish Migrants' Civic Participation in the UK* at the Center for European Studies, Jagiellonian University, Kraków, Poland. He is currently writing a monograph on Polish migrants' social class and ethnicity in London (co-authored with John Eade). His interests include long-distance nationalism, white immigrant groups' racism, contestation of nationalism in Poland, EU integration, immigrant civic participation and the informal labor market strategies of marginalized groups.

ROBERT GIBB is lecturer in sociology at the University of Glasgow (Scotland). His doctoral research examined the relationship between antiracism, republicanism and party politics in France through an ethnographic study of the association SOS-Racisme. More recently, he completed a pilot study of inter-group relations and racism in a 'multicultural' area of Copenhagen (Denmark). He is currently working, in collaboration with Professor A. Good (University of Edinburgh), on a two-year comparative study of the processes of cultural translation involved in converting asylum applicants' accounts of persecution into legal language by lawyers in France and the United Kingdom.

NINA GLICK SCHILLER is the founding director of the Research Institute of Cosmopolitan Cultures and a member of the social anthropology faculty of the University of Manchester. She also serves as a research associate of the Max-Planck-Institute for Social Anthropology Halle, Germany. Glick Schiller is founding editor of the international journal *Identities: Global Studies of Culture and Power* and serves on the editorial board of several other journals. Her recent publications focus on migration theory, transnational migration, ethnicity, racialization, long distance nationalism, methodological nationalism, imperialism, migrant simultaneous incorporation, rescaling of city space and migration, and fundamentalist Christianity. She has conducted ethnographic research in the United States, Haiti, and Germany. Glick Schiller's books include the co-authored volumes *Nations Unbound: Transnational Projects, Postcolonial Predicaments, and Deterritorialized Nation-States* and *Georges Woke Up Laughing: Long Distance Nationalism and the Search for Home*, and the co-edited book *Towards a Transnational Perspective On Migration*.

DAVIDE PERÒ is lecturer in sociology at the University of Nottingham where he convenes the Identity Citizenship and Migration Centre (ICMiC). Previously he was researcher at the Centre on Migration, Policy and Society of the Institute of Social and Cultural Anthropology (Oxford University). Però has conducted ethnographic research on politics and migrants in Britain, Italy, and Spain. His recent publications include the book *Inclusionary Rhetoric / Exclusionary Practices: Left-wing Politics and Migrants in Italy*.

DEBORAH REED-DANAHAY is a professor of anthropology at SUNY Buffalo. She has conducted fieldwork in France and in the United States on topics such as education, youth, citizenship, personal narrative, health, and immigration. Her most recent work is among Vietnamese diaspora populations in the United States and France. She also works on anthropological theory, and on narrative and autoethnography. She is author of *Education and Identity: The Politics of Schooling* (1996) and *Locating Bourdieu* (2005), and editor of *Auto/ Ethnography: Rewriting the Self and the Social* (1997).

KAREN E. RICHMAN is a cultural anthropologist who studies religion, migration, transnationalism, performance, gender, labor and consumption in the United States, Haiti and Mexico. She is the director of the Migration and Border Studies center at the Institute for Latino Studies at University of Notre

Dame. Her book *Migration and Vodou* (2005) explores migration, religious experience and ritual transformation in a far-flung Haitian community. Among her recent and current journal articles and book chapters are "Peasants, Migrants and the Discovery of African Traditions: Ritual and Social Change In Lowland Haiti" (*Journal of Religion in Africa*, 2007), "Innocent Imitations? Mimesis and Alterity in Haitian Vodou Art, Tourism and Anthropology"(*E thnohistory*, in press), "Miami Money and the Home Girl" (*Anthropology and Humanism*, 2002) and "The Protestant Ethic and the Dis-spirit of Vodou" in *Immigrant Faiths: Transforming Religious Life in America* (2005). Her current book projects are a study of migration and religious conversion and an ethnographic biography of a Mexican immigrant woman. She has worked as an advocate for refugees and migrant farm workers in the United States.

PAUL A. SILVERSTEIN is associate professor of anthropology at Reed College. His research and writing focus on questions of immigration, racial politics, and ethnic nationalism between France, Algeria, and Morocco. He is author of *Algeria in France: Transpolitics, Race, and Nation* (2004), and editor (with Ussama Makdisi) of *Memory and Violence in the Middle East and North Africa* (2006). He is also an editor of the journal *Middle East Report*.

ANGÈLE SMITH is an assistant professor in anthropology at the University of Northern British Columbia, Canada. Her articles have been published in such periodicals as *International Journal of Historical Archaeology* and *Archaeological Dialogues*. She is co-editing a book with Amy Gazin-Schwartz, entitled *Landscapes of Clearance: Anthropological and Archaeological Perspectives*. She currently has a three-year Social Science and Humanities Research Council of Canada grant to undertake the research project "Articulating Place and Identity: Social and Spatial Exclusion/ Inclusion of Nigerian Asylum Seekers in Ireland."

FLAVIA STANLEY is a doctoral candidate in anthropology at the University of Massachusetts-Amherst. She also holds an MSW in Community Organizing from the University of Michigan. Her research interests include immigration, the cultural politics of 'race,' the anthropology of social work, and applied and public interest anthropology.

BERNARD P. WONG is professor of anthropology at San Francisco State University. He has conducted fieldwork on the Chinese in Peru, the United States, Japan, and the Philippines. His research interests include the family, ethnic identity, cultural citizenship, globalization and ethnic entrepreneurship. He is the author of six scholarly books, many book chapters and journal articles.

# Index

Committee of 100, 198–199
Common European Asylum System
  (2004), 63–64
Communism, 88–89, 91, 109, 124, 132–
  133, 136. *See also* anti-Communism
community, 62, 79, 96n1, 111, 113, 199,
  202, 218; online, 227–228, 240, 242n1;
  of practice, 78–87, 93–95, 228; transnational, 183–184
community organizations, 14, 94, 112,
  114, 192
conspiracy theories, 100, 132, 144–145,
  148, 151–156, 160
contributions, 185, 230
Convergence 84, 147–148, 150, 153
Coutin, Susan Bibler, 7
Creole, 164, 170–171, 174
Cubitt, Geoffrey, 151–152, 154–155
cultural intimacy, 81–84, 95, 96n5
cultural politics, 109
"cybercultural politics," 241
cyberspace, 3, 228, 230, 234
cyberspace family, 241

Dallas/Fort Worth, 85, 87–88, 242n1
Davidson, Alistair, 2–3
De Genova, Nicholas, 27, 30
demonstrations. *See* protests
denizen, 3
deportation, 30, 37, 63, 68, 71–73, 119,
  177, 228
Désir, Harlem, 147–155, 157, 161n4
diaspora, 10, 32, 85, 89, 93–94, 100–101,
  124–128, 131–137, 139–141, 164–167,
  175, 178
"diasporic public sphere," 226
Direct Provision Accommodation Centres, 66–67
discrimination, 11, 14, 40, 62, 66–67, 71,
  116, 154, 158, 159, 185–186, 188, 194,
  201, 205, 248
divided loyalty, 189
*Dixième Département* (Tenth Province),
  165, 178

Do, Hien Duc, 14
Dorsina, Linda, 163
Dray, Julián, 149–157
dual citizenship. *See* citizenship: dual
dual nationality. *See* citizenship: dual

economic migrants, 63, 100, 104, 108,
  129–130, 133, 142n3
Eighty/Twenty (80/20) Project, 198–199
employment. *See* work
England, 99–100, 103–123, 124–143
entrepreneurs, entrepreneurship, 111,
  184–190, 192–193, 198, 200, 202
Escobar, Arturo, 12, 106
establishing roots, 185, 192–194, 198–199,
  202, 245
European Council of Tampere, 63
European Court of Justice, 68–69
European Social Forum, 118
European Union, 1, 4, 45–46, 54–58,
  62–64, 68, 70–71, 124, 127–128, 132,
  135, 140
Evangelical Christians, 182, 203, 208–218;
  and U.S. imperialism, 219–223
exclusion, 2, 21, 27, 61, 77, 84, 94, 99, 108,
  119, 121, 125–126, 131, 134, 139, 141,
  178, 204, 245, 247, 249

family reunification, 3, 28, 74, 225–229,
  231, 233, 235, 237–242, 242n2
Federation of Poles in Great Britain, 134,
  136, 138, 142n8, 143n11
flag symbolism, 31, 81, 90–94, 182, 199,
  221
flexible citizenship. *See* citizenship, models
  of: flexible
Flores, William V., 9
football, 20, 23–24, 41nn1–6
"Fortress Europe," 70–71
Fouron, Georges E., 11, 166
Fox, Vicente, 166–167, 170, 172
*Français de souche,* 25, 29
France, 19–21, 23–42, 100–101, 144–161,
  178